Democracy and Knowledge

_____

Democracy and Knowledge

INNOVATION AND LEARNING
IN CLASSICAL ATHENS

Josiah Ober

PRINCETON UNIVERSITY PRESS

PRINCETON AND OXFORD

Library of Congress Cataloging-in-Publication Data

Ober, Josiah.
Democracy and knowledge : innovation and learning
in classical Athens / Josiah Ober.
p.   cm.
Includes bibliographical references and index.
ISBN 978-0-691-13347-8 (cloth : alk. paper)
1. Democracy—Greece—Athens—History—To 1500. 2. Political participation—
Greece—Athens—History—To 1500. 3. Athens (Greece)—Politics and government.
4. Greece—Politics and government—To 146 B.C. I. Title.
JC75.D36O25 2008
320.938′5—dc22   2008007928

British Library Cataloging-in-Publication Data is available

This book has been composed in Sabon

Printed on acid-free paper. ∞

press.princeton.edu

Printed in the United States of America

1 3 5 7 9 10 8 6 4 2

For my families

Liberty cannot be preserved without a general knowledge among the people, who have a right, from the frame of their nature, to knowledge. . . . The preservation of the means of knowledge among the lowest ranks, is of more importance to the public than all the property of all the rich men in the country. . . . Let us tenderly and kindly cherish, therefore, the means of knowledge. Let us dare to read, think, speak, and write. Let every order and degree among the people rouse their attention and animate their resolution. Let them all become attentive to the grounds and principles of government. . . . Let us study the law of nature . . . contemplate the great examples of Greece and Rome. . . . In a word, let every sluice of knowledge be opened and set a-flowing.
　　　　—John Adams, "A Dissertation on the Canon
　　　　　　　　and Feudal Law" (1765)

The problem [of dispersed knowledge] which we meet here is by no means peculiar to economics but arises in connection with nearly all truly social phenomena . . . and constitutes really the central theoretical problem of all social science. . . . The practical problem arises precisely because facts are never so given to a single mind, and because, in consequence, it is necessary that in the solution of the problem knowledge should be used that is dispersed among many people.
　　　　—Friedrich A. Hayek, "The Use of Knowledge
　　　　　　　　in Society" (1945)

The servant and messenger of the Muses, if he should have any exceptional knowledge, must not be stinting of it. . . . What use would it be for him if he alone knows it?
　　　　—Theognis, lines 769–72

CONTENTS

ILLUSTRATIONS

TABLES

PREFACE

ATHENS STOOD OUT among its many rivals in the ancient Greek world. No other city-state was as rich, as resilient, or as influential. This book shows how democracy contributed to Athenian preeminence: Innovative political and economic institutions enabled citizens to pursue their private interests while cooperating on joint projects, coordinating their actions, and sharing common resources without tragedy. Anticipating one of the great insights of modern social science, ancient Athenian democracy harnessed the power of dispersed knowledge through the free choices of many people.

Democracy and Knowledge completes a trilogy on the theory and practice of democracy in classical Athens, a historical, social-scientific, and philosophical undertaking with which I have been engaged for most of my career. Athenian history is worth a life's work because it shows how participatory and deliberative democracy enabled a socially diverse community to flourish in a highly competitive and fast-changing environment. Athens proves that democratic productivity is not merely a contingent result of distinctively modern conditions. That is an important conclusion if one supposes, as I do, that our modernity is not the end of history and that democracy is uniquely well suited to human flourishing—both in the sense of material well-being and in the Aristotelian sense of happiness as *eudaimonia*.

No real-world democracy can claim to be a fully just society. Athens, with its slaves and male-only political franchise, certainly could not. Yet democracy promotes just and noble actions by self-consciously ethical agents. Through participating in common enterprises and deliberating with their fellows on matters of great moment, democratic citizens come to recognize themselves as free and equal individuals and as the joint creators of a shared destiny. Democracy is the only form of government in which the inherent human capacity to associate in public decisions can be fully realized. Understanding the conditions that have allowed for the emergence, flowering, and spread of productive democratic practices in the past is, therefore, of fundamental moral, as well as practical, importance.

I did not know that I would be writing a trilogy when, in the late 1970s, I began gathering notes for the book that became *Mass and Elite in Democratic Athens*. It was only some twenty years later, as I was completing *Political Dissent in Democratic Athens*, that I realized that my portrait of Athens still lacked a proper account of the relationships among democracy, state performance, and useful knowledge. Yet the goal of explaining democratic knowledge proved frustratingly elusive. As I struggled to identify the true object of my inquiry, the project was transformed by two seminal experiences. The first was to work intensively as a member of a small team of consultants seeking to redesign the governance system of a large professional service firm. That work—which led to a book advocating a citizen-based governance model for firms (Manville and Ober 2003)—led me to focus on the relationship between knowledge management and organizational performance in highly competitive environments. The second transformative experience was a fellowship year (2004/5) at the Center for Advanced Study in the Behavior Sciences in Stanford, California. Conversations with my fellow CASBS residents and with Stanford faculty persuaded me to reorient the book around problems of public action and rational choice, and convinced me of the potential value of quantification.

I have received a great deal of support in writing this book. I developed the preliminary framework during a sabbatical year (2000/1), spent first in Paris, under the auspices of the marvelous Centre Gustave Glotz (Université de Paris 1: Panthéon-Sorbonne), and then at the University of California at Irvine, as Nichols Visiting Professor in the Humanities. Meanwhile, my two institutional homes, Princeton University and, since 2006, Stanford University, supported the interdisciplinary work that this book demanded, both with research funds and by providing superb intellectual environments for teaching and scholarship. Princeton's Department of Classics and University Center for Human Values, and Stanford's Departments of Classics and Political Science have been as near to ideal environments for sustained work on this project as it is possible to imagine. Each summer I have returned to Bozeman, Montana, my refuge for almost three decades. Much of this book was written between hikes, picnics, and evenings on rivers and streams, with friends who have become like family.

I presented preliminary results at a number of scholarly venues. I am deeply grateful to the organizers of lectures and to attentive and critical audiences at these colleges, universities, and research institutes: Bergen, Bristol, Brown (Watson Institute), California (Berkeley, Irvine, San Diego, Santa Cruz), CASBS, Columbia, Duke, Emory, Florida State, Georgia, Harvard, Indiana, Lausanne, Michigan, New England (Armidale), Nottingham, Onassis Foundation (NYC), Oslo, Paris I (Sorbonne), Penn, Princeton, Soonsgil (Seoul), South Florida, Southern Virginia, Stanford, Sydney, Syracuse, Toronto, Tufts , USC, Victoria, Virginia Tech, Wabash, Washington (St. Louis), Washington (Seattle), Wellesley, and Wisconsin. Joshua Cohen and Christian List invited me to publish preliminary versions of chapters 4 and 5 in, respectively, *Boston Review* and *Episteme*;

their comments and suggestions led to very substantial improvements. My students in seminars at Princeton and Stanford were extraordinarily insightful, and helped me to reframe many aspects of the argument.

I have contracted many personal debts of gratitude to scholars who shared unpublished work, commented on drafts of chapters, and responded helpfully to my often-naïve queries. Thanks for making my stay in Paris so enjoyable and productive are due to Vincent Azoulay, Jean-Marie Bertrand, Paul Demont, and Pauline Schmitt-Pantel. Among my fellow residents at CASBS, Bill Barnett, Jon Bendor, Michael Heller, Mary and Peter Katzenstein, Nan and Bob Keohane, Brad Inwood, David Konstan, Doug McAdam, Nolan McCarty, Sam Popkin, Susan Shirk, and Kaare Strøm were particularly helpful. Lynn Gale, the CASBS statistician, was extraordinarily helpful in teaching me how to set up and to analyze the databases on which chapter 2 is based.

I have benefited greatly from conversation, comments, and unpublished work from Danielle Allen, Ryan Balot, Ed Burke, Joshua Cohen, John Ferejohn, Sara Forsdyke, Charles Hedrick, Bruce Hitchner, John Keane, Jack Kroll, Susan Lape, Christian List, John Ma, Steve Macedo, Gerry Mackie, James March, Terry Moe, Philip Pettit, David Pritchard, Rob Reich, Molly Richardson, Mona Ringveg, Doug Smith, Peter Stone, Barry Strauss, Claire Taylor, and many others. Numerous colleagues generously offered their special expertise, including Chris Achen (theater distribution statistics), Michele Angel (graphics), Michael Bratman (philosophy of action), Rob Felk and Andy Hanssen (agricultural economics and Hayek), Maggie Neale (work teams), Peter J. Rhodes (Athenian political institutions) Billy G. Smith (statistics for historical argument), and Peter Van Alfen (numismatics). I owe an especially deep debt of gratitude to Paul Cartledge, Bob Keohane, Emily Mackil, Ian Morris, Barry Weingast, and two anonymous readers for Princeton University Press, for critical comments that influenced both form and content in fundamental ways. David Teegarden entered most of the data for the charts and has been an indispensible collaborator. Rebecca Katz as bibliographer, Alice Calaprice as copy editor, and Barbara Mayor as proofreader, brought discipline to an unruly manuscript. Chuck Myers, my thoughtful and patient editor at Princeton University Press, saw the essence of the project from the beginning and persuaded me to discard everything that distracted from it.

The following pages would not have have been written but for countless hours of conversation on politics, culture, economics, and much else, with two close friends and mentors. Gerald C. Olson, a brilliant polymath, died in a tragic accident in 2006; his unbounded curiosity and profound intellectual generosity are deeply missed. Brook Manville's deep insights about organizations and his passionate dedication to citizen self-governance remain a constant source of inspiration. More recently, Eleni

Tsakopoulos and Markos Kounalakis unexpectedly and wonderfully set my life on a new course, through their vision and generosity in establishing the Constantine Mitsotakis Chair at Stanford and their passion for the real and enduring value of Hellenic culture. Adrienne Mayor is my best reader, my life partner, my center. This book is dedicated to my families, kinfolk by birth and choice, who never let me forget that I study the past for the sake of the future.

ABBREVIATIONS

Ath. Pol.	=	*Athēnaiōn Politeia*
F	=	Fragment (of a lost work by an ancient author)
IG	=	*Inscriptiones Gracae.* Berlin, 1873–
LSJ	=	*A Greek-English Lexicon*, compiled by Henry George Liddell and Robert Scott, revised and augmented by Sir Henry Stuart Jones, 9th ed., with supplement. Oxford: Oxford University Press, 1968
RO	=	Rhodes, P. J., and Robin Osborne. 2003. *Greek Historical Inscriptions: 404–323* B.C. Oxford: Oxford University Press
SEG	=	Supplementum Epigraphicum Graecum. *1923–*
West	=	Martin L. West, *Iambi et elegi graeci*, 2nd ed. 2 vols. Oxford: Clarendon Press, 1991–92.

ATHENIAN MONEY, TAXES, REVENUES

6 obols = one drachma (dr)

4 drachmas = tetradrachm (standard silver coin: weight = ca. 17 grams)

100 drachmas = one mina

6000 drachmas = one talent (T)

Pay rate for government service (per day) = 3–9 obols

Property tax (*eisphora*) paying estate = ca. 1 talent (ca. 1200–2000 estates)

Liturgy paying estate = ca. 3–4 talents (ca. 300–400 estates)

Athenian state revenues = ca. 130–1200 talents (per year)

Democracy and Knowledge

Chapter 1

INTRODUCTION: DISPERSED KNOWLEDGE

AND PUBLIC ACTION

How SHOULD a democratic community make public policy? The citizens of classical Athens used a simple rule: both policy and the practice of policy making must be good for the community and good for democracy. A time-traveling Athenian democrat would condemn contemporary American practice, on the grounds that it willfully ignores popular sources of useful knowledge.[1]

Willful ignorance is practiced by the parties of the right and left alike. The recipe followed by the conservative George W. Bush administration when planning for war in Iraq in 2002 was quite similar to the liberal William J. Clinton administration's formula for devising a national health care policy a decade earlier: *Gather the experts. Close the door. Design a policy. Roll it out. Reject criticism.* Well-known policy failures like these do not prove that the cloistered-expert formula inevitably falls short. But the formula can succeed only if the chosen experts really do know enough. Our Athenian observer would point out that the cloistered-experts approach to policy making—insofar as it ignores vital information held by those not recognized as experts—is both worse for democracy and less likely to benefit the community. Contemporary political practice often treats free citizens as passive subjects by discounting the value of what they know. Democratic Athenian practice was very different.

The world of the ancient Greek city-states is a natural experimental laboratory for studying the relationship between democracy and knowledge: By the standards of pre-modernity, the Greek world experienced remarkable growth (Morris 2004). Growth is stimulated by innovation,

---

[1] I refer to American policy making *exempli gratia*. The Athenian visitor would likewise disapprove of policy-making practices in other contemporary democratic systems, whether parliamentary or presidential. The Athenian conviction that policy (especially when codified in law: *nomos*) and public practice (the process of lawmaking: *nomothesia*) must benefit the community of citizens (*dēmos*) and democracy (*dēmokratia*) is neatly summed up by Eukrates' anti-tyranny law of 337/6 B.C. with its formulaic preamble describing the institutional practice by which the law came into being and its oft-reproduced relief sculpture depicting personified Demos being crowned by personified Demokratia; see discussion in Ober 1998, chapter 10; Blanshard 2004; Teegarden 2007.

and key innovations in the area of public knowledge management emerged, I will argue, from democratic institutions developed in classical Athens—the most successful and influential of all the thousand-plus Greek city-states. The distinctive Athenian approach to the aggregation, alignment, and codification of useful knowledge allowed Athenians to employ resources deftly by exploiting opportunities and learning from mistakes. The Athenians' capacity to make effective use of knowledge dispersed across a large and diverse population enabled democratic Athens to compete well against non-democratic rivals. Athens did not always employ its knowledge-based democratic advantage wisely or justly. Its misuse of state power caused great harm, at home and abroad. Yet, over time, the Greek city-state culture benefited from the diffusion of innovative Athenian political institutions.

Athens offers alternatives to the cloistered-experts approach to policy making, alternatives that are consistent with some of the best modern thinking on democracy and knowledge. This book suggests that John Adams (2000 [1765]) and Friedrich Hayek (1945) were right: liberty *does* demand "a general knowledge among the people," and the use of knowledge "dispersed among many people" *is* "the central theoretical problem of all social science." The second president of the United States and the 1974 Nobel laureate in economics each called attention to useful knowledge that is—and ought to be—distributed across all levels of society. Making good policy for a democratic community dedicated to liberty and social justice, whether in antiquity or today, requires a system for organizing what is known by many disparate people. By demonstrating the truth of Adams' startling claim that "the preservation of the means of knowledge among the lowest ranks is of more importance to the public than all the property of all the rich men in the country," this book argues that democracy once was, and might again become, such a system.

A willingness, with Adams, to "let every sluice of knowledge be opened and set a-flowing," matched with an ability to organize useful knowledge for learning and innovation, builds democracy's core capacity. When policy makers rely too heavily on like-minded experts, they blunt democracy's competitive edge. Hayek realized, as had Pericles before him, that access to social and technical knowledge, widely distributed among a diverse population, gives free societies a unique advantage against authoritarian rivals. The history of Athenian popular government shows that making good use of dispersed knowledge is the original source of democracy's strength. It remains our best hope for sustained democratic flourishing in a world in which adherents of fundamentalist systems of belief express violent hostility to diversity of thought and behavior and in which new political hybrids, "managed democracy" and "authoritarian capitalism," pose economic and military challenges.

Democratic societies, faced with rising authoritarian powers and non-state networks of true believers, may be tempted to imitate their challengers. Elected officials seek to counter emerging threats by centralizing executive power, establishing stricter lines of command, increasing government secrecy, and controlling public information. They mimic their enemies' fervor by deploying the rhetoric of fear and fundamentalism. Citizens who allow their leaders to give in to these temptations risk losing their liberties along with the wellspring of their material flourishing. A liberal democracy can never match the command-and-control apparatus of authoritarians, nor can it equal the zeal of fanatics. The bad news offered here is that it is only by mobilizing knowledge that is widely dispersed across a genuinely diverse community that a free society can hope to outperform its rivals while remaining true to its values. The good news is that by putting knowledge to work, democracy can fulfill that hope.[2]

THEORY AND PRACTICE

Since the time of Aristotle, democracy, as a field of study, has invited the integration of value-centered political theory with the scientific analysis of political practices. Yet the project of uniting democratic theory and practice remains incomplete, and Adams' urgent plea that we attend to the vital public role of knowledge has too often been ignored. Much academic work on democracy still tacitly accepts some version of Tocqueville's early nineteenth century claim that "the absolute sovereignty of the will of the majority is the essence of democratic government." While impressed by the vibrancy of American civil society, Tocqueville argued

---

[2] Elizabeth Anderson (2003 and 2006) offers a philosophical account of "epistemic democracy," drawing upon Amartya Sen, Friedrich Hayek, and John Dewey, that is compatible with the portrait of Athenian deliberative/participatory democracy I develop here. Anderson emphasizes the positive value of dispersed knowledge and experimentalism. Anderson's empirical cases are drawn from modernity, and she focuses in the first instance on the value of gender diversity. The lack of gender diversity in the Athenian citizenship is among the moral and practical flaws of the Athenian democracy; see further, below. The term "epistemic democracy" was coined by Joshua Cohen (1986) according to List and Goodin (2001). Page 2007 develops a formal model to show how epistemic diversity can improve problem solving. The approach I develop here seeks to extend work on epistemic diversity and democracy by showing how a democracy can use diverse knowledge to improve its organizational performance. This includes, but is not limited to, doing better at discovering truths about the world. Focusing on epistemic processes does not require slighting institutional and cultural factors; see Mokyr 2002: 285–87, and below.

that the "tyranny of the majority" promotes mediocrity (especially in military endeavors), legislative and administrative instability, and a general atmosphere of unpredictability.[3]

Working within the framework of democracy as majoritarianism, mid-twentieth-century social choice theorists updated Tocqueville's concerns about democratic instability by identifying what appeared to be fatal flaws in the structure of democratic voting. Kenneth Arrow (1963, [1951]) demonstrated that the potential for voting cycles among factions rendered the stable aggregation of diverse preferences mathematically impossible. Anthony Downs (1957) showed that ignorance about political issues was a rational response among voters. The scientific rigor with which these findings were established seemed a devastating rebuttal to anyone offering more than "two cheers for democracy" (Forster 1951). In the last half-century, much of the best work on democratic politics has taken knowledge as a burdensome cost of participation, and has emphasized strategic bargaining among elites within the framework of an imperfect voting rule. While acknowledging that there is no better alternative, political scientists offered little reason to regard democracy as anything better than a least-bad, in Churchill's famous dictum, "the worst form of government except all those other forms that have been tried from time to time."[4]

Meanwhile, contemporary political philosophers often regard democracy as a normative ideal. Democracy, they suggest, ought to be valued insofar as it furthers values of freedom, equality, and dignity along with practices of liberty as non-interference and non-domination, procedural fairness, and fair distribution of power and resources. Participatory forms of democracy ought to expand the scope for human flourishing through the exercise of individuals' political capacity to associate with others in public decision making. Democratic commitment to deliberation requires decisions to be made by persuasive discourse and reciprocal reason-giving, while democratic tolerance for political dissent allows critics to expose inconsistencies between core values and current practices. Democratic culture encourages civic virtue in the form of consistent and voluntary social cooperation, yet democratic government does not demand that its citizens or leaders be moral saints. Churchill was right to say that democracies are inherently imperfect, but a participatory and deliberative democracy is in principle self-correcting, and ought to become better over

---

[3] Tocqueville 2000 [1835]: I.227–31; quote 227. Tocqueville also had much to say in favor of local democratic associationalism; see further, chapter 4.

[4] Costs of gaining knowledge: Sowell 1980; R. Hardin 2002. Page 2007: 239–96 reviews and summarizes the literature on preference diversity and aggregation. Churchill quote: Hansard, November 11, 1947.

time. These desirable attributes should emerge from the logic of collective decision making, follow-through, and rule setting in a socially diverse community if its members treat one another as moral equals.[5]

Looking at democracy through a classical Athenian lens suggests how the normative "ought" can be more closely conjoined with the descriptive "is." Participatory and deliberative government, dedicated to and constrained by moral values, can be grounded in choices made by interdependent and rational individuals—people who are concerned (although not uniquely) with their own welfare and aware that it depends (although not entirely) on others' behavior. Bringing normative political theory together with the philosophy of joint action and the political science of rational choice creates space for conceptual advances in democratic theory and social epistemology: it leads to defining democracy as the capacity of a public to do things (rather than simply as majority rule), to focusing on the relationship between innovation and learning (not just bargaining and voting), and to designing institutions to aggregate useful knowledge (not merely preferences or interests).

The potential payoff is great. Insofar as it promotes better values and better outcomes, a participatory and deliberative democracy is rightly favored over all other forms of political organization. Yet before embracing participation and deliberation, we must answer a practical question: Do good values cost too much in fiercely competitive environments? Given that participation and deliberation are inherently costly processes, can government *by* the people (as well as of and for them) compete militarily and economically with managed democracy, authoritarian capitalism, statelike networks, and other modern hybrids? Is democracy equal to the challenges of the future—climate change, natural resource depletion, demographic shifts, and epidemic disease?

Few democratic citizens, ancient or modern, would willingly tolerate the elimination of democracy as such. But by the same token, they expect their states to compete effectively with rivals and to address urgent issues of the day.[6] Do the imperatives to seek competitive advantage and to solve global-scale problems mean that democratic states will best preserve their values by turning over government to a managerial elite of experts? That question was engaged in the mid-twentieth century, when democracy's

[5] The foundations for the sketch of democratic theory offered above can be found in Dewey 1954; Rawls 1971, 1996; Pettit 1997; J. Cohen 1996; Gutmann and Thompson 2004; Ober 2007b.

[6] Competition among communities (at various levels) may be for (1) military advantage, economic stature, and international prestige; (2) the services of talented and mobile people; (3) the dissemination of cultural forms—including values, ideas, practices, and modes of expression. My thanks to Rob Fleck for help in clarifying these three types of competition.

rivals were fascist and communist regimes: Joseph Schumpeter (1947) and
Walter Lippmann (1956), among others, advocated a managed system of
"democratic elitism," while John Dewey (1954), whose commitment to
knowledge mirrored Adams', argued that an experimental and fallible
democratic public could overcome its own problems.[7] The collapse of the
Soviet bloc in 1989 reanimated scholarly interest in the deeper roots of
the "democratic advantage"; in the early twenty-first century the relationship of democracy to outcomes remains an issue for policy makers and a
problem in democratic theory.[8] The question of the relationship between
democracy and performance becomes even more trenchant when we look
beyond the nation-state, to local governments and to non-governmental
organizations. While democracy may have become a universal value (Sen
1999), it remains a rarity, even as an aspiration, within the organizations
in which most of us spend most of our working lives (Manville and Ober
2003).

By assessing the relationship between economic and military performance, public institutions, knowledge, and choice, this book argues that
democracy can best compete with authoritarian rivals and meet the challenges of the future by strengthening government by the people. If, in
practice as in theory, democracy best aligns rational political choices with
moral choices, and if that alignment promotes outstanding performance,
then democracy could fairly claim to be the best possible form of government. In that case, choosing democracy would mean much more than
settling for a least-bad—it would express an informed and justifiable preference for a political system that promotes valued ends, including (but
not only) liberty, justice, and sustainable material prosperity, and is rightly
desired as a valuable end-in-itself.[9]

RATIONAL CHOICE AND JOINT ACTION

My thesis, that democracy can align political choices with moral choices
to produce outstanding results, rests on a set of arguments about knowledge, institutions, and state performance. The following chapters offer a

---

[7] On Dewey and his intellectual rivals on the topic of democracy, see further Westbrook
1991; Ryan 1995.

[8] "Democratic advantage": Schultz and Weingast 2003; cf. Stasavage 2003. See below,
note 18.

[9] Although it does not employ formal economic models, this book's ambition of explaining complex historical developments by reference to social-scientific theories of choice
and collective action is similar to that of Bates et al. 1998 (see especially Introduction);
Rodrik 2003; and Greif 2006. By the same token, it is intended only as a partial explanation.
For a fuller explanation of how Athenian democracy worked, this book may be read in

historical case study of democratic practice, grounded in an extensive body of empirical evidence and informed by both normative (value-centered) and positive (causal explanation-centered) political theory. It describes how, in ancient Athens, government by the people enabled a large and socially diverse citizenship to find surprisingly good solutions to seemingly intractable social problems involving joint action and requiring shared value commitments. These problems arise whenever groups of self-interested and interdependent individuals seek to develop and carry out cooperative plans. Joint action problems confront all states—and indeed all other purposeful organizations, ancient and modern.[10]

Cooperation would be politically unproblematic if a group actually possessed a unitary general will of the sort Rousseau postulates in his *Social Contract* (2002 [1762]). But as Michael Bratman (1999: 93–161) argues, intentions are held by individuals: saying that "we intend" to do something means that our intentions are shared, but shared intention, unlike a general will, allows for substantial disagreement and competition. Bratman argues that joint action can be explained philosophically as a shared cooperative activity among individuals. In order to act jointly, individuals must not only share certain intentions, they must mesh certain of their subplans, manifest at least minimal cooperative stability, and possess relevant common knowledge. Philip Pettit and Christian List (in progress), drawing on Bratman's reductively individualistic argument, suggest that joint action requires four basic steps:

1. The members of a group each intend that they together promote a certain goal.
2. They each intend to do their assigned part in a salient plan for achieving that goal.
3. They each form these intentions at least partly on the basis of believing that the others have formed similar intentions.
4. This is all a matter of common knowledge, with each believing that the first three conditions are met, each believing that others believe this, and so on.

---

conjunction with the analysis of rhetoric and power in Ober 1989 and the intellectual history of dissent in Ober 1998. See below, this chapter.

[10] The general problem of joint action, which underlies all economic and political behavior, engages the philosophy of action, philosophy of mind, and moral psychology. Here I adopt the frame developed by Philip Pettit and Christian List (in progress), who draw upon (inter alia) Bratman 1999 and 2004, Pettit 2002, and Pettit and Schweikard 2006. The primary difference between my work and that of Pettit and List is one of emphasis: they are concerned in the first instance with voting procedures for aggregating group judgments in situations in which there is a presumptive right answer (e.g., jury trials), whereas I focus on procedures for aggregating social and technical knowledge for setting public agendas and making public policy.

In a democracy lacking both command-and-control governmental apparatus and an "all the way down" political ideology, it is initially difficult to see how free and equal individuals would be able to form such compatible intentions, would come to share beliefs about others' intentions, or could gain common knowledge. Yet the Athenians must have done so. As we will see, democratic Athens featured highly participatory and deliberative institutions, formulated and carried out complex plans, and was, by various measures, a leading Greek city-state for most of its 180-year history as an independent democracy. Explaining democratic joint action in classical Athens will require conjoining cultural, historical, and social-scientific approaches to explaining why and how people come to act in certain ways under certain conditions.[11]

Institutions, understood as *action-guiding rules*, are an important part of the story. Institutional rules might, under some imaginable circumstances, become so strongly action-guiding as to determine people's choices. At this point, social structure overwhelms individual agency; autonomy (understood as free choice) disappears along with the possibility of endogenous change. Yet even in the most rule-bound situations of the real world, agency persists; in a democracy, autonomy is positively valued and individual choices remain fundamental. Choices are always affected, but never fully determined, by the rules governing formal institutions (notably, for our purposes, legislative, judicial, and executive bodies), as well as by ideology, and by cultural norms. Meanwhile, institutions are recursively brought into being, sustained, revised, or discarded by the choices made by individuals.[12]

Joint action in the real world is easier to understand when it is predicated on hierarchy, in which the rules are strong and unambiguous. When an authoritative command is issued by an empowered individual, each of

[11] Morris and Manning 2005 lay out the methodological issues involved with the kind of study that is attempted here.

[12] Recursive relationship between choice-making agents and social structure: Giddens 1979, 1990: esp. 28–32, 184–86 (autonomy in democracy), 1992. The relationship between structure and agency is central to several fields and the subject of much debate. See, for example, Leifer 1988 (sociology: social roles and local action); Baumol 1993: esp. 30–32, 40–41; North 2005 (economics: rules of the game change over time, in response to changed intentions arising from social learning); Orlikowsky 2002 (organizational theory: knowledge is both capability and expressed in practice); Wolin 1994 (political theory: solidification of structure corrupts agent-centered democracy); Sewell 1996 (historical anthropology: events affect social structure); Pettit 2002 (philosophy of action: rule following is response dependent). Avner Greif (2006) emphasizes the necessity of focusing on individual agency in order to understand institutions (pp. 3–14) and offers an expansive definition of institutions, which includes ideology and culture. Here I focus more narrowly on formal institutions, because I have treated ideological and cultural questions in detail elsewhere. On the relationship between the study of institutions, ideology, and critique, see further, below, this chapter.

the multiple recipients of that command has certain ends set for him or her. If all have, and believe that others have, a prior intention to obey commands issued by the empowered individual, and if the order is publicly communicated and so a matter of common knowledge, each of Pettit and List's conditions may be adequately met. Yet the problem of joint action does not disappear because individual agency is never reduced to zero. Those who are under orders ought not be regarded simply as passive instruments of another's will, as they are, for example, in Taylorist management theory.[13]

To move from an order to a shared intention among its multiple recipients, and to shared belief about others' intentions, the command must be taken by each of those commanded as having effective force. In the terms of J. L. Austin's (1975 [1962]) theory of speech acts, it must be performed felicitously: it must be "taken up" such that a new social fact (people under orders) is brought into being. If that felicity condition is met, at least some of the group-agency difficulties regarding intention, belief, and commonality that come to the fore when thinking about *democratic* joint action drop away. Some version of this line of thought undergirds the claim by twentieth-century social theorists (e.g., Michels 1962 [1911]; Williamson 1975, 1985: see below) that large-scale participatory democratic organizations must inevitably be defeated by more hierarchical rivals. Yet even the most authoritative speech acts are liable to subversive misperformance; like other sorts of rules, the social rules governing felicity in speech are liable to interpretation and emendation.[14]

Three problems involving public goods and joint action will recur in our investigation of Athenian democratic institutions: collective action, coordination, and common pool resources.[15] Although, as we will see, these three problems overlap in actual social practice, each has somewhat different formal properties and different implications for politics. Each concerns certain difficulties that social groups experience in fully reaping

[13] Taylorism (on which see Rothschild 1973, and chapter 3) ignores the problem that order givers ("principals") and order takers ("agents") are differently motivated—the "principal/agent problem" lies at the heart of discussions of organizational management; see Roberts 2004, and chapter 3.

[14] I discussed the application of Austin's speech-act theory to political action (and especially Athenian democracy) in Ober 1998, chapter 1. See, further, Petrey 1988, 1990; Ma 2000. Misperformance: Butler 1997; Ober 2004. On the distinction between social facts that may be brought about by speech acts and "brute" facts of nature that cannot, see Searle 1995.

[15] The terminology for what I will be calling "public-action problems," deriving from game theory, is employed variously by different scholars. "Collective action" may be (as here) restricted to free-rider problems; it is sometimes used to describe a wider range of social choices modeled by non-cooperative games, or in reference to both non-cooperative and cooperative games. For a review of the field, see Mueller 2003.

the benefits of cooperation. Difficulties arise for two reasons: First, individuals rationally interested in their own welfare do not necessarily answer "yes" when they ask themselves, "Is it reasonable for me to cooperate with others?" Second, even when the answer would be "yes, so long as they cooperate with me," people may lack the relevant knowledge of others' intentions (i.e., the answer to the question, "Is it reasonable for them to cooperate with me?"), and so the chance for productive cooperation is lost. Contemporary theories of rational choice making assume that we ordinarily answer self-queries about cooperation by reference to incentives ("Given our goals, has each of us been given an adequate reason to cooperate?") rather than from motives of altruism ("Do we have reason to believe that our cooperation would enable others to achieve their goals?").[16]

The self-interest-centered rational choice model discounts other-regarding benevolence as an independent motivation. Yet it is essential to keep in mind that the perfectly rational actor is a convenient methodological fiction: an over-simplification of human psychology that gains analytic power by reduction—by stripping away, as analytically irrelevant, many complexities of real-world human motivation. Moreover, to the extent that she empathetically experiences others' pleasures and pains as her own, the good of others may be a positive incentive even for a perfectly rational individual. Here, I adopt a fairly parsimonious (non-altruistic) approach to rationality in order to sharpen the analytic problem presented by democratic joint action. I do not, however, assume

[16] On collective action problems as a product of rational choice, see Olson 1965 and R. Hardin 1982. On common pool resources, see G. Hardin 1968 and the essays collected in Ostrom et al. 2002. On coordination, see Chwe 2001; democracy as a coordination problem among citizens: Weingast 1997. Rational choice theory assumes that a rational actor is motivated by "expected utility" rather than altruism and is centrally concerned with the problem of defection (or free-riding) from cooperative agreements. Utility is the sum of an agent's preferences, which may include a preference for public policies that are not in his or her narrow self-interest. The question of how rationality is *bounded* by cultural or ethical norms, or by cognitive constraints (H. Simon 1955), is a key problem for choice theorists. Ferejohn 1991 underlines the necessity of conjoining rational choice with cultural interpretation, both because values and utility are influenced by culture and in order to limit the range of equilibria possible in repeated games. In brief, while I suppose that each Athenian's rationality was bounded by cultural and ethical norms, I also suppose that we must seek to understand the behavior of collectivities like classical Athens in terms of choices made by individuals who willingly cooperate with one another only if they believe that doing so has a reasonable chance of fulfilling their own aspirations. Rational choice can aid in historical explanation when it focuses attention on how complex systems emerge from and are sustained by individual choices. But historians must not confuse automata or "model actors" with actual human agents, whose motivations and cognitive capacities are much more complex; cf. the critiques of choice theory by Green and Shapiro 1994; Gaddis 2002; Mackie 2003; Mueller 2003: 657–70 (literature review).

that robust egoism is or ought to be an adequate basis for anyone's moral psychology.[17]

The first of our three problems involving joint action concerns *collective action*. The problem arises because, although a substantially better collective outcome would emerge from mutual cooperation, it is rational for each individual to defect (i.e., act in narrow self-interest) rather than to cooperate. Collective action is modeled in game theory by the "Prisoners' Dilemma," in which two prisoners end up serving long sentences as a result of their rational unwillingness to cooperate with each other in a course of action (refusing to reveal information to the authorities) that would gain short sentences for each. Neither prisoner is willing to risk the "sucker's payoff"—that is, the cooperator receives a very long sentence while the defector goes free—that he would receive by cooperating while his partner defected.

The second problem is one of *coordination*. It differs from the first type in that there is no sucker's payoff: people have good reason to want to cooperate, but they may have difficulty in doing so. In the coordination problem, there is no payoff to anyone without general cooperation in a course of action. The choice is between two (or more) different cooperative equilibria. If either equilibrium is equally good (for example, if we all drive on either the left or the right side of the road), no deep political problem emerges. The problem arises when many prefer a cooperative equilibrium different from the current one but remain ignorant of others' preferences and intentions. This can be exemplified by the "despised but stable dictatorship." Most of the dictator's subjects would be willing to assume some personal risk to get rid of the dictator, but the action threshold for each remains too high until and unless each potential actor has good reason to believe that others will act in concert with her. Because each lacks that good reason, due to an absence of common knowledge regarding preferences and intentions, all stay quiet and the dictator remains in power.

The third problem, which returns to reasons people have for not cooperating, concerns *common pool resources*. Here the problem arises because it is rational for each individual in a group to cheat on agreements regulating use of shared resources by taking more than his or her share. The eventual result, a general degradation of the resource, is often referred

---

[17] The moral psychology of reason, empathy, and altruism is a field that engages political theory, psychology, and economics as well as moral philosophy; see, recently, Frank 1988; Mansbridge 1990; Sen 1993; Elster 1999; Nussbaum 2001, 2006; Gintis et al. 2004; Pettit 2002:167–69, 222–44; Haidt 2006. Defense of robust egoism, on Aristotelian grounds: T. Smith 2006. Bad social consequences attendant upon reducing all value to economically measurable forms: D. Smith 2004.

to as the "tragedy of the commons." It is modeled by a pasture commonly owned by a group of shepherds. They know how many sheep can be sustainably grazed on the pasture, so by mutual agreement each is permitted to graze only a certain number of sheep. Yet each shepherd has a high incentive to cheat by grazing an extra sheep. It is rational for him to do so because, in the short run, he receives a much higher return for his extra sheep than he loses from the marginal bad effects of introducing one sheep more than the grazing ground can sustainably support. But since all have the same incentive, the pasture is soon badly overgrazed and therefore the commonly owned resource is ruined. Readers unfamiliar with these sorts of "rational choosing and acting" problems will find further discussion of them in chapters 3–6.

In the following pages I refer to the joint action problems of collective action, coordination, and common pool resources as *public action problems*, because my concern is with democracy. In its original Greek form (*dēmokratia*), democracy meant that "the capacity to act in order to effect change" (*kratos*) lay with a public (*dēmos*) composed of many choice-making individuals (Ober 2006a). While problems involving joint action are endemic to organized human communities, political solutions to those problems, that is, ways of generating and sustaining cooperation, are various. Solutions may be better or worse when judged in moral terms and economically more or less efficient. I seek to show how distinctively democratic solutions to public action problems can be economically efficient while remaining morally preferable to despotic or oligarchic alternatives. Here, the emphasis is on efficiency—on the argument that robust forms of participatory democracy need not be traded off for competitiveness. The ultimate reason for preferring democracy is, however, because it is morally preferable: more liberal in the sense of better promoting individual liberty, dignity, and social justice, and, by offering people a richer opportunity to associate in public decisions, more supportive of the expression of constitutive human capacities (Ober 2007b).

Premises and Problem

The following paragraphs set out the book's major premises regarding human nature, competition, culture, and power, along with the hypothesis that my argument seeks to test.

Humans are highly sociable (group-forming and interdependent), fairly rational (expected utility optimizing and strategic), and extremely communicative (language-using and symbol-interpreting) animals. As such, we live in communities in which we create meaning for ourselves and others through social interaction; in which we pursue interests based in part on our expectations of others' actions; and in which we exchange goods of various kinds, including ideas and information.[18] The sum of the choices made by individuals living in (and otherwise involved with) a viable community defines a self-reinforcing social-economic equilibrium. A given equilibrium may be relatively more or less cooperative, relatively adaptive or relatively inflexible. Because social cooperation produces economic value (as well as being valuable in non-material ways), more cooperative and (in changing environments) more dynamically adaptive equilibria perform relatively well in economic terms. Less cooperative and inflexible equilibria perform poorly. An equilibrium may be judged *robust* if it is capable of maintaining coherence in the face of substantial environmental changes.[19]

Communities (including states) exist in multicommunity ecologies in which they compete with one another for scarce resources, even as they cooperate by exchanging goods and services and in other ways. In more competitive environments, a given community must gain greater economic benefits from social cooperation or suffer the consequences of its failure. Because of persistent intercommunity competition there is constant, more or less intense, pressure for each community to achieve a higher-performing equilibrium. Competitive pressure rewards strong forms of state organization and drives out weaker ones (Waltz 1979). We might, therefore, expect states that gain and hold leading positions in highly competitive ecologies like the ancient Greek world (chapter 3), to

---

[18] Meaning-seeking is a necessary part of any full-featured account of human social life; this has been the focus of much of my earlier work on Athens and democracy (see especially Ober 2005b), but meaning-seeking, as such, is not my main concern here.

[19] In game theory a "Nash perfect equilibrium" is reached when no actor with full knowledge of costs and payoffs has any better (higher individual payoff) move to make. But it is important to keep in mind that when applied to actual societies, the self-reinforcing equilibrium is another convenient fiction: an ideal type of perfect stability unattainable in the real world. Moreover, in a perfect equilibrium there is no endogenous impulse to change (cf. critical comments of D. Cohen 1995, esp. 12), and the sort of democracy I seek to explain is dynamic—that is, it contains within itself the tendency to innovation and melioration. Finally, the so-called Folk Theorem in game theory demonstrates that in multiplayer repeated games (the relevant category for historical case studies of political communities), there is an infinite number of possible equilibria, which vary widely in their capacity to capture the potential gains arising from cooperation (i.e., to "Pareto optimize"). Real-world social equilibria remain imperfect, but some imperfect equilibria are better (offer higher aggregate payoffs) than others. On the theory of multiple-party repeated games, and the multiplicity of possible better (higher aggregate payoff) and worse equilibria, see Binmore 1994, 1998: esp. 293–398. The question of *social justice* concerns how the goods that result from cooperation ought to be distributed (notably, Rawls 1971). On this moral question, game theory is silent.

be better than their less successful rivals at coordination, at avoiding deadly commons tragedies, and at addressing collective-action problems in effective ways—for example by increasing the credibility of commitments, lowering transaction costs, and reducing the incidence of free-riding. Historically, more successful Greek *poleis* ought, in short, to have been better organized.

Competition under changing environmental conditions rewards innovation and punishes rigid path dependency, that is, collectively sticking to a given way of doing things over time, despite its declining efficiency. On the other hand, competition among states can lead to imitation of valuable innovations and enhanced potential for interstate cooperation. Because stronger states may dominate weaker states, coerced cooperation and cultural convergence can be produced by power inequalities. Interstate cooperation and emulation may also, however, be voluntary and based on a recognition of compatible interests and advantages. In either case, shared cultural norms and interstate institutions can extend across an ecology of states, potentially enabling a culture as a whole to better compete against—and in turn to cooperate with, to emulate, and to be emulated by—other cultures. The era of the Greco-Persian Wars of the fifth century and the pre- and postwar history of Aegean/western Asian interaction exemplifies this interactive process.[20]

If carried to its logical end, imitation and convergence might eliminate cultural diversity altogether. Yet no state or culture has yet achieved a performance advantage great enough to drive all rivals into extinction or slavish emulation. Public action problems have been addressed in quite different ways in different communities over the course of human history; the historical record offers a rich and still largely unexplored repository of more and less successful experiments in public action.[21]

Within a given community, culture and ideology serve (inter alia) as instruments by which individuals are persuaded to make more cooperative choices than they would make in a game-theoretic "state of nature."[22]

---

[20] For cooperation among poleis, see Mackil 2004; Mackil and van Alfen 2006. On states as "societal cultures" embracing a variety of subcultures and existing within an "umbrella culture" that extends across an ecology of states, see Ober 2005b, chapter 4. On emulation after the Persian Wars, see M. Miller 1997.

[21] Greif 2006 is an example of how much can be learned by looking in detail at a historical case study of public action.

[22] The problem of how to move rational actors from an uncooperative and undesirable state of nature to a collectively advantageous cooperative situation *without* invoking ideology or culture is the central problem of contractarian political theory, as exemplified by Hobbes' *Leviathan* of 1660, Rousseau's *Social Contract* of 1762, and Rawls' *Theory of Justice* of 1971; the tradition is critically surveyed in Nussbaum 2006, chapter 1.

Cultural persuasion may take a hard form by making a given set of choices appear inevitable, or a soft form by making certain choices appear more desirable or morally preferable than known alternatives. Because of the ideological work done by culture, neither utility nor the social information on which expectations about utility are developed can simply be taken for granted. One important effect of culture is to help to shape individuals' conceptions of utility and to filter social information regarding how utility is best achieved.[23]

Power, in this intracommunity context, should be understood as including (although not as limited to) direct or indirect control over how the additional outputs of goods and services that are generated through social cooperation are managed (e.g., through democratic choice or authoritarian command), how those outputs are distributed, and how they are deployed in ongoing competitions with rival communities and to address other problems. States, like firms and other purposeful organizations, are integrated systems in which control of cooperation-derived surplus is organized, held (or lost), and wielded by certain individual and institutional actors.[24]

Democracy, then, is a sociopolitical system featuring relatively soft forms of cultural persuasion, thereby offering individuals a broad range of choices and relatively full social information. Power in a democracy is not monopolized by an individual or a small elite nor is it exercised uniquely within formal institutions. The question of how the benefits of social cooperation are to be managed, distributed, and deployed must be negotiated (e.g., through deliberative decision making or voting) among relatively large and diverse groups of citizens, rather than being mandated by a small and exclusive leadership elite. In a competitive ecology, a state organized as a democracy must find ways to compete with more hierarchical and hard-ideology rivals. Hierarchical rivals appear to enjoy substantial advantages in respect to the employment of culture for addressing incentive problems. Democracies seem, on the face of it, particularly vul-

---

[23] For further discussion on democracy and culture, see Ober 2005b. It is important to keep in mind that a person's culture (in the sense I am using it here) is never unitary or homogeneous, in that no given individual is the product of a single culture. In addition to what we might think of as a primary (e.g., national) culture, all individuals are members of multiple subcultures, and primary cultures are in turn related to overarching "umbrella cultures."

[24] I concluded Ober 1989 by suggesting that in Athens, democracy meant that the power to assign meanings to symbols was retained by the people. This is an example of an indirect, but extremely important, form of power that had very substantial effects on distribution and employment of resources. See further, Ober 1996, chapter 7. Power and political institutions in the framework of rational choice: Moe 2005.

nerable to free riders, hard-put to make their commitments credible, confused about the relationship between decision-making principals and the agents assigned to carrying out orders, and insufficiently attentive to expert judgment.[25]

Based on the premises sketched out in the preceding paragraphs, one might suppose that, all other things being equal, democracies would perform relatively poorly in competitive environments. And yet, while some contemporary democratic states do underperform, others do very well indeed. As we shall see, there is good reason to believe that some ancient Greek democracies fared less well than some of their more hierarchical rivals. Yet in antiquity, as in modernity, certain democracies performed extremely well; classical Athens is a case in point—it was the preeminent Greek city-state on a variety of measures (chapter 2). The problem this book seeks to answer is why and how democratic Athens came to perform so comparatively well.

Because democracy is morally preferable to its alternatives, specifying the conditions under which democracies do well is a matter of great importance. The problem of democratic flourishing has attracted substantial attention from economists and political scientists, but there is as yet no clear consensus about *why* high-performing democracies do extraordinarily well. Comparative historical cases of high-performing democracies are valuable in that they enable us to test theories about the relationship between social choice, culture, and power by analyzing specific institutions under different conditions. The competitive world of the ancient Greek city-states is a particularly good laboratory in that it allows us to hold constant a variety of exogenous environmental and cultural factors that complicate attempts to gauge democracy's role in the flourishing of modern nations.[26]

This book contributes to the literature on democracy and performance in two ways. First, it analyzes the working of the institutions of an ancient state that has received sustained attention from historians since the midnineteenth century, but remains understudied by contemporary social scientists.[27] Next, it seeks to show how certain institutions that promoted

[25] Military discipline problems: Wallace 2005; inattentive to experts: Cary 1927/28. Democratic disadvantages arising from the costs of participation (the other side of the "democratic advantage" discussed by Schultz and Weingast 2003): below, this chapter.

[26] Comparative democratic performance on various success measures (especially economic and military): Putnam 1993; Sen 1999; Barro 1996; Rodrik 1999, 2000a, 2000b, 2003; Przeworski 2000; Tavares and Wacziarg 2001; Reiter and Stam 2002; Schultz and Weingast 2003; Rodrik and Wacziarg 2005; Friedman 2005: 327–45; Acemoglu and Robinson 2006.

[27] Recent and notable exceptions to the relative neglect of Greek antiquity by social scientists include North 1981: 102–7; Lyttkens 1992, 1994, 1997, 2006; Schwartzberg 2004;

the state's economic success also fostered a vibrant civic culture and (in certain spheres) admirable social arrangements. There are, of course, limits to our admiration for any society that exploited the labor of slaves, excluded women from political participation, and used violence and the threat of violence to extract resources from unwilling subjects—as did classical Athens. But those fundamental moral failings, which were common to other Greek city-states, should not foreclose attempts to understand aspects of Athenian social life that promoted procedural and distributive justice and expanded the scope of individual liberty and human flourishing.

My hypothesis (which is stated more formally at the end of this chapter) is that in classical Athens, superior economic and military performance was, at least in part, a product of democratic institutions and civic culture. Democracy, ancient and modern, is associated with an array of economically beneficial institutions, notably those committing governments to protecting rights in respect to property, citizenship, and legal processes. These commitment features have been the primary focus of recent social-scientific studies attempting to explain the "democratic advantage." Commitment features of various kinds were common to a number of Greek republics, oligarchies and democracies alike, and can certainly help to explain both Athenian flourishing and the overall flourishing of the Greek city-state ecology. But our special concern here is with Athenian exceptionalism within the city-state ecology. I therefore focus primarily on the *epistemic function* of democratic institutions, positing that exceptional Athenian performance is best explained by what Friedrich A. Hayek (1945) called "the use of knowledge in society."

In arguing against centralized economic planning by a small body of experts, Hayek pointed out that "the practical problem [of promoting economic rationality] arises precisely because [the relevant] facts are never so given to a single mind, and because, in consequence, it is necessary that in the solution of the problem knowledge should be used that is dispersed among many people" (1945: 530). Hayek emphasized that the knowledge with which he is concerned is not reducible to scientific knowledge (in which expertise is the key issue); he pointedly included unique information about particular circumstances in his definition. Useful knowledge in Hayek's sense is possessed not only by experts, but by "practically every individual" (1945: 521). Hayek focused on microeconomics, and thus on price, as immediately communicated social information about changes in supply and demand. He argued, however, that "the problem [of dispersed

---

Fleck and Hanssen 2006; Kaiser 2007; Karayiannis and Hatzis 2007. Contemporary neglect of classical antiquity is ironic in light of the interests of the founders of social science, including Marx and Engels, Weber, and Durkheim.

knowledge] which we meet here is by no means peculiar to economics but arises in connection with nearly all truly social phenomena . . . and constitutes really the central theoretical problem of all social science" (1945: 528).[28]

Politics differs from economics in that there is no neat analog to the price mechanism for seamlessly converting a mass of dispersed information into a single instantly communicable solution.[29] But Hayek's insistence that widely dispersed social knowledge inevitably escapes and defeats the best attempts at central planning by small groups of experts is germane to the question of why a democracy might compete well against hierarchical governments. I will argue that participatory democracy has the potential to behave more like a market and less like a central planning board in respect to useful knowledge. Democracies in the Athenian style can gain competitive advantage by devising institutions that respond to change through knowledge in action.

By *knowledge in action* I mean making information available for socially productive purposes through individual choices made in the context of institutional processes, and involving both innovation and learning.[30] The key to successful democratic decision making is the integration of dispersed and latent technical knowledge with social knowledge and shared values. Athens achieved higher than otherwise-expected performance through better-than-usual information processing—by transforming raw data and unprocessed information into politically valuable knowledge.[31] That transformation was carried out through processes that aggregated, aligned, and codified knowledge while balancing the poten-

---

[28] Cf. Hayek 1937. On the value of Hayek's insight about dispersed knowledge for understanding the social epistemology of democracy, see, further, Anderson 2006; Sunstein 2006: 118–45, 2007. On social epistemology, see Goldman 1999 and the articles published in the first three volumes (1–3: 2004–2006) of the journal *Episteme*.

[29] The outcome of occasional elections in a modern representative system of democracy is a poor analogy for the price mechanism; see below, chapter 3.

[30] While this definition borrows from philosophical pragmatism, it need not contradict the ordinary analytic definition of knowledge as "justified true belief." It acknowledges the basic insight of social epistemology, that the quest for truth is strongly and inevitably influenced by institutional arrangements that affect what belief-holding human agents hear from and say to each other. See further discussion in Goldman 1999 (analytic social epistemology) and Rorty 1979 (pragmatic social epistemology).

[31] The terms "data," "information," and "knowledge" are variously defined by organizational theorists. Davenport and Prusak (1998: 1–6) suggest that data are facts about events, information is data that have been given relevance and purpose, and knowledge is a matrix of experience, values, insight, and contextual information that allows for the incorporation of new experiences and information. See also Dixon 2000: 13; Brown and Duguid 2000: 119–202; Page 2007, on problem solving and prediction through diverse perspectives, interpretations, heuristics, and predictive models; and below, chapter 3, on social, technical, latent, and tacit knowledge.

tially contradictory drives for *innovation* as generation of new solutions and *learning* as socialization in routines of proven value.

The organizational theorist James March and his collaborators have shown (through studies of how business firms are organized) that innovation and learning are potentially contradictory drives: social learning is valuable in that learning allows routinization and routinization increases returns to effort. But the capacity for innovation, which is essential for success in changing competitive environments, depends on people's socialization in established routines remaining incomplete. In volatile environments, too much learning can compromise competitive advantage, as can too little learning when conditions are more predictable.[32]

When the innovation/learning balance, whether in a firm or a state, is right, its productive capacity will be high, and robustly so. We may describe such a system as exhibiting *good organizational design*. It is important to note that "design," as I use the term, need not imply a designer. A political system may be the product of unguided processes of experimental adaptation over time (on the analogy of the British "constitution"), or the product of formal planning (like the postwar West German or Japanese constitutions). Or it may be some combination of experimentation and formality (like the U.S. Constitution). In later chapters I will touch on, but not try to solve, the question of how much of the organizational design evidenced by the Athenian political system arose from a series of adaptive experiments, and how much can be attributed to an intelligently chosen top-down blueprint.[33]

Figure 1.1 presents a schematic and intentionally static model of the factors of knowledge at play in an ideal-type democracy. The burden of the following chapters will be to put these various factors into a dynamic relationship with one another—to bring the system to life by explaining its endogenous capacity for change. This will entail showing, first, why rational individuals would choose to share and exchange useful knowledge within particular institutional contexts. Next I must show how

---

[32] Levitt and March 1988, March 1991, pointing to the dangers of "competency traps" in which people learn an inferior process too well and thus fail to experiment with superior processes, "superstitious learning" arising from too much success or too much failure, the difficulty of accurately recording and routinizing what is known, and differing interpretations of history. See, further, Brown and Duguid 2000, 95–96; Chang and Harrington 2005; and chapter 3, below.

[33] Davies 2004 argues that ancient democracy was not the product of a formal theory, but a set of responses to particular situations and crises. Pettit 2002: 170–72, 245–56, discusses the issue of explaining how effective social equilibria can emerge without a designer and in the absence of a quasi-biological selection mechanism. Non-political systems that emerge and flourish by a combination of formality and experimentation include the Internet and many of its products (especially "wiki's": Sunstein 2006). See, further, chapters 3 and 7.

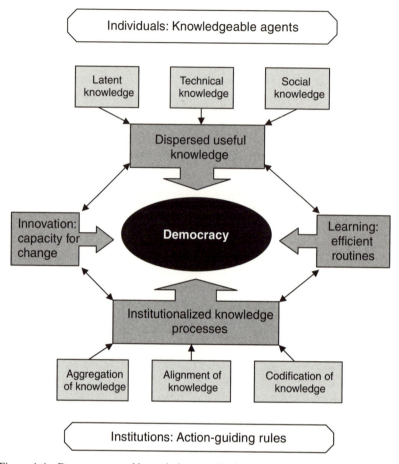

Figure 1.1. Democracy and knowledge. An ideal-type epistemic democracy incorporates individual agency and institutional structure. The knowledge possessed by individuals is organized by institutionalized processes. Social learning and ongoing innovation are outcomes of agency and process, and inputs to democracy.

action-guiding institutions both promoted the development of social learning and stimulated innovation. Finally, I will need to explain how Athenian institutions avoided ossification while remaining predictable enough that ordinary people—concerned with the everyday business of devising, refining, and pursuing their individual and collective life-plans—would choose to invest substantial time in learning how those institutions worked and in "working the machine" of Athenian self-governance.

In Athens, with its effective democratic institutions and vibrant civic culture, superior organization of knowledge became a key differentiator that allowed the community to compete effectively against its rivals.

There is no reason to believe that Athens' democratic productivity was a unique result of an irreproducible set of historically contingent circumstances. Although scale differences between Athens and any modern nation-state render direct comparisons inappropriate, some Athenian democratic institutions are structurally similar enough, in relevant ways, to those found in modern organizations to allow certain conclusions about the Athenian case to be extrapolated to contemporary circumstances. Among this book's ambitions is to demonstrate the value for democratic theory of a focus on public action. I also hope to show the value of ancient history for social science and vice versa. Finally, I hope to help persuade political scientists and historians alike that there is much to be gained from closer attention to dispersed knowledge, innovation, and learning.

Classical Athens offers a particularly good case for studying democracy and economic performance. It is historically complete, featuring long and reasonably well documented predemocratic, democratic, and postdemocratic periods (chapter 2). The relatively well-integrated, Mediterranean-centered world of the ancient Greek poleis (Horden and Purcell 2000; Morris 2003) allows us to hold cultural and environmental variables constant, strengthening the argument for the endogeneity of democratic productivity—which is to say that increased state capacity is produced by democracy rather than by some external cause. The world of the poleis was characterized by intense interstate competition (as well as cooperation) and was not a "small pond." Greece manifested remarkably strong overall demographic and economic growth over the course of the period in question (ca. 600–300 B.C.). Classical Greek standards of living and population densities are unusually high for premodern societies, and, in at least some geographic regions of the Greek world, appear to have approached modern levels (see, further, chapters 2, 3, and 7).

The need for effective public solutions to the problems of public action was acute in democratic Athens because of its relatively great size, the social diversity of its citizenry, and its culture of personal freedom and individual choice. As a society, Athens was sufficiently complex to make it interesting to students of the contemporary world—indeed, it is possible to speak without whimsy or paradox of ancient Athens as, in certain ways, "modern."[34] Of course, one need not be a political theorist, ancient historian, or social scientist to regard the success of democratic Athens as an interesting puzzle. How could a system of policy making by open

---

[34] Harris 2002 rightly points to the wide range of technical specializations among Athenians involved in market exchanges and offers a preliminary catalog of some 170 Athenian occupation titles. Modernity of Athens: Ober 2006, using Anthony Giddens' (1990) definition of modernity.

discussions in public assemblies attended by hundreds, or thousands, of non-expert decision makers have contributed so much to "the glory that was Greece"?[35]

CAVEATS AND METHOD

No case study is perfect, and there are limits to what the Athenian case can tell us. I will attempt to demonstrate that innovative solutions to public-action problems helped the Greek city-state culture to flourish and enabled democratic Athens to become richer and more powerful (on the whole and over time) than its city-state rivals. Ian Morris, Geoffrey Kron, and others have collected evidence showing that in comparison with other premodern cultures, classical (ca. 500–320 B.C.) Greeks in general and classical Athenians in particular were remarkably well off on a per capita basis (notably in terms of nutrition and house size), and much better off than they had been in the preceding "dark age" (ca. 1150–750) and the archaic era (ca. 750–500).[36] It is not possible, however, given the state of our evidence, to track short-term changes in well-being or wealth or to measure differences in per capita wealth or income between poleis. I focus here on the comparative overall performance of communities, as an admittedly imperfect proxy for their general economic welfare. The terms "flourishing" and "capacity" will be employed as shorthand for a given polis' actual and potential *economic and military performance when compared to rival poleis* and its *ability to accumulate resources, ensure security, and influence other states* in a competitive environment.[37]

---

[35] Of course the high culture that is typically associated with "the glory that was Greece" was not uniquely a product of democratic Athens (Boedeker and Raaflaub 1998; Robinson 2007), but to a remarkable extent classical Greek high culture was in fact produced by Athenians (both citizens and by foreign residents). Morris 2005b documents Athenian cultural dominance in the fifth century B.C. A growing body of work on musical performance (Wilson 2000; J. Shear 2003) suggests continued Athenian dominance, in at least some cultural areas, in the fourth century.

[36] Morris 2004, 2005a; cf. Kron 2005; Reden 2007a, table 15.1 (average heights of skeletons with breakout of data for late classical Athens). The post-classical period, in which Greek-speakers conquered and colonized parts of Asia and Egypt, appears to have continued high economic standards for some Aegean Greeks (notably the island-polis of Rhodes), although many parts of the Greek mainland saw steep declines in local rural economies after the fourth century. See Alcock 1993; Reger 1994; Gabrielsen 1997, 1999; Eich 2006. Prosperity continued in the imperial Roman era, but both economy and demography crashed in late antiquity; the sharp decline began in the third century. After a partial recovery, decline was precipitous after the sixth century: Scheidel 2004; Hitchner 2005; Jongman 2006.

[37] There is no way to measure gross domestic product for any Greek polis. A set of proxies for standard modern economic measures is described in chapter 2 and in the appendix.

Material well-being matters a lot, but it is far from the whole story. Prevailing in competition with rivals through superior economic and military performance was only one of the Athenians' goals in the era of democracy. Honoring the gods through appropriate rituals and preserving the freedom, equality, and dignity of citizens were regarded as vitally important ends. Economic and military performance may be regarded as a "satisficing condition," in that the necessity of achieving at least a minimum level of deployable wealth and power was a constraint on the resources and social energy that the Athenians—or the citizens of any other state in a competitive ecology—could afford to devote to achieving their other ends. There were some trade-offs, but pursuing the goals of higher performance and promoting other valued ends should not be regarded as zero-sum. The economic success of the state enabled temple building, numerous and splendid festivals, and other communal expressions of civic identity and religious feeling. Moreover, as I suggested above, social choices that promoted state performance were compatible with moral choices that preserved the goods of individual freedom, equality, and dignity for many (although certainly not all) Athenians.[38]

I will attempt to demonstrate, in the chapters that follow, that Athenian flourishing, especially in the post-imperial fourth century, rested less on rent seeking (that is, using power to extract remuneration beyond what a competitive market would provide) than on the development of Athens as a desirable and accessible center for exchange. Athens differed in important ways from premodern "natural states," which achieve a stable social, political, and economic equilibrium through strategic agreement by a small group of power holders to share rents with an exclusive body of specialists in violence. Natural states focus their economic activity on extracting rents and narrowly curtail access to legal rights and redress. By contrast, Athens flourished and thereby gained state capacity in part by creating conditions favorable to entry into institutions of exchange

---

While the proxies I have employed are rough, they are adequate to make the basic point that Athens did better in a material sense, overall and over the course of the classical period, than any of its polis rivals.

[38] Treating material success as a satisficing condition is to regard Athens in the terms used by behavioral economists, who work in the tradition established by Herbert Simon to explain profit seeking in the business firm: see Simon 1976 [1947], 1955; Cyert and March 1963. Participation in religious ceremony and ritual was a significant aspect of the lives of most Athenians (as it was to other Greeks) and properly honoring the gods was an important function of the Athenian state (as it was of other poleis); see Garland 1992, Parker 1996, 2006; Munn 2006. While Athens had an exceptionally dense ritual calendar (see chapter 5), it requires excessive special pleading to claim either that discovering the will of the gods and acting accordingly was the *primary* purpose of the Athenian democracy (as does Bowden 2005) or, alternatively, that democratic Athens was unusually *lacking* in religious expression (Samons 2004).

and law by diverse categories of persons—to lower-class citizens and ultimately to some non-citizens. The development of Athens as a trade center was thus promoted by the same institutionalized practices that sustained its democratic values of procedural fairness and free access to political institutions. Focusing on knowledge in action clarifies the relationship between democracy, fairness, and access across political, legal, and economic domains.[39]

There were limits to Athenian fairness and openness in regard to entry. Athenians remained attached to practices that were morally indefensible and economically unproductive. Classical Athens never approached its threshold of optimal performance in part because the Athenians failed to promote political equality beyond the ranks of native males. Much dispersed and potentially useful social and technical knowledge remained publicly inaccessible because the Athenian male citizens refused to accept women as full participants in the participatory political order, were too slow to naturalize long-term residents as citizens, and remained committed to slaveholding. While the rules governing Athenian slaveholding suggest that Athenians recognized the fundamental injustice of slavery, they were unwilling to abandon slavery as a culturally acceptable form of rent seeking.[40] These failings must be weighed heavily when judging Athens as a moral community, and they arguably contributed to Athens' eclipse in the late fourth century by the national empire of Macedon. But, insofar as these failings were common to the Greek city-states, they did not degrade Athens' performance *relative to its polis rivals*.

The question remains: Did the costs of Athens' commitment to political participation have a deleterious effect on Athenian economic and military performance? While difficult to quantify, there were certainly substantial financial costs associated with bringing many people with a wide range of specific and general competence into positions of relatively great public

[39] Definition of rent seeking: Krueger 1973; literature review: Mueller 2003: 333–58. On pre-modern states and rent seeking, see North 1981. While retaining features of a "natural state," Athens may be taken as an early and incomplete example of what North, Wallis, and Weingast (in progress) describe as the "open-access order"; see below, chapter 6.

[40] The question of the conditions under which slavery was economically efficient is vexed; J. Cohen 1997 reviews the evidence for the economics of slavery with reference to the social recognition of slavery's injustice and slavery as rent seeking. White 2006 argues that slavery should be regarded as rent seeking only if we assume universal self-ownership as the initial starting point. Greek practices of slavery do seem to assume this (Aristotle's peculiar doctrine of natural slavery is the exception; runaways were a persistent problem, and the motivation of the runaway was obvious to the Greeks). Greek slavery was therefore a form of rent seeking under the basic definition I am employing here, even though some specific examples of Athenian slavery (e.g., slaves engaged in banking), in which innovation and productivity were emphasized, do not fit the definition. Cf. the different approaches to the economics of ancient slavery and conclusions of Osborne 1995; Garlan 1995; Garnsey 1996; E. Cohen 2000; Scheidel 2005b; S. Morris and Papadopoulos 2005.

responsibility. The majority of Athenians who worked for a living could not afford to engage in public service without pay.[41] The cost of individual incompetence was sometimes high. I argue in detail, below, that these participatory costs were controlled by good institutional design, and that, over time, they were overbalanced by the knowledge gains that the Athenians reaped from participatory practices. Yet it is important to keep in mind that participation was in some ways costly, and that those costs did sometimes compromise short-term competitive advantage.[42] Along with financial costs and costly mistakes, there were certainly substantial losses of opportunity that resulted from Athens' open and participatory system of government. The high costs of doing democratic political business could have led to the general failure of the polis had Athens' social equilibrium not proved robust enough for Athens to be able to survive crises. The fact that there were crises that had to be survived points to the obvious fact that Athens was not consistently successful.

Moreover, although the Athenians liked to think of themselves as uniquely innovative and quick to take advantage of new opportunities, Athens was not in every sense unique in its own historical context. Overestimating their own capacities on the basis of overstating Athenian exceptionalism contributed to arrogance in the fifth century—and thus to bad public decisions. Although the Athenians sometimes spoke and acted as if their system were inimitable, Athens had no monopoly on good institutional design; some of this book's conclusions should help to explain the relative success of other classical and Hellenistic Greek poleis and non-polis collectivities— including the Macedonian kingdom that ultimately came to dominate the Greek poleis.

Successful institutional imitation by other states reduced Athens' performance advantage during the classical age, notably in the later stages of the Peloponnesian War and in the mid-fourth century, the era of the so-called Social War. In the Hellenistic period, public institutions and cultural practices first pioneered by democratic Athens were widely adopted by other poleis, especially in western Asia.[43] Imitation contrib-

---

[41] Burke 2005 surveys the history of democratic Athenian subsidization of the poor, through pay for public service and other means. M. H. Hansen 1999: 315–16, estimates the costs to the state of pay for public service. See below, chapter 6.

[42] Costs of participation: Dahl and Tufte 1973: 66–68. Williamson 1975: 46–54, includes decision-making inefficiency and failure to achieve economies of communication among the problems of participatory "peer group" governance, noting that "full group discussion . . . is time consuming and may yield little gain." Furthermore, he suggests, the lack of effective command and control mechanisms leads to opportunistic exploitation of shared information and malingering. See also below, chapter 3.

[43] Obvious examples include drama, theater architecture, the "epigraphic habit," and public decree formulas; see, for example, Hedrick 1999 and below, chapter 7. A full-scale historical treatment of the Hellenistic afterlife of Athenian-style institutions and political

uted to Athens' failure to retain its preeminence indefinitely. Yet by the same token, imitation of Athens almost certainly had an overall long-term positive effect on the Greek world. Although it is a difficult hypothesis to test, it seems likely that the vitality of the Greek polis as an organizational form, well into the periods of Macedonian and Roman rule, can be attributed in some part to the widespread and successful imitation of institutional solutions for public-action problems that were originally devised in Athens.

The Athenians' shortcomings—their moral failings, tendency to arrogance, mistakes of judgment, vulnerability to incompetence, and unwillingness to acknowledge their own limitations and imitability—are unlikely to be forgotten anytime soon. These issues have been repeatedly rehearsed since antiquity; the history of Athens must be reconstructed in large part from the literature written by its sternest ancient critics. The history of the Greek city-states has long been a matter of interest to political innovators, as a potential repository of valuable institutional forms. Yet many practice-oriented students of Greek history, including the American Founders, have been fearful of adopting Athenian-style participative and deliberative institutions. Their unease arose in part because Athens' historical record seemingly featured too many mistakes, which were attributed by critics to the ignorance of popular assemblies.[44]

Popular ignorance is a poor explanation for Athens' failings; Hayek's attention to dispersed knowledge suggests that elite ignorance is a more serious problem, because it is less often recognized. I will argue that the positive effect of democratic knowledge in action is what allowed Athens to survive its mistakes. By analyzing the function of democratic knowledge-based processes, this study aims to lower the perceived and actual risk of incorporating practices of participation and deliberation into contemporary systems of organizational governance.[45]

In arguing that the unusually robust and productive Athenian solution to the problems of public action depended on discovering effective means to organize what was known by a large community's diverse membership, I focus on three epistemic processes, each involving innovation and learning. First is *aggregation*, by which I mean the process of collecting the

---

culture would add a good deal to our understanding of the post-classical polis. See, meanwhile, Rhodes and Lewis 1997, a collection of decrees of Greek states.

[44] Athens as a negative example: J. T. Roberts 1994. Athens was, however, a source of positive inspiration for J. S. Mill: Urbinati 2002.

[45] It is in this spirit that Manville and Ober 2003 was written, albeit for an audience of business practitioners. My debt to Brook Manville for all that follows in this book is profound; without his urging, advice, and example, I would not have become engaged in the set of problems addressed here.

right kinds of dispersed knowledge in a timely manner for purposes of decision making. The second process is *alignment*, enabling people who prefer similar outcomes to coordinate their actions by reference to shared values and a shared body of common knowledge. Third is *codification*, the process by which implemented decisions become action-guiding rules capable of influencing future social behavior and interpersonal exchanges.

Each of these epistemic processes has been studied in depth by social scientists, but most often in isolation from the other two. Thus, for example, the literature on knowledge aggregation (often focusing on deliberative practices) typically treats common knowledge and information cascades as decision-making pathologies. Yet, once a decision has been reached, common knowledge and cascading must come into play in order to enable non-hierarchical groups to move from decision to implementation. Likewise, the extensive literature on the role of rules in lowering transaction costs tends to slight the question of how rules come to be made and revised in democratic contexts. Because we are seeking to explain the role of knowledge in the performance of a democratic organization, we must keep in mind the overall epistemic situation and attempt to grasp the dynamic interaction among epistemic processes. The three processes are schematically illustrated in figure 1.2 and explained in greater detail in chapter 3.

Exploring why an ancient democracy can be said to have an active and in some ways even *modern* approach to the aggregation, alignment, and codification of knowledge helps to explain the historical puzzle of Athenian exceptionalism. The approach taken in the following chapters varies between the synchronic approach of treating "democratic Athens" as a single entity, and a diachronic approach that breaks the long history of Athens from the seventh through the second centuries B.C. into twelve distinct periods (see chapter 2). The question of "why did Athens stand out from its rivals?" is more pointed because democratic Athens did not succeed "once and for all" by mastering a single economic domain: Athens rebounded from a series of shocks by adapting to changed circumstances and succeeding in new domains of collective endeavor. A key part of the answer to the question of how classical Athens flourished over time will be that democratic institutions, originally established to address particular problems at a specific historical moment in the late sixth century B.C., proved highly adaptive over the next six human generations. Institutional innovations served to ensure that Athens' capacity for solving public-action problems was preserved in the face of a changing environment. The net result was a sustained level of state wealth, power, and cultural influence—an outcome that could not have been fully anticipated by the democratic institutions' original framers.

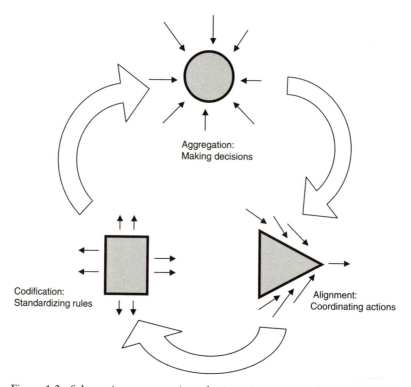

Figure 1.2. Schematic representation of epistemic processes (shapes) and knowledge flows (small arrows) in Athenian governmental institutions. The large arrows illustrate the dynamically recursive relationship among processes.

THE ARGUMENT AND ITS CONTEXTS

The following chapters employ a variety of methods for interpreting social behavior and public action. The deployment of well-tested theories for explaining the operation of social networks, the function of common knowledge, and the role of state institutions in lowering transaction costs can, I believe, help to reveal the wellsprings of Athens' record of accomplishment. The residents of ancient Greece had no comparable body of social theory to draw upon in explaining how and why democracy worked. Yet prominent ancient writers with direct experience of Athenian democratic practices have something to tell us about the relationship between democracy, knowledge, and action. Ancient Greek authors recognized incentive problems, and shrewdly perceived that democratic flourishing over time and in multiple domains was a product of institutionalized processes promoting cooperation, learning, and innovation. Moreover, because ancient writers tend to view public action and knowledge within a moral framework, they point the way to an integration of history, positive theory, and normative theory.[46]

This introductory chapter sets out the book's central hypothesis about democracy, public action, and knowledge organization, and then situates that hypothesis in the broader interpretive framework in which this book came to be written. Chapter 2 treats the history of Athens as a twelve-era "multiperiod case study" and empirically demonstrates two propositions. First is that Athens was highly successful (in terms of its material flourishing over time) when compared with peer polities and rivals—that is to say, with other major Greek poleis. The second proposition is that democracy played a causal role in Athens' success. Chapter 3 introduces competition, scale, and the organization of knowledge. I argue that knowledge organization, in its relationship to public action, at scale and in a competitive environment, is a critical factor in explaining why Athenian democratic institutions proved to be productive in the ancient Greek context. The chapter defines the relevant kinds and processes of knowledge with which we will be concerned, and confronts the doubts raised by organizational theorists about the very possibility of democratic productivity.

Chapters 4–6 examine in detail the three knowledge processes (aggregation, alignment, and codification) identified in chapter 3 as especially relevant to productivity. Each of these three central chapters describes particular democratic institutions and practices in Athens. We will look closely at the problems that institutions were meant to solve when they were first established, and how they functioned and evolved in the context of the democratic community and its changing competitive environment. Attention to how the Athenians developed and revised institutions in response to environmental challenges will in turn help to explain how the democratic order fostered innovation and learning within and across domains of endeavor, rewarded cooperative behavior, sanctioned misbehavior, and addressed incentive problems. In methodological terms, the theory of knowledge in action laid out in chapter 3 should (and does) predict the kinds of institutions that we find to be prevalent in Athens in chapters 4–6.

The concluding chapter 7 conjoins this book's findings about institutions and practices with some of my earlier work on the roles played by Athenian democratic ideology and political dissent in building and sustaining a large, diverse, and participatory democratic community. The result is a more fully rounded explanation of "how and why Athens performed as well as it did."

---

[46] Ober 2006, 2007, and in progress.

This book stands on its own, but it also completes a trilogy on the theory and practice of politics in democratic Athens. In the two previous installments (Ober 1989, 1998: outlined below), I deliberately slighted formal institutions of government and exchange in favor of an emphasis on power, rhetoric, ideology, and dissent. This book fills an institutional gap in my account of Athens, but it takes for granted that formal institutions are only one part of the story. I sketch the main arguments of the two previous parts of the trilogy below, but because the focus here is on the role of formal institutions and public practices, this book has relatively little to say about topics that I treated in detail in earlier work. Ideology and critique, and the discursive forms in which they were expressed, were fundamental aspects of Athenian political life and tightly interwoven with the formal institutions of democratic government.[47] If we are to comprehend the choices made by Athenians, as individuals and as collectivities, we must keep in mind that formal institutions are both affected by and are platforms for the expression of ideological commitment and critical challenge. If our goal is to sculpt an "in the round" portrait of Athenian political life in order to grasp the potential of participatory and deliberative democracy, we must integrate analysis of ideology and critique with rational calculation and ethical responsibility.[48]

Athenian state performance is of more than antiquarian interest because Athens was a diverse society governed by a genuine and robust democracy for some six generations (from 508 to 322 B.C.) and periodically thereafter. Athens would be uninteresting as a case study of democratic success if, counterfactually, popular participation were ephemeral, or a façade masking elite rule. Athens would be equally uninteresting if it were predicated on such a high level of homogeneity of thought and

[47] William Baumol's warning about causal explanation in economic history is relevant here: "Many economic historians set a booby trap for themselves when they attempt to explain particular historical developments in their entirety. . . [natural] scientists focus their search on what are, in effect, partial derivatives rather than seeking to account for complex phenomena of reality in their entirety" (Baumol 1990: 1715, quoted with approval in King, Keohane, and Verba 1994: 218, n. 7). My two earlier monographs and this one might be thought of as "partial derivatives"—each seeks to explain discrete but related aspects of the complex historical phenomenon of democratic performance.

[48] Williamson 1985: 268–71 gestures at this conjunction; Handy 1998, Brennan and Pettit 2004, Friedman 2005, and Greif 2006 address it in detail, from different but complementary perspectives. In each volume of this trilogy, in order to drive forward the double project of coming to a better *theoretical* understanding of participatory democracy and its *historical* role in Athenian political life, I have acted as a landscape photographer, deliberately holding the primary focus steady on a single plane in order to reveal some important but necessarily incomplete aspect of my subject. This allows me to produce relatively fine-grained "two-dimensional" studies, but it risks temporary blindness to essential dimensions of democracy and Athenian politics.

culture that diversity and free choice—hallmarks of modern democracy—were irrelevant. Since Athens offers a sustained example of a state that was indeed governed by the people and was characterized by high levels of epistemic diversity and individual agency, it is invalid to preempt the question "how does participatory democracy work?" by treating it as analytically equivalent to asking "how does a Pegasus fly?"—that is, as applicable only to imaginary entities.[49]

The most important preemptive claim about democracy is famously set out in Robert Michels' "iron law of oligarchy" (Michels 1962 [1915]). In his influential study of the historical development of European labor parties of the nineteenth and early twentieth centuries, Michels dispensed with the question "how does participatory democracy work?" by analytic fiat: democracy, as a sustainable form of participatory self-government by a mass of ordinary people in a large association, could never exist for long (and certainly not for anything like six human generations) because it predictably and rapidly devolves into the rule of a managerial elite. That devolution is driven by the requirement of large collectivities for organization in order to achieve (or indeed even seek to achieve) their ends. The intensity of that requirement and the apparent impossibility of organization arising from direct forms of mass decision making led Michels to state his sociological hypothesis about elite domination as an "iron law." Of course, if ever effective organization did arise and was sustained over time in a participatory democracy, such that a mass of people could consistently achieve their collectively chosen ends, the "iron law of oligarchy" would be refuted as such—even if Michels' general claim about the need for elite leadership remains valid under most conditions.[50]

In *Mass and Elite in Democratic Athens* (Ober 1989) I argued that there is no historical evidence for devolution to elite rule in Athens. In the fifth and fourth centuries alike, the *dēmos* as a body (the citizenry as a

---

[49] The depiction of Athens as both genuinely democratic and as intellectually and socially diverse is defended in Ober 1989, 1996, 1998, 2005b. Athens thus poses a challenge for both liberal (Miller 2000) and conservative (Schmitt 1985 [1926]) political theorists who suppose that participatory democracy demands full homogeneity.

[50] Michels' "Iron Law" builds on Max Weber's arguments about bureaucracy and rationality and anticipated mid-twentieth century theories of democratic elitism developed by Joseph Schumpeter (1947), Walter Lippman (1956), and Seymour Lipset (1981 [1960]): see Scaff 1981; T. Shaw 2006. A version of Michels' thesis became an article of faith among some Anglophone ancient historians (see, for example, Fornara and Samons 1991), especially in the wake of the seminal work of Ronald Syme (1939). Syme conjoined a commitment to the principle of inevitable oligarchy with the prosopographical study of aristocratic elite networks, associated in English history with Louis Namier (1957), in order to explain the process whereby the choices made by elite Romans in the late Roman republic allowed for the transformation of Rome into a monarchy. For discussion of the application of Michels' theory in the context of Athenian democracy, see Finley 1985.

whole, exemplified by the citizens at a given assembly) and the ordinary citizens, as individuals and working in small groups, actually ruled via direct participation in the primary institutions of governance. This does not mean that there were no leaders, or that there were no elite leaders with special expertise in domains relevant to organized governance.[51] It means that democratic leadership was built on a model of the volunteer expert adviser constantly seeking public attention and approval through direct communication with the citizenship, rather than on a model of the authoritative expert class of rulers who occasionally seek legitimation through elections. Socially elite Athenians retained their private wealth; the demos' political power was not used to impose equality of outcome by systematic violations of established claims to private property. Wealthy citizens could and did achieve political prominence, and thus positions of leadership, by demonstrating, through speech and action, both their expert credentials and their commitment to democratic cultural norms and aspirations. They did not, however, become a Michels-style ruling elite. In the present book I return to the issue of the roles played by elites and masses in democratic organization by specifying in more detail the institutional conditions under which public actions were carried out by a participatory citizenry over time.

I concluded *Mass and Elite* by stressing the importance of the ideological hegemony of the ordinary citizens— the control of the discursive contexts in which public behavior of individuals was judged and in which abstractions (such as freedom and equality) were evaluated and associated with political practices. That conclusion left open the possibility of another easy answer for Athenian democratic success: that the citizen-centered (and thus adult, native, male-dominated) Athenian political culture was so massively hegemonic as to eliminate diversity of thought or behavior, and with it many of the public action problems we associate with diverse communities of individuals capable of identifying and seeking their own good.

On this potential line of argument (which can be stated positively in Rousseauian terms, or negatively in Orwellian terms), it was not really democracy as it is normally understood that produced the result of successfulness, but rather it was a sort of communal "one-mindedness" that did away with individual agency and obscured intracommunity diversity. Athens might thus be explained in terms of a homogeneity that could be regarded as worthy of praise by strong communitarians or blame by liberals. Yet, as a corollary, it is generally supposed that such homogeneity is

---

[51] Kallet-Marx 1994 erroneously states that in Ober 1989 I described Athens as a community in which expert leadership was entirely lacking; her error is based on ascribing to me a claim made in a speech of Demosthenes that stakes out one pole of a continuum of Athenian opinion on the proper role of public speakers; see Ober 1989: 163–65, 314–27.

(for better or worse) only sustainable under conditions of premodernity. A homogeneous Athens would be of little interest in thinking about democracy as a modern system of organizational governance because all modern democratic systems must accommodate epistemic and social diversity, and must be predicated on the choices of individuals freely seeking to fulfill their own aspirations.[52]

In *Political Dissent in Democratic Athens* (Ober 1998) I argued that Athenian democracy cannot be explained in terms of cultural normalization and epistemic homogeneity. I focused on the development of an influential dissident "critical community" among Athenian intellectuals and on the form and content of their written work. The dissidents recognized Athens as a socially diverse political association, made up of individuals willfully pursuing individual aspirations through individual actions. Far from supposing that Athenian cultural norms rendered public action simple, the dissidents worried about how good public decision making was possible in the face of individual self-interest and that ethical norms had too little purchase on members of a community that celebrated individual freedom. They sought to explain how a "bad" (or at least misguided) popular regime could be so apparently successful, and what sort of alternatives to it might be devised, in theory or in practice. Their efforts resulted in much of the literature (including Thucydidean history, Platonic and Aristotelian political philosophy) that we now tend to regard as typical of classical Greece.

I concluded *Political Dissent in Democratic Athens* by arguing that an important component of Athens' democratic capacity to change over time in response to new challenges was realized within the space democracy left open for the development and voicing of openly dissident opinion. Here I return, briefly and in passing, to Thucydides, Plato, and Aristotle as theorists of democracy, focusing on their explanations for how solving public action problems and organizing useful knowledge allowed participatory democracy to exceed expectations, despite what they regarded as its very serious failings as a system of government.[53]

In sum, we ought not seek preemptively to answer the question of how Athens' participatory democracy worked by reference either to a cryptic ruling elite of experts, or to a homogeneous premodern mass culture that eliminated potential public action problems by normative fiat. Yet two other obvious answers for explaining democratic flourishing will occur to readers familiar with modern discussions of democracy. First is the

---

[52] Positive version of this communitarian argument: Barber 1984; negative version: Philipps 1993. Victoria Wohl (1998, 2002) develops a strong version of this ideological hegemony line of argument for Athens.

[53] I offer a much fuller account of classical Greek writers as theorists of information exchange and collective action in Ober, in progress.

free-market economist's belief that democracy succeeds because it allows for the development of open markets and robust economic growth.[54] Next is the classical republican's claim that democracy benefits from high morale and civic virtue, as well as a sense of patriotism, shared identity, and communal solidarity among the citizenry.

Markets and morale do indeed help to illuminate the Athenian democratic case and help to explain the overall positive correlation between generically republican (non-despotic) constitutional form and success among Greek poleis (see chapter 2). Each will receive a good deal more discussion in the chapters that follow. It is now widely (although not universally) acknowledged that, especially in the fourth century, the Athenian economy was market oriented in some important ways.[55] And it is certainly the case that democracy promoted a relatively strong sense of citizen identity, based in part on shared values of liberty, political equality, and security.[56] But market economy and citizen-centered morale effects are themselves only two aspects of the organization of knowledge. Athens' market economy and the morale of its citizens seem to me inadequate, *in themselves*, to explain Athenian exceptionalism within the city-state ecology. The growth of Athens' market was stimulated by institutionalized public knowledge processes (see chapter 6). Meanwhile, rival republican Greek states (such as Sparta) featured non-democratic systems of governance specifically designed to maximize morale effects. If morale adequately explains polis flourishing, then democratic Athens should not have competed against its non-democratic republican rivals as well as it demonstrably did.[57]

Experts and Interests

The focus on social epistemology, on *knowledge* as a key to a democratic state's success, may, on the face of it, seem peculiar, given that success

[54] Friedman 2005 makes the case in detail.

[55] Athens' economy as market oriented: W. Thompson 1978; Burke 1985, 1992; E. Cohen 1992, 2000; Christesen 2003. Doubts: Millet 1991; Reed 2003. For critical assessments of the "ancient economy debate," see Morris 1994; Bresson 2000; Andreau 2002; Cartledge 2002; Reden 2002a, 2002b; Engen 2004; Saller 2005; Amemiya 2007.

[56] There is a large and valuable literature on Athenian civic identity stimulated, in large part, by the seminal work of W. R. Connor; see, for example, Connor 1987; Manville 1990; Boegehold and Scafuro 1994; Wolpert 2002; Low 2002; Lape 2004; Christ 2006.

[57] Spartan education and morale: Cartledge 2001, chapter 7; Ducat 2006. The morale argument is one reason that classical republicans, such as Rousseau, have long turned to Sparta rather than to Athens as a model. There are a variety of other "easy answers" for the success of Athenian democracy, notably that exploitation of slave labor and/or building male solidarity through the oppression of women was of decisive importance. I address these arguments in Ober 1989; 22–35. See further, below, chapter 6.

demands expertise and participatory democracy places much responsibility for public affairs in the hands of non-experts. Commentators have rightly pointed out that democratic institutions and culture contribute to citizen morale and to the credibility of a government's commitment to repay its debts. These democratic features translate into advantages in the vital areas of military mobilization and raising capital. Yet, in light of the expertise issue, it is often assumed that successes enjoyed by a participatory democracy like Athens must be in spite of, rather than because of, its approach to the organization of useful knowledge. Plato's *Republic* provides the paradigm case.[58]

Plato famously argued in the *Republic* that democracy was systematically flawed as a form of governance because (inter alia) it was based on a bad relationship between knowledge (understood as justified true belief) and political authority. He reasoned that the practice of democracy requires a capacity for good judgment about the basic question "what choices are most conducive to the human good?" on the part of non-expert ordinary citizens, operating both in groups and individually. Plato denied that ordinary men had the capacity to make judgments about the human good, or could ever gain it. He held that in any given domain (be it shoemaking or ruling), judgment ought to be left to experts with the specialized knowledge that would render their judgments valid. Plato argued that in an ideal state only philosophers would rule. His argument was based on his assumption that the domain of ruling required expert philosophical knowledge of the Form of the Good. Because only a very few people had the capacity ever to develop philosophical expertise, and even then only by dint of long training, rulership must always be left in the hands of a tiny elite of the wise.[59]

Few subsequent commentators on the theory and practice of government have followed Plato in making philosophical knowledge of the Form of the Good a prerequisite for ruling, and Plato himself offered alterna-

---

[58] Morale and mobilization: Machiavelli, *Discorsi*, and literature cited by Ferejohn and Rosenbluth 2005. Reiter and Stam 2002 demonstrate that modern democracies tend to win wars. Their explanation for this phenomenon combines the standard morale argument (soldiers with a stake in the regime fight better) with an argument that the discipline of needing to win and retain a popular mandate prompts democratic leaders to fight wars that they are pretty sure they can win. Mobilization and Greek republics: Morris 2005c; Scheidel 2005a. For democracy and Athenian military performance, with special reference to the early stages of the Peloponnesian War, see Ober 2007a. Schultz and Weingast (2003) focus on the credibility of the commitment of democratic states to repay their loans and their subsequent advantage in securing reliable funding during extended periods of interstate conflict. On the question of democracy and military success, see, further, chapter 2.

[59] Plato on knowledge and democracy: Sharples 1994; Hitz 2004, chapter 2; Schofield 2006. On Plato as a commentator on democracy: Anton 1998; Ober 1998, chapter 4; Monoson 2000; Wallach 2001; Euben 2003; Saxonhouse 2006.

tives in his later political dialogues, *Statesman* and *Laws*.[60] But Plato's general argument in the *Republic*, that ruling is primarily a matter of specialized expertise, and that the capacity to develop the relevant expertise is limited to relatively few people and requires special training, is widespread. Plato drew a sharp divide between opinion and knowledge, holding that those who are not expert in a given domain can have only opinions about it, not actual knowledge of it. His theory of governance is predicated on a strict separation between the spheres of opinion and knowledge. Modern political and social theorists tend to agree with Plato on the knowledge/opinion distinction. Most break with Plato by asserting that in order to be legitimate, a political system must find a way to give non-expert opinions a certain weight. Approached from this direction, democratic government can be understood as a system for accommodating non-expert public opinion within a domain of expert knowledge. Modern democracies achieve that accommodation primarily through the majoritarian voting rule and structures of representation. This leaves considerable room for arguments in favor of limiting popular participation in favor of efficiency.[61]

In an influential (and explicitly anti-Platonic) model, Robert Dahl (1989) predicates democracy on the widely shared conviction (regarded by Plato as false) that each individual is the best judge of his or her own interests. But that presumption does not entail supposing that the individual is capable of formulating or even deciding among the actual governmental policies that would best facilitate the achievement of her interests. Without that capacity, the opinionated individual cannot be a competent direct legislator of her own interest. This suggests that the role of non-expert opinion in governance is likely to be detrimental, unless it is very carefully controlled—and thus, well-designed structures of representation are required. In Dahl's theory, like most theories of republican government from James Madison onward, if a government is to be legitimate, the non-expert citizen must be permitted to vote for represen-

---

[60] For a range of views on Plato's late political thought, see, for example, Piérart 1974; Bertrand 1999; Bobonich 2002.

[61] Estlund 2007 argues against Platonic-type "epistocracy"—the rule of those who know—while accepting that there probably are only a few people who really do know best. Estlund's argument necessarily pits efficiency (the few-who-know-best rule without undue interference) against legitimacy (the rule of the knowledgeable elite must be acceptable from all reasonable points of view). Caplan 2007 argues for institutional changes in democracy that would limit the role of "irrational voters" in favor of policy made by expert economists (like himself). Organizational theorists sympathetic to workplace democracy, e.g., Fitzgerald 1971 and Putterman 1982, sometimes regard the scarcity of managerial expertise, and the alignment of managers' interests with hierarchical forms of organization, to be a potentially fatal weakness of democratic organizations in competitive environments; but see now Orlikowsky 2002, esp. 265–69; Locke and Romis 2006.

tatives: that is, to make a choice among various possible rulers based on his opinion of which of them will work most effectively to further his interests. The actual ruling is left to experts. This line of thought eliminates, by definition, directly participatory democracy as a form of governance.[62]

Democratic theory brings in representation and experts for two reasons: to accommodate the problem of scale, and as a prosthetic institutional mechanism to accommodate the incapacity of non-experts to rule directly in their own interests. The scale problem is a serious one; it is addressed in chapter 3. Because the scale of most modern states is vastly greater than that of the largest Greek polis, the Athenian case cannot be held to offer a participatory *alternative* to representation for any modern democratic state. But the prosthesis of representation is often clumsy in practice. Athenian deliberative and participatory institutions, with their emphasis on employment of diverse sources of knowledge for problem solving, might offer a valuable *supplement* to existing forms of representative government, especially at local levels. Of course, the political experience of Athens will be valuable as a supplement to modern representative practice only if Athenian institutions can be shown to have distinctive and valuable features that could potentially be abstracted from their original ancient setting. This conjoined theoretical and descriptive enterprise is undertaken in this book.

HYPOTHESIS

The hypothesis explored in the following chapters can now be framed as follows:

> *Democratic Athens was able to take advantage of its size and resources, and therefore competed successfully over time against hierarchical rivals, because the costs of participatory political practices were overbalanced by superior returns to social cooperation resulting from useful knowledge as it was*

[62] Of course, the actual representatives for whom one votes need not be legislative experts; they must only defer to experts in formulating policy. On contemporary theories of representation, see chapter 3. Theoretical critiques of representation, favoring more participatory forms of democracy, include Dahl 1970; Pateman 1970; Mansbridge 1983; Barber 1984; Wolin 1994, 1996. These critiques do not have as much traction as they might, in part because of performance failures of participatory experiments of various kinds. The argument of this book suggests that those failures can, at least in part, be attributed to poor organization in respect to useful knowledge. Successful local participatory processes are documented by Fung and Wright 2003; Fung 2004; Baiocchi 2005.

organized and deployed in the simultaneously innovation-pro-
moting and learning-based context of democratic institutions
and culture.

The hypothesis can be tested, and potentially falsified, by reference to Athenian government institutions and history. If the hypothesis is correct, then distinctive and otherwise anomalous design features of Athenian in-tuitions should be parsimoniously explained by reference to their role in organizing and deploying useful knowledge. Furthermore, it should be possible to show that democratic institutions did in fact organize dis-persed useful knowledge, in ways that are plausibly related to general material flourishing. Finally, if the hypothesis is right, Athenian institu-tions, individually and taken as a system, should demonstrably have served to promote social learning and thus to facilitate productive routin-ization. They should also have adapted to change over time as a result of steady innovation. The hypothesis would be falsified if Athenian institu-tions manifested the strong path dependency associated with robust forms of socialization, or if they changed in the whimsical and undisciplined manner that Tocqueville (among others) associated with democracy as majoritarianism. Yet before testing the democracy/knowledge hypothesis, we need to confirm that there really is a substantial problem that it might solve. Was democratic Athens, in fact, an especially successful polis?

Chapter 2

ASSESSING ATHENIAN PERFORMANCE

ATHENS WAS A POLIS, a city-state that existed in an interstate milieu defined, in the first instance, by other city-states.[1] Athenian performance should, therefore, be measured in the first instance by reference to the performance of other city-states. This entails defining the standard of performance typical of ordinary city-states and of the city-states that were Athens' primary rivals, and then setting Athenian performance against those benchmarks. Below, I offer three comparative indices of polis performance: aggregate material flourishing, distribution of minted coins, and prominence in classical Greek literature. The data are "noisy" (containing relatively high levels of random error) in each case, but not so noisy as to be without heuristic value. The basic results are consistent and unambiguous: in each index Athens ranks as the preeminent Greek polis by a very substantial margin. This is especially notable given that the world of the Greek poleis was densely populated and the economy of the Greek world appears to have been unusually strong by pre-modern standards. Thus, Athens was the outstanding competitor in what was, for its time, a highly demanding environment.[2]

Athens stands out starkly from the quotidian poleis on each indicator of performance, but also dominates the top group of poleis, including its major rivals, Sparta and Syracuse. This general conclusion is in line with mainstream professional opinion and is not in doubt. At the end of the chapter we will look at the more difficult question of correlating quantitative evidence for polis performance with democracy. Although the data are harder to interpret, it appears that changes in Athenian performance

[1] The Greek city-states in turn existed in a larger Mediterranean/western Asian context, a context that included prominent non-Greek city-states (notably Carthage). In an influential study, Horden and Purcell 2000 emphasize the long-term continuities (especially movement of people, fluid exchange relations, and cultural interconnection) of the Mediterranean context. Morris 2003 notes the difficulty involved in delimiting "the Mediterranean," warns against timeless "Mediterraneanism" as an analytic construct, and underlines the necessity of paying attention to how political and sociological processes led to "winners and losers."

[2] Unusually strong Greek economic and demographic performance: Goldstone 2002; Morris 2004, 2005a; Kron 2005; Scheidel 2006; M. H. Hansen 2006b (the most recent and plausible estimate of total population of the Greek world).

capacity are strongly and positively correlated with changes in the direction of democratic government.

What is it about Athenian democracy that produces the positive result? When compared to other Greek poleis and to its own pre- and post-democratic eras, classical Athens stands out not only for its very highly developed and innovative participatory institutions, but also for the relatively open access it offered to key economic and legal institutions. Moreover, the conjoined preference for institutional innovation and open access grew over the course of Athenian history, and is especially evident in the notably prosperous late classical era of 354–322 B.C. Athenian historical development is surveyed later in this chapter. In the wider universe of Greek poleis, the relationship between performance and democracy in the Tocquevillian sense—a political system characterized by an inclusive citizenry and majority rule—is relatively weak. Strong democracy is correlated with moderately good performance but not with *outstanding* performance. Because classical Athens remains an exceptionally high performing state when compared both to other Greek democracies and to non-democratic periods of Athenian history, we will need to analyze distinctive institutional and cultural features of Athenian democracy in more detail in the chapters that follow.

HISTORICAL EVALUATION

It would not, I think, be regarded as tendentious by most Greek historians to say that over the period 508–322 B.C., taken as a whole, Athens was a very successful polis if we specify two conditions of evaluation: First, the relevant measures of polis success should be wealth, power, security, stability, and cultural influence—as opposed to moralistic criteria, such as virtuousness (as adherence to traditional values) or piety (as it is understood in monotheistic traditions). Second, the comparison group ought to be other real Greek poleis over the full course of the late archaic and classical period—as opposed to hypothetical ideal states or national empires.[3]

---

[3] Brock and Hodkinson 2000: 9–13 express the *communis opinio* of professional historians: compared to other Greek poleis, Athens was exceptionally populous, wealthy, urbanized, and politically stable. While I am very concerned with assessing Athens in the moral terms employed by the fields of contemporary democratic theory and analytic political philosophy, I am not concerned with answering Samons 2004 (see review of M. H. Hansen 2006d) or other ideological social conservatives who find both ancient Athens (especially in the post-imperial fourth century) and modern America deficient in "traditional" values of reverence for God, family, and nation, and who despise as shallow and contemptible the

Athens is sometimes compared to ideal poleis described by ancient political philosophers—Plato's Callipolis of the *Republic*, Aristotle's "polis of our prayers" of *Politics*, book 7—or to an ideal and counterfactual error-free Athens. In comparison to these imaginary entities, Athens was, of course, unsuccessful, but deviation from perfection is not the relevant criterion. Democratic Athens was highly experimental, and a good many of its experiments failed, sometimes in spectacular and costly ways. It is easy to point to Athenian errors and miscalculations, without which Athens would certainly have been *more* successful. The litany of Athenian failures is long and varied, and has provided much ammunition for those who argue that participatory democracy in the Athenian style should be considered inefficient, immoral, or both. Yet measuring Athens against an imaginary ideal is no more historically meaningful than measuring a real investment record against an ideal investor who always buys at the bottom of the market and sells at the top. To say that such an ideal type investor would soon control all the money in a perfect market is true but irrelevant to the project of rating an actual investment record. Likewise, in rating Athenian successfulness, the question is not whether, in hindsight, Athens might have done better, but how Athens stacked up against its real-world rivals.[4]

The other category of state entity with which Athens is sometimes misleadingly compared is the ancient national empire (e.g., Assyria, Persia, Macedon, Rome).[5] It is certainly true that poleis did not define the sum of political entities with which Athens and other Greek poleis periodically contended. At several key moments in Greek history, the Greek poleis militarily confronted large-scale national empires that sought (unsuccess-

---

(classical and modern) democratic regard for freedom, choice, and diversity. Given our sharply divergent evaluative standards, there is little ground for productive debate.

[4] Notable Athenian failures include the disastrous Egyptian expeditions of the 450s, the failed attempt to take over Boeotia in the 440s, the crowding into the city after the outbreak of the Peloponnesian War that worsened the effects of the plague of 430–29, the catastrophe in Sicily in 413, the mass trial of the Arginusai generals in 406, followed by defeat at Aigospotami in 405 and surrender to Sparta in 404, executing Socrates in 399, the debilitating Social War of the 350s, and the defeats at the hands of Macedon at Chaeronea in 338 and in the Lamian War in 322. The historical trope that "Athenian democracy was a failure because it made mistakes" dates back to antiquity and has been frequently repeated ever since; see J. T. Roberts 1994.

[5] See, for example Runciman 1990, arguing, inter alia, that Greek poleis were structurally "doomed to extinction" because, in comparison with successful pre-modern empires, the Greek poleis were far too democratic and thus failed to develop institutions allowing for elite consolidation of power. Runciman draws upon the familiar but false notion that democracy suffers from inherently poor institutional design (failure of the authority relation) and so must invariably be beaten in competition with hierarchies. See, further, chapters 3 and 7.

fully in the case of Persia, successfully in the case of Macedon) to dominate them. In an interesting counterfactual, Ian Morris (2005b) has suggested that had the Athenians not made the single human error of invading Sicily in 415, Athens might have transcended the scale limitations of the polis by evolving into a national empire. Yet in the event, Athens remained a polis and, like all other poleis, Athens operated within an environment defined, in the first instance, by other individual poleis or by groups of poleis (e.g., *koina*)—that is, within a "city-state culture."[6]

Comparing the performance of a city-state to that of a national empire is not a very meaningful exercise, in light of the differences of both scale and organizational form. Yet historians have often posed the question, "Why did Athens fail to stop the king of Macedon in 338 B.C.?" Various answers have been offered. But the fact that fifteen years after 338 B.C. the king of Macedon ruled much of what was (as far as the Greeks were concerned) the known world suggests that the independent variable of "Athenian performance" is unlikely to explain very much about the dependent variable of Macedonian expansion. In seeking to assess Athenian performance, the relevant question is not, "Why did a city-state fail to defeat a given national empire?" Rather it is, "How well did a polis respond over time to the challenges presented by national empires?" Responses ranged from military confrontation, to diplomatic negotiation, to accommodation. At any point in Greek history and over time, it is possible to assess how a given polis ranks relative to its polis rivals in terms of achieving its endogenous goals in the face of threats and opportunities—including those associated with the presence of national empires in the larger competitive ecology.

The historical record clearly demonstrates that when compared to its rivals, Athens was, at various points in its democratic history, outstanding in various ways. In 435 and in 335 B.C. alike, Athens certainly boasted the largest economy among the Greek poleis and was the center of eastern Mediterranean trade: this was not the case in 535 (before the democracy was established) or 235 (after democracy was suppressed). In both 435 and 335 Athens had unmatched capital resources (state treasure and taxable base), and an unequaled navy of warships. Athens was defended by mighty fortification walls, could summon a large land army, featured a stable government and a reliable system of dispute resolution. In both years Athens was unquestionably the cultural capital of the Greek world. Athenian literature, art, and architecture were preeminent—more widely admired, and more frequently imitated than the cultural products of any other polis.

---

[6] See M. H. Hansen 2000, 2006a for the concept of "city-state culture," and other historical examples.

It is also notable that Athens became and remained a magnet for voluntary immigration. It seems unlikely that any other Greek state could come close to Athens in the size and diversity of its resident-alien (metic) population across the classical period. To the extent to which a polis' flourishing can be modeled by its "all things considered desirability as an immigration destination," Athens again stands out. Although there was considerable variation over time in Athens' desirability as an immigration destination, if it could be averaged over the course of the democratic era (508–322), Athens would probably rank at the top of the list of all poleis as a chosen destination. That would not be the case in the two centuries preceding or following the democratic era.[7]

Aggregate Flourishing

The historical judgment of Athens' relative standing is borne out by the material collected in the *Inventory of Archaic and Classical Poleis* (Hansen and Nielsen 2004), a recently compiled catalog of the evidence available for the approximately one thousand Greek city-states during the archaic and classical periods. Quantifying evidence from the *Inventory* allows us to develop statistical profiles of some aspects of individual polis performance. The following discussion is based on a database compiled from the raw evidence available in the now-standard *Inventory*.[8] The text and indices to this comprehensive collection allow cross-polis comparisons of various sorts of state activity and accomplishment, including (as here) fame (count of *Inventory* text columns), territorial size (in square kilometers), interstate activity (measured by *proxenoi* given and received, *theorodokoi* established, and count of Panhellenic victory locales), and number of public buildings.

We can also compare poleis on the basis of their average reported constitutional form (on a 1–5 scale from tyranny to democracy), and some aspects of their reported political history (experience of regime types [democracy, oligarchy, and tyranny], civil conflict, and destruction). The *Inventory* includes some evidence of constitutional regime for 199 poleis (thus, about one in five of all known poleis) and includes territory size for

---

[7] Athenian metics: Whitehead 1977; E. Cohen 2000. Lexicon of known Athenian metics: Osborne and Byrne 1996. See, further, chapter 6.

[8] Hansen and Nielsen 2004 is more comprehensive in its coverage of minor states than other encyclopedic works of reference, but where comparison is meaningful (coverage devoted to individual poleis as measured by columns of text: i.e., "fame" score), the correlation between the *Inventory* and two other recent and standard works of reference (*Oxford Classical Dictionary*, third edition; *Neue Pauly*) is reassuringly high; see appendix table A.4 for details.

164 of those. These statistics contain very considerable selection bias, in that the evidence was compiled from literary and archaeological records. Literature was produced in some poleis but not in others; some poleis have been thoroughly excavated while others have not. The next statistical measure (coin hoards) we will consider, below, is much less affected by systematic bias, but it is also less complete. The *Inventory* evidence permits a preliminary ranking of poleis, which can then be tested against other data.

The following discussion is based on ranking these 164 poleis on an 80-point scale, in which fame, territory size, extent of interstate activity, and number of public buildings are equally weighted (maximum of 20 points for each category). The aggregate numerical score for each polis serves as a rough proxy for its "overall material flourishing."[9] Figure 2.1 displays the range of aggregate scores (with broken out fame scores as a control) for the 164 poleis in the sample.

We will consider the 20 highest-ranking Greek poleis (the poleis on the far-left side of figure 2.1); but in order to put Athens and other leading poleis in their proper geopolitical context, we should first consider the "middling group," composed of the 80 poleis in the two middle quartiles of the ranked poleis (i.e., those ranking 41st to 120th overall: the poleis in the center of fig. 2.1). The middling group of 80 poleis has a median aggregate score of 18.4 on the 80-point scale.[10] The group includes many poleis well known to Greek historians, as well as a few that are fairly obscure. The poleis in this middling group were often prominent regionally, but were unlikely to be serious rivals to the states in the top group of 20. The poleis in the middling group are, therefore, closer to approximating the "ordinary Greek polis"—more reasonable approximations, in terms of size and standing (if not for virtuousness), for Aristotle's moderately sized "polis of our prayers."[11] It is important, however, to keep in mind that the poleis of this middling group were much more prominent than the great majority of Greek poleis. Most of the ca. 850 known classi-

---

[9] The database was compiled under my direction by David Teegarden. My thanks to Lynn Gale of the CASBS for assistance in organizing and analyzing the data. See appendix A for details on how the scoring was done. It should be kept in mind that the specific flourishing of the individual poleis took place in the context of overall economic growth across the Greek world, from 800 to 300 B.C.—a level of sustained growth (measured, inter alia, by rising population, increasing age at death, and increasing size of houses) that is quite remarkable by pre-modern standards. See Morris 2004.

[10] Aggregate score range: 10.68 (Massalia) to 25.34 (Karystos); standard deviation = 4.23.

[11] Aristotle's "polis of our prayers" is to be small enough so that the citizens can know one another, and the herald need not have superhuman powers. It is to be walled and capable of defending itself, with modern technology as appropriate: see *Politics*, book 7. On the problem of defining the ordinary polis, see, further, Hansen 2006a, chapter 13.

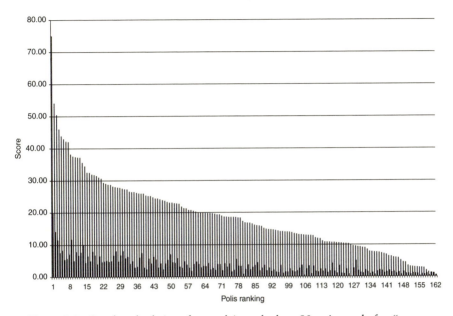

Figure 2.1. One hundred sixty-four poleis ranked on 80-point scale for "aggregate material flourishing" (fame + territory size + international activity + public building = higher bars) and on 20-point scale for "fame" (measured by *Inventory* text columns = lower bars). The spikiness of the fame scores shows that aggregate flourishing is not simply a function of fame (Pearson correlations: Appendix A.1).

cal poleis that remain unranked in my database are historically obscure.[12] Although information is lacking, they are likely to be, on the whole, smaller than those in the middling group, less involved in interstate activity, and with fewer public buildings. The rankings are tabulated in more detail (and how the counting was done is described) in appendix A.

In the classical era the standard middling polis (i.e., the median polis of the middling group) had a territory of some 200–300 square kilometers, with a total population not exceeding a few tens of thousands.[13] Its constitution averaged out to oligarchy, but it is quite likely (40 percent chance) to be known to have experienced tyranny, and somewhat more

[12] Some well-known poleis (e.g., Amphipolis, Magnesia, Melos) are left out of the database because the *Inventory* is agnostic in terms of either territory size or constitutional form. With some more work by historians, these and other states could probably be added to an expanded database, but the overall results would not be much different.

[13] It is difficult to estimate actual population. If we take the low and high area figures, and multiply by a low of 50 persons/km and a high of 100 persons per km, we arrive at a population of ca. 10,000–30,000, which must be in the right general range. See, further, Hansen 2006b.

likely to have experienced actual oligarchy (50 percent) and democracy (55 percent). Of the 80 poleis in the middling group, 26 are known to have had an assembly of citizens; 28 had a government council; but only 6 are known to have had a system of law courts. Of the 80, 50 minted coins of both silver and bronze (or some other metal); 23 others minted only silver; 3 minted only bronze; only 4 are not known to have issued coinage. In terms of "interstate" activity, just over half (46) are known to have received *proxenoi* (i.e., one or more of its citizens was offered diplomatic courtesies) from other poleis, while only about a quarter of the middling poleis (23) offered *proxenos* status to citizens of other poleis. *Theorodokoi* (hosts of ritual ambassadors en route to a sanctuary) were established by 28 poleis, very occasionally more than once. Citizens from 28 of the 80 middling poleis won a total of at least 40 victories in Panhellenic games. Of the middling poleis, 46 had one or (quite often) more temples; 27 are known to have had one or (very occasionally) more public buildings; 22 had a theater; 13 had one or more *stoas*. Of the 80 middling poleis, only 2 had a stadium; and none is known to have had a gymnasium. On the other hand, almost all (72) of the middling poleis were fortified by a wall around the central town; 3 had only a fortified Acropolis; 5 are not known to have been fortified. Half of the middling poleis (41) suffered civil war (*stasis*) one or more times in its recorded history. It is particularly notable that 30 percent of them (24) were destroyed (totally or partially) at some point in their archaic or classical history. For details, see appendix A.

Limiting ourselves for the time being to information available in the *Inventory*, Athens appears similar to the "standard middling" polis in some ways: it was a walled city, coining silver and bronze, with the historical experience of democracy, oligarchy, and tyranny. Like many of the middling poleis, Athens suffered civil conflict and the city was physically destroyed (by Persia in 480 B.C.). It had a well-documented Assembly and a Council (see chapter 6), but also a system of law courts and special constitutional "lawmakers" (*nomothetai*, otherwise attested only at Syracuse; see chapter 6). Athens was much larger than the standard middling polis—2,500 square kilometers with a total population estimated at ca. 250,000. Athens was highly active in international affairs, both giving and receiving proxenoi, establishing *theorodokoi*, and its citizens won athletic victories at all four major Panhellenic festivals. Athens stands out sharply from the middling poleis in the number of its public buildings: multiple substantial buildings were devoted to government purposes, along with temples, theaters, stoas, gymnasiums, and stadiums.[14]

---

[14] Data based on the *Inventory* index substantially underreports actual Athenian public buildings, due to the index counting methods. See further discussion below.

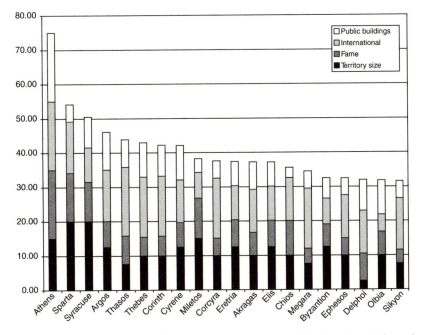

Figure 2.2. Comparisons of the twenty most prominent Greek poleis. Balanced 80-point scale based on the aggregate of territory size, fame (columns of *Inventory* text), international activity, and public buildings.

With an aggregate score of 75 (out of 80 possible), Athens wins overall in the polis rankings of aggregate material flourishing, beating its closest rivals by a substantial margin. Indeed, as figure 2.2 shows, Athens wins in every measured category except territory size (see appendix A for details), standing out not only from the middling polis average, but from its highest-performing rivals.

The "top 20" group listed on figure 2.2 includes most of the poleis likely to be familiar to a lay audience, and Greek historians are likely to describe these 20 poleis as leading states of the classical era.[15] This top 20 group gives a good sense of the poleis that were Athens's primary rivals. Athens, with its aggregate score of 75, is the outlier, doubling the top 20 median score of 37.4—just as the top 20 median doubles the "middling group" median score of 18.4. The other 19 top poleis of the top 20 are grouped quite tightly around the mean, with only two other poleis—Sparta and Syracuse—scoring higher than 50 and none falling below 30 (standard deviation = 6.5). Of course, Athens is much better documented

---

[15] Aigina is notably missing from the list of the top 20, but see below for coinage.

than any other polis in terms of ancient literary texts, epigraphic documents, and archaeological evidence. But the counting method used for the rankings, based on the *Inventory* text and indices, corrects (if imprecisely) for this because the *Inventory* devotes relatively more text to less well documented poleis, and its indices systematically underreport both level of international activity and number of public buildings of the best-known poleis.[16]

Distribution of Coinage

The concern that the high Athenian ranking on the aggregate score measure is simply a function of selection bias is allayed by considering a second body of quantifiable data: the count of coins minted by various poleis and subsequently discovered in hoards around the Greek world. The coin hoard data are considerably less affected by selection bias, but Athens is similarly outstanding when compared to other leading Greek city-states. Moreover, the coin hoard data allow rankings across a time series, rather than the synchronic measurement of the aggregate data.

A coin hoard is a group of coins intentionally gathered as a group in antiquity and subsequently discovered by modern investigators. The burial dates of hoards can usually be determined within a quarter century. The standard *Inventory of Greek Coin Hoards* (Thompson et al. 1973) lists 852 hoards from all across the Greek world (146,099 coins) dating to the period 550–300 B.C. A substantial number of the coins in those hoards (40,508) were issued by the 80 poleis in the two upper quartiles of the 164 polis group, discussed above.[17] By determining in which hoards a polis' coins appear, and how many of that polis' coins appear in each hoard, we can determine the distribution of a given polis' coins over time and across regions.

Individual polis scores were calculated for the following variables: hoard count (total number of hoards in which a polis' coins appear), coins total (total number of a polis' coins in all hoards), date range count (number of quarter-centuries, from 550 to 300 B.C., in which a polis' coins appear in hoards: maximum 10); region count (number of geographic

---

[16] Columns of *Inventory* text per polis can be compared, for example, to the number of times a polis name appears in classical Greek literature (using the *TLG* as the database). By this comparison, classical Athens appears vastly more prominent than its leading rivals; only Sparta is even close. See below and appendix C. Reasons for undercounting are described in appendix A.

[17] Many coins in archaic and classical Greek coin hoards were issued by non-polis authorities, especially eastern monarchies such as Lydia and Persia; by the late fourth century, coins of Macedonian kings and dynasts are very prominent in hoards. The following results

TABLE 2.1

Coin hoard median and mean scores for 80 poleis (top two quartiles of the 164 polis sample, as ranked by "aggregate material flourishing" score)

	Hoard Count	Coins Total	Date Range Count	Region Count	Extra-Region %
Median	13.0	123	4.0	2.0	21
Mean	17.0	506	4.6	2.5	26
Std. deviation	18.3	1098	3.0	1.7	25

regions within the Greek world in which a polis' coins appear in hoards: maximum 9); extraregional percent (percentage of hoards in which a polis' coins appear that lie outside that polis' home region). See appendix B for details.

Distribution of a polis' coins in hoards cannot accurately measure that polis' *overall* economic performance.[18] Yet counting coins in hoards is a good proxy for what we might call "currency performance"—which is certainly one part of economic performance—for two reasons: First, the choice to select a given coin for retention (hoarding) was in each case made directly by an individual (or group) in antiquity who had acquired that coin, at a given time and place, through some sort of exchange. We may assume that coins were typically retained for economically rational reasons—because they were valued, in the first instance, for their monetary worth and as a redeemable store of financial value. Second, hoards are frequently discovered by non-archaeologists, and so their known distribution is not determined by modern professionalized choices about which sites are worthy of excavation. In short, post-classical selection bias is relatively low, at least for hoard counts.[19] The median and average scores for the 80 polis sample are listed in table 2.1.

As in the case of the material flourishing index, there is a substantial difference between a few top-ranked poleis and the median polis (the bot-

---

are based on database based on Thompson et al. 1973, compiled under my direction by David Teegarden in 2005.

[18] For an introduction to Greek coinage, see Howgego 1995. On the difficulties involved with moving from the evidence of hoards to historical conclusions regarding currency production, monetization of economies, patterns of commerce, and the comparative strength of ancient states, see Howgego 1990; Buttrey 1993, 1999; Picard 1997; Callataÿ 1997, 2006.

[19] The primary systematic bias with which we need to be concerned comes in counting the numbers of a given polis' coins in a given hoard: some hoards are better recorded than others, and in relatively ill-recorded hoards, very common coin types (notably Athenian "owls") are listed simply as "present" or "numerous," whereas rarer coins are counted more carefully. The "total coin numbers" for the top-ranking poleis (Athens, Aigina, Syracuse) are therefore certainly (and probably substantially) underreported.

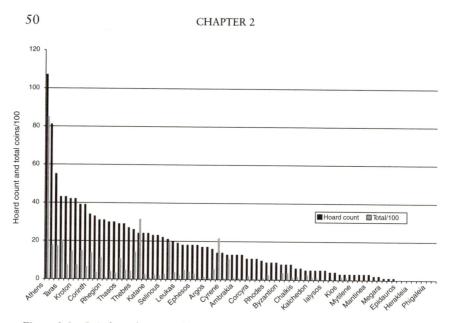

Figure 2.3. Coin hoard counts (black bars) and 1 percent of total coins in hoards (gray bars) for eighty poleis. Note that the labels on the x-axis list only every third polis.

tom-ranked poleis scored zero on both hoard count and total coins, because no coins minted by them appear in hoards). Using "hoard count" as the primary indicator, and "coins total" as a secondary indicator, the 80 poleis in the sample are distributed as shown in figure 2.3.

Although the y-axis scales and sample sizes are different, it is instructive to compare figure 2.3 with figure 2.1: in both cases the primary indicator (high bars) tracks a sharp drop-off in performance after the few highest-ranking poleis (far left of the figure). This initial sharp drop is followed by a fairly even decline through the third quartile, with a tail-off to very low rankings in the lowest quartile. The general similarity is maintained when we look at the top 20 poleis (ranked according to hoard count). These are shown in figure 2.4.

The top 20 poleis all score comfortably above the 80-polis median hoard count of 13. In all but one case (Rhegion) they also score well above the "coins total" median of 123. Coins from each of the poleis in the top 20 circulated over a relatively long period of time, and so the date range count for this group is fairly narrow, from six quarter-centuries to ten.[20] By contrast, the coins of some high-ranking poleis circulated only regionally, whereas others were distributed more globally. Region counts vary

[20] Date range count of 6: Taras, Gela, Rhegion, Sybaris, Thourioi, Thebes. Count of 10: Aigina, Samos.

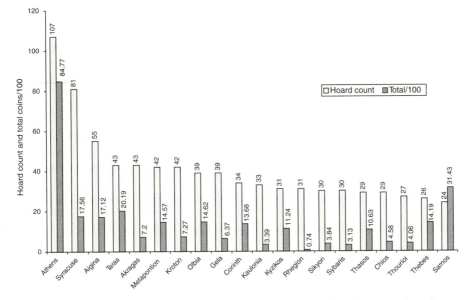

Figure 2.4. Coin hoard counts (left bar) and 1 percent of total coins in hoards (right bar) for top-ranking twenty poleis (ranking by hoard count).

widely, from 1 (Taras, Olbia) to 8 (Athens). Extraregional percentages manifest a similarly wide distribution, from zero (Taras, Sybaris) to 78 percent (Athens). Nine of the twenty poleis listed in figure 2.2 (i.e., the top 20 according to aggregate material flourishing score) reappear here in figure 2.4. Overall correlation between the material flourishing aggregate scores of the 80 poleis and their hoard count scores is substantial (r = 0.57), although far from complete.[21] Aigina and several states from Magna Graecia and Asia Minor, for example, rank much higher on hoard count than they do in material flourishing aggregate.

Athens once again leads the list by a substantial margin. Syracuse, ranked third in material flourishing aggregate score, behind Athens and Sparta, here ranks second.[22] Clearly the coinage of both Athens and Syracuse was in considerable demand in the Greek world; their coins were chosen for retention by many individuals, and thus they appear in significant numbers in many hoards, over time and across disparate regions. Athenian coins appear in hoards in nine of ten quarter-century ranges and in eight of nine regions; Syracuse also scores high on both measures: eight

[21] Other Pearson correlations with material flourishing aggregate: total coins, 0.53; regional count, 0.43; date range count, 0.34; extraterritorial percent, 0.18.

[22] The second-ranking material flourishing polis, Sparta, did not issue coins of any kind during the classical period, as a matter of deliberate state policy, and so is out of the picture.

of ten in quarter-centuries and six of nine in regions. There is a great difference, however, in extraregional hoards score: 78 percent of hoards containing Athenian coins are located outside Athens' home region of Greece, whereas only 17 percent of hoards containing Syracusan coins are outside Sicily. This difference seems to point to diverging but similarly successful currency strategies. Each of these strategies was evidently also followed by other high-ranking poleis. Clearly there was more than one route by which a polis might develop a successful currency policy.[23]

ATHENS VERSUS SYRACUSE AND SPARTA

Athens, Syracuse, and Sparta were clearly outstanding poleis, arguably the three leading poleis of the classical period.[24] Comparing their scores with one another on several key indicators, and with the mean scores of the top 80 poleis (the two upper quartiles of the material flourishing sample = the total coin hoard sample) allows us to better define the extent of Athenian exceptionalism (table 2.2).

On the various measures, Athens ranges between 2.5 and 7.3 standard deviations from the 80-polis mean.[25] On the two most significant indicators, material flourishing aggregate and hoard count, Athens' divergence from the mean is 4.9. This is a remarkably consistent showing, given the complete independence of the databases from which each figure derives. Syracuse scores consistently below Athens, ranging from 0.3 to 3.7 standard deviations from the 80-polis mean. Yet once again, Syracuse's showing on the two most significant indicators is quite close: 2.4 standard deviations for aggregate material flourishing and 3.7 for hoard count. Sparta did not mint coins; its other standard deviation scores rank from −0.1 to 3.0. Sparta's aggregate flourishing standard deviation score is quite comparable to that of Syracuse; its fame and international activity scores rank between those of Athens and Syracuse. Sparta has relatively

[23] Aigina, the third-ranked polis in hoard count, splits the difference, with an extraregional score of 38 percent.

[24] In the later fifth century, Athens and Syracuse were similar in various other respects, notably in terms of constitution and military power. Thucydides makes a point of comparing Athens and Sparta on various measures. See further, Ober 1996, chapter 6.

[25] The mean is the average score of a group (in this sample, it is invariably higher than the median); the standard deviation is the numerical variation from the mean necessary to cover the two middle quartiles of a ranked group. Thus, for the eighty-polis group (ranking order is different, of course, for each variable), adding the standard deviation to the mean score covers the forty poleis ranking 21–60. The data on which table 2.2 is based are listed in appendix table A.5.

TABLE 2.2
Athens, Syracuse, and Sparta, standard deviations from "top 80 polis" mean scores

	Material Fl. Aggreg.	Fame (text cols.)	Internat'l Activity	Public Buildings	Hoard Count	Coins in Hoards
Athens	4.9	5.1	2.5	5.4	4.9	7.3
Syracuse	2.4	2.1	0.3	1.4	3.7	1.1
Sparta	2.7	3.0	1.4	−0.1	Not valid	Not valid

few recorded public buildings, indeed its score is lower than the 80-polis mean. But here it is important to note Thucydides' famous caveat (1.10) regarding the lack of fit between physical splendor and actual power of Athens and Sparta: he predicted that, based on the physical remains alone, Athens would be judged twice as powerful as it actually was and Sparta would be seriously underestimated. Yet even if we follow Thucydides' advice by cutting Athens' public buildings score in half, the Athenian public building score would still be 1.8 standard deviations above the mean.

Given the loose fit between "material flourishing" and the variables that can be measured statistically, and the noisiness of the data for ancient city-states, these numbers must be regarded as only suggestive. They do not accurately assess comparative power or overall state capacity, much less the overall well-being of residents or economic growth over time. Nonetheless, the general conclusion that Athens stands out, even when measured against its two closest competitors, seems inescapable.

CITATIONS IN GREEK LITERATURE AND OTHER MEASURES

A third body of quantifiable data deserves brief consideration: polis "citation ranking"—that is, the number of times the name of a given polis is mentioned in works written in classical antiquity by Greek authors (the database is the standard *Thesaurus of Greek Literature*). This measure may be taken as a rough index of "classical era fame," although the citation-ranking measures the prominence of poleis in *surviving* literary texts, which constitute only a fraction of the texts actually written in classical antiquity. The citation-ranking is strongly biased in that a disproportionate quantity of surviving fifth- and fourth-century Greek literature was originally produced in Athens, by Athenian citizens (for example, Thucydides, Plato, Demosthenes) or long-term residents (Aristotle, Lysias). Yet that fact alone is indicative of an aspect of flourishing, in that it underlines Athens' role as a major cultural center.

In the archaic period (eighth through sixth centuries B.C.), that is, before the inauguration of democracy, Athens (score of 40) is one among a small group of poleis (all from the mainland) with 20 or more cites: Archaic Athens is beaten by Sparta (47) and tied by Argos (40). In the fifth century, however, after democracy had been established, the situation changes radically: all major polis scores rise sharply, but Athens (2622 cites) now completely dominates all others; only Sparta (1555) is even close. In the fourth century, many prominent poleis, including Sparta (still second at 1316), decline somewhat in citation count. Athens, however, substantially *increases* its count (3273). As in the case of the evidence of datable coin hoards (see table 6.3), the "citations in Greek literature" score not only suggests Athens' standing relative to its rivals, but points to the resilience of Athenian performance over time. According to both measures Athens is more dominant in the post-imperial fourth century than in the imperial fifth. For details, see appendix C.

Moving beyond aggregate material flourishing, distribution of coinage, and prominence in ancient Greek literature as indicators of performance, it is certainly true that by some measures of raw power Athens was rivaled by Syracuse (number of long- and short-term colonial enterprises) as well as by Sparta (military power and diplomatic influence).[26] Yet by various other potentially quantifiable measures of polis activity and influence in the classical period—number of public inscriptions, number of writers and artists in residence, number of known names of persons in residence, number of mentions in modern classical scholarship—Athens would certainly dominate its rivals by a substantial denominator.[27] Each of these measures would be subject to the issues of selection bias that affect the aggregate flourishing and the "citations in literature" scores. Athens was in antiquity and is today an exceptionally well-known polis. The relatively unbiased coin hoard data suggest, however, that Athens' fame is indicative of its actual standing rather than of its celebrity status alone. Insofar as it can be tested empirically, the historical evaluation appears correct: Athens was, relative to its Greek rivals and over time, an outstandingly successful

[26] Hansen and Nielsen 2004, Appendix 27 (Colonization and Hellenisation) has 18 Classical-era listings for Syracuse as a colonizer, 26 for Athens. But 19 of the Athenian listings are for the special category "Athenian short term occupation by klerouchs or colonists." No other polis in the top 20 "rivals" group is known to have engaged in substantial colonial activity in the classical period, although a number were very active in the archaic period.

[27] The raw data on which a statistical argument could be made can be found in the following collections. Inscriptions: Hedrick 1999 (with preliminary conclusions on Athenian pre-eminence: pp. 389–91, 395); cf. Davies 2003: 326–27. Names: *Lexicon of Greek Personal Names*. Writers and artists in residence: *Oxford Classical Dictionary* (3d ed.) and *Neue Pauly*. Citations by modern scholars: *Database of Classical Bibliography* and *L'Année Philologique*.

polis during the period of the democracy, and not before. The question then becomes, what factor or set of factors *explains* Athens' relatively high capacity to achieve and sustain public outcomes?

ATHENS × 12: A MULTIPERIOD CASE STUDY

The following sections sketch twelve eras of Athenian history—from the pre-democratic period to the generation in which democracy was founded and Athens first rose to prominence in Greek affairs, through the establishment of democratic Athens as a great imperial power, to an era of crisis in which the democracy faced catastrophic losses in war and was twice overthrown, through a period of recovery in which Athens confronted new financial problems and aggressive non-polis rivals, transformed itself into a wealthy center of Mediterranean trade but lost its independence in foreign policy, and finally to the post-democratic era of Macedonian and Roman domination. The approach of subdividing Athenian history on the basis of its institutional development has good ancient precedents: the Aristotelian *Constitution of Athens* ([Aristotle] *Ath. Pol.*, and Rhodes 1981), breaks Athenian political history into eleven eras (through the third quarter of the fourth century).

In each period, I have emphasized (1) institutional continuity and change; (2) Athens' responses to challenges and developments indicative of its capacity to carry out major projects in the three general areas of foreign policy, domestic policy, and public building; and (3) Athenian political development, in the three areas of citizenship, majority rule, and authority of law. In the first period Athens emerged as a "natural state" characterized by systematic rent seeking on the part of a well-entrenched elite. Throughout its independent history, the polis of Athenians remained committed to some forms of traditional rent seeking. Yet in a historical process beginning in the early sixth and culminating in the late fourth century, Athenian society was in certain ways transformed into a surprisingly "modern" open-access state that valued and promoted personal freedom, individual choice, and social diversity. This historical development, at least in its autonomous and democratic aspects, was aborted by the consolidation of Macedonian and then Roman domination of the Greek world as a whole.

The methodological point of subdividing Athenian history into multiple phases is to transform a single case study into a series of cases— "Athens I–XII" can function as at least partially distinct observations of a polis confronting a variety of challenges, and thus can help us to isolate democracy as a causal factor at work across an extended historical era.[28] Table 2.3 sums up the twelve periods, and relevant aspects of each period are detailed below. Many new institutions were introduced and substantial changes were made in the areas of legal procedure, military recruitment, taxation, trade policy, welfare provisions, and state finance. Certain historical developments touched on only briefly here will be addressed at more length in chapters 4–6. Detailed historical narratives are available in standard accounts of Greek history and in specialist studies of particular periods and institutions. A few of the most important of these are cited below.[29]

Era I. 700–595: Eupatrid Oligarchy

Athens emerged in the early archaic period as an exceptionally large polis by consolidating the towns and villages of the Attic peninsula (i.e., the territory east and south of the Kithairon-Parnes mountain zone). Yet early Athens did not stand out from polis rivals in terms of its economic or military performance. Athens did not participate in the large-scale overseas colonial projects sponsored by Corinth, Eretria, Chalcis, and other leading states of the period. Formal leadership positions (the several archonships) were monopolized by a loose coalition of leading families, later known as the *Eupatridai*, the "well born." The Eupatrid oligarchy dominated the society politically and economically. While some overseas trade was carried on, economic activity was overwhelmingly based on rent seeking, especially in the domain of agriculture where the exploitation of various forms of unfree labor provided surpluses for the wealthy elite of large landowners. Institutional political infrastructure was rudimentary. Large-scale military actions were rare. With the exception of occasional and short-duration "mass levies" (notably one in the later seventh century, against an attempt at tyranny), military forces were evidently raised by

---

[28] For this multipart case-study approach for qualitatively analyzing historical material with the goal of developing defensible descriptive and causal inferences, see King, Keohane, and Verba 1994: esp. 221–23.

[29] General histories of Greece including Athens: *Cambridge Ancient History*, second edition, volumes 3–6. More concisely: Morris and Powell 2005; R. Osborne 1996 (eras I–IV); Ehrenberg 1973 (II–VIII); Welwei 1999 (III–XI); Hornblower 2002 (V–XI); Buckler 2003 (IX–XI). Recent and detailed survey of Greek economic history: Eich 2006. Greek temple building and comparative economic performance: Salmon 2001. Histories of Athens, including foreign policy: Meier 1998; Meiggs 1973 (V–VIII); Powell 2001 (V–VIII); Mossé 1962 (IX–XI). Public buildings: Boersma 1970; Camp 2001. Taxation and public duties: Christ 2006. Domestic policy and institutional development: Andreades 1933: 197–391; Rhodes 1981; M. H. Hansen 1999 (with emphasis on X–XI); Raaflaub, Ober, and Wallace 2007 (II–V). I have cited, below, a small selection of era-specific works focusing on Athens for each era, but this is only a tiny fraction of a massive literature.

TABLE 2.3
Twelve eras of Athenian history

Date B.C.	Era	Challenges	Response
I. 700–595	Eupatrid oligarchy	State formation, regional rivals, social conflict.	Emergence of a complex "natural state." Domination and aggressive rent seeking by a narrow elite of birth and wealth.
II. 594–509	Solon and tyranny	Intra-elite conflict, rise of Sparta as dominant polis.	First open access institutions: written laws, citizen immunities, communal identity-building. Promotion of industry, trade.
III. 508–491	Foundation of democracy	Attacks by rivals, civil conflict, collapse of traditional authority structures.	New fundamental institutions established. New processes for civic participation. Public spaces, buildings for new regime.
IV. 490–479	Persian Wars	Conflicts among ambitious elites. Invasions. City attacked and sacked.	Ostracisms, warships built, city evacuated and reoccupied after victory, leadership of Themistocles.
V. 478–462	Delian League and postwar rebuilding	Persian threat. Shattered infrastructure, conflicts among ambitious leaders.	Areopagus powers limited. Establishment of major anti-Persia Aegean alliance system. Attacks on Persia.
VI. 461–430	High empire and struggle for Greek hegemony	Transformation of League to Empire. Growth of wealth and power. War with Sparta. Costs of military adventurism.	Judicial system elaborated, pay for jurors, imperial institutions elaborated. Ostracisms. Attempts to break up Spartan alliance. Major architectural program.
VII. 429–416	Peloponnesian War, phase I: Stalemate	Plague, invasions, revolts of subjects. Conflicts among ambitious leaders.	Complex land-sea military operations, diplomacy. Truce with Sparta.
VIII. 415–404	Peloponnesian War, phase II: Crisis	Military setbacks, huge losses of men and material. Oligarchic coup, revolts in empire. Spartan domination; oligarchy imposed.	Rejection of oligarchy, reestablishment of democracy, rebuilt military capacity. Law code consolidation begun.
IX. 403–379	Post-Peloponnesian War	Severely reduced manpower, lost empire, fleet. Vulnerability to Spartan-Persian axis. Anger over oligarchs' crimes.	Democracy restored. Amnesty. Law code rewritten; new formalized procedures for lawmaking. Pay for assemblymen. Alliances with former rivals. Infrastructure rebuilding.
X. 378–355	Naval Confederation and Social War, financial crisis	External threats on multiple fronts. Complex foreign policy situation. Restive allies. Funding shortfall in military and domestic budgets.	Major new anti-Sparta coalition; consolidation of border defenses. Generals in the field improvise ways to raise funds necessary to pay their troops. Army recruitment reform. Tax system reforms, Approvers of coins.
XI. 354–322	Confronting Macedon, economic prosperity	Financial crisis in mid-350s. Rise of imperial Macedon. Military defeats. Loss of foreign policy autonomy.	Financial reforms. Maritime courts and other benefits for non-citizens. Growth of silver mining and trade revenue. Reforms in legal jurisdiction, recruitment of jurors, assembly procedure. Major military and civic architecture. Acme as an open access state.
XII. 321–146	Macedonian and Roman domination	Imperial powers end autonomy. Disenfranchisements, expulsions. Emergence of rival markets.	Maintenance of some democratic institutions, occasional revolts, accommodation, negotiation, reduced expectations.

local big men. There was probably no national army as such. Athens in era I was in many ways a typical undeveloped "natural state."

Megara and Aigina, much smaller but better-coordinated regional rivals, posed serious threats to Athenian control of its western marches and contested control of the strategically important island of Salamis. Athens had a city center of some sort, but with the possible exception of a temple on the Acropolis (for which there is scant evidence in this period), there is no reason to suppose that there was any large-scale public building. Toward the end of this period, social coherence came close to breaking down entirely as tensions grew, both between the Eupatrid nobility and wealthy but non-noble Athenians and between wealthy landowners and poorer Athenians. The practice of enslavement of local residents for non-payment of debts had apparently increased by the first years of the sixth century. Athens seemed to be on the brink of either tyranny or developing a Spartan-style masters/serfs solution to large-polis social organization, in which the native-born community would be strictly divided into free and unfree populations.[30]

Era II. 594–509: Solon and Peisistratid Tyranny

The sixth century was characterized by experiments with quasi-monarchical forms of rule and saw substantial improvement in Athens' relative standing. In 594 the growing social crisis led to the appointment of Solon as archon and mediator with special powers for institutional reform. Rejecting the opportunity to convert his office into a tyranny, Solon carried out fundamental social and political reforms, including a one-time cancellation of debts, the abolition of enslavement of Athenians by Athenians, and measures intended to attract immigrants with desirable skills. He also restructured access to political office, making wealth (annual income, measured in agricultural produce) the basis for differential access to public office. In the legal domain, he established the principle of formal accountability for magistrates and gave all citizens legal standing as potential prosecutors of criminal malefactors. His new law code was written down and made public. The Solonian reforms turned Athens decisively away from any Sparta-style solution to the problem of large-scale coordination, but did not end the threat of tyranny.

In 546, in the third of a series of coups, Peisistratus established himself and his sons after him as sole rulers of the polis. In the era of the Peisistratid tyrants, Athens overtook Corinth as the dominant Greek producer and exporter of painted pottery. Following the lead of regional rival Aigina, Athens began to mint silver coins. Athens' first monumental temples

---

[30] Snodgrass 1980; Morris 1987.

were begun, on the Acropolis and in the lower town; the Agora was better established as the city center and provided with a major altar and public fountains. Athens consolidated its hold over Salamis and some border regions, and Athenian forces were involved in occasional military and colonial actions in the Cyclades and Hellespontine region. Overall, Athenian foreign policy remained relatively unambitious when compared to its leading rivals—especially Sparta, which during this era came to control the whole of the Peloponnese. There was still no coordinated national system for recruitment of armed forces, and outlying regions of Attica remained only loosely tied to the center. The tyrants sought to increase social cohesion, degrade regional patronage networks, and enhance Athens' prestige by the sponsorship of new civic rituals, athletic games attracting competitors from across Greece, and large-scale national parades. Development loans were made available to individual farmers. The tyranny remained relatively benevolent until 514, when one of the sons of Peisistratus was assassinated. Supported by disaffected Athenian aristocrats, the Spartans invaded Athens and expelled the increasingly paranoid and disliked last of the Peisistratids in 510.[31]

Era III. 508–491: Foundation of Democracy

Under the shadow of Spartan domination, political control of Athens was contested among rival aristocrats. Losing out to a pro-Spartan rival, Cleisthenes sought popular support among lower-class Athenians. This led, however, to a renewed Spartan occupation of Athens and to Cleisthenes' expulsion. Threatened with a reversion to something like an "era I" Eupatrid oligarchy, the Athenian demos rose up, expelled the Spartan forces, and recalled Cleisthenes. He then instituted a series of fundamental political changes that amounted to the institutional foundation of democracy. Citizenship was extended in the first instance to all adult resident males; subsequently it would be limited to their descendants as confirmed by public votes in 139 villages and neighborhoods newly designated as "demes." The residents of three non-contiguous sets of demes were aggregated as members of one of ten new tribes—thus each Athenian's citizenship was constructed at a local, regional, and national level (this extremely important reform is described in detail in chapter 4). The tribe system quickly became the backbone of Athens' first truly national army. Subsequent reforms established ten generals (one from each tribe) as the elected leaders of this new national army and a system of "liturgies"

[31] Solon: Blok and Lardinois 2006; Peisistratids: Lavelle 2005. Hölkeskamp 1992, 1999 notes that *comprehensive* law codes are rare in archaic Greece, known only at Athens and Gortyn.

whereby the very wealthiest residents of the city were assigned the duty of sponsoring theatrical and choral performances.

New political institutions were established, notably an agenda-setting Council of 500, selected by lot from across the citizenry, and ostracism, a process by which the demos decided each year whether to expel a leading individual and selected the "winner" by balloting. Substantial new public buildings for the new officers of the democratic government were erected in the Agora, and work on new temples began on the Acropolis. Now, or late in era II, Athens began minting its famous "owl" series of silver coins.

This era saw a steep rise in the capacity of Athens as a state to effect its ends: in 506 Athenian land forces defeated a major Spartan-led coalition that had launched a multipronged invasion of Athenian territory. The historian Herodotus (5.78) notes this victory as a clear sign that Athens had turned a corner toward greatness in Greek international affairs. The first moves were made to fortify the port at Piraeus, suggesting an increased attention to the potential of overseas activity. Athens signaled its new standing as a major power by sending twenty warships to aid the revolt of Ionian poleis from Persia in 499 B.C. Although external threats remained, Athens was now a force to be reckoned with—the latent potential of Athens' large territory and population was becoming manifest. Meanwhile, Athenian painted pottery was characterized by the striking artistic experiments of the so-called Pioneer group of painters and dominated Mediterranean markets for fine pottery.[32]

Era IV. 490–479: Persian Wars

In 490 the full national Athenian infantry levy, a force of some nine thousand men organized according to the new tribal system, won a notable victory over Persian invaders at the battle of Marathon. In the aftermath of that victory a series of distinctive war monuments was erected. The new democracy continued to experiment with its institutions; the 480s saw the first actual ostracisms. The decade of the 480s was also marked by considerable large-scale building activity, especially on the Acropolis, but work was also begun on a new treasury at Delphi, and on temples in Attica—at Sounion and Rhamnous. The most notable new enterprise of the decade, however, was the construction of a huge navy. In the mid-480s, the silver mines in southern Attica came more fully on line, resulting in a substantial windfall profit to the state. At the initiative of Themistocles, the Athenian assembly turned down a move to distribute the windfall as a one-time payoff to each citizen in favor of a proposal to build

---

[32] Anderson 2003, and Pritchard 2005; Forsdyke 2005. Pottery: Neer 2002.

a huge naval force: two hundred oared ships, according to Herodotus (7.144.1–2). The silver windfall was not sufficient to man the ships with mercenaries. The navy-building plan necessarily assumed that citizens unable to afford hoplite armor (perhaps two-thirds of the citizen body) would be available to row the ships. This force was initially intended to allow Athens to dominate longtime regional rival and naval power, Aigina, but was used in the renewed war against Persia.

The massive overland invasion of Greece by Persian forces in 480 led to an alliance between Sparta (with its Peloponnesian League) and Athens, the two leading mainland Greek states. When the Greek coalition was unable to stop Persia in northern Greece, the Athenians evacuated Athenian territory, again on the motion of Themistocles, and the city was sacked. Yet a Greek naval victory off Salamis, made possible by the large Athenian navy and Athenian strategic leadership, turned the tide. The Persian land forces were subsequently crushed by Greek coalition forces at Plataea. Athens had become a leading Greek power, a near-equal to Sparta.[33]

Era V. 478–462: Delian League and Postwar Rebuilding

The Persian sack had left the city in ruins; the pace of Athenian silver minting was slow in the immediate postwar generation. Yet the population was intact and work commenced immediately on rebuilding the city, beginning with a new city wall. The Persian threat was not ended; Athens quickly assumed leadership of a coalition of island and coastal Greek states, known as the Delian League, with the goal of maintaining naval superiority in the Aegean. Most members of the League provided funds; Athens built and manned the bulk of the ships. The League's navy engaged in successful operations against Persian forces, and severely punished recalcitrant League members and Aegean states that were considered Persian sympathizers.

By the 460s, the Athenian economy had recovered from the sack, and Athens returned to large-scale building projects, notably in the Agora. The city and its port region to the southwest were conjoined in a single fortified enclave by the construction of Long Walls to the sea. In western Attica, the major town of Eleusis was also fortified. The *patrios nomos*, a new state ritual honoring the year's war dead with common public burial and a funeral oration, was inaugurated. At the end of this period, tension between Athens and Sparta flared up. The leading advocate of accommodation with Sparta was ostracized and the Areopagus council

---

[33] Persian Wars: P. Green 1996; Strauss 2004. Themistocles and the navy: Labarbe 1957.

of former archons, which had played a key role in the evacuation of the city during the Persian wars, was stripped of political authority and reduced to a judicial body. Athenian tragedy matured, notably featuring the early works of Aeschylus.[34]

Era VI. 461–430: High Empire and the Struggle for Greek Hegemony

In this period the Delian League became more explicitly an Athenian empire, and the Athenian economy boomed. Minting of silver coins, which had remained at a low level in era V increased dramatically, reaching an all-time high in the 440s and 430s.[35] The Athenian population and its military forces also reached record highs: in addition to the great navy and a large reserve force of infantry, Athens created a large permanent body of cavalry, establishing a system for partial pay of the upkeep of a mount. Both wealthy and lower-class Athenians benefited materially from the enhanced opportunities for imperial rent seeking. Athenian power was increasingly employed to establish garrisons on "allied" territory, and to appropriate lands that were controlled by Athenian rentiers (*clerouchs*). Total revenues from the empire may have been in the region of 1000 talents per year, some 400–600 talents of that total in direct tribute. Traditional rival Aigina was forced to join the "alliance" in 458; in 431 Aigina's population was expelled and replaced by Athenians. Pressure was put on Megara by the imposition of trade restrictions, an act that ultimately helped to precipitate the Peloponnesian War. Pericles was a leading figure in Athenian politics throughout this period; although Thucydides (2.65) overstates his position, Pericles was influential in many aspects of Athenian policy.

In the so-called First Peloponnesian War (460–445) Athens successfully engaged Sparta's allies at sea, but land operations carried out against the poleis of Boeotia, to Athens' north, failed to bring Boeotia into the Athenian sphere of influence. Major naval expeditions were launched against Persian holdings, including Cyprus and Egypt, with mixed results and massive Athenian casualties. Revolts in various parts of the empire were confronted and suppressed, notably in an expensive but successful war with the island state of Samos. Athenian colonies were founded at

---

[34] Fornara and Samons 1991.

[35] Total mint output cannot be measured for this period. The standard method of measuring mint output is to estimate the number of obverse and reverse dies used, which can be calculated by die links between individual coins; see, for example, Starr 1970 for Athenian coinage 480–449. The mid-fifth-century Athenian output of owls is so great that no die link study has ever been attempted and is regarded as impossible by experts. Thanks to Peter van Alfen for discussion of this point.

Thourioi (Italy) and Amphipolis (Thrace), and Athens sought allies in Sicily. The end of this period saw the outbreak of renewed conflict with Peloponnesian states, especially Corinth; this ultimately drew in Sparta and led to the outbreak of the great Peloponnesian War. In 430, in the second year of the war, plague broke out in Athens, killing a quarter to a third of the population within a few years.

Athens meanwhile became a judicial center for the empire, mandating that various offenses be judged in Athens by Athenian juries. The revenues of the empire enabled an extraordinary public building boom, especially on the Acropolis, but also in the lower city and in the towns of Attica. A third long wall was built to the port of Piraeus, which became the center of both Athenian naval and commercial activity and the center of eastern Mediterranean trade.

The institutions of the democracy were considerably elaborated. Pay was introduced for jury service and introduced or expanded for various kinds of magisterial services. The assembly met more regularly (perhaps thirty times per year), and the production of inscriptions to record public decisions increased dramatically. Ostracism was employed quite frequently, especially in the 440s. Orphans of citizens who died in military service were raised as wards of the state. Athenian theatrical and performance culture entered its "golden age."[36]

Era VII. 429–416: Peloponnesian War, Phase I. Stalemate

Despite the demographic catastrophe occasioned by the plague, Athens continued its war with Sparta, using its naval superiority to engage in successful land-sea operations against Peloponnesian cities and fleets, and to suppress revolts among the subject allies—notably by Mytilene in 428–27. The conduct of war became increasingly brutal, featuring mutilations of prisoners of war and large-scale executions of combatants and noncombatants alike by both sides. The capture of a several hundred Spartan soldiers on an island off the southwest coast of the Peloponnesus in 425 led to a cessation of the annual Spartan invasions of Attica, but these were replaced by Spartan attacks on Athenian imperial assets in northern Greece, notably the strategically vital Athenian colony of Amphipolis. Neither side in the conflict was capable of gaining a decisive advantage; a peace was arranged in 421. This led to a temporary halt to the fighting, but was followed by destabilizing realignments in the Peloponnesus, which in turn created opportunities for the ambitious Alcibiades and other Athenians eager to recommence hostilities. In 416 Athens attacked

[36] Samons 2007. Origins of Peloponnesian War: de Ste. Croix 1972.

and ultimately eliminated, by execution and deportation, the entire population of the island state of Melos. Athenians took over the land.

The institutions of democracy were maintained intact. To augment imperial revenues, a direct tax was levied on Athenian property (*eisphora*). The Athenians passed a decree (probably now, possibly in era VI) mandating the use of Athenian coinage, along with standard Athenian weights and measures, throughout its empire. Although the initial impetus for this reform may have been to increase Athenian revenues (notably by charging reminting fees), the longer-term result was a more consolidated and integrated trade zone in the eastern Mediterranean (see chapter 6). Meanwhile, building continued in the Agora (south stoa), at various sites around Attica, and on the Athenian-controlled sacred island of Delos.[37]

Era VIII. 415–404: Peloponnesian War, Phase II. Crisis

In 415, urged on by Alcibiades, the Athenian assembly authorized a massive seaborne expedition to Sicily, with the ill-disguised goal of conquering Syracuse and annexing the island. The spectacular failure of the expedition in 413 was a terrific blow to Athens. It led to a major change in the way imperial revenues were collected—the forced "contributions" of subject allies were replaced with a 5 percent tax on overseas trade. It also precipitated revolts among Athens' subject allies. The first wave of revolts was largely suppressed by 412. Meanwhile, having paved the way by a series of assassinations, Athenian oligarchs effected a coup d'état that concentrated power in a body of four hundred men. Yet "the Four Hundred" proved incapable of winning the loyalty of the sailors of the fleet, or retaining the loyalty of the heavy-infantry *hoplites*. The narrow oligarchy was deposed and replaced by a more moderate oligarchic government, "the Five Thousand." That government in turn gave way to restored full democracy by 410. In the same year, the Athenians established a commission that spent a decade gathering and publishing the laws, resulting in a substantial revision of the legal system. Also in 410 a two-obol welfare benefit was established for Athenians reduced to indigence by the conditions of the war, and the 5 percent imperial trade tax was dropped in favor of restored tribute payments.

In 413 Sparta had occupied a stronghold in Athenian territory to which more than 20,000 Athenian slaves fled. Sparta also received massive Persian funding for fleet building. An indecisive see-saw conflict in the northern Aegean proved extremely costly in terms of lives and treasure. Athens came near to exhausting its capital reserves and resorted to issuing a fiduciary silver-plated internal currency. This phase of the war

---

[37] Kagan 1974, 1981; Mattingly 1996.

finally culminated in a decisive Athenian loss at Aegospotami in 405 that was followed by the surrender of Athens to Sparta in 404. The Spartans destroyed the remnants of Athens' fleet, slighted the fortification walls, divided Athens' imperial holdings with Persia, and installed a pro-Spartan oligarchic government, "the Thirty," in Athens. The Thirty executed many citizens, expelled others from their homes, seized property of wealthy citizens and resident aliens (*metics*), and borrowed substantial sums from the Spartans to pay for a garrison that sustained their harsh and arbitrary rule. In the years before the surrender, some building continued on the Acropolis; a new Council house was constructed in the Agora. By the end of this era, Athens was at its lowest point in terms of material well-being and international standing since the foundation of democracy. As a result of disease and war, the native male population stood at less than half of its era-VI level.[38]

Era IX. 403–379: Post-Peloponnesian War

Pro-democratic forces (including citizens, metics, and slaves) rallied outside the city, defeated the forces of the Thirty in a series of skirmishes, and restored the democracy. The democrats then quickly declared an amnesty and decreed that the loans taken by the Thirty would be repaid. Persia, responding to Spartan overreaching in western Anatolia, provided funds for rebuilding the city walls and a fleet. The wartime plated coinage was recalled, certainly by the late 390s and perhaps immediately upon the reinstitution of democracy. Athens joined former Spartan allies Thebes and Corinth in an anti-Spartan coalition to fight the so-called Corinthian War. Athenian naval operations in the northern Aegean during this period suggest that many Athenians hoped to regain control of parts of the old empire, but this proved a futile hope. Athenian overseas possessions were for the most part limited to the three strategic Aegean islands of Lemnos, Imbros, and Skyros, which provided some ongoing revenue in the form of a tax on grain. Persia again switched sides in 387; with Persian backing, Sparta resumed its position of military dominance on the mainland.

The legal reforms begun in 410 were completed by 400. The upshot was a formal code of "primary" laws (*nomoi*), which were now distinguished from decrees of the Assembly (*psēphismata*); new laws would now be made by large lotteried boards of *nomothetai*. The Assembly no longer made fundamental law as such, but voted annually on the question of whether changes in each section of the law code were called for, thus balancing legal stability with revisability. Pay for attending the assembly

[38] Kagan 1987; Munn 2000.

was introduced for the first time; by 392 it stood at 3 obols, thus equal
to juror's pay. A new mint building was constructed in the Agora, and
the Pnyx (the meeting place for the Assembly) was reconstructed. A new
Pompeion (ritual parade building) was constructed at a major entrance
to the city. Statues were erected in the Agora in honor of individual Athenians whose military exploits helped to fuel the restoration, and elaborate
monumental private tombs were constructed in the Kerameikos.[39]

Era X. 378–355: Naval Confederation and
Social War, Financial Crisis

In 378 Athens established a new anti-Spartan naval confederation; the
founding charter included guarantees intended to reassure potential allies
that it would not repeat the history of the Delian League by devolving
into a second Athenian empire. Meanwhile, new and robust forms of
inter-polis cooperation were beginning to change the political landscape.
Thebes rose to increased prominence as the hegemon of a revived Boeo-
tian Confederation and defeated Sparta decisively at Leuctra in 371. By
the 360s, Thebes had replaced Sparta as Athens' leading polis rival. At
the fringes of the Greek world—in Thessaly, Cyprus, Macedon, and
Caria—local dynasts were gaining increased regional influence, in part
by borrowing and adapting Greek and Persian institutions and political
techniques. In 359 Philip II took control of Macedon and began threaten-
ing Athenian interests in the northern Aegean. Mausolus of Caria challenged Athens in the central Aegean. Athenian naval forces were called
upon to deal with these and other threats, all the while securing the vital
grain route to Thrace. Without the empire, funding for extensive overseas
military operations was tighter than it had been in the imperial fifth century. In order to secure the funds necessary to carry out their missions,
some Athenian generals resorted to extortion of Athenian allies. The tacit
acceptance by the Assembly of these quasi-imperial/quasi-piratical actions on the part of Athenian commanders led to the debilitating Social
War (i.e., war versus the allies) of the mid-350s.

Compulsory military service for the hoplite class was put on a new
footing by 366, with infantrymen now being recruited by age classes; the
new system was both more efficient and more equitable. In 378 the eisphora property tax system was overhauled, with taxes now being paid
by syndicates of wealthy men; in 373 a follow-up reform provided for
prepayment of the tax (*proeisphora*) by the three hundred wealthiest
Athenians. In 358 the trierarchic system was likewise reformed, using the

---

[39] Strauss 1986.

syndicate model that had proved successful for the eisphora tax. As in the recruitment system, concerns for efficiency and equity of taxation were simultaneously addressed.

Substantial minting of silver coins recommenced in this period (although perhaps as early as the 390s). Athenian silver tetradrachms had by now become a standard means of exchange throughout the central and eastern Mediterranean, which precipitated widespread and large-scale imitation, by individuals and by foreign governments, of the familiar "Athenian owls." In Athens new magistrates were appointed as "Approvers" of silver coinage. With offices in the main markets in Piraeus and the Agora, they were charged with guaranteeing the quality of the coins exchanged by merchants trading in Athenian territory. Meanwhile, a new law reorganized the farming of taxes on grain from Lemnos, Imbros, and Skyros (see chapter 6). By the early 360s (and probably before), silver mining leases were being offered by the state, but the level of mining activity remained relatively low. Athens appears to have retained its position, gained in the imperial fifth century, as a leading center of Mediterranean trade. Yet because of the extraordinary expenses of the Social War and related military expenses, by the later 350s Athens was facing a financial crisis. Total annual revenues at the end of this period amounted to about 130 talents.

Most major Athenian public building in this era was military in nature and outside the city proper. In the aftermath of a Spartan raid in 378 and then stimulated by the renewed military threat posed by Thebes, a series of fortresses and watchtowers were built or renovated along the northern and western frontiers. As the fleet was rebuilt, so too were the dockyards and shipsheds in the Piraeus.[40]

Era XI. 354–322: *Confronting Macedon, Economic Prosperity*

Along with the other mainland and Aegean Greek poleis, Athens lost its independence in foreign policy as imperial Macedon became the dominant power in the Greek world. Athenian policy toward Macedon varied over the course of the period, from a hostile stance in the early 340s, to an uneasy peace in the mid-340s, and back to open hostility culminating in the decisive battle of Chaeronea where a Theban-Athenian coalition, urged by the leading anti-Macedonian Athenian politician, Demosthenes, was defeated in 338. Athens was required to join the Macedonian-led

---

[40] Buckler 1980; Cargill 1981; Ober 1985. Tax reforms and military recruitment reforms (the latter taking place sometime between 386 and 366): Christ 2001, 2006: 144–70. Trierarchic reforms explained in specifically economic terms: Kaiser 2007.

League of Corinth, which supported the Macedonian invasion of Persia under Alexander the Great. After Alexander's death in 323, Athens led a coalition of Greek states in a revolt against Macedon, but was decisively defeated in the Lamian War in 322.

Although this period was marked by foreign policy failures, it also saw the introduction of a series of innovative economic measures that solved Athens' financial problems and restored the polis to a level of prosperity comparable to that of the pre-Peloponnesian War imperial era. By the late 340s, annual revenues were up to 400 talents; by the mid-330s they stood at 1200 talents—comparable to the imperial era VI. Newly established financial offices enabled a series of highly competent elected officials, notably Eubulus in the 340s and Lycurgus in the 330s, to develop innovative and sound fiscal policies for the state. The annual cost of running the democratic government in this period (mostly in the form of state pay for participation) was something like 100 talents.

New measures were introduced to enhance Athens' standing as a trade center; the 2 percent harbor tax provided a major source of public funds. A commercial law code allowed metics and perhaps even slaves to litigate over contracts on equal footing with citizens. There was a sharp increase in special grants (*enktēsis*) allowing non-citizens to own real estate, and some foreigners active in overseas trade were granted full citizenship by special decrees of the assembly. In 354/3, apparently in conjunction with plans for a massive new issue of owls (the "pi series"), more aggressive measures may have been introduced to ensure the soundness of Athenian coins circulating in the city (Kroll 2006; also see chapter 6). Silver mining had returned to high levels by the 340s. The navy was employed to suppress piracy, and late in the period a naval station was established in the Adriatic to that end (see chapter 4).

The trierarchic taxation system was again reformed in 340, in ways that discouraged free riding and better distributed the burden among wealthy Athenians. Various changes were made in legal jurisdiction (e.g., charges of treason were no longer heard by the Assembly and the Areopagus Council gained a new investigative role), in the system by which jurors were randomly assigned to courts, and in the procedures used to assure orderly debate in the assembly. Assembly pay was doubled to one drachma (tripled to 9 obols for ten meetings each year). Substantial changes were also made in recruitment and training of young soldiers (reorganization of the *ephēbeia*, the two youngest age classes), and greater functional specialization was introduced within the board of the ten annually elected generals. As in era X, the goal behind these reforms seemed to be making the democratic system at once fairer, more reliable, and more cost effective. This era saw Athens' closest approach to becoming an "open-access state" (see chapter 6).

There was a great deal of public building. The city walls were modernized and provided with outworks; new shipsheds for a much-expanded fleet of warships and an arsenal for naval stores were constructed in Piraeus. In the city, the theater of Dionysus and the Pnyx were rebuilt, both on monumental scales, and a new Panathenaic stadium was constructed. The Agora was provided with new temples, law courts, and other monuments, including a prominent water clock. Outside the city, new work was begun at the Lyceum, on the Telesterion at Eleusis, and on theaters in some demes.[41]

Era XII. 321–146: Macedonian and Roman Domination

After the Lamian war, Macedon mandated the end of democracy in Athens. Although a deep cultural commitment to democracy remained, and for the next two generations the Athenians would use every opportunity presented them to seek to restore democratic institutions, notably in 317 and 307, democracy would never be securely reestablished. Oligarchic governments mandated by Macedonian kings eliminated the People's Courts and other key democratic institutions, and disenfranchised and expelled large numbers of lower-class citizens. Newly created state offices (e.g., the *gunaikonomoi*, controllers of women) sought to regulate various aspects of private life. Athens lost its position as a significant military power in the Greek world; the island-polis of Rhodes became the most important independent naval power in the Aegean, and took over Athens' role in suppressing piracy. Military endeavors were for the most part limited to concerted but ultimately futile attempts to escape Macedonian domination.

By the early third century, Athens had been largely replaced by Rhodes and Alexandria, and later by Delos, as the center of eastern Mediterranean trade. After a final major program to rebuild the city walls in 307/6, relatively little new large-scale public building was undertaken until the second century, when foreign benefactors built major new stoas in the Agora. Athens remained a highly influential cultural center. Philosophical and rhetorical schools flourished, and Athenian theatrical productions (especially New Comedy) were widely admired and imitated. Athenian-produced literature made up a substantial part of the great library collected in Alexandria. In this period, institutions and practices first devel-

---

[41] Cawkwell 1963; Montgomery 1983; Buckler 1989; Hintzen-Bohlen 1997; Burke 2005.

oped by the Athenian democracy were adopted and adapted by a number of Greek poleis, especially in western Anatolia. Athenian owls were overshadowed by coins issued by Macedonian mints in other cities, but the Athenian tetradrachm weight standard was retained for most of the major coinages in the eastern Mediterranean.[42]

DEMOCRACY AS AN EXPLANATORY VARIABLE

In era I, the seventh century B.C., Athens was not remarkable among the Greek poleis for large-scale public activity, internationally or domestically; other poleis were unquestionably more prominent. In era II, the sixth century, Athens rose in prominence, moving into a dominant position in the international market for painted pottery, engaging in some large-scale building projects, and competing militarily with some success against its regional revivals. Yet Athens remained in the shadow of Sparta throughout this period and was limited in its scope of action by the military strength of its smaller neighbors. In era XII, the post-democratic era, Athens remained a cultural center and was eventually able to undertake substantial building initiatives with the help of foreign benefactors, but was overshadowed economically by rival poleis and dominated militarily by Macedon. By contrast, throughout the democratic era (eras III–XI) and in the face of sometimes-severe financial and military pressure, Athens sustained a capacity to carry out very large scale projects in the areas of foreign policy, domestic policy, and public building (see further, appendix E).

If we ignore short-term rises and dips, both "Athenian democracy" (as defined by native male franchise, majority rule, and authority of law) and "Athenian capacity" (as defined by the ability to undertake projects in the areas of foreign policy, domestic policy, and public building) describe similar bell curves: these curves start out low in era I, rise modestly in II and steeply in III, remain high in IV through XI, then tail off sharply in XII. Other poleis, with different constitutional histories, would manifest very different "capacity curves" over the same five and a half centuries of history.

In each of the nine phases of democratic history surveyed above (III–XI), Athens confronted diverse internal and external challenges—in some cases these included threats to its political system, in other cases threats to its very existence. The Athenian response to these challenges was likewise

---

[42] Habicht 1997; Shipley and Hansen 2006: 66–68; Oliver 2007, noting the sharp downturn in number of inscriptions (chapter 3.4) and archaeological evidence for public building (chapter 3) in the third century.

diverse—in each era the mix of political, social, economic/financial, military, and diplomatic responses was somewhat different. Athens experienced substantial changes over time in terms of its demography, sources of wealth, international prestige, and built environment. And yet, with the exception of two brief oligarchic interludes in 411/10 and 404, throughout the 185-year democratic period (508–322 B.C.), core political principles (free speech, equal votes, mixing) remained intact, as did central political institutions established in the founding generation (e.g., council, assembly, demes, tribes). These democratic institutions, and others (notably legal and financial) that were added over time, played a very substantial part in the lives of all Athenian citizens and their families. Athens III, the Athens of Cleisthenes around 500 B.C., was different in many ways from the Athens (VI) of Pericles in 435 or the Athens (XI) of Demosthenes in 335 B.C. Yet if Cleisthenes had been transported forward in time to the ages of Pericles and Demosthenes, he would have found key aspects of the democratic government familiar, and in each case he would have found himself in a wealthy, culturally influential, architecturally impressive, internationally active community that was a highly desirable immigration destination.

Athens clearly stands out among the Greek poleis in terms of its record of accomplishment and its political history. Athens' high performance as a state and its democratic political culture and government (*politeia*) are what distinguished Athens from its rivals in the era 508–322, and from Athens itself in earlier and later periods. Athenian state capacity and democracy appear to be related, but how? There are, reductively, three possibilities:

1. Enhanced capacity enables democracy.
2. Exogenous factors explain the growth of capacity and democracy.
3. Democracy promotes capacity.

While acknowledging that these are not mutually exclusionary scenarios, and that in reality there must have been complex feedback loops between state capacity, democracy, and external factors, I argue here that the third of these options best explains the multipart historical case: taking democratic institutions and practices as an independent variable does much to explain the dependent variable of increasing capacity.[43]

---

[43] Gaddis (2002) criticizes approaches to explanation that rely on explanatory (independent) and dependent variables, preferring literary narrative to modeling and statistics and advocating a flexible (some might say, murky) notion of "interdependence," that is drawn loosely from chaos theory. Gaddis is certainly right that any rigid attempt to find a single independent variable that adequately explains all other variables in a given historical situation is an inherently absurd undertaking (see Baumol's comments in chapter 1, note 47).

Explanation 1—capacity enables democracy—fails on historical grounds: democracy was first established when Athens was in the midst of a security crisis and at a low point in its international prestige. Athens remained democratic through the Persian sack of the city in 480, the demographic catastrophes of the plague years and the last years of the Peloponnesian War, and the financial crises of the late fifth and mid-fourth centuries. It is true that the two oligarchic interludes were preceded by catastrophic declines in state capacity—the Sicilian disaster of 413 precipitated the oligarchic coup of 411, and the major military defeat at Aegospotami in 405 led quickly to surrender to Sparta and the imposition of the oligarchy of the Thirty in 404. But in each case, democracy was quickly restored, and the city returned to prosperity, security, and influence. Democracy likewise survived the military defeat at Chaeronea in 338. Athenian history from 700 to 146 B.C. offers no warrant for claiming that preexisting capacity to achieve public outcomes led directly to the emergence of democracy or was required for the persistence of democratic government.

Explanation 2, that both capacity and democracy are the result of some external cause, cannot be positively disproved, given our incomplete knowledge of the past. There is, however, no very plausible candidate. Athens was quite similar to its rivals in terms of climate, location, geology, ethnicity, background history, and general culture.[44] Athens did possess an extraordinary resource in the silver-bearing geological strata of southern Attica. But resource endowments, in and of themselves, do not spur high performance. Indeed, students of development economics have posited a "resource curse": by lowering incentives for innovative forms of social cooperation, an exceptionally rich resource endowment may actually depress economic growth. Not all resource endowments prove to be curses; whether mineral resources are a curse or a blessing is a matter of knowledge organization. As economic historians Gavin Wright and

---

He is right to say that some social science falls into this trap; but he is wrong to imply that this is the undertaking of all (or of the best) contemporary social science. Compare, for example, the work of social scientists who integrate historical narrative and modeling, e.g., Haber 1989; Bates et al. 1998; Rodrik 2003; Manning and Morris 2005; Greif 2006.

[44] Fleck and Hanssen 2006 argue that the somewhat different topographies and rainfall patterns experienced by different Greek poleis are more favorable to the emergence and persistence of democratic institutions. They correlate democracy in Greece with the difficulty of monitoring agricultural labor in broken hill land favoring olive cultivation such as Attica (ergo Athens); oligarchy with the greater returns to monitoring activity in more open terrain suited to wheat cultivation, such as Laconia and Messenia (ergo Sparta). They conclude, therefore, that exogenous factors having to do with agricultural regimes can influence both democracy and economic performance. Their agricultural economics argument helps to explain why in the late sixth century Athens and not Sparta had arrived at the point at which a transition to democracy was a possibility. But as we have seen, agriculture in Attica was only one part of the larger the Athenian economy (especially in the democratic period).

Jesse Czelusta (2002) demonstrate, "What matters most for resource-based development is not the inherent character of the resources, but the nature of the learning process through which their economic potential is achieved." Without the cooperative decision following Themistocles' motion to manage the common pool resource of silver for public purposes (to ensure security and other common goods; see eras IV, XI, above), there would be no correlation between the presence of silver ore deposits in south Attica and enhanced Athenian state capacity. Other Greek states possessed outstanding mineral resource endowments but failed to achieve a comparable performance level.[45]

Except in its production and export of especially fine black- and red-figured pottery, Athens does not stand out among its main rivals in the pre-democratic era. Nor did Athens stand out in the post-democratic period. Macedonian actions after 322 can certainly be considered an external cause, in that they led to simultaneous declines in Athenian democracy and capacity. Yet the fact that rulers of Macedon imposed oligarchy on Athens after the Lamian War suggests that they considered Athens' democracy as inimical to their interests. On the other hand, both Demetrius Poliorcetes, who sought to employ Athens as a base against rival dynasts in the last decade of the fourth century, and Mithradates of Pontus, who sought allies among the mainland Greek poleis in his early first-century war against Rome, sponsored the restoration of democracy at Athens. It is reasonable to suppose that Demetrius and Mithradates imagined that democracy would enhance Athens' military capacity.

The most commonly cited exogenous cause of democracy, imperial power, is a relevant factor for only certain parts of the democratic era (strongly in VI and VII, weakly in V and VIII). Had Athens risen to prominence only once, an exogenous explanation might be persuasive. But since there are multiple periods of "robust democracy/high capacity" that must be explained, such explanations must offer multiple exogenous factors. The challenges faced by Athens and the means employed to confront those challenges varied considerably across the nine democratic periods. Two general trends are noteworthy: *democracy temporally leads capacity growth*, and *democracy is less volatile than capacity*.

These trends are illustrated schematically in figure 2.5. The chart somewhat impressionistically tracks changes over time in the state's capacity to accomplish substantial ends (aggregating military activity, public-building activity, and domestic programs) and in the level of democracy

---

[45] The "resource curse": Fleck and Hanssen 2006: 135, with literature cited; Wright and Czelusta 2002. Other poleis with exceptional mineral resources include Thasos (aggregate rank 5, score 48.3: gold and silver), Paros (rank 51, score 23.1: fine marble), Sinope (rank 54, score 22.82: realgar), and Siphnos (rank 144, score 6.5: gold and silver).

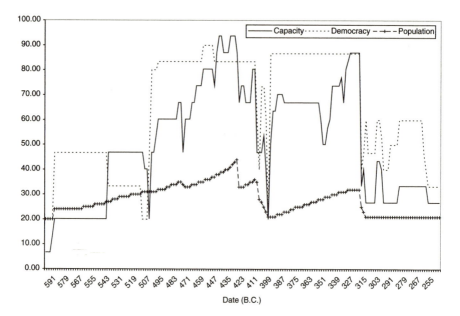

Figure 2.5. Athenian state capacity (aggregated military activity, public building, and domestic programs), democracy (aggregated citizenship, majority rule, law), and population (native and naturalized adult male) from 600 to 250 B.C. See appendix E for details.

(aggregating portion of native adult male population with full citizenship, the political power of the demos, and authority of law). Capacity and democracy are construed in percentages, with 100 indicating a top score in each of the three components. Estimated population (adult native males and naturalized male citizens) is included as a control and is measured in thousands.[46]

Overall, with the notable exception of the early Peisistratid tyranny in the mid-sixth century (when democracy falls as capacity rises), the lines described by state capacity, democracy, and population track fairly

---

[46] Each of the three components of state capacity and democracy was scored 1–5 on a biennial basis. A score of 5 indicates the highest level that Athens achieved in that component. These scores are subjective; another Greek historian might assign higher or lower scores to a specific component in a given biennium. Yet my scoring is based on the historical outline offered above; to the extent that the outline is accurate, the general trends are not in doubt. These scores were then converted to a 100-point scale; a capacity score of 100 on the chart would therefore indicate that during a given two-year period the Athenian state was in my view operating at its highest capacity in each of the component areas of military activity, public building, and domestic activity. Similarly, a 100 score on democracy would mean that the highest Athenian level of citizenship portion, majority rule, and authority of law had been achieved. See appendix E for details. Likewise, general Athenian population

closely. When we look more closely, the trend of "democracy leading growth in capacity and population" is clear, especially in the years following the establishment of democracy in 508 and the re-establishment of democracy in 403 and the years following. The same trend of democracy as a leading indicator is evident in the short term in Athens' capacity to rebuild military capacity after the disaster in Sicily in 413–12, and in the rebuilding of institutional and physical infrastructures in 410–406 following the collapse of the oligarchy. The second trend of "democracy less volatile than capacity" is evident in eras when democracy remains high and steady during sharp drops in capacity and through the recovery periods in which capacity returns to high levels. Democracy remains high through the sack of the city by the Persians in 480 and the subsequent era of rebuilding, following the plague of 430 and years following, through the costly Social War of the 350s, and after the loss of foreign policy independence to the Macedonians in 338.

While it would be absurdly overreductive to claim that this series of rises and recoveries in the dependent variable of aggregated state capacity is *fully* explained by the independent variable of democracy, the history of Athens over the twelve eras surveyed above supports a political explanation for a substantial part of the polis' exceptional performance. It seems safe to conclude that participatory democratic institutions and practices were an important contributing factor in Athens' relative success over time.

Republics, Democracies, and Athenian Exceptionalism

Athens was a democracy of a distinctive and highly participatory kind. Although there were many other Greek democracies (Robinson, forthcoming), many of Athens' political institutions are unparalleled in classical Greece. Most legislative and judicial functions of government were carried out by very large bodies of ordinary citizens: judicial bodies numbering in the hundreds and legislative assemblies in the thousands. Executive responsibility lay with magisterial boards (often of ten members) staffed for the most part by amateurs chosen by lot; a few executive officers (including the board of generals) were elected annually. All officials, however selected, were subject to strict accountability rules, enforced, once again, by bodies of citizens.[47]

---

trends are fairly clear, although absolute numbers remain hotly debated and highly uncertain. See discussion in M. H. Hansen 1986 and 2006c: 19–60; Oliver 2007, chapter 3.

[47] Democracy in the classical period outside Athens: Piérart 2000: Argos; Robinson 2000: Syracuse; Robinson, forthcoming: full survey. Detailed treatments of Athenian democratic

Direct governance by ordinary people seems, at least at first glance, to offer insufficient scope for expert leadership and to introduce a welter of problems in respect to coordination between individuals, institutions, and processes of governance. These considerations have led many observers, in antiquity and modernity alike, to suppose that sustained success is impossible for any organization directly governed by its people (see chapters 1 and 3). The facts of Athenian history prove this notion, at least in its simple form, is wrong. The basic questions, "Can participatory democracy ever succeed in a competitive ecology?" and "Does democratic government ever help promote success?" are answered by the Athenian case. This leads to the harder questions of *how* democracy promoted Athenian success and under what conditions that positive conjunction might be replicated.

There is reason to suppose that among other Greek poleis, democracy, in the basic sense of "public decision-making by majority rule among an extensive citizenry," was at least weakly correlated with flourishing. When we aggregate the evidence for 164 Greek poleis for which we have some (usually, however, fragmentary) evidence of constitution and some sense of territory size, more democratic constitutional histories are positively correlated with higher polis capacity (as measured by the aggregate score). This can be expressed by a simple statistical measurement: "Degree of democracy" (i.e., higher ranking on the 1–5 constitution scale), as an explanatory variable, proves to have a modest but significant positive effect on aggregate material flourishing ($r = 0.31$). This suggests that there actually is a positive link in the posited direction—that is, "more democracy can lead to higher capacity" (see further, appendix D).[48]

Yet the story becomes more complicated when we break down the data. The correlation between degree of democracy and level of performance is not linear. Poleis with constitution types 1 or 2 (averaging out to tyranny or monarchy) indeed generally score quite poorly. Those averaging around 3 (oligarchy) do better. Those averaging 4 (moderate oligarchy) do better yet. Poleis with constitution types verging on 5 (more fully dem-

---

institutions include Hignett 1952; Bleicken 1985; Mossé 1986; Sinclair 1988; Kinzl and Raaflaub 1995; M. H. Hansen 1999; Camassa 2007.

[48] The correlation rises to 0.39 if we limit the success criteria to the raw scores for international activity and buildings. Aristotle, working from a similar-sized "data set" (158 states) and with much more anecdotal evidence for each of them, thought that democracy was, on the whole, more stable than either tyranny or oligarchy, and that under the conditions of his era it was not easy for any regime type other than democracy to emerge. The question of exactly where Aristotle placed Athens' government on the spectrum of relatively good to extremely bad forms of democracy is vexed. For all of these issues, see Ober 1998, chapter 6. I have found no meaningful statistical correlation between constitutional form and distribution of coins in hoards.

ocratic) perform at about the level of type 3 (oligarchy) and do somewhat *less* well than the constitutional type 4 (moderate oligarchy) group. The current state of the evidence for the 164 poleis does not support the claim that, on the whole, "the more democratic a polis, the higher its capacity." It does, however, suggest that "republican" (oligarchic through democratic) constitutions beat despotic (monarchical or tyrannical) regimes. This result is strengthened by considering political histories.

Poleis known to have complex political histories (experience of all three constitutional types, which includes many poleis in the best-scoring "constitutional type 4" group) are on the average considerably more successful than poleis with less complex histories. This is, in part, a function of fame: poleis with more complex preserved constitutional histories tend to be those that are in general better known. Yet these data are telling us something. While the experience of tyranny boosts average scores if it is conjoined with the experience of democracy and oligarchy, when we isolate democracy, oligarchy, and tyranny we find that the experience of tyranny is comparatively depressing. Overall, the data consistently show that tyranny and monarchy, as forms of polis government, are negatively correlated with material flourishing when compared to the "republican" forms of oligarchy and democracy. Tilting a polis' constitution away from the autocratic forms of tyranny and kingship and toward the republican forms of oligarchy or democracy promotes the likelihood that the polis will rank higher in terms of its material flourishing. But the effect is not especially strong. Across the sample, the variable of territory size is more strongly correlated with aggregate material flourishing than is constitutional form or history.[49]

The evidence that can be gleaned from analyzing statistical correlations between aggregate flourishing and what is known of constitutional history among the sample of 164 relatively well-documented Greek poleis supports the conclusion that having a generically republican constitution contributed something to Athenian capacity. But this does not get us very far. Most of Athens's key polis rivals also featured republican constitutions, yet none of them came close to matching Athens' performance record. Likewise, the simple fact of being democratic, in the familiar majoritarian sense, is insufficient to explain exceptional Athenian performance. If, as the evidence of Athenian history suggests, democracy was an important factor in the growth of Athens' outstanding capacity to achieve

---

[49] Fame: $r = 0.83$; territory size: $r = 0.77$. Note, however, that fame and territory size are each part of (25 percent) the overall aggregate score. There is only a slight correlation between territory size and constitution ($r = 0.12$), and no meaningful correlation between constitution and civil conflict ($r = -0.04$). See, further, appendix tables A.1, A.2, and A.6 for statistical breakdowns.

public outcomes, then we may guess that Athenian democracy had special features that were not fully replicated in the governments of other, less successful, classical Greek states. The rest of this book attempts to identify those special features.

To sum up the argument so far: Given the general parity of background physical and cultural conditions among the Greek poleis, differential economic performance is most plausibly explained by differences in each polis' institutionalized capacity to capture the social benefits of cooperation by addressing public action problems. When compared to its polis rivals, Athens was an outstandingly successful state. Participatory democracy seems, on the face of it, to be especially vulnerable to free riding, to problems arising from principal-agent coordination, and in terms of making its commitments appear credible. Yet there are strong reasons to believe that the historical emergence and development of Athenian democracy are causally related to the growth and persistence of high Athenian capacity. Comparative data shows that neither the fact of being generically republican (non-despotic) nor being generically democratic (inclusive citizenship and majority rule) can account for exceptional Athenian performance.

The question remains: Just how does democracy promote flourishing? Athens' democratic era coincided with the elaboration of institutions and practices that, as a growing body of work in institutional economics has demonstrated, can help to explain enhanced state performance: commitment to property rights, respect for individual liberty, open markets, extensive citizenship with high mobilization rates, and increased authority of written law.[50] These institutional features were, however, shared, to a greater or lesser extent, by other Greek republican states. The spread of these performance-enhancing institutions across the ancient Greek city-state ecology helps to explain why that ecology as a whole performed relatively well when compared to other premodern societies. Yet we are left with the puzzle of apparent Athenian exceptionalism within the ecology. The hypothesis developed in chapter 1 assumes that the participatory and deliberative institutions that are particularly associated with democracy in the Athenian style (and not with generic Greek republicanism) were costly. If Athens reaped no beneficial performance returns from those costly institutions, Athens should have been dominated by Greek republics that did not assume those costs.

The next four chapters seek to explain how certain special features of Athens' participatory and deliberative form of self-governance could have

---

[50] See, for example, North and Weingast 1989; Morris 2004: esp. 732; Acemoglu and Robinson 2006; Greif 2006.

contributed to the Athenians' superior capacity for solving public-action problems and thereby gaining greater social benefits from higher levels of cooperation.[51] One important means by which the Athenians captured the benefits of cooperation was, I will argue, their distinctive system for organizing useful knowledge.

[51] Given the current state of the evidence for other democratic poleis (Brock and Hodkinson 2000: 14–15), it is impossible to demonstrate just *how* distinctive Athenian institutions were—but they were certainly *thought of* as distinctive by ancient authors (Ober 1998, 2007a). The Athenian "epigraphic habit" also points to a distinctive institutional history: Hedrick 1994, 1999. Classical democratic institutions outside Athens are the subject of a comprehensive study by Eric Robinson, forthcoming.

Chapter 3

COMPETITION, SCALE, AND VARIETIES

OF KNOWLEDGE

CLASSICAL ATHENS, as a Greek polis, is rightly understood as a "state" in the ordinary historical and social-scientific sense of the term.[1] Yet democratic Athens was in certain respects quite different from most other Greek poleis, and all poleis are different in various ways from contemporary nation-states. Most obviously, while it was very large for a polis, Athens, with its territory of 2,500 square kilometers and population of about 250,000, would be a tiny nation-state.[2] Equally important, if less obvious, is the consideration that Athens, like other Greek poleis, existed in a hypercompetitive environment and was constantly at risk of elimination. As theorists of international relations point out (Waltz 1979), inefficient forms of state organization are unlikely to survive indefinitely in a competitive interstate environment.

COMPETITION AND ITS CONSEQUENCES

The Greek city-state culture of about one thousand states, sharing a language and other cultural features and geographically concentrated around the Mediterranean and Black Seas, appears to have undergone a period of strikingly rapid and sustained economic growth in the period circa 800–300 B.C. The standard of living rose substantially even as the population of the Greek world grew rapidly. Overall growth continued across this period, although not all poleis fared equally well.[3] The competitive environment faced by a given city-state is in some ways analogous to that faced by a modern firm in an expanding and highly competitive market. As in the case of competing firms in growing markets, there were substantial advantages associated with greater size. The three most prominent

---

[1] Polis as a state: M. H. Hansen 2002a, with specific reference to the argument of Berent (1996 and 2000) that the ancient Greek polis is best understood as an "acephalous" stateless political society.

[2] Sizes of nation states: Dahl and Tufte 1973; Alesina and Spolaore 2003.

[3] Growth of the Greek economy: see chapter 2, note 2.

Greek poleis—Athens, Syracuse, and Sparta—were among the largest poleis, in territory and population (see chapter 2). Yet, as managers of modern firms have long realized, scale introduces problems in respect to coordination; coalitions of nimble small organizations may outcompete slower behemoths. The scale-rewarding competitive environment stimulated ambitious Greek city-states to seek ways to increase their populations and the territory under their control, while the complex public action problems that arose with increased scale demanded innovative solutions.[4]

Like most modern firms, but unlike most contemporary (post-1945) nation-states, a Greek polis confronted a meaningful chance of being destroyed, either by rivals (other city-states) or by an outside power (e.g., Macedon or Persia). By destruction I do not mean merely loss of autonomy or regime change, but the temporary or permanent end of the polis as a physical or as a social entity as a result of the sack of the central city and/or the extermination, enslavement, or forced resettlement of the entire population. Close to 12 percent (120) of 1035 known poleis are recorded as having suffered destruction in the course of the later archaic and classical periods. This number certainly underrepresents the actual danger faced by poleis. Among the 120 relatively well-documented poleis in the first three quartiles of the 164 polis group discussed in chapter 2, the chance of suffering destruction was as follows: first quartile, 33 percent; second quartile, 30 percent; and third quartile, 30 percent. These are strikingly consistent figures.[5] There is no reason to suppose that more obscure

---

[4] Examples of growth strategies include Sparta's conquest of Messenia, Syracuse's forced assimilation of the populations of Sicilian cities, Athens' empire and measures to attract foreign residents. I focus here only on the issue of the problem of coordination and scale within individual poleis, but this is only part of the story. Mackil 2004, 2008 assesses the ways in which the scale problem was addressed by institutionalized regional coalitions of poleis (koina). The development of Macedon under Philip II as a large national empire, which overcame its endemic coordination problems in part by successfully borrowing and adapting certain of the institutional innovations of the most successful fourth-century Greek poleis, offers a case study in scale. For a now-classic account of how a modern corporate "elephant learned to dance," see Gerstner 2003.

[5] The destruction rate for the fourth quartile drops to 15 percent. The destruction rate for the "top 20" group is 25 percent. It is notable that, although destruction rates do not drop across the first three quartiles, the rates for other recorded historical events (experience of various constitutional forms and civil conflict) do drop quite regularly from quartile to quartile. See appendix table D.4 for details. Assuming that the steady drop in the other event numbers from quartile to quartile is in part a function of fame (less high-ranked poleis having less fully preserved histories), it would appear that record of destruction, perhaps because it is a particularly notable event, may be less subject to "memory decay" than other events. Athenian orators disagreed as to the finality of destruction: Lycurgus 1.61 equated destruction with state death; Hypereides 2.8 claimed that destroyed poleis had often returned to prominence.

poleis (the 44 poleis in the fourth quartile and the 800+ unranked poleis) were *less* likely to be destroyed, although their destruction is less likely to be recorded. It therefore appears likely that a Greek polis confronted something like a 1:3 chance of suffering destruction at some point in its archaic/classical history.

Some poleis, including Athens in 480, suffered the destruction of urban and rural infrastructures but were able to rebuild. Others, like Olynthus in 348, were driven out of existence. It is significant that the consequences of intra-Greek competition were not always fatal. When destruction was at the hand of an outside power, local rivals were not always willing or able to take advantage of a city-state's post-destruction weakness to "finish the job." Consequently, many of the more successful city-states that suffered destruction managed to survive (like Athens and Miletus) or were subsequently refounded (like Sybaris, Aigina, and Thebes). The general point is that endogenous political choices of the sort that resulted (directly or indirectly) in greater material flourishing might not allow a given state to avoid destruction, but might improve the odds that destruction would not entail permanent state death.[6]

Competition among the city-states during the classical and archaic periods did not result in the consolidation of the Greek world into a few very large states, nor did it drive out republican/democratic states in favor of highly centralized governments. Although Sparta did successfully conquer neighboring Messenia in the early archaic period, and Syracuse forcibly incorporated Sicilian poleis in the late archaic and early classical periods, subsequent Athenian, Spartan, Syracusan, and Theban attempts to absorb their neighbors in the mid-fifth and fourth centuries ultimately failed. Political authority in the Greek world remained distributed among a large number of independent or semi-independent states, many of which were more or less democratic.

The historical pattern of state emergence and persistence within the Greek-city state culture was strikingly different from other well-studied

---

[6] See appendix table D.4; evidence drawn from Hansen and Nielsen 2004, index 20. On the extreme rarity of modern (post-1945) states going out of existence, see Dahl and Tufte 1973: 120–22. Fazal 2007 confirms that "state death" is rare post-1945, but points out that only about half of the states in existence in 1816 are still in existence. The point is not that antiquity experienced more horrification than modernity: there is no reason to suppose this is the case (see, e.g., Glover 2000). Rather, the point is that the nature of risks faced by people were different and that, while many people today risk (and experience) terrible suffering, that suffering is less likely to be the result of a state being destroyed by rival states. The question of what exogenous and endogenous factors affect differential outcomes following destruction events among the Greek poleis demands more study. It is a difficult question because destruction obviously has a bearing on success ranking, and thus it is hard to say, given the state of our evidence, if a state was eliminated rather than surviving destruction because it was relatively low ranking, or vice versa.

examples of ancient and modern state formation. Ancient Rome, for example, emerged as a great and centralized state by following a predatory logic of ongoing territorial expansion. The process of Roman state formation in many ways resembles the emergence of nation-states under centralized authority in early modern Europe.[7] The likelihood of destruction faced by any given state is indeed a significant difference between the ancient Greek city-state culture and the contemporary world order. Yet viewed as a multistate system, the Greek world, with its widely dispersed authority structure, prevalence of republican/democratic regimes, and interstate institutions that allowed for competition while promoting some forms of cooperation, more closely resembles the contemporary post-hegemonic (Keohane 1984, 2002) international situation than does ancient Rome or any other centralized empire of the past. I suggest some possible implications of this similarity in chapter 7.

The failure of endogenous Greek attempts to build and maintain stable and large-scale structures of centralized imperial authority in the classical period may be attributed in part to the effectiveness of institutionalized interstate cooperation among the city-states. Cooperative institutions included federations of states (*koina*), multistate treaties and alliances capable of balancing would-be dominant states, along with more or less effective formal and informal rules governing the conduct of interstate warfare. These arrangements served to reduce the day-to-day risk of destruction and the negative consequences of temporary weakness while promoting valuable economic exchanges. By the same token, however, the potential of productive cooperation made political choices, and the institutionalized processes by which they were made, more salient: as the options for productive cooperation among states multiplied, the menu of public policy options faced by any given polis expanded. The question was not simply "how best to destroy our rivals and survive their attempts to destroy us?"—but also "which rivals ought we cooperate with, to what extent, and in what domains?" The answer to those questions was likely to favor some interests within the polis over others. As Thucydides points out in his exemplary narrative of civil war at Corcyra, a change of alliance could fatally undermine a state's sociopolitical equilibrium and lead to self-immolation.[8]

---

[7] Some thirty-five other city-state cultures have been documented across world history (M. H. Hansen 2000, 2002b), but none was nearly so extensive or long lived as the thousand-state Greek culture. Roman state formation resembles that of European states: Eich and Eich 2005.

[8] Cooperation and reciprocity in Greek interstate relations: Low 2007. *Koina*: Mackil 2003, 2008. Greek diplomatic strategies in light of contemporary international relations literature: Lebow and Strauss 1991. Thucydides on Corcyra: 3.70–85, and Morrison 1999; Ober 2000a. Cooperation among rival firms is now common in highly competitive business ecologies: Baumol 1993: 193–222; Gomes-Casseres 1996.

Competition between Greek states was not expressed uniquely in destructive organized violence: competition among rivals was played out in athletic games, in public-building projects, and in musical performances. Greek interstate competition was not always zero-sum. Competition promoted innovation in the waging of war, but also in various other domains: in performance culture, architecture, and, notably, in institutional design. A similar pattern of competition and cooperation leading to innovation and overall growth of the system is manifest in relations among rival firms. Firms compete with one another in rule-bounded environments, build cooperative partnerships with rivals, and engage in competitive emulation in ways that are not invariably zero-sum. Yet the problem of "when to cooperate and with what other organizations?" is not easily resolved, especially in the face of entrenched intraorganizational interests. Meanwhile, the realistic possibility of destruction remained as a motivator of individual and collective behavior, both for the ancient city-state and the modern firm.

The stakes were certainly higher for city-states than they are for firms. Managers of business organizations do not expect their physical plants to be sacked or their personnel to be killed and enslaved by victorious rivals. Yet they do regularly confront the negative consequences of organizational failure. They know that failure can mean not just lowered profit margins or lower ranking, but the elimination of their firm. Furthermore, they know that this outcome can follow from a failure on the part of the organization's decision makers to manage knowledge and information properly. The problem of organizing knowledge increases with scale. Like a modern firm, in seeking to maximize competitive advantage by coordinating "human capital"—that is, the activities of its people—the Greek polis confronted the problem of how to balance the competitive advantages that accompanied larger scale with the problems of organizing knowledge at scale. This chapter looks at the public-action problems faced by Greek poleis, and solutions they devised with reference to contemporary democratic nation-states and non-state organizations.

PARTICIPATION AND SCALE

Size was clearly an advantage in Greek interstate competition: the twenty highest-ranking poleis in terms of aggregate flourishing (see chapter 2) had territories that were, on the average, about three times the size of the poleis in the middling group, and the middling group was, on the average, considerably larger than the mass of unranked poleis. These relationships generally hold even when territory is removed from the aggregate score. While we have only very limited evidence for the actual human population of most Greek poleis, it is likely that population correlated fairly closely with territory size.[9]

The majority of the approximately one thousand Greek states that existed during the archaic and classical period were not, when compared to the "top 20," particularly large, rich, or powerful. A substantial number appear to have been what E. Ruschenbusch (1985) has called *Normalpoleis*—which means that they had very small populations (averaging a few hundred to a several thousand persons) and controlled very small territories (below 100 square kilometers). Such communities tended in the direction of true face-to-face societies, in which people actually knew (for good or ill) a lot about one another's characters and habits.[10] Many of these Normalpoleis were not fully independent: some were forced to join alliance systems (e.g., the Peloponnesian League or Athenian Empire); others organized themselves into sophisticated regional systems (*koina*), sustained by shared economic interests, religious practices, and political institutions.[11] The ecology of large and small poleis is illustrated in figure 3.1.

Figure 3.1[12] shows graphically that more than half of the poleis in the sample (344 of 590) were level 1 (25 km² or smaller), or level 2 (25–100 km²)—and thus good candidates for Normalpolis status. As we have seen (chapter 2), the median size of "middling poleis" (second and third quartiles of the sample group of 164 poleis) is somewhat larger on average: at the lower end of size level 4, so about 200–300 square kilometers. A few very well known poleis (like Delphi and Aigina) were category 2 and certainly had populations that were out of proportion to their territory size. Yet most historically prominent poleis were level 3 (100–200

---

[9] Nixon and Price 1990 offer a thoughtful analysis of the resources of big and small poleis, based on the lists of tribute payers to the Athenian empire. The top-20 group has an average territory level of 5.7, which corresponds to approximately 800–900 square kilometers. In the extended group of 164 poleis, territorial size correlates fairly strongly with success as measured by public buildings + international activity: $r = 0.51$. For a survey of the evidence for the size of polis territories, see M. H. Hansen and Nielsen 2004: 70–73. Estimated correlation between polis populations and territory size: M. H. Hansen 2006b. Among modern states, which vary much more than did Greek poleis in their climate and geography, territory size correlates quite strongly with population ($r = 0.69$): Dahl and Tufte 1973. On the effect of extreme size differentials on international relations in the modern world, see Dahl and Tufte 1973: esp. 120–22.

[10] On face-to-face communities, see the classic study of Laslett 1973.

[11] Total number of poleis: M. H. Hansen and Nielsen 2004: 53–54. The inventory of 1035 poleis compiled by Hansen and Nielsen (2004: 71) yields the following breakdown of territory size: 60% of poleis = under 100 km²; 80% = under 200 km²; 90% = under 500 km²; + only 13 poleis = greater than 1000 km².

[12] N = 590. Number of poleis = the number of poleis in M. H. Hansen and Nielsen 2004 of each size rank (1–7, ranks 8–10 assimilated to 7). Actual size/10 = size of territory of each size rank in km² divided by 10. See M. H. Hansen 2006a, chapter 13, who arrives at similar conclusions using a slightly larger database.

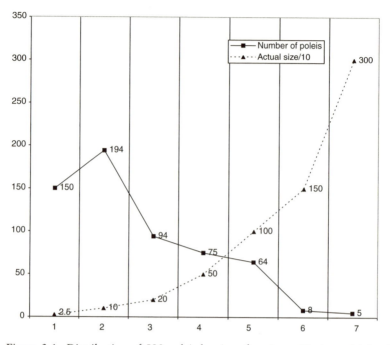

Figure 3.1. Distribution of 590 poleis by size of territory. Horizontal (*x*) axis is rank of territorial size (1–7 scale). Vertical (*y*) axis is number of poleis at each rank and (estimated average) actual size (in km^2/10) of each rank. N = 590. Number of poleis = the number of poleis in Hansen and Nielsen 2004 of each size rank (1–7, ranks 8–10 assimilated to 7). Actual size/10 = size of territory of each size rank in km^2 divided by 10. See Hansen 2006a, chapter 13, who arrives at similar conclusions using a slightly larger database.

km^2) like Tegea, Plataea, or Paros; level 4 (200–500 km^2) like Megara or Samos; or level 5 (500–1000 km^2) like Corinth, Thebes, and Chios. Only thirteen of all known poleis were level 6 (1000–2000 km^2) or 7 + (2000 km^2 and over). The super-poleis, those with territories over 2000 square kilometers, are limited to a handful of the best-known classical cities, including Miletus, Syracuse, Sparta—and, of course, Athens.[13] With a total population of perhaps a quarter-million and a home territory (not counting imperial possessions) of some 2500 square kilometers, Athens was perhaps twenty-five to fifty times the size of a Normalpolis and ten times the size of the median "middling" polis.

[13] M. H. Hansen and Nielsen 2004 list the territories of some of these states as follows (in km^2): Syracuse, 12,000 (in the fourth century); Sparta 8400 (before 371: "two-fifths of the Peloponnesus"); Athens 2500 (excluding overseas possessions); Argos 1400, Corinth 900 (total est. pop. 70,000); Thebes 650–800.

The organization of knowledge changes dramatically with changes in political scale. For most of human history, community size was limited by environmental constraints. Before the consolidation of sedentary agriculture (some 10,000 years ago), people lived in foraging bands with populations measured in dozens and (if anthropological evidence is any guide) fairly egalitarian social norms.[14] Even after the food surpluses generated by agriculture began to repay economies of scale, and thus made larger and more hierarchical communities potentially more efficient, many people continued to live and work in small, relatively homogeneous, face-to-face communities in which the individual residents knew one another's characters and domains of expertise. This appears to be a tolerably good description of the Normalpolis, of the active-citizen body in many mid-sized Greek oligarchies, and (see chapter 4) of the constituent villages and neighborhoods of classical Athens.

In an influential study of collective action, Mancur Olson asserted that "unless the number of individuals is quite small, or unless there is coercion or some other special device to make individuals act in their common interest, *rational, self-interested individuals will not act to achieve their common or group interests*" (his emphasis).[15] In a small community, such as the Normalpolis or the oligarchic active-citizen body, some collective action and knowledge organization problems are quite easily solved: interpersonal knowledge serves to keep transaction costs low, and ongoing communication facilitates exchange of information and goods among the members of the group. Common knowledge is generated quite readily in public rituals, and collection of useful information is facilitated because people are likely to know who is skilled within what domain. Deliberations about matters of importance to the community can take proper account of both social and technical knowledge.[16] Education (formal and

---

[14] Foraging bands egalitarian: Boehm 1993, 1999, 2000a, 2000b. Band size: Dunbar 1993, based on a sample of anthropological evidence for nine foraging societies. Recent archaeological work suggests that some forms of agriculture may date back to 13,000 years ago (but were interrupted by climate change) and band size of pre-agricultural foraging groups varied considerably over the fifty or so millennia between the emergence of *Homo sapiens sapiens* and the development of agriculture. It is, however, very unlikely that any human community exceeded 150 members before ca. 9000 B.C. (Morris, in progress, chapter 2). There is no doubt that the human brain and human sociability evolved in a small group setting.

[15] Olson 1965: 2. Olson also noted that an "intermediate sized group"—that is, one in which each individual's actions are quite noticeable—may sometimes provide collective benefits. See, further, R. Hardin 1982: 48–49; Keohane 1984: 76–77; Ostrom 1990: 5–6; Davenport and Prusak 1998: 18. Ostrom 2003: 29–34 and Kopelman, Weber, and Messick 2002, esp. 134–37 summarize psychological literature on factors contributing to cooperation, emphasizing two-way communication.

[16] Coase (1988: 178) notes that "in a zero transaction cost world . . . all parties have an incentive to discover and disclose all the adjustments which would have the effect of increas-

informal) encourages individuals to internalize group norms with respect to making and keeping commitments. Meanwhile, behavioral norms and sanctions, triggered by easily observed misbehavior, serve to control the tendency of individuals to free-ride on others' cooperative behavior or to take more than their share from common-pool resources.[17]

In light of the very long human history of social life in small face-to-face groups (bands, villages) and Olson's argument about the advantage of smallness for solving collective action problems, it not surprising that smallness appears to be positively correlated to participation rates in democratic organizations. In his detailed study of town meetings in Vermont, Frank Bryan employs an extensive data set (1435 individual meetings) to demonstrate that the single variable with most weight in explaining the level of participation in Vermont towns is scale. After correcting for all other potentially relevant factors, Bryan concludes that "real democracy works better in small places—dramatically better." In smaller towns, with bodies of citizens under about 350 (keeping in mind the attendance at any given meeting is much smaller, averaging 20.5 percent of the citizen body across the sample), the level of participation in town meetings is consistently higher than it is in larger towns.[18]

Bryan's findings correlating small size with increased political participation are consistent with a general claim about scale that Malcolm Gladwell makes in his well-known book *The Tipping Point* (2000). On the basis of work in cognitive psychology and the experience of actual organizations (from Menonnite communities to high-tech business firms), Gladwell postulates that 150 active members is a maximum for organizations that depend for their success on the close cooperation and personal relationships that emerge within egalitarian face-to-face communities. Gladwell suggests that as purposeful communities grow in size beyond about 150 active members, it is no longer possible for everyone to know everyone else, and thus the community loses the close coherence that emerges only with personal familiarity. Public-action problems emerge and performance declines.[19]

---

ing the value of production." Coase (1988: 174–75) was careful to specify that there is no such thing as a world without transaction costs; the point is that as transaction costs are lowered, the incentives Coase alludes to here are increased.

[17] On the role of moral education and sanctions in building cooperative behavior, see, further, Dietz et al. 2002; Kopelman, Weber, and Messick 2002, esp. 135–36. This basic conjunction is at the center of much communitarian political theory. Liberal theorists point out that strong norms can stifle pluralism (e.g., Waldron 1992). Economists (e.g., Baumol 1993) note that strong norms can stifle innovation. My thanks to Paul Edwards for sharing unpublished work and for discussion related to this issue.

[18] Bryan 2004: quote p. 83. Percentage average attendance: Bryan 2004: 105.

[19] Gladwell 2000, chapter 5; on cognitive psychology, Gladwell cites the work of Dunbar 1993. Bryan 2004: 62–64 notes that the average highest attendance throughout the day at a Vermont town meeting (averaged over all meetings studied) is 137.

Aristotle (*Politics* 1326a) makes a similar general point about the "best achievable polis," which he says must be small enough to ensure that the citizens will all be able to know one another's character and virtues. In this sense, at least, Aristotle's best possible polis would not have been radically different from many actual poleis. In the small-scale Normalpolis, people were able to solve some public-action problems by reference to habits that may be in some sense "natural" within small human communities. The apparent scale limitation for effective and cooperative aggregation and alignment of useful knowledge via personal information and face-to-face deliberation posed no particular problem for a midlevel oligarchic polis community. In a midsized oligarchy, the number of adult male native "potential active citizens" might be counted in the hundreds. Property qualifications for the full exercise of citizenship restricted the active political participation of many native residents and decreased the social and epistemic diversity among political participants. The problem that oligarchies faced was not so much internal coordination within the decision-making body, but rather demands by natives outside that body for fuller participation rights. This was one important reason Aristotle regarded oligarchies as more prone to civil conflict than democracies.[20]

Scale poses a very serious challenge to a relatively large and highly participatory democracy like Athens. Indeed, the scale problem might seem to obviate the value of participatory democracy as an explanation for the success of any organization with a large and diverse active membership. As a super-polis, Athens did not share the "natural" advantage in respect to collective action enjoyed by the tiny Normalpoleis and by oligarchic midsized poleis with limited active-citizen bodies. Like other large organizations, Athens was under competitive pressure to develop cultural practices and institutions capable of addressing its public-action problems. Along with small size, Olson notes "coercion" and "other special devices" as possible answers to the problem of achieving common purposes. Yet, unlike other super-poleis, Athens did not resort either to the special device of "ideology all the way down" (mandatory social indoctrination in strong traditionalism) as did Sparta, or to the coercive mechanisms of a command-and-control hierarchy as did Syracuse during its tyrannical interludes.[21]

I argued in chapter 1 that Robert Michels' conclusion, that the problem of organizing coordinated activity at scale must in and of itself render

[20] Oligarchic size advantage for organizational efficiency: Brock and Hodkinson 2000: 19–20. Civil conflict problem: Ober 2000a, 2005a.

[21] Dahl 1970: 59–103 and Dahl and Tufte 1973: 20–22, 66–88 emphasize the correlation between larger scale and higher communication costs, and thus the difficulty—or even impossibility—of scaling up participatory forms of democracy. Note, however, that they assume that full participation means *each citizen* must speak in public assembly. Institutional alternatives to that unworkable ideal are discussed in detail below.

participatory democracy an *impossibility*, is disproved by the Athenian case. But the scale issue highlights the vital importance of institutional design. A large democratic organization in a competitive environment must develop ways to take advantage of the enhanced potential for cooperation and organization of useful knowledge that occurs more or less naturally in egalitarian communities with small and relatively homogeneous bodies of participants. Given that the special devices of "all the way down" ideology and coercion are unavailable to democracies, a large-scale participatory democracy must devise ways to organize itself such that the small face-to-face community is a fundamental part of its institutional architecture.[22]

Scale management (via the deme/tribe/polis system discussed in chapter 4) was a key operational feature of Athenian democratic institutions, just as it is in much larger modern representative democracies. Athenian approaches to managing scale appear in some ways more akin to the knowledge-centered practices of successful contemporary non-state organizations than to the political systems typical of modern states (Manville and Ober 2003). Successful modern firms—with employee bases ranging from the hundreds to the tens of thousands, and occasionally to the hundreds of thousands—operate at a range of scales roughly comparable to that of the Greek poleis. Contemporary work on modern nation-states and international regimes is enlightening for explaining many aspects the Greek poleis. Yet, given the issues of limited size and the fiercely competitive environment confronted by city-states, certain aspects of the Greek poleis, including the organization of knowledge, may be better modeled by branches of social and organizational theory that focus on human behavior in the context of firms and other non-state organizations in highly competitive environments.

Social, Technical, and Latent Knowledge

Three premises about organizations undergird the arguments in this and the next three chapters:

1. States (and a fortiori poleis) are purposeful organizations whose members jointly pursue collective flourishing, as well as other shared and individual goals.[23]

---

[22] Importance of maintaining face-to-face interaction in organizations: Davenport and Prusak 1998: esp. 12, 22; Dixon 2000: 3–5; Brown and Duguid 2000, chapter 8. The value to citizens of the experience of local participatory self-governance is a key conclusion of Dahl 1970: 153–66, but Dahl is very pessimistic about the potential of making local governance an integral part of a larger state system. See, however, Fung 2004; Baiocchi 2005.

[23] Flourishing: see chapter 2. In some cases, succeeding in accomplishing the "other goals" may be essential to the organization's flourishing (building good automobiles is es-

2. Organizations typically exist within competitive (as well as sometimes cooperative) ecologies shared with other, more or less similar, organizations. The more competitive the environment, the
   more severe are the consequences of failure.[24]
3. Effective employment of useful knowledge is a key differentiator
   among organizations; other things being equal, organizations
   with more effective epistemic processes are more likely to flourish
   under competitive conditions.[25]

In sum, the issue addressed in chapters 3–6 is "the role of knowledge in
the comparative flourishing of a complex organization in a competitive
environment."

In chapter 1, "knowledge in action" was defined as the structuring of
information for productive social action through processes of innovation
and learning. We may gloss that definition as follows: Politically relevant
knowledge consists of people's beliefs, capabilities, experience, and information, organized in ways that can be reproduced and shared within and
among collectivities. When put to use through routinization and innovation, this sort of knowledge produces substantial political and economic
effects that are relevant to competitive performance.[26] Politically relevant
knowledge conjoins social/interpersonal and technical/expert forms of
knowledge that are possessed by the organization as a whole (in the form
of institutionalized processes and formal codes) and by individuals (both
explicitly and latently).

Social knowledge includes knowledge of people, norms, institutions
and their characteristic practices. It includes answers to questions like
these: Who is my friend/foe? Whom should I trust/distrust and under

---

sential to the flourishing of Ford Motor Company); in other cases the "other goals" sought
by the organization may be independent from its own flourishing (failing to end famine in
the Sudan may not compromise the flourishing of Oxfam as an organization).

[24] There is some evidence to suggest that competition is positively correlated to the fitness
of organizations; organizations that exist for a long period of time in a monopolistic condition may compete less successfully when placed into a competitive situation: Barnett and
Pontikes 2006; Barnett 2008.

[25] There is a vast literature on organizational learning and knowledge; useful introductions include Levitt and March 1988; March 1991; Davenport 1998; Wenger 1998; Dixon
2000; Garvin 2000; and Brown and Duguid 2000. Other studies are cited below.

[26] This expanded definition of knowledge in action approximates what Russel Hardin
(2002: 214–16) calls "street level epistemology," which he describes as "economic; it is not
generally about justification but about usefulness. It follows John Dewey's 'pragmatic rule':
in order to discover the meaning of an idea, ask for its consequences. In essence, a street-
level epistemology applies this idea to knowledge, with consequences broadly defined to
include the full costs and benefits of coming to know and using knowledge." While Hardin
uses this definition to show that participatory democracy is incoherent, I believe that it helps
to explain how a knowledge-centered participatory democracy can work.

what circumstances? How ought I to behave in public? What sorts of redress do I have if I am wronged? Social knowledge is a prerequisite for meaningful participation in a democratic community. It is possessed, in one way or another and to a greater or lesser degree, by everyone. That said, some people are much better at accumulating and using social knowledge than others, and an especially high level of social knowledge may be regarded as a sort of expertise. Social knowledge thus merges into technical or expert knowledge.[27]

Technical knowledge may be defined as specialized knowledge about how to use tools and processes to gain desired ends in a given domain of endeavor. The highest level of technical knowledge is characterized by difficult-to-acquire expertise within a specific domain. In a given domain (chess and violin playing are often cited as examples), there are only a small number of persons with the highest level of expertise—call them "true experts." But because there are many domains in which expertise of one sort or another may be gained, any large and complex society is likely to contain a substantial number of true experts. It will also contain many people whose mastery of a domain falls short of true expertise, but is much greater than that of most other people.[28]

I argue that the *interaction* of social and technical aspects of politically relevant knowledge, within the context of democratic institutions, played an important role in making the participatory Athenian democracy a sustainable form of political organization—despite the "iron law of oligarchy." It helped Athens to become a comparatively wealthy, secure, and powerful polis. The iteration of the practices of knowledge exchange led, over time, to the emergence of a new domain of "democratic political action" in which many ordinary Athenians became highly competent, and some became true experts. The exchange of social and technical knowl-

[27] Social competence (the capacity to acquire useful social knowledge) is innate and manifest in infants: Premack and Premack 1995. It can be measured as "emotional intelligence": Goleman 1995. Of course, some people may be innately without the capacity to easily acquire social knowledge (e.g., persons with Asperger's syndrome), but these are exceptions that prove the rule.

[28] Expertise: Leifer 1988 (example of positional play in chess); Ericsson and Smith 1991, Introduction: esp. 27–32, on the importance of practice and feedback in the development of expertise; Salthouse 1991, on expertise as circumvention of ordinary limits; Ericsson 1999 (literature review). Expert political judgment and its limits: Tetlock 2005. Mokyr 2002 is an important study of the relationship between the economic prosperity and the growth of propositional (what) and prescriptive (how) knowledge (especially after A.D. 1800). Mokyr concentrates on the broadening of the epistemic base of experts (18–19) but concludes that "for better or worse, the history of the growth of useful knowledge is the history of an elite" (291). Harris 2002 shows that a very wide range of technical skills was possessed by individual Athenians.

edge within democratic institutions yielded better decisions, more effective routines, and more innovative solutions—and therefore contributed to Athens' competitive success as a state.

The claim that the effective use of specialized technical knowledge is an important part of a state's success is unsurprising. It is obvious to anyone with experience of complex organizations that some kinds of expertise are at once fairly rare and essential to governance. It is an easy move from this intuitive premise to the conclusion that participatory forms of organization are impossible, and that organizational success depends entirely on expert leadership—that is to say, on the choices made by technically expert rulers.[29] If the successful organization of useful and politically relevant knowledge were entirely a matter of entrusting decisions to leaders who were true experts in rulership, a mass of non-experts would have nothing of value to add. Including non-experts in decision making would be, at best, a costly waste of time.[30] Participatory democratic processes should, therefore, consistently fail in competitive environments, and democracies should be eliminated by competitive pressure. This train of thought is what led to Michels' conclusion about the inevitability of oligarchy, which I suggested (chapter 1) is refuted by the history of Athens. As we have seen (chapter 2), Athenian decision-making practices *were* costly and Athenian democratic bodies *did* make some bad decisions, and yet Athens still outperformed its hierarchical rivals.

Michels' influential conception of the role of organization leads to the assumption that it would *always* be better, from the point of view of efficiency, if non-experts accepted whatever the experts decided and followed orders from above without demur. In the industrial realm, this is the principle of "Taylorism," famously expressed by Henry Ford's reported regret that the hands he hired were attached to heads.[31] As noted in chapter 1, Plato's Callipolis is an ancient example of an imaginary state organized on a similarly strict hierarchical assumption about the division of labor between experts in governing and the rest of society. It is their unique expert knowledge of the Form of the Good, a knowledge that is not communicable to non-experts, that provides Callipolis' philosopher-kings

---

[29] The huge modern business literature on organizational leadership suggests just how easy and seemingly natural that move is.

[30] It is not, however, the case that experts always make good decisions even within their own domains: Camerer and Johnson 1991; Ericsson 1999, with review of literature; Tetlock 2005. See further, below.

[31] Ford and Taylorism: Rothschild 1973. Historical study of Taylorism in action: Aitken 1985.

with their unique capacity to rule the ideal polis and to maintain through their rule the conditions of its flourishing.[32] The culture of Callipolis (including censorship and "noble lies") is designed to ensure (through education and indoctrination) that those who are not expert in ruling will not question the decisions of the true-expert rulers.

Although there is no real human community that models Plato's Callipolis, the belief in the value of a strict hierarchy based on expert knowledge of "rulership as management" has been widespread in the modern world. Taylorist industrial factories have their totalizing analogs in modern states run as hierarchies based on the putative expertise of rulers. Various large-scale technocratic sociopolitical experiments of modernity have confidently proceeded as if specialized managerial knowledge, possessed by a handful of technically proficient experts in positions of leadership, were the primary, indeed perhaps the only, determinant of success. Grandiose social experiments run on these lines have failed catastrophically, resulting in great human suffering (Scott 1998). Although the reasons for the spectacular failure of grandiose schemes designed by experts and carried out by authoritarian states are no doubt complex, some part of the failure must be attributed to a willful refusal of non-democratic governments to take into account the social knowledge of ordinary people.

Leadership undoubtedly makes a difference—in a potentially positive as well as a potentially negative sense—and it certainly has some things in common with expertise. Yet, from Greek antiquity to the present, rulership, "general expertise in the domain of political leadership" (in Greek, politikē technē), has eluded formal definition and has proved to be difficult to learn. Approaches to leadership that are highly effective in some contexts prove catastrophic in others.[33] The question then arises: Should leadership be regarded as a domain of expertise in the ordinary sense of the term? I suggest that it should not: although leadership typically involves *coordination of* multiple forms of expert knowledge, leadership in the real world is not itself properly characterized *as* a form of expert knowledge. If this is right, it means that politically relevant knowledge cannot rightly be redescribed as expertise in the domain of leadership. It is among the recognized virtues of democracy that the common sense

[32] The other residents of Callipolis presumably appreciate the conditions under which they do flourish. It is worth noting that each resident of Callipolis is assumed to be expert in some specific domain, and it is a fundamental principle of Callipolis that expertise is not transferable between domains. See below.

[33] This point is reiterated in classic studies of leadership in business organizations; for example, Barnard 1948, chapters 2 and 4; Collins 2001; Drucker 2003, and in biographies of American presidents. Leadership, as such, is not a major field in contemporary political theory; a work in progress by Nannerl Keohane aims to fill this notable gap.

(that is, the aggregated social and technical knowledge) of the citizenry can be politically expressed. Leaders who are accountable to citizens capable of expressing that common sense in their votes are likely to be more hesitant about embarking upon potentially disastrous projects for remaking society according to a master plan.

In addition to its salutary *negative* function of resisting overly ambitious attempts at top-down social engineering, democracy, in its participatory form, can add *positive* value to policy making and execution. It does so by bringing various forms of social knowledge to bear on difficult problems and by expanding the range of technical knowledge available for decision making. There are several reasons that adding diverse sorts of social and technical knowledge to political decision making, through costly processes of democratic participation, may add enough value to the outcome to overbalance the cost.

First, the technical knowledge necessary to make the best possible decision on a complex issue may be possessed by a large number of experts, whose expertise lies in a wide variety of sometimes non-obvious domains. Participatory government systematically brings diverse experiences and knowledge-sets to deliberative decision-making processes. Diversity of input brings to the fore *latent knowledge* possessed by individuals who would not be recognized by elite power holders as experts. People from various walks of life possess pertinent information and expertise that potentially promotes productive innovations. Latent knowledge includes explicit local knowledge that can readily be transferred once it is brought to the surface and recognized (by its possessors and others) as valuable. But it also includes forms of "tacit knowing" (Polanyi 1966)—"know-how" (the standard examples are swimming and riding a bicycle)—that are not easily written down, but can be learned by experimentation and personal instruction. Tacit knowledge is often at the heart of team-based organizational processes; the fact that it is hard to codify (and thus imitate) makes tacit knowledge an important source of competitive advantage.[34]

Dispersed latent knowledge is unlikely to surface in deliberations among a limited body of "expert rulers" and their circle of specialist advisers because it is not recognized by them as relevant. Under the right circumstances, potentially useful latent knowledge, possessed by knowledgeable informants and experts in domains previously considered irrelevant (and whose participation would therefore be counted only as a cost), may come to be recognized as highly relevant. When it is transformed into *active knowledge* that promotes the organization's purposes, latent

---

[34] Davenport and Prusak 1998: 68; Osterloh and Frey 2000; Dixon 2000: 11–13; Brown and Duguid 2000: 122–24.

technical knowledge of this sort comes to count as a substantial benefit; organizational investment in participation on the part of those who possess valuable local and tacit knowledge becomes profitable. Large-scale and broad-based participation makes more sense because potentially important latent knowledge is various, widely dispersed, and difficult to identify in advance. Given the high potential value of latent knowledge, and the difficulty of bringing it to the surface in a systematic way, institutionalizing the process of identifying sources of latent knowledge and transferring it to others is a major challenge of organizational design.[35]

Along with the identification of latent knowledge, costly participatory processes, often although not always involving deliberation, are potentially effective at bringing diverse varieties of social knowledge into the same "solution space" with various kinds of technical knowledge. The intermixture of the right kinds of social knowledge with the right kinds of technical knowledge can lead to more realistic and sustainable policy. It can also serve to lower implementation costs, by identifying sources of friction in advance and giving decision makers a more accurate sense of the social costs likely to be incurred as the result of a given action. On the other hand, the deliberative process can, again under the right conditions, give an extensive body of decision makers a better appreciation for the benefits of a given course of action. Policies that demand sacrifices on the part of the citizenry may therefore be carried out with less popular resistance.[36]

Finally, as processes of surfacing latent knowledge are standardized and routinized over time, some of the costs associated with participation should drop and the benefits should rise. Many of the skills necessary for good governance may be developed to quite a high level by ordinary citizens who have adequate chance to learn and practice those skills. Citizens who become familiar with public decision-making processes are likely to make fewer costly mistakes. At the same time, participation on the part

---

[35] On latent knowledge and its potential transformation into action, see Hargadon and Fanelli 2002. The general issue of how organization manages what it knows, promotes routinization and/or innovation, and thus helps or hinders short- and long-term productivity is a primary concern of the sociological subfield of organizational learning: see, for example, Levitt and March 1988; March 1991; Baumol 1993, 2004; Osterloh and Frey 2000; Grandori and Kogut 2002; Orlikowsky 2002.

[36] Ruzé 1997 is the most detailed treatment of ancient Greek deliberation. Modern advocates of deliberative practice include Fishkin 1991; Ackerman and Fishkin 2004. Critics of deliberation often point to the tendency for deliberation to increase group polarization (e.g., Sunstein 2000, 2002; Mendelberg 2002). For a review of empirical work on the effects of deliberation, see Delli Carpini et al. 2004 and the essays in Fishkin and Laslett 2003. Modern deliberation experiments typically lack relevant features (in terms of duration, salience, potential for iteration and reputation effects) that characterized Athenian deliberative processes; see, further, chapter 4.

of many reasonably highly skilled amateurs in the routines of political process lowers costs insofar as it helps keep the processes of government transparent and thereby lowers the opportunity for corruption. Transparency makes it more difficult for power holders and political insiders to design and manipulate a "black box" system. Thus they are limited in their opportunity to use the system in ways that will promote their own personal and partial interests to the detriment of the interests of the less powerful or the general interest of the organization as a whole. The democratic advantage in respect to political corruption was duly noted by the "Old Oligarch" (Ps-Xenophon, *Ath. Pol.* 3.7) and Aristotle (*Politics* 1286a31–35).

In sum, broader participation potentially enables diverse sorts of technical expertise to be made available for devising innovative solutions to problems, while simultaneously distributing some of the benefits associated with routinization and learning across an extensive membership and over time. If both innovation and learning can be optimized and brought into an appropriate balance, the benefits of participation may substantially exceed its costs. The expected result is higher levels of organizational performance. Yet in order to achieve this desirable goal, participation must bring latent knowledge to the surface and must intermix social with technical knowledge in ways that are relatively seamless. Contemporary work on organizational learning emphasizes the difficulty of finding and maintaining a productive balance between innovation and routinization and the right blend of social and technical knowledge. This book is meant to explain how the Athenian participatory system worked in practice to achieve that balance and blending through epistemic processes of aggregation, alignment, and codification. While these Athenian processes are indeed political and democratic, they are quite different from core political processes of modern democratic nation-states.

PREFERENCES, PARTIES, AND COSTLY INFORMATION

In modern democratic states, the practice of voting for representatives brings public opinion into the political process as a means of ensuring legitimacy; it is much less clear that the process of voting for representatives also adds value to outcomes by contributing something that could properly be understood as *knowledge*.[37] Indeed, the ignorance of individ-

---

[37] Influential and recent discussions of democratic representation include Pitkin 1967; Manin 1997; Przeworski, Stokes, and Manin 1999; Urbinati 2006; D. Runciman 2007. The lack of substantial impact on U.S. federal policy of mechanisms for soliciting public input (e.g., on environmental issues) may be taken as indicative of the tendency of governing

ual voters about what choices will actually promote their best interest is frequently cited as a problem for representative government—perhaps even as its fatal flaw. The problem is that information about how to vote in order to optimize individual utility is relatively costly to acquire, and the impact of an individual's vote on his or her utility is low, so that the cost exceeds the benefit. Voting is, on this argument, strictly irrational.[38]

Representative government requires the practice of voting in that the appeal to public opinion in the form of the election is what imparts legitimacy to the rule of elected leaders. These leaders in turn are expected to make decisions that promote the preferences of those who voted for them, and that promote the common good, based on their expert mastery of the political system and their privileged access to sources of information and expert knowledge. By contrast, voting for candidates is a relatively unimportant part of participatory democracy in the Athenian style, which was predicated not on the legitimacy of elected leaders but on the assumption that value is added in political decision making via the aggregation of technical and social knowledge that is widely distributed within the citizenry itself.

In terms of the organization of knowledge, representation can be understood as a means of identifying and electing to office persons who possess the specialized knowledge necessary for ruling a complex state. I have suggested, above, that "true experts in the domain of rulership" do not exist. In any event, the job of a leader in a representative democracy is famously contradictory: she must somehow accurately represent (i.e., "make present") the interests and preferences of her constituency in policy making, while simultaneously making the best choices for her constituents and for the state as a whole on the basis of her special access to expertise.[39] Although elected representatives in a constitutional democ-

---

elites to treat public opinion as something other than knowledge. Stasavage 2007 notes that transparency in representative systems (i.e., making decision processes a matter of public knowledge) can lead to worse policy, because it encourages representatives to stick to established positions as a signal of their loyalty to their core constituencies. Urbinati 2002 suggests that J. S. Mill's original conception of representative democracy was centered on mechanisms for developing and distributing useful knowledge among the citizenry.

[38] Fatal flaw: Downs 1957, with discussion in Grofman 1993; R. Hardin 2002: esp. 225. For different approaches, see Page and Shapiro 1992 (public opinion is rational and consistent over the long term); Gordon and Segura 1997 (if cognitive ability is supplemented by incentives and access to information, masses of ordinary voters can choose rationally and well); Caplan 2007 (voters are irrational in that they misperceive economic reality). Lohmann 1994 demonstrates the complexity of aggregating dispersed political knowledge in voting-centered systems, focusing on the surprising result that pre-vote political action by individuals seeking to educate their fellow citizens may add "noise" to the process, and that this may be deleterious to the goal of aggregating actual preferences.

[39] Representation as "making present": Pitkin 1967.

racy employ both social and technical forms of knowledge in the performance of their offices, citizens are seldom direct participants in the process of deciding on the merits of particular courses of public action—the expression of political knowledge by citizens is ordinarily limited to choosing representatives. When citizens in modern democracies do vote directly on issues, as in American state ballot initiatives, the process is subject to elite capture and manipulation; the results are often counterproductive.[40] This history has contributed to a tendency among political scientists to discount the possibility that genuine "government by the people" could ever work.[41]

Much contemporary work on democracy and knowledge has tended to suppose that democracy is best understood as a non-cooperative game in the following sense. The primary purpose of democracy is deciding between (or giving the appropriate weight to) mutually incompatible interests (or preferences) held by the individuals who constitute the citizen body. The primary means of determining the relative weight of conflicting interests is voting. Political parties (and the individual politicians who lead them) thus serve to aggregate diverse preferences and compete to offer policies that will (or that will seem to) further the interests of some part of the electorate. The goal of electoral politics is to win out over rivals by successfully appealing to some subset of the public. This approach certainly makes sense under circumstances of political life that have come to be regarded by many contemporary political scientists as normal: that is to say, within a stable constitutional framework and in the absence of exogenous or endogenous threats that must be contained by resort to actions that potentially endanger the existence of the community (e.g., the United States after ca. 1945).[42]

My concern here is with circumstances of political life that vary in some ways from the contemporary conception of political normalcy.[43] Individ-

---

[40] Modern direct democracy (via referendum and ballot initiative, now employed in a number of American states: Cronin 1989; Budge 1996) *seems* participatory in that people are voting on an issue rather than for an individual, but it lacks most of the organizational design and educational features that, as I will argue in chapter 4, may enable participatory democracies to succeed in the difficult process of efficient aggregation.

[41] This argument is made explicitly by Dahl 1970: 67–71 and 143–47 in respect to Athens, and is repeated in some of his later work, e.g., Dahl 1989, 1998.

[42] Attempt to transcend the "normal" assumption can be found in the historical essays collected in Bates et al. 1998 and in Greif 2006. Cf. Padgett and Ansell 1993: esp. 1301–1302, and 1307–8 (in reference to politics in fifteenth-century Florence): "Given fixed role frames, self-interests (and attributions) are clear, but in complicated chaos . . . the games themselves are all up for grabs. Rational choice requires a common metric of utility for footing, but revealed preferences (the basis for inferring trade-offs across goals/roles) only exist post hoc."

[43] This line of argument is not leading to a claim that the difference between normal and extraordinary politics leads to the desirability of unfettered executive authority, along the

ual Athenians certainly had different interests, and those interests could be aggregated into definable interest groups—notably "the wealthy elite" and "the working many."[44] But, in the face of endemic threats to state existence from external rivals and internal civil war, there was a widespread agreement among the Athenians on the answer to the high-level question of "must our state seek to be relatively more prosperous, secure, and powerful in relation to its rivals?" Of course, the same may be true of contemporary nations. The difference lies in the salience of the question and the predictable consequences of failure. The general agreement of Athenians on this question, its centrality in policy making, and thus its relative importance for how Athenians thought about their individual interests, were conditioned by the fact that the high level of competition that characterized the Greek polis ecology meant that Athens regularly faced meaningful threats to its existence.[45]

As we have seen, destruction of the polis was a very real possibility, as was devolution into a destructive cycle of debilitating civil war. Many Greek poleis suffered these catastrophes in the classical period.[46] Much of the work of the democratic Athenian government was aimed at policy making that would allow Athens to avoid these ghastly, easily imagined, and realistically possible alternatives. An essential aspect of the ideology and cultural practice of the polis was reminding members of a diverse and free citizenry that they should in fact share a preference for a polis that was rich and powerful enough to fend off threats to its survival—and that excessive polarization along the lines of factional or class interest would jeopardize that goal.[47]

---

lines of Carl Schmitt (2004 [1932]). Rather, I suppose that in Greek antiquity, the definition of normal politics was different, in part as a result of the high level and serious consequences of competition.

[44] Aristotle's *mere* or *moria* ("parts" of the "whole" that is the polis) in the *Politics* are interest groups based on economic class or some other quality; a prevailing and historically realistic concern of ancient political theory is that such parts will come into conflict (*stasis*) and thus weaken the state, leaving it vulnerable to overthrow by rivals. The relative political stability of democratic Athens (other than in the period 415–403) suggests that interest-group politics was not dominant. See, further, Gehrke 1985; Ober 1989, 2000a, 2005b. But cf. Burke 2005.

[45] Cf. Funke 1980, on the prevalence of the term *homonoia* (same-mindedness) in Athenian public discourse after the Peloponnesian War.

[46] The destruction rates discussed above do not include poleis forced by rivals into unequal alliances or other forms of subjection. Mackil 2004 discusses various social and political strategies developed by Greek poleis for reducing the human costs of natural catastrophe. Frequency of civil conflict: see details in appendix table A.1; further information: M. H. Hansen and Nielsen 2004, appendix 19; Lintott 1982; Gehrke 1985.

[47] Plato's Socrates notably dissents from this consensus; e.g., *Gorgias* 518e–19c (Socrates describes wealth, ships, and walls as "trash"). This is indicative of how self-consciously radical Plato's critical position really was. See further, Ober 1998: 209–10.

The corollary to a shared preference for the flourishing of the community in the face of a general recognition of the catastrophic alternative was a general *lack* of fixed ideological commitments of the sort that sustain a system of organized political parties. The absence of parties and party platforms meant that there were no party-supported candidates and nothing like party discipline in public votes on matters of policy. In comparison to the coalition politics and "cheap talk" characteristic of modern democratic legislative assemblies, Athenian public debates manifested an open texture in which debate mattered. Athenian citizens were free to attend to and to follow or ignore the advice of a diverse range of would-be leaders of the moment.[48] Athenian public speakers sought to demonstrate to audiences of politically experienced decision makers that they possessed relevant knowledge, and succeeded or failed in their policy goals at least in part on the basis of how well they made their case. In the absence of parties, public rhetoric was a meaningful part of deliberations on public policy (Ober 1989).

Because there were no organized political parties in Athens, voting for candidates seeking public office was a relatively small part of the overall political activity undertaken by the ordinary Athenian citizen. The common contemporary equation of "political participation" with "voting for candidates" makes no sense in an Athenian context. In terms of costly information, this situation might seem to make participation in Athens even less rational than participation in a modern democracy. The Athenian citizen could not employ a low-cost approach to answering the question, "Which choice is more likely to maximize my expected utility?" by reference to his predetermined loyalty to a party that he imagined as advocating policies likely to be especially favorable to himself.[49]

Suppose that an Athenian were convinced by the ideology and culture of the polis that he should frame the personal utility question partly in terms of the public interest. He should then ask himself, "Which choice is more likely to secure the security and prosperity of the state, such that my individual interests can safely and effectively be pursued?" In this case he would need to decide how each of his political choices affected the general welfare. Making fully informed choices of that sort seems, on the face of it, ridiculously costly. Given that a politically active Athenian citizen might make hundreds of them in the course of a given year, the level of irrationality might seem extraordinarily high. Nonetheless, I will

[48] Cheap talk: Austen-Smith 1990. Diversity of speakers in Athenian public assemblies: M. H. Hansen 1983, 1984; Taylor 2007; Rhodes, forthcoming. On how leaders of the moment might determine the direction of a group, see chapter 5.

[49] Costly information paradox: R. Hardin 2002. But cf. Popkin 1991, who argues that voters can be quite skilled at using social and cultural "cues" in making their decisions.

argue below that the design of Athenian institutions allowed the individual citizen to make choices that were, if not fully informed, nonetheless fundamentally rational. Moreover, those decisions were *right* often enough that the aggregate of individual decisions, over time, promoted state flourishing.

There was considerable public debate (and much private grumbling) about the political regime itself—some Athenians despised democracy on principle or doubted its ability to keep the state strong. Some among the wealthier minority feared (without justification, as it turned out) that the poorer majority would use the democratic government to radically redistribute private wealth. Given this endemic dissatisfaction, there was always the chance that the Athenian democracy could be replaced by a nondemocratic regime. Some of the energy of Athenian popular government was devoted to preventing the overthrow of the people as collective ruler.[50] But the day-to-day workings of democracy were not driven by electoral competition among parties or ideological competition among party lines. The driver was instead the imperative of deciding which knowledge and whose knowledge was most likely to ensure a common good (the survival and flourishing of the polis qua community) that was recognized by most as an essential prerequisite for the free pursuit of private interests by each individual.

In Athens religious, ethnic, regional, and tribal identities were not reified as divisive group-based political interests.[51] Questions about how to distribute public goods and burdens did periodically threaten to destabilize decision-making processes based on shared core preferences. But competition among leaders was primarily in terms of offering the community the best way forward to continued survival (i.e., security) and common flourishing (i.e., power and wealth). In this sense, Athens is in some ways unlike a secure great-power modern democracy in peacetime. On the other hand, Athens may be in some ways analogous to modern democracies faced by existence-threatening wars and to non-state organizations that confront the realistic possibility of being eliminated in the course of competition with more successful rivals.

HIERARCHY, DEMOCRACY, AND PRODUCTIVITY

Robert Michels' reasoning about the effects of scale and the need for organization in political contexts, along with his conclusion about the "iron law of oligarchy," were updated in an influential body of work on institu-

---

[50] See Ober 2005b, chapter 10; Teegarden, 2007.

[51] As, indeed, at least in the case of regional and tribal identities, they might have been; see, further, chapter 4.

tions and the costs of transactions by the economist Oliver E. Williamson. In an explicitly process-centered analysis, Williamson sought to analyze the relative productive capacity of organizations in light of their governance structures. He concluded that transaction costs (on which, see further, below this chapter and chapter 6) are best controlled by firms with hierarchical governance regimes, that is, with unambiguous and non-rotating leadership positions and clear lines of command and control. Williamson argued in his 1975 book that more participatory and democratic forms of governance fall victim to standard collective action problems: to decision-making inefficiencies and to opportunism—free-riding, malingering, and exploitation of access to valuable information. By contrast, he suggested that hierarchy, which emerged in response to market failure (see below, this chapter), also helped prevent organizational failure in several ways: by allowing for specialization of decision making and thereby economizing on communication expense; curbing the tendency to opportunistic self-seeking of individuals via command and control; coordinating response of subunits to unforeseen circumstances; resolving bargaining indeterminacies among subunits and individuals by fiat; closing information gaps between autonomous agents; and in general creating a less calculative exchange atmosphere.[52]

A decade later Williamson published a second book on organizations and transaction costs (Williamson 1985). Here Williamson's earlier model of relatively inefficient democratic governance structure, "the Peer Group relation," was revived and defined as follows:

> Peer Groups: [work stations are owned in common], but workers are paid on the average product of the group. . . . Workers may rotate among stations or specialize at one or a few stations. Moreover, so as to avoid the need for full group discussion whenever an adaptation has to be made and/or to assure better coordination among the members . . . Peer Groups may elect temporary "leaders," who make *operating—but not strategic—decisions* on behalf of the group. *It is important, however, that leadership rotate among group members if rigid hierarchical relations are to be avoided.* Ernest Mandel's (1968, p. 677) proposal for self-management "in which everybody will take a turn to carry out administrative work in which the differences between 'director' and 'directed' will be abolished" is in that spirit. The

[52] Control of transaction costs best by hierarchical firms: Williamson 1975, esp. chapter 3; 1985, esp. chapter 10. Democracies as victims of collective action problems: Williamson 1975: 41–56. Hierarchy prevents organizational failure: Williamson 1975, summary on 257–58. Granovetter 1985: 493–504 offers a sociological critique of Williamson 1975, arguing (499) that "Williamson vastly overestimates the efficacy of hierarchical power . . . within organizations." See also Kogut and Zander 1992, 1996; Grandori and Kogut 2002: 229–30; J. Roberts 2004: 106–15.

joining of a nonmarginal productivity sharing rule [i.e., all share in the profits that come from everyone's work, rather than each being compensated on the basis of his own work] with democratic decision-making is what characterizes Peer Group organization. (Williamson 1985, 217–18, italics added).

The scare quotes Williamson places around "leaders," the prohibition on temporary leaders making strategic decisions, the rotation of leadership roles, the abolition of the distinction between directors and directed in administration, and the specification that decision making is democratic all point to quite a strong form of participatory democracy. Indeed, although Williamson had in mind something like an industrial factory rather than a city-state, his Peer Group is a tolerably good description of classical Athens.

Strikingly, in Williamson's comparison of various forms of organization, "Peer Group" turns out to rank almost as highly in terms of overall efficiency as the explicitly hierarchical "Authority Relation." Out of eleven "simple efficiency properties," Peer Group receives a positive score in eight; Authority Relation scores positively in nine—Williamson's other four forms of ownership/governance structure all score much lower.[53] Authority Relation beats Peer Group at the properties of "appropriate station assignments" and "leadership." But Peer Group wins over Authority Relation in terms of its superior capacity for "local innovation."[54] The apparent contradiction of the earlier finding, in which peer-group democratic organization was described as hopelessly inefficient, is glossed by the new (and on the face of it, surprising) claim that Peer Group is actually a sort of hierarchy: Peer Group and Authority Relation both "rely extensively on decision-making hierarchy—which indeed goes far to explain the superior performance" of these two relative to other forms of ownership and governance structure (1985: 231). Paraphrasing Michels, Williamson concludes that it "is no accident that hierarchy is ubiquitous within all organizations of any size ... non-hierarchical

[53] Both receive positive marks for transportation expense, buffer inventories, interface leakage, contracting, equipment utilization, and system responsiveness. Both receive negative marks for work intensity. Williamson 1985, table 9–1 on p. 226.

[54] Local innovation is driven, in part, by individuals who have the incentive and opportunity to transfer specialized knowledge gained through work experience in one domain (i.e., one "station assignment"—in Athens this might be, for example, a year's service on the Council of Five Hundred) to another domain (e.g., a collegial board of ten magistrates, such as the Dispatchers—chapter 4). Processes that have become routine in one domain may be revolutionary when transferred to another. Some contemporary business firms make deep capital investments in programs designed to give employees substantial experience in multiple domains, with the explicit goal of fostering local innovation arising from cross-domain transfer of knowledge. See Hargadon and Fanelli 2002; Osterloh and Frey 2000.

modes are mainly of ephemeral duration" and this in turn raises "serious doubt that efforts to effect participation can be justified on profitability grounds" (1985: 270).

Williamson's work was undertaken in the spirit of Michels' Iron Law of Oligarchy; he notes that "efforts to weaken this Law notwithstanding, it has so far resisted repeal" (1985: 264). Intellectual context may also help to explain Williamson's conclusion that participation is unjustifiable—he was seeking to refute certain "Radical" economists who claimed that the sole purpose of organizations was the establishment of power relations (Williamson 1985: 206–12), and he was not concerned with the success potential of ancient (or modern) democratic states. But the high efficiency ranking he gives the quite Athens-like "Peer Group relation" suggests, *contrary* to his general conclusion, that a transaction-cost-centered analysis might explain why a participatory and democratic organization could succeed, even against more explicitly hierarchical rivals.

It is significant in Williamson's scheme that Peer Group wins over Authority Relation in the area of local innovations, which "involve process improvements at individual stations. Modes that promote local cost economizing process changes are preferred" (Williamson 1985: 225). If we imagine a competitive situation in which process innovation is an especially important differentiator, this factor might make up for whatever inefficiencies in regard to station assignments and leadership are properly associated with democracy. The situation becomes clearer when we drop Williamson's implied mid-twentieth-century model of the heavily capitalized industrial factory—with its fixed work stations and vertical information-communicating structure. Instead of industrial factories, we should, I believe, think of states (at least ancient Athens) in comparison with contemporary "knowledge-based organizations."[55] These are organizations (canonical examples include for-profit computer-building or Internet firms such as Hewlett-Packard or Google and military services such as the U.S. Army) in which the personal knowledge (or "human capital") possessed by the members of the organization is regarded as its most important asset, a networked organizational structure rewards those who

[55] Roberts 2004 argues that the structural changes in the firm as a form of organization since 1985 are as profound as the changes of the early twentieth century, when the multidivision corporation was pioneered by GM and other major firms. Yet Rothschild 1973, a business history focusing on the case of the American automobile industry, shows that the old industrial model was already becoming obsolete by the early 1970s. Williamson (1985: 11) cites Chandler 1962 as an example of a business history that ran well ahead of more formal economic analysis: "Chandler clearly established that organizational form had important business performance consequences, which neither economics nor organizational theory had done (nor, for the most part, even attempted) before." This precedent offers some justification for my extensive citation of business-history literature in this book.

accumulate social capital, and *learning* is acknowledged to be among its most important features in terms of promoting success.[56]

In many contemporary knowledge-based organizations much of the work is done by task-specific teams, and information is meant to flow horizontally (or better, omni-directionally), with little concern for hierarchical authority relations. A great deal of attention is placed on learning: both in terms of ongoing skills acquisition by individual members of the organization, and the growth of the aggregate knowledge base of the organization as a whole. The "knowledge-based, learning organization" model for Athens will be developed in more detail in subsequent chapters. Two points are important here. First, process innovation *is* highly valued by knowledge-based organizations, specifically because it offers a competitive advantage. And next, there is good reason to believe that hierarchy *does* impede the knowledge flows necessary to sustain innovation. A rigid hierarchy may be very good at promoting the learning of routines, but favoring learning-as-routinization at the expense of learning-as-innovation is harmful to the long-term productivity of organizations in highly competitive environments.[57]

Knowledge Processes as Public-Action Strategies

The background issues and interpretive framework for testing the democracy/knowledge hypothesis set out in chapter 1 are now in place. This section introduces the next three chapters and presents, in a preliminary way, their main conclusions.

Through the development of democratic institutions and cultural practices the Athenians devised effective strategies for addressing three major problems in the organization of knowledge, and thereby promoted the success of the state:

> 1. *Dispersed knowledge problem*: How to bring together the latent knowledge that is dispersed among diverse individual members

---

[56] P. B. Manville (1996) was the first to suggest that Athens should be understood on the model of the knowledge-based and learning organization. On contemporary knowledge-based and learning organizations, see the literature on organizational learning cited in note 35, above. Burt 1997: 359–61 reviews the recent shift from command and control hierarchical organization to network organization. King 1994 argues that human evolution, and the success of modern humans as a species, should be understood in part in terms of a dramatic growth (relative to monkeys and apes) in "social information transfer," that is, information acquisition (by apprentices), and especially information donation (intentional teaching by more experienced individuals). This hypothesis suggests that the linkage of organizational success with knowledge organization may be part of a bigger story.

[57] Levitt and March 1988. Baumol 1993 offers a powerful argument for the vital role of innovation.

of the community, such that individuals sharing a common preference can both learn and innovate and thereby arrive at the best possible answer on a given matter? *Strategy*: Networking and teaming. Athenian institutions fostered the growth of a dense and large-scale knowledge network by interconnecting small-scale social networks by both weak and strong ties. They arranged for much of the work of governance to be carried out by small teams of amateurs who learned basic routines and had easy access to expert knowledge.

2. *Unaligned actions problem*: How to enable individuals sharing a common preference for coordinating their actions to be reasonably secure in their knowledge of what others know, what others know that they know, and so on? *Strategy*: Common knowledge among citizens was built up via publicity and interpresence. The architectural design of public-meeting spaces fostered intervisibility among large numbers of participants; public monuments, notices, and ritual performances built common knowledge about matters of public concern.

3. *Transaction costs problem*: How can the expected costs to individuals of making potentially profitable transactions (contracts, bargains) be minimized such that profits from transacting (to individuals and to the community at large) are maximized? *Strategy*: Standardization of rules and exchange practices and wide dissemination of knowledge of them. Public and well-enforced standards, especially commercial law, but also a reliable coinage, built trust and ensured a relatively secure exchange environment.

These three problems and their solutions are addressed individually in the next three chapters. Yet they are closely related, in that the solution to each of the three problems involves integrating social with technical knowledge. Moreover, each of the three problems is an aspect of the general public action dilemma: How can the useful knowledge and capacity for judgment possessed by *individuals* be brought together in the service of a *collective* good (group flourishing) rightly regarded as necessary to the flourishing of each individual—and how, in the language of game theory, can this result be stabilized as an equilibrium, such that each individual participant has no more advantageous move to make in the game? Because the problems of dispersed knowledge, unaligned actions, and transaction costs are interrelated, it will be helpful to consider them together, in a preliminary way, before embarking on the more detailed analysis of each process in chapters 4–6. Table 3.1 sums up the ensuing discussion, which reconsiders the three knowledge organization problems under the headings of the processes by which they were addressed in Athens.

TABLE 3.1
Epistemic processes as strategies for addressing public-action problems

Process	Problem	Strategy	Institutions
Aggregation. "If Athens only knew what Athenians know." Chapter 4.	Information dispersed across the organization is hard to get to the right place at the right time.	Networking face-to-face communities via weak and strong links for knowledge sharing. Teaming for on-job learning and morale.	Council of 500 = 10 tribal teams of 50. Magisterial boards of 10. Rotation. Standard practices across institutions.
Alignment. "I'll only attend the meeting if I know you will too." Chapter 5.	Preference-sharing individuals unable to coordinate actions to achieve desired goals.	Common knowledge, credible commitments built via widespread participation in public practices, publicity, interpresence.	Architecture featuring intervisibility. Highly public clear-message monuments. Public rituals: parades, feasts, dances. Oaths.
Codification. "Let's make a deal—but only if it doesn't cost too much." Chapter 6.	High transaction costs reduce the number and value of bargains, depressing productivity.	Transaction costs are lowered by reducing information inequalities and power inequality arising from privileged access to public institutions.	Well-publicized law code emphasizing procedural fairness; trustworthy coinage, standard weights, measures. Opening access to legal redress.

AGGREGATION

Knowledge aggregation is the most mysterious of the three processes, and so merits a somewhat longer introduction. If the problem of collecting dispersed knowledge is pressing for all large organizations, it is especially so in democracies. The problem is particularly difficult to solve if it is expressed in terms of aggregating diverse preexisting individual preferences by voting procedures. But if we assume that some core preferences are held in common, that most group members come to decision-making processes without party loyalties or predetermined policy assumptions, and that the question is therefore how to aggregate available knowledge so as to get the right (or best possible) answer, the problem may be soluble.[58]

One means by which the aggregation of what is known among a large body of non-experts may lead to valid judgment was presented by the

---

[58] See esp. Arrow 1963 [1951], for the "impossibility theorem": given the potential for voting cycles, there is no acceptable way to stably aggregate individual preferences by voting; cited by Hardin 2002: 212 to show that well-informed participatory democracy is impossible; cf. Elster 1989: 90–91. Christian List (2005, with literature cited) and his collaborators have adapted Arrow's result to the aggregation of group judgments. They show that judgment aggregation, like preference aggregation, is subject to cycling, but also

Marquis de Condorcet in his famous "jury theorem" of 1785. Condorcet sought to demonstrate the conditions under which decisions made by a group of individuals with common preferences but diverse information would be better (more likely to be right) than decisions made by a dictator: he postulated voters in a formally egalitarian decision-making situation (each vote weighs the same), who sincerely attempt to decide rightly among two choices (e.g., guilty/not guilty in a jury trial). Each of Condorcet's voters is further assumed to be at least marginally more likely to be right than wrong in his choice. Condorcet's theorem demonstrates that, although each individual may be 49 percent likely to choose wrongly, the aggregated majority opinion is more than 51 percent likely to be right, and that likelihood grows, ultimately approaching mathematical certainty, as the size of the majority increases.[59]

In its original form, Condorcet's jury theorem is limited to binary judgments made by voters who are marginally likely to be right in their choices. If we grant the premise of individual marginal likelihood of correctness, Condorcet's theorem applies to jury trials in criminal cases, where the decision is the binary question of guilty or not guilty and there is a presumption that jurors are sincerely trying to find the right answer to that question. Yet Condorcet's theorem is incapable of explaining the decision-making processes of the Athenian Assembly, where a very large body of persons, some of them expert in various domains relevant to the issue of the day, often decided among a variety of possible policy options after listening to a series of speeches. In the Athenian real-life situation, unlike Condorcet's thought experiment, the audience judged both the persons giving speeches and the content of their speech.

Condorcet's theorem can be generalized and modified so as to be more valuable for democracies (List and Goodin 2001) and experimental evidence points to various other ways in which the "wisdom of crowds" is manifest (Surowiecki 2004). Under some circumstances the simple expedient of averaging non-expert guesses about an objective fact (the classic case is guessing the dressed weight of a slaughtered ox) will outperform

---

demonstrate how collective judgments can be stabilized by relaxing formal conditions under which judgments are made.

[59] Or if the marginal likelihood of individual correctness increases. Mathematically, if v = individual likelihood of rightness, h = correct choices, k = incorrect choices, then if $v = 0.51$ and $(h - k) = 20$, the probability of correctness = 0.69; when $(h - k)$ rises to 200 then the probability of correctness rises to 0.9997. For the demonstration, see McLean and Hewitt 1994: 36–37, who also note that in 1785, when he published the jury theorem, Condorcet was not yet a democrat and doubted that most groups of ordinary persons were actually likely to meet the marginal likelihood of correctness criterion. For application of Condorcet's theorem to contemporary issues in political theory and practice, see, further, Young 1988; McLennan 1998; List and Goodin 2001.

most or all experts. Like Condorcet's original jury theorem, these findings are highly relevant to democratic governance. If a group is to make good policy it will need methods of judgment capable of getting facts about the world right. Yet, because it is concerned with an inherently uncertain future, policy making requires much more than accuracy in regard to objective facts about the world—it requires, for example, agenda setting to determine the relevant question, the range of culturally acceptable solutions, the relevant set of facts to be brought to bear, and how much weight ought to be given to each.

Aristotle, who knew a great deal about classical Greek decision-making processes, offers a sketch of a theory of knowledge aggregation that addresses complex decision making situations, and thus allows us to imagine how widely dispersed useful knowledge might be effectively aggregated by a large and diverse group of Athenian decision makers confronted with a variety of possible answers. Aristotle claims that under certain conditions judgments of large bodies of decision makers will be superior to those made by an expert individual or small group. Aristotle describes a process, sometimes called "summation," whereby diverse "knowledge/expertise sets" are taken into consideration by a large group:

> The many (*hoi polloi*), of whom none is individually an excellent (*spoudaios*) man, nevertheless can, when joined together, be better than those [the excellent few], not as individuals but all together [*hōs sumpantas*], just as potluck [*sumphorēta*] dinners can be better than those provided at one man's expense. For, there being many, each person possesses a constituent part [*morion*] of virtue and practical reason, and when they have come together, the multitude [*plēthos*] is like a single person, yet many-footed and many-handed and possessing many sense-capacities [*aisthēseis*], so it is likewise as regards to its multiplicity of character [*ta ēthē*] and its mind [*dianoia*]. This is why the many [*hoi polloi*] judge better in regard to musical works and those of the poets, for some judge a particular aspect [*ti morion*], while all of them judge the whole [*panta de pantes*]. (*Politics* 3.1281a40–b10. Trans. C. Lord, adapted).[60]

Aristotle offers two analogies to explain summation: first, the "potluck dinner," to which each brings a different dish, resulting in a superior

---

[60] Waldron 1995 underlines the importance of this passage and emphasizes its deliberative character. In a book in progress, Paula Gottlieb, argues persuasively that Aristotle is neither being ironic nor presenting someone else's argument here. She shows that the optimistic account of democratic decision making in this and related passages is compatible

dining experience for every contributor; next, the judgment of "musical and poetic" (certainly including dramatic) performances, an undertaking that requires aggregating a variety of sensibilities. In the case of tragedy, for example, it would require an appreciation of the six elements of plot, character, diction, thought, spectacle, and song (for the six elements, see Aristotle, *Poetics* 1450a6–10).[61] It is only when the decision-making group is of the right sort that the democratic summation process yields superior judgments. In order to be of the right sort, the group must be mindful of the common good (thus meeting the baseline Aristotelian criterion for acting justly) and sensitive to the locus of relevant expertise among its membership. That is to say, the group's members must be concerned with getting the best solution overall, and each of them must pay attention to the opinions/responses of those who are (in the dramatic example) musically adept in respect to the singing, to those adept at visual art in respect to the spectacular staging, and so on.

Aristotelian summation arrives at right answers in a way that is in some ways similar to but in other ways quite different from Condorcet's jury theorem. Like Condorcet, Aristotle begins with an assumption of a group of preference-sharing decision makers, each of whom believes that there is a best choice and sincerely seeks that best choice. Neither Aristotle nor Condorcet confronts the question of divergent interests or "legitimately factional" voting. Unlike Condorcet, Aristotle acknowledges the role played by intragroup diversity in respect to knowledge and thus to the group's judgment capacity. Moreover, unlike Condorcet, Aristotle can assume that most of the individuals would be likely to choose wrongly (were they to decide as individuals) and Aristotle's decision makers can choose among multiple options (e.g., among three competing tragic poets). Instead of directly aggregating the marginal likelihood of individual correct judgment on the issue itself, Aristotle assumed that each individual takes his lead from the response of those persons in the crowd who are known to be most capable of rightly judging a particular aspect of the issue. This, I believe, is the sense of "some judge a particular aspect while all of them judge the whole."

Aristotle's theory replaces Condorcet's assumption of marginal likelihood of correctness *on the matter being decided* with an assumption that

---

with the discussion of the unity of the virtues in *Nicomachean Ethics* and *Eudemian Ethics*, because "vices are a disunited lot whereas only the virtues cohere in a unified and coherent way." See Ober 1998: 319–24 for discussion and bibliography.

[61] On the summation argument, see Keyt 1991. The "summation" passage strongly recalls Aristotle's analysis of tragedy in the *Poetics*, with its discussion of how "parts" make up the whole, and of the essential roles in action and judgment played by *dianoia* and *ēthos*.

people have diverse forms of expertise and a relatively accurate knowledge of who is expert at what. The assumption of "marginal likelihood of correctness" is deferred: away from highly demanding technical knowledge about the substance of the matter to a less demanding form of social knowledge, a judgment about "who is expert at what." Most individual decision makers need not be accurate judges of, for example, the quality of the singing, so long as they pay attention to the reaction of someone in group who is an adequate judge of singing and who is both clear and trustworthy in signaling that expert judgment.[62]

The final vote in the summation process will be right under the following circumstances. The correct choice lies in the center of the distribution of judgments regarding weighting, and the majority represents this center. It is in the process of judging the relative weight to be given to various expert judgments by finding the center of the distribution that the value of large-group democratic voting is most clearly manifest. It explains why, in the "judging a musical contest" case, a small group of six experts (one specialist in each of the six Aristotelian elements of tragedy) would not do better: each expert would be unlikely to give the right weight to the other experts' domains in making the overall judgment; the song expert can be expected to overrate the role of singing and so on. As contemporary work on expertise has shown, expert competence is often limited to judgments made within a given domain, and experts are not necessarily good public decision makers even within their own domains. Neither a single expert nor a small but diverse group of experts is likely to come to the right decision on a complex matter like judging a drama.[63]

What is needed is a body of decision makers capable of recognizing (through social knowledge) who really is expert, and capable of deciding (by voting) how much weight to give various domains of expertise in "all things considered" judgments. Exactly how that two-stage process works in actual practice is not easy to specify, but the experience of it is common. Imagine you are in the audience of a dramatic performance. Suppose that

---

Athenian audiences as judges of drama: Csapo and Slater 1994; Wallace 1997; Marshall and van Willigenburg 2005.

[62] This approach systematically violates the independence of individual judgment criterion, which grounds Condorcet's jury theorem and contemporary approaches to judgment aggregation. List and Pettit 2004 note that violation of independence could lead to free-riding on others' judgments, with negative results for achieving right choices. Once again, however, the actual result will depend on institutional design and the political expertise of the group in question. See, further, chapter 5.

[63] Ericsson 1999: 298 makes the point that "the superior performance of experts is often very domain-specific, and transfer outside their narrow area of expertise is surprisingly limited." We will consider the conditions necessary for small groups of experts to act as "true teams" capable of highly effective decision making across domains in chapter 4.

the audience is made up of fairly experienced theatergoers, includes some acknowledged experts in various technical aspects of drama, and that the applause of the crowd constitutes its collective judgment. The group does the work of gauging expert response and weighing the various elements of its "all things considered" judgment without much conscious thought on the part of each of its members. The decision does not require formal discussion: the clapping is sustained or brief, focused on a particular actor or aimed at the whole group, depending on the group's judgment. You may disagree with that judgment, but the chances are that the audience as a whole knows better than you do because it is drawing on a more diverse internal body of expertise and is more capable of weighing the value of various elements.

In Aristotle's scenario, the process of aggregation works because the group in question is diverse in the right way and not diverse in any wrong way. If the group were diverse in the wrong way, the summation process will not get off the ground. If each member of the group has a pre-conceived notion of the outcome it desires and is proprietary in regard to what it knows, then the group's members will not pay appropriate attention to the various experts in their midst. In order to judge well, the membership must have a certain level of political ability: each member of the group must possess a minimum level of (to use Aristotle's conceptual vocabulary) civic virtue and practical reason. But the levels need not be extraordinarily high—in this context civic virtue is a matter of choosing cooperation, and practical reason means doing so for rational reasons.[64]

As well as avoiding the wrong sort of diversity, the group must be diverse in the right way—it must include a diversity of distinctly different expertise-sets.[65] If the group were perfectly homogeneous, each of its members would have precisely the same knowledge as every other member, and so the decision could be made just as well, and more efficiently, by any one of its members. Likewise, there would be no qualitative culinary benefit in a common feast to which each diner brought the same dish. The process of summation adds value to large-group judgments only

---

[64] See, further, Ober 2007b.

[65] Cf. [Aristotle] *Eudemian Ethics* 1216b31: "Everyone has something of his own (*oikeion*) to contribute to the truth." This leads to a question that cannot be adequately answered here: What is the origin of diversity in knowledge sets and expertise sets? Suffice it to note that if a community were to take each human infant as a tabula rasa, and submit him or her to a perfectly standardized upbringing and education, such diversity would not emerge; the Spartan attempt to create a community of "similars" was based on this sort of ideological indoctrination as social engineering. The sort of desirable democratic diversity pointed to here assumes that the community's members have different abilities and different life experiences.

when people bring things "to the table" that are both different and valuable. Although decision making in high-stakes political forums may seem a long way from judging musical contests and enjoying potluck dinners, the Athenians put something quite like the summation process to work in everyday political practice.

The process of alignment is connected to aggregation, in that it is concerned with how individuals with shared preferences can achieve their purposes in group situations. But rather than being about getting the right answer to a given question, it concerns the problem of how a mass of individuals, with a common interest in coordinating their actions, can do so effectively. Simple coordination problems can be solved non-cognitively by reference to a basic preference algorithm (as in the movements of a school of fish), or by a rational agreement to abide by certain basic rules that are in everybody's interest (in America, we all drive on the right side of the road). These simple mechanisms can result in highly coordinated movement at great scale, but do not, in and of themselves, explain coordinated political activity.

More complicated coordination problems can be solved by reference to "common knowledge." Suppose, to take a familiar example, that I want to attend a political rally because my purpose is to overthrow a dictator. And suppose that many other people also want to attend the same rally for the same purpose. But none of us will actually attend (fearing arrest or the consequences of failure) if we do not know that many others also plan to attend. If I know that others will go, and each of them knows the same thing about me and about the others, and we each know that the others know *that* we know (and so on), then we share *common knowledge* regarding our shared preferences and intentions. As a result we all attend and so have the chance to achieve our individual and shared purposes. Common knowledge makes coordination into a straightforward matter of rational agreement—a "right-side driving rule." Yet *lacking* that common knowledge, we will all stay home—despite our shared desire to attend the rally—and the dictator will remain in power.

The key to solving complex coordination dilemmas like the "rally problem" is publicity, but it must be publicity of a certain kind. In order to attract others to the political rally, I might put up a poster urging people to attend and hope others will see the poster and act according to its message. But publicity of this sort will solve the problem only under special conditions: I must know that (enough) others have in fact seen the poster, and each of them must know that others have seen it, and we must all know that others know that we have seen it, and so on. So the space in which my poster appears must be very public, and the poster must be very noticeable and its message clear. This sort of publicity consideration is one reason that tyrannical regimes seek to stop dissidents from publicly posting messages. It is also the reason that advertisers whose products depend upon solving coordination problems (say a new Internet service that no one will use unless many people use it) will pay a premium for television advertisements during mega-events like the American Super Bowl. The goal is not just reaching a large audience, but reaching a lot of people, each of whom knows that a lot of other people are receiving the same message at the same time, and each of whom knows that others know the same thing. The premium is based not just on the value of many individual people seeing the advertisement (it is cheaper per viewer to run more ads in less prominent venues), but on the value of creating common knowledge among that large audience (Chwe 2001, 49–60).

Common knowledge arising from publicity has a major role to play in public action. Timur Kuran (1991 and 1995) has demonstrated how alignment cascades helped to precipitate the sudden and unexpected collapse of autocratic regimes in Eastern Europe in the late 1980s. But common knowledge can also sustain regimes. Michael Chwe (2001) argues persuasively that many cultural rituals (e.g., royal parades, religious gatherings) are important not only in conveying a particular meaning to each viewer, but also in the creation of common knowledge. He points out the importance of intervisibility in common-knowledge producing rituals— when I attend a particular cultural event and see the other members of the audience who are attending the event, and when I can observe their response to the event itself, common knowledge is built up both quickly and deeply—a great deal of complex and valuable common knowledge can be generated in this sort of intervisible situation. Chwe plausibly associates certain architectural forms (especially round seating areas) with an implicit social recognition of the value of intervisibility in building common knowledge. Highly public and visible announcements of various sorts, and architectural forms featuring intervisibility, are strongly associated with Athenian democracy.

CODIFICATION

Why should complex organizations exist in the first place? Neoclassical economics, with its focus on "cost-free" transactions (exchanges, based on bargain or contract), predicated entirely on price (value as determined by supply and demand) in an open market, offers no answer to this question. In a pathbreaking article R. H. Coase (1988 [1937]) pointed out that cost-free transactions are as imaginary as frictionless machines. In addressing the general problem of market failure, Coase showed that it always costs something, in terms of time and effort, to engage in a bargain or to make a contract. Under some circumstances, for example in the case of complex exchanges of labor and goods, the costs of creating individual contracts become unacceptably high due to information asymmetries. Costs can efficiently be lowered by bringing the transactions out of the open market, into a codified, rule-bounded system characterized by authoritative non-market mechanisms. Hence, Coase argued, the emergence of the firm.[66] Coase's insight was generalized as transaction-cost economics by Williamson (1975, 1981, 1985). Douglass North (1981, 1990, 2005) subsequently applied transaction-cost analysis to explain the emergence and development of states. States, along with some international institutions (Keohane 1984), can be understood as large-scale complex organizations that emerge and persist because of the need to address market failure and to keep transaction costs reasonably low by internalizing them.

As in the case of aggregation and alignment, explaining the emergence of states and their codified practices as a response to high transaction costs involves thinking about knowledge and public action. Knowledge is a central issue in transaction cost analysis: organizations lower transaction costs by regulations that lower the cost to individuals of gaining information, and that lessen costly knowledge asymmetries among contracting parties. This is accomplished through imposing rules, including general codes of conduct, standards of value and measurement, and fair mechanisms for dispute resolution.[67] In Athens cost-reducing rules included a uniform code of law and rules governing exchange media.

Rules are structural features that influence how people make choices, but as in aggregation and alignment, agency is exercised in response to a codified rule at an individual level. The lower-cost equilibrium should not be imagined as being achieved in a simple top-down manner—as might be suggested by the Greek philosophical metaphor of the political community as a human being consisting of a "mind" (elite rulers) giving rational direction to "limbs" or "bellies" (ordinary persons). Rather, the self-reinforcing equilibrium position is achieved via a great number of individual decisions made by more or less rational individual persons. In Athens, as in other societies (Greif 2006), individual rationality was bounded by cultural and ethical norms, rules, and protocols. Athenian (male) citizens were notable beneficiaries of the democracy's legal regime.

---

[66] Coase 1988, chapter 2; see esp. 43: "by forming an organization and allowing some authority . . . to direct the resources, certain marketing costs are saved." For a thoughtful update of Coase's argument, see J. Roberts 2004: esp. 74–117.

[67] See Barnard 1938 for an early expression and the helpful discussion of these issues, with Keohane 1984: 82–109.

But the law increasingly took into account the commercial interests of foreign visitors to Athens (whether long or short term). Athenian women and even slaves remained choice-making agents (even though their range of choice was fundamentally unsatisfactory) and were covered by certain legal immunities.[68]

Over the course of its democratic history, Athens deviated from the ordinary premodern and relatively unproductive conditions of the rent-seeking "natural state" in favor of the more productive conditions typical of a modern open-access order (North, Wallis, and Weingast, in progress). The next three chapters seek to explain why and how this happened, by looking at how Athenian institutions and political culture encouraged the growth of productive epistemic processes.

[68] Rules and agency: see chapter 1. Immunities of non-citizens: Ober 2005b, chapter 5, and below, chapter 6.

Chapter 4

AGGREGATION: NETWORKS, TEAMS, AND EXPERTS

AGGREGATING DISPERSED knowledge posed a steep epistemic challenge for Athens. How could a large community of active citizens arrange to have relevant information consistently brought forward to the right place, at the right time, and have it recognized *as* right by those empowered to make decisions? How, in brief, can "Athens know what the Athenians know"? Knowledge aggregation requires complex joint action and is complicated by political scale and social diversity. The relevant information, along with the social and technical knowledge necessary for processing it, is lodged in the minds of many individuals from different walks of life. Collecting knowledge in a participatory democracy demands communication among people who are often, at least in the first instance, strangers to one another. Communication among strangers requires overcoming a basic public action problem: Why should a rational individual freely communicate potentially valuable information to a someone who might be a free-rider?

INSTITUTIONAL DESIGN: INCENTIVES, LOW COST, SORTING

If the problem of knowledge aggregation is to be solved, individuals possessing potentially useful information must have some reason for sharing it. Moreover, they must have access to appropriate communications media—a low-cost means for bringing forward what they know and making it available to the community. The community, for its part, must have a sorting method, a means of discriminating between information that is more and less useful in any given decision-making context.

Because knowledge has exchange value it can profitably be hoarded under conditions of scarcity. Unique information and technical expertise may, for example, take the form of proprietary trade secrets that are valuable only so long as those in the know are few (e.g., the secret formula for Coca-Cola). In other cases, for example open source computer software, information gains in value when it is widely known and used. In either case, if a productive epistemic equilibrium is to be achieved, incentives for communicating useful information must somehow correspond to the value of what is shared. Examples of attempts to arrive at an epistemic equilibrium through material incentives include police detectives contracting with paid informants or a corporate CEO hiring a management consulting firm. In each case, the buyer willingly pays for specialized knowledge that he believes will help his organization to fulfill its purposes.[1]

Incentives need not be material. An implied contract between the knowing agent and those who desire access to her knowledge may be built into the common culture. Information sharing may be promoted by established relationships of reciprocity in an "economy of esteem" (Brennan and Pettit 2004). In a competitive culture, like that of ancient Greece, in which the publicly expressed esteem of others was an important part of individual utility, some incentives for knowledge communication could be cast in the form of public honors for winning victories in state-sponsored "knowledge aggregation contests"—that is, tournaments that could be won only by those willing to share what they know and capable of persuading others to do likewise. We will consider examples of such contests later in the chapter. The general point is that public incentives for knowledge sharing must be valuable because knowledge is recognized as having value to individuals and groups, as well as to the community as a whole. The first principle of institutional design for an organization attempting to solve epistemic public-action problems should be providing incentives to knowledgeable individuals so that they will choose to share what they know.[2]

Next, the communication media—the means available to agents for communicating useful knowledge—should be as nearly costless as possible (i.e., easy to use and readily at hand) because the greater the costs associated with the act of communicating, the higher the incentives must be for doing so. The imperative for reducing communication costs in order to facilitate knowledge transfer explains why, for example, law enforcement agencies set up toll-free and anonymous "hot lines" soliciting information about criminal activities that are likely to be observed by bystanders (e.g., drug dealing or poaching game). If potential informants knew they would have to pay for the call and risked being called to testify in court, they would be less likely to report crimes. Reducing the cost of

---

[1] Trade secrets: Davenport and Prusak 1998: 16–17. Incentives as essential for effective knowledge sharing: Sunstein 2006: 69–70, 201, 203–5.

[2] On the vocabulary of "honor-loving" and Athenian public practices associated with it, see Whitehead 1983, 1993. Non-material incentives for knowledge sharing: Davenport and Prusak 1998: 22–51; internal "knowledge markets": Osterloh and Frey 2000. Walker 2004 discusses modern "word of mouth" marketing techniques, suggesting that for at least some people the experience of sharing some kinds of information (in this case about new products) with others is valued in itself, and that material incentives are relatively less important. Similarly, Dixon 2000: 6–7.

public communications means lowering the cost to individuals of communicating what they know by compensating them for the burdens they incur in moving information to the point in an organization where it will do some good.[3]

Finally, there must be an epistemic sorting device, a means for distinguishing not only truth from falsity, but what sorts of expertise and what information may (in any given context) actually prove useful. If those involved in decision making are incapable of weeding out false or irrelevant information and disregarding inappropriate expert knowledge, they will be unable to produce good policy. The sorting mechanisms must be context sensitive: some technical knowledge that is of great value to a national assembly deliberating on matters of foreign policy will be useless to a village assembly discussing lease arrangements for communally owned land. In the participatory Athenian context, social knowledge served as a sorting device. Experienced citizens learned habits of discrimination, of recognizing whom to attend to and whose opinion to trust in what context.

The conjoined imperatives of incentives, low communication costs, and sorting mean that designing an aggregation process is inherently difficult. The difficulty increases with the complexity of what must be decided, the volume and diversity of the information necessary for decision making, and the multiplication of kinds of expert knowledge that must be brought to bear. Knowledge collection becomes more complicated as organizations grow larger and more diverse. Yet the costs to an organization of *failing* to collect and attend to the right kind of information before making major policy choices can be extraordinarily high, as the Athenians were reminded, for example, in the course of the catastrophic Sicilian expedition (415–413 B.C.).[4]

One solution to the problem of collecting knowledge is routinization, capturing the organization's past experience by archiving data, establishing standard protocols, and socializing members into "the ways we do things around here." Routinization can make work processes more efficient, and thus more productive. Yet, deep socialization in established routines becomes counterproductive when circumstances change. Making effective use of archived data is difficult, and an overemphasis on routines can lead to process ossification and a decline of productive capacity. In

---

[3] Communications costs can be regarded as part of the general issue of transaction costs, which are treated in more detail in chapter 6.

[4] A well-known business history example is the failure of Xerox Corporation to recognize the commercial potential of the breakthrough graphical user interface (GUI) originally developed in the mid-1970s at its Palo Alto Research Center subsidiary. See D. Smith and Alexander 1988.

order for an organization to remain competitive under new conditions, it must be able to innovate: it must break with established routines and draw upon information sources outside the standard banks of data. Innovation depends on tapping latent knowledge held by people who have not been fully socialized into routine patterns of behavior. This in turn means that organizations in competitive and fast-changing environments must maintain a diversity of experience, expertise, and social knowledge among their membership.[5]

Leaders of modern organizations are well aware that access to knowledge is essential to success. They recognize that it is hard for a large organization to know, in an active way, even a sizable fraction of what its diverse members know in a latent sense. They recognize the difficulty an organization is likely to have in accessing even its own archived historical experience. This epistemic dilemma is summed up in a comment attributed (perhaps apocryphally: Sieloff 1999) to a former CEO of Hewlett-Packard: "If only HP knew what HP knows, we would be three times as profitable."

This chapter looks at the design of certain Athenian political institutions, arguing that Athenian democratic institutions and practices, when viewed in their social context, can be understood as a kind of machine for aggregating useful knowledge. Moreover, the "machine" reaped some of the benefits of routinization while maintaining a capacity for innovation. The machine of Athenian government was fueled by a variety of incentives, oiled by lowering communication costs and developing efficient means of information transfer, and regulated by formal and informal sanctions. The machine served to build, over time, a special kind of social knowledge, a heightened capacity for discrimination in respect to sources of information among a large segment of the Athenian population. That heightened capacity may be understood as a sort of political expertise, an expertise in the operations of self-government. The chapter argues that Athenian performance benefited as more citizens gained that kind of expertise.

The machine was refined and recalibrated over time. Some of its original parts, designed and put in place in the post-revolutionary era of the late sixth and early fifth centuries, proved remarkably durable. Other parts were added, dropped, or modified over time, as successful and failed experiments led the Athenians to retool their approach to the collection of knowledge. Refinements included new incentives for knowledge sharers, sanctions for hoarders, and enhanced access to low-cost means

---

[5] Difficulty of making effective use of archived data: Brown and Duguid 1991, 2000. Routinization versus innovation in organization theory: Levitt and March 1988; for further discussion and bibliography, see chapter 3.

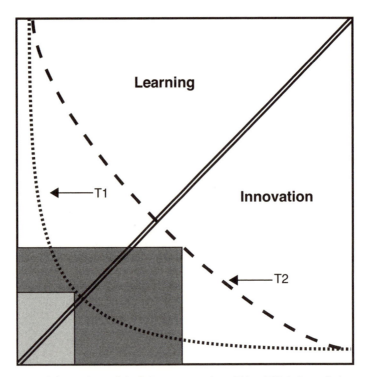

Figure 4.1. Schematic model of change over time (T1 to T2) in knowledge-aggregation capacity (gray boxes) in an organization characterized by both learning and innovation.

of communication. Over time, with the ongoing refinement of governmental institutions and the diffusion of political expertise, the learning/innovation horizon was pushed outward, and so the Athenians were able to capture more useful knowledge. This development is illustrated schematically in figure 4.1.

In the figure, the double-line perpendicular divides the domains of learning (upper left) and innovation (lower right). The curved lines (dotted—first state "Time 1"; and dashed—second stage "Time 2") represent earlier and later horizons of knowledge-aggregation capacity. The distance between the two curved lines thus represents growth over time in an organization's potential capacity to gain from institutionalized processes of learning and innovation. The boxes (light and dark grey) represent the value to the organization of innovation (below the double line) and learning (above the double line). The smaller, light-gray box is the value of aggregated knowledge at the earlier stage, when the aggregate was less and drawn more from learning. The larger, dark-gray box represents the increased value of aggregated knowledge at the later stage, after the learning/innovation horizon has been pushed outward, and as the organization develops institutions that encourage innovation. The main question we seek to answer in this chapter is *how* the epistemic horizon was broadened over time. The answer will be that the horizon expanded as institutional innovations allowed knowledge to be collected more efficiently as more individual citizens gained greater expertise in polis self-governance.

This chapter pays close attention to two features of Athenian decision-making institutions: social/knowledge networks and task-specific work teams. Networks and teams are important to the functioning of many modern organizations, and are much studied by organizational theorists and practitioners. Networks and teams operated in distinctive ways within the participatory democratic context. Networks and teams were, I will argue, highly relevant to the Athenian process of knowledge collection, and helped to instantiate the design principles of incentives, low costs, and sorting.

Through its day-to-day operations, the Athenian system sought to identify and make effective use of experts in many different knowledge domains. It also provided citizens with an ongoing—indeed, potentially life-long—practical education in the workings of the democratic machine, thereby conjoining the innovation-promoting and routinization aspects of organizational learning. The result was that individual Athenians became more politically capable—still amateurs in that they served occasionally and in rotation, yet possessing some of the decision-making characteristics associated with experts.

The system required that the diverse participants upon which it depended grasp the value of certain political practices, including transparency and accountability. These practices were common to many of the institutional operations of Athenian government. Yet the effective operation of democracy did not require each participant to be completely socialized into the routines of government or to understand all of the machine's complex workings. Indeed, it seems unlikely that any Athenian had the sort of general political mastery that Thucydides (2.65) attributed to Pericles, much less that of Plato's philosopher-kings. The single most noteworthy aspect of Athenian government may be its capacity to operate in the absence of system-level grand masters.[6]

Much of this and the next two chapters will be devoted to reverse engineering the machine of Athenian self-governance, pulling out pieces of the democratic system in order to analyze how particular institutions worked and how they fit together. But before we begin tearing it apart,

---

[6] See, further, Ober 1996, chapter 6; Ober 2006.

we should first take a close look at the machine in action. The unexpectedly strong performance of Athenian democracy is the phenomenon that this book seeks to explain; the better our grasp of how Athenian institutions worked in practice, the better grounded will be our explanations for overall organizational performance. Having a specific example of "knowledge in action" to refer back to will also help us to track the relationship of the various moving parts to the whole once we begin the task of reverse engineering the system.

ESTABLISHING A NAVAL STATION, 325/4 B.C.

In the Athenian (July–June) year 325/4 B.C., the citizen Assembly passed a decree authorizing a major military expedition to be deployed well to the west of mainland Greece. A historically minded Assemblyman might have recalled with dread the debate between Nicias and Alcibiades and the decrees that had authorized the ultimately disastrous military expedition to the same region ninety years earlier. Yet this new expedition aimed not at the military conquest of all Sicily, but at the more modest goal of establishing an Athenian naval station (*naustathmos*) in the form of a colony somewhere in the Adriatic. The colony was to be founded by Miltiades of the Athenian deme (township) Lakiadai, a homonymous descendant of the hero of the battle of Marathon in 490 B.C.[7] Sometime after the authorizing decree, a supplementary decree was passed by the Athenian citizen Assembly, detailing which warships were to be dispatched to the colony. A copy of this second decree survives on stone; it was recorded as part of an extensive list of naval equipment published (that is, inscribed on a publicly displayed marble stele) by a collegial board of magistrates: the curators (*epimelētai*) of the shipyards for that year. After listing the specific ships to be dispatched on the expedition, along with their current operational status, and the persons responsible for their reoutfitting, the Assembly's decree is reproduced on the stele, apparently in full.[8]

This "dispatching decree," as it is embedded in the context of the curators' equipment list, offers a snapshot of knowledge in action in the institutional framework of democracy in later fourth-century Athens.

---

[7] Ironically, after playing a key leadership role in the victory at Marathon, the earlier Miltiades persuaded the Athenians to support a secret plan to attack Paros, and was tried and fined for misleading the Assembly when the plan went wrong (Herodotus 6.133–36); his son, Cimon, was a leading figure in the buildup of the Athenian empire until his ardently pro-Spartan policy led to his disgrace and ostracism (Plutarch, *Life of Cimon*). On the archaic tone of the language of colony foundation employed here, see commentary to RO 100.

[8] The inscription: RO 100, lines 165–271, with valuable commentary. There is lacuna (due to damage to the stone) in the middle of the text. Cargill 1995: xxiv–xxv, 31–34, sets

The decree calls for a large number of officials and public bodies to work in concert to carry out a complex and potentially risky new venture, one that has both military and commercial implications. Unlike the Sicilian expedition of 415 B.C., which precipitated the crisis of the late fifth century (chapter 2, era VIII) and in which commercial considerations were tertiary, in 325/4 the concern with Athenian commerce was paramount. The dispatching decree was passed at a time when Alexander the Great had extended his conquests to India and Athenian foreign policy was constrained by the Macedonians. The Athenians had declined to aid Sparta in an attempted rebellion against Macedonian domination a few years before (331–330 B.C.). The decision to embark on a new overseas enterprise demonstrates Athenian determination to retain a measure of control over the polis' own destiny, even as the focus on the intended role of the naval station in protecting Athenian and non-Athenian traders underlines how Athenian priorities had changed over the course of a century.

The decree is preceded on the stele by a (now damaged) list of the ships, including two horse-transport vessels, that were to be dispatched to the naval station. It is introduced by a statement that it was in accordance with this decree that Miltiades took over (from the curators of the shipyards) the triremes and quadriremes and triaconters (three classes of warship) along with their equipment. The transcript below boldfaces the names of the fourteen public bodies and officials referred to in this document at their first mention, and renders the document in outline form for ease of reference.

> Cephisophon son of Lysiphon of [the deme] Cholargos made the proposal. For the good fortune of the Athenian **demos**, in order that what the demos has resolved concerning the colony to the Adriatic [in a previous decree] may be done as quickly as possible, be it decreed by the demos that:
>
> 1. The **curators of the shipyards** are to hand over the ships and the equipment [to the trierarchs] in accordance with the [authorizing] decree of the demos,
> 2. and that the **trierarchs** [ship commanders/equippers] who have been appointed are to bring the ships up to the dock [in Piraeus] in the month of Mounichion, before the 10th of the month, and are to provide them equipped for sailing.
> 3. The demos is to crown the first [trierarch] to bring his ship [to the dock] with a crown of 500 drachmas and the second with a crown of 300 drs and the third with a crown of 200 drs,

the Adriatic colony in the context of the relatively few other known Athenian fourth-century settlements outside of Attica.

a. and the **herald** of the **Council** [of 500] is to announce the crowns at the contest of the Thargelia [festival],

b. and the *apodektai* ["receivers" of public funds] are to allocate the money for the crowns,

c. [all of this is] in order that the competitive zeal [*philotimia*] of the trierarchs towards the demos may be evident [*phanera*].

4. In order that pleas for exemption [from trierarchic service] may be heard, the ***thesmothetai*** [judicial magistrates] are to man *dikastēria* [people's Courts] with 201 jurors for the **general elected to be in charge of the symmories** [boards of trierarchs] on the 2nd and 5th of the month Mounichion.

a. The **treasurers of Athena** are to provide the money for the courts in accordance with the law [*nomos*].

5. In order that

a. the demos may for all future time have its own commerce [*emporia oikeia*] and transport in grain [*sitopompia*],

b. and that the establishment of their own naval station [*naustathmos oikeios*] may result in a guard [*phulakē*] against the Tyrrhenians [i.e., Etruscan pirates],

c. and Miltiades the founder [of the naval station colony] and the settlers may be able to use their own fleet [*oikeion nautikon*],

d. and those Greeks and barbarians sailing the sea and themselves sailing into the Athenians' naval station will have their ships and all else secure, knowing that . . . [lines missing, due to damage to the stele] [.]

6. . . . but if anyone to whom each of these things has been commanded does not do them in accordance with this decree, whether he be a magistrate [*archōn*] or a private individual [*idiōtēs*], the man who does not do so is to be fined 10,000 drs, [the money to be] sacred to Athena, and the **euthunos** [magistrate in charge of accountability proceedings] and the ***paredroi*** [his assistants] are of necessity to condemn them or themselves owe the money.

7. The Council of 500 is to look after the dispatch [of the ships], punishing any lack of discipline among the trierarchs in accordance with the laws.

a. The ***prutaneis*** [a tribal subset of the Council] are to arrange for the Council to be in session continuously on the dock [in Piraeus] in connection with the dispatch, until the dispatch takes place.

b. The demos is to choose from the whole body of Athenians ten men as **Dispatchers** and those chosen are to look after the dispatch as the Council has ordered.

8. It is to be possible for the Council and the *prutaneis*, when they have looked after the dispatch [of the ships], to be crowned by the demos with a gold crown of 1,000 drs.

9. If there is anything lacking in this decree about the dispatch [of ships], the Council is to have authority to pass a decree, provided it does not annul any of the measures decreed by the demos.

10. All this is to be for the security of the homeland [*eis phulakēn tēs chōras*]. (Translation Rhodes and Osborne 2003, slightly modified.)

The document continues with an indication that the council used its delegated authority (in §9) to requisition an additional quadrireme for the expedition, and then goes on to enumerate the total number of warships and oars taken over by the curators of the shipyards in 325/4 (297 ships) and passed on to the next year's board (289 ships). The discrepancy between the number of ships taken over by the curators and those passed on seems (at least in part) to be accounted for by the ships dispatched to the naval station. This is in turn a good indication that the support fleet actually sailed, although we know nothing further about the fortunes of the new colony.[9]

The dispatching decree points to a number of ways in which useful knowledge was aggregated and put into action by the democratic state. Even without worrying too much about the specific duties of each of the official bodies mentioned in the document, it is immediately obvious that we are confronted with a complex governance system. The decree takes cognizance of the areas of legislative policy making, law and legal judgment, and executive responsibility for follow-through. The primary decision-making and authorizing body is the demos, the Athenian citizenry in the guise of the approximately eight thousand citizens who attended the relevant Assembly.[10] The decree was moved by Cephisophon of Cholargos. In accordance with standard Athenian practice, Cephisophon is recorded simply as an individual citizen who chose to speak out during the Assembly and made the successful motion. The Assembly's

---

[9] The curators of the shipyards took over three horse transports and passed on only one, to the next year's board. The list of ships dispatched includes two horse transports. The obvious inference is that the ships are not available to be passed on to the next year's curators because they were now posted at the new naval base (assuming they had not been lost en route, or in action).

[10] Numbers in attendance: the top end figure of eight thousand is indicated by the fact that this decree "in respect to homeland security" (see below, note 14) was certainly passed at a designated "principal" (*kuria*) meeting at which especially important matters were addressed and pay for Assembly attendance was increased by half: [Aristotle] *Ath. Pol.* 43.4, 62.2.

decree gives orders to a wide variety of government agents: in the first instance to the curators of the shipyards at Piraeus—a board of ten magistrates, one selected from each of the Athenian tribes. The Assembly's orders also concern some of the trierarchs—a certain number of the richest Athenian men who, acting as individuals or on boards (symmories) of two to ten men, were required each year to take on the expensive public service of putting a warship into sailable condition.

The curators of the shipyards and the trierarchs have primary responsibility for seeing to it that the right ships are provided to Miltiades and his settlers, in good sailing condition and in a timely manner. But the decree directly involves many other magistrates and public bodies as well, and it specifies a variety of incentives as well as sanctions for malfeasance. Incentives include rewards in the form of honorific crowns offered to individuals or groups who do their jobs well. Punishments are in the form of potentially crippling fines for those persons who fail in their duties. Among noteworthy incentives are the gold crowns offered as first (500 drachmas), second (300 dr), and third (200 dr) prizes to the three trierarchs who are quickest to get their ships to the dock and ready for dispatch (§3). The "race to the docks" set up by the incentive of winning notable honors is a prime example of an "aggregation/coordination contest." The winners will obviously be those trierarchs who can most quickly assemble the necessary team of experts for service on their ships: men capable of getting the ship properly rigged and outfitted, a full complement of expert rowers, an expert steersman, and so on. The conjunction of knowledgeable trierarch, well-equipped ship, and skilled crew would be the key to victory in the race to the docks. The employment of a race points to a concern with maintaining the complex matrix of specialized knowledge that had enabled the Athenian fleet to dominate the Aegean in the fifth century.[11]

The honors for the winning trierarchs are to be publicly proclaimed by the herald of the Council at a major festival (§3a). The proclamation was meant to reward honor-loving individuals who had done their duty with particular dispatch, but it had another public purpose as well: it was explicitly intended to publicize "the competitive zeal (*philotimia*) of the trierarchs in respect to the demos." The structure of competition and public

---

[11] The value of the crown is the honor rather than its monetary value to the recipient (it would likely be dedicated back to the state in the form of an offering to Athena; see Harris 1995). The monetary value specified in the inscription allows the extent of the honor to be precisely calibrated: first, second, and third places have an honor value of 5:3:2. A law-court speech by the prominent Athenian politician Apollodorus ([Demosthenes] 50), offers a vivid portrait of an ambitious trierarch's attempt to secure the best men and equipment available (50.7) and the prizes he won by doing so (50.13). Trierarchic system: Gabrielsen 1994.

reward thus cements and celebrates a reciprocal exchange relationship with deep psychological resonance for Athenians: the elite officials appointed by the state compete for the esteem of the mass of ordinary citizens who appointed them.[12] The public proclamation builds common social knowledge of who among the elite is especially worthy of esteem. Money for the three crowns (a total of 1000 drachmas) is to be dispensed by the relevant board of financial controllers (the *apodektai*). We later learn (§8) that the full Council and one of its ten constituent parts (the tribal teams: see below, this chapter) are themselves likely to receive a substantial collective honor (a crown of 1000 dr) if they are deemed by the demos to have acted well at the conclusion of the naval station support project. Aggregation contests were played and won by institutionalized groups as well as by individuals.

The demos next (§4) specifies that the *thesmothetai* (six of the nine annually appointed archons or "chief magistrates") are to call into session People's Courts (*dikastēria*), each staffed with 201 jurors, in order to allow the "general in charge of the symmories" (i.e., syndicates for financing trierarchic duties) to deal efficiently with legal challenges by those individuals upon whom the responsibility of a trierarchy has fallen. This general (one of the ten military leaders elected each year by the Assembly, and one among several of the generals to be assigned a specific sphere of responsibility) is thus provided with the legal apparatus he will require in order to complete his part in coordinating the assignment of trierarchs to ships.

Meanwhile, those individuals who had been assigned to undertake trierarchies, yet believed that their estates were being unfairly burdened relative to the estates of other wealthy Athenians, are assured the opportunity of timely legal appeal. The procedure for such an appeal (*antidosis*: "property exchange") took the form of a challenge. The man called upon to undertake a trierarchic liturgy challenged some other wealthy individual either to take over the liturgy or voluntarily to exchange properties. The ground for such a challenge was the claim that the second man's estate had been lightly burdened relative to the challenger's. If the recipient of the challenge refused both options (neither took on the liturgy nor agreed to exchange estates), a trial ensued and the jurors decided which man's estate was responsible for paying the liturgy.

This legal procedure, which has sometimes been regarded by modern scholars as simply bizarre, effectively leveraged the comparatively expert knowledge of members of the wealthy elite regarding one another's financial affairs and thereby eliminated the need for intrusive and probably

---

[12] See, further, Ober 1989 (mass-elite reciprocity at Athens); Brennan and Pettit 2004 (reciprocity in economies of esteem).

ineffectual investigations into individual finances by amateur magis-trates.[13] The funds for setting up these courts (mostly for the jurors' pay) is to be provided, in accordance with the established law (*nomos*), by yet another magisterial board with substantial financial responsibilities: the treasurers of Athena.

After a helpful digression (§5), explaining that the *reasons* for the naval station and its fleet were to guarantee Athenian commerce and en-sure the grain supply for the demos, by providing security for Greek and barbarian ships alike against Etruscan pirates (de Souza 1999: 33–42), the decree returns to specifying the role of official agents, moving from rewards to punishments (§6). Any individual, whether private citizen or public official, who shares some responsibility for the success of the dis-patch of the ships and who is discovered to have been derelict in his duty (in the case of an official, this would be at his formal scrutiny upon leaving office: his *euthuna*) is fined 10,000 drachmas. This is a substantial penalty that only the wealthiest Athenians could afford to pay; anyone who could not pay the fine would become a state debtor and lose some part of his civic rights. Again the relevant public officials (the euthunos and his assis-tants) are charged with doing the investigation and are themselves subject to fines if they fail to assess fines upon others guilty of dereliction of duty. These sanctions complement the incentives of crowns and honors and were clearly regarded as being equally important to the efficient working of the system.

The decree next (§7) circles back around to the issue of general over-sight for the project. This is assigned to the Council of 500, which is to meet in plenary session on the dock until the dispatch of ships has been completed: a tribal team of fifty councilors (see below, this chapter) is to arrange for this. But then, seeming to recognize that this extended period of direct oversight by five hundred officials who were simultaneously re-sponsible for a great deal of other government work is a cumbersome arrangement, the decree mandates (§7b) the creation of a new (presum-ably temporary) magistracy: ten Dispatchers, to be chosen from the entire citizenry, who are to see to it that the Council's orders are carried out. The legislative language of the decree concludes (§9) by authorizing the Council to pass supplementary decrees related to the dispatch of the expe-dition, carefully noting, however, that the Council lacks the authority to annul any decree of the Assembly. The decree ends (§10) by stating suc-

---

[13] The logic of *antidosis* procedure: Christ 1990; Gabrielsen 1994: 79; Kaiser 2007. Its role in discouraging class solidarity among the Athenian elite: Ober 1989: 242–43. On "in-visible" (i.e., liquid, non–real estate) goods and the ease with which they could be hidden from ordinary public scrutiny, see Gabrielsen 1986.

cinctly that the measures providing for the dispatch of the ships were passed in the interest of "homeland security."[14]

The dispatching decree gives a vivid sense of a system of public administration with a large number of moving parts, concerning, inter alia, inspection, supervision, transfer of funds, dispute resolution, possession, usufruct, reward, and punishment. The goal and motivation for establishing the new colony is quite different from archaic Greek colonization efforts, which typically sought to address population pressure by establishing completely independent new cities in areas featuring good agricultural land.[15] Here it was a matter of setting up a permanent military outpost as a colony staffed with permanent settlers and with adequate support in terms of well-equipped warships. The motivation (§5) is to neutralize a threat to vital overseas trade, and the goal is to guarantee Athenian commerce and strategically vital grain supplies from the relatively distant Adriatic. This undertaking is comparable in complexity to a miniature Sicilian Expedition, although given its much smaller scale it entailed lower risk to the polis as a whole. The importance of the project is evident in its engagement of each of the major branches of the Athenian governmental apparatus. It clearly called for the mobilization of considerable social knowledge—for example, about the incentive value of rewards and punishments, about ownership and rights to property (note the reiterated reference to that which is *oikeion*, "personally owned"), and about distinction and overlap between public and private realms.

Even more striking, however, is the need to bring to the complex project a diverse body of expert technical knowledge. The decision to found a naval station points to some kind of overarching cost-benefit analysis. Clearly a military outpost would be expensive in terms of money, manpower, and the attention of government officials. The danger represented by piracy to Athens' "own commerce" (*emporia oikeia*: §5a) and to essential grain shipments sent to Athens from the Adriatic region evidently justified the expense. Protecting Athenian interests demanded not just that Athenians be able to sail the seas without fear, but also a general sense of security on the part of all those engaged in overseas trade in the region, both Greeks and non-Greeks.

---

[14] The designation "for homeland security" (*eis phulakēn tēs chōras*) was in this period sometimes appended to decrees that have nothing obviously to do with the defense of Attica, although in this case the designation seems relevant insofar as Athenian security interests were directly affected by its capacity to sustain overseas trade. See further, Oliver 2007: 209–12.

[15] Cargill 1995 reviews the evidence for fourth-century overseas colonization, noting the great difference between this period and earlier eras.

What positive steps might accomplish this goal of ensuring the security of Adriatic trade? Answering that general policy question required bringing together expert knowledge of military, sociological, and diplomatic matters capable of answering a series of subsidiary questions: How big should the permanent colony be? What sorts of people should be enlisted as settlers, and what incentives might they be offered? Where should the colony be put, and what sorts of natural and human threats might it face? How independent would the colony be, and how would the Athenians be able to assure the long-term alignment of the interests of the colonists and those of the mother city? These issues, among others, must have been addressed in the deliberations leading to the original authorizing decree (a document which, sadly, we do not have).

Turning to the dispatching decree itself, we confront the need to aggregate military, financial, climatological, and legal knowledge. What should be the size and makeup of the supporting naval contingent? The answer was that it must be composed of several distinct classes of ships, including horse-transport vessels. Evidently military operations were anticipated that included the use of cavalry. The specialized knowledge of naval matters that went into the planning is indicated by the specification of particular ships for the expedition (in sections of the inscription not reproduced above). These ships are designated by ship name, by shipbuilder (as a standard feature) and in at least one case by age (lines 272–76). When should the expedition sail? This was an important detail in light of the relatively short annual window for safely rounding the Peloponnesus en route to the Adriatic. Answer: all ships must be ready to go by the 10th of Mounichion (§2: that is, about mid-June), which meant that all challenges to trierarchic duty must be settled on two court dates earlier in the month (§4). All of these preparations demanded prior knowledge of where the money would come from, who would be keeping track of each transaction, and how accountability would be maintained through the course of the project.

In sum, founding a naval colony—like many other important enterprises undertaken by the Athenians—required that many diverse sorts of knowledge be brought to the right place and at the right time. In hierarchical organizations, it is generally assumed that comparably important operations must be managed by a centralized executive authority, employing a control and command structure, capable of coordinating and monitoring the work of a large number of experts. Yet, of the many individuals and public bodies designated in the Athenian dispatching decree as having responsible roles, very few could be regarded as professionals or as experts in the ordinary sense of those terms. Much of the work is done and oversight is provided by the Council of 500, a body whose membership was annually chosen by lot. Most of the rest of the project was to be the responsibility of collegial boards of magistrates chosen for a year's service by lot, by popular election (in the case of the generals and the Dispatchers appointed under this decree), or according to a principle of fair rotation among a particular sociological segment of the population (the trierarchs).[16]

The demos that mandated the establishment of the colony and authorized the naval support consisted in practice of whichever Athenians chose to show up at the Assembly on the relevant day. Although magisterial boards were provided with quasi-professional "staff secretaries," the responsible officials were amateurs. There was very little in the way of executive-level command and control, and it is hard to define anything like a formal hierarchy in the operation of the various moving parts. This brings us back, of course, to the question of how the participatory Athenian system of self-governance actually worked.[17] From the perspective of a standard command-and-control organization, proliferation of responsible bodies, and the densely interwoven legislative, judicial, and executive functions, might be taken as evidence that the system was simply dysfunctional. The burden of this chapter is to demonstrate, to the contrary, that Athenian government can best be understood as a complex and effective machine designed (*ab initio* and through much subsequent experimentation) to identify and collect relevant social and technical knowledge.

The sections that follow assess some of the various "moving parts," beginning with the basic structural elements of the *deme* (a village, town, or urban neighborhood) and the *tribe* (a group of demes from different parts of Athenian territory). We then analyze the origins and workings of a particular institution, the Council of 500 (*boulē*). At the end of the chapter we will turn, more briefly, to the workings of the collegial boards of magistrates, and to the systematic relationship between Council, boards, and Assembly. Throughout, the focus will be on the choices made by the individual citizen—on how Athenian organizational design promoted choices that were in the interests of both individuals and the polis, and on how free-riding was monitored and sanctioned.

[16] Of course, many operations carried out by modern states are much larger scale and more complex than those contemplated by Athens and call on more specialized forms of knowledge. The point here is not that Athens was as complex as a modern state, but that the Athenian case puts some pressure on standard intuitions about the scale and complexity of operations that might successfully be managed and governed by non-experts.

[17] We do not actually know how well it did work in this case: this inscription is the sole evidence for the naval station in the Adriatic, and no archaeological traces have ever been identified. The point is not the success or failure of a given enterprise, but that the Athenian state flourished through carrying out many complex policies by a similar process.

Demes and Tribes as Social Networks

Consider a typical village (deme) of Athens, near the end of the sixth century B.C., just before the Athenian Revolution of 508 and the institution of the democratic political order (see chapter 2: era III).[18] Prasiai was a settlement on the south side of the bay of Porto Raphti, on the east coast of Attica. Prasiai was some 25 kilometers from the city of Athens as the crow flies, but perhaps twice that distance by the overland route skirting Mount Hymettos. It is likely that there was a town center of some sort, although it has not been excavated, and some of Prasiai's residents ("the Prasieis") probably lived in isolated farms scattered through the local area. Farming, supplemented with some fishing and mostly local trade, formed the economic base, although the village featured a local Apollo sanctuary and may have profited from historic ties to Delos. In addition to some slaves and perhaps a few resident aliens, the total free population of Prasieis was probably in the range of 700 persons. Of these, perhaps 180–200 were adult native males—citizens of Athens who had enjoyed limited privileges in regard to participation and certain legal immunities since the reforms of Solon in 594 B.C.[19]

---

[18] Osborne 1990 answers the question, "What is a deme and why does it matter?" in the context of an analytic history of the large and important deme of Rhamnous, on the northeast coast of Attica. Some other demes had extraordinary resources (Acharnai: population; Piraeus: major port; Eleusis: major sanctuary; Thorikos and Sounion: silver mines and industry) and are therefore exceptionally well documented in the literary, epigraphic, or archaeological records. Moreno 2008, chapter 2, analyzes the resources and population of the large deme Euonymon. I focus on relatively small and obscure Prasiai because it is closer to the "median deme" in size, resources, and fame. An ongoing debate concerns the extent to which demes were densely settled villages (Osborne 1985a) or scattered farmsteads (Jones 2004: 17–47).

[19] On Prasiai, see Vanderpool, McCredie, and Steinberg 1962; Whitehead 1986, index s.v.; Camp 2001: 281. *Population and typicality*: The main evidence is the quota (evidence of quotas is from the fourth century and later) of councilors later sent annually by each deme to the Council of 500. On these data and their interpretation (especially in reference to the question of the original Cleisthenic quotas), Traill 1975 and 1986 remain fundamental; Whitehead 1986 is a particularly helpful survey. Prasiai's quota of 3 is near the mean quota size (3.6, median 2) of all 139 Attic demes: 76 demes were smaller, 46 larger. Again, judging by quota size, about a third of Athenians lived in Prasiai-sized demes or smaller, about two-thirds in larger demes. Prasiai is among the 44 demes from which one or more inscriptions are known and among the 45 demes known to have had politically active residents. It is not among the 14 demes with known theaters or the 24 demes with known *demarchs* ("mayors"). In terms of fame, measured by index references in Whitehead's standard book (1986), Prasiai, with its 12 references, is very close to the mean of 11.8, but well above the median of 5. *Documents*: (1) IG II² 2497. Land lease of the Prasieis, after the mid-fourth century: name of demesman Kirrhias, son of Poseidippos, supplied by Vanderpool, McCredie, and Steinberg 1962: 56. (2) SEG 21.644 = Vanderpool, McCredie, and Steinberg 1962: 54–

After the democratic Revolution of 508, the adult male Athenian residents of Prasiai, as in the other villages and urban neighborhoods of Athens, would be regarded as full citizens with extensive participation rights in central institutions of the polis government. They would also have the opportunity to meet periodically in a local village assembly in order to vote on admitting new citizens and to decide on various matters of local concern. By the late sixth century, many of the families of the village had lived there for generations. A century and a half later, by the middle of the fourth century, a number of Prasieis will have moved away, to the city or elsewhere in Athenian territory. Yet by Athenian constitutional law they maintained membership in their ancestral deme, and we can assume that many of them would still have attended deme meetings.[20]

As a result of their long history of steady interaction—social, economic, and religious if not yet extensively political—the men of late-sixth-century Prasiai knew quite a lot about one another. By comparative reference to other small and relatively egalitarian pre-modern rural communities, we can assume that many of the ties between adult male citizens of Prasiai were *strong*, in the formal sense of the term as it is used by modern theorists of social networks. That is to say, the local social network by which the Prasieis were connected to one another would be based on regular face-to-face interaction and would feature a good deal of overlap and redundancy. Many of a man's friends and relations were also friends and relations of one another.

As a result of this *strong-tie* linked network of social relationships, the general level of mutual social knowledge in Prasiai was very high. People for the most part knew, for example, who was technically skilled in vari-

---

56, no. 138: fragmentary land lease of the Prasieis; second half of the fourth century. (3) Vanderpool, McCredie, and Steinberg 1962: 54, no. 137. Fragment of inscribed stele, with relief: someone crowned with a gold crown by the deme of [Prasiai?] dedicates it to Artemis. Late fourth century. *Prosopography*: (1) Kirrhias Poseidippou, above. *IG* II² 7286 is a grave monument of Kirrhias and (2) his father Poseidippos Kirrhiou (= Kirchner 1966 [1901] 12132): syntrierarch between 356 and 346/5 B.C.: *IG* II² 1622, line 711), and presumably their wives, found at Markopoulo/Prasiai. Davies 1971: 469 discusses the family, although Kroll 1972: 200, no. 100b, doubts Poseidippos' possession of a juror's *pinakion* (allotment plate). (3) Poseidippos' brother ". . . ros" was involved in the leasing of temple property on Delos in mid-fourth century. (4) Posyssthenes [*sic*]: *SEG* 21.644, a land lease. He is the lessee of land from his deme (assumed to be a demesman although this is not certain). His name is consistently erased from the document, which suggests that he defaulted on the agreement.

[20] Deme life and diachronic history of residence patterns in rural Attica: Osborne 1985a, 1987; Whitehead 1986; Jones 1999. In addition to the citizens and their families we can assume that there would be some slaves and perhaps some long-term foreign residents, although we cannot guess how many. Moreno 2008, chapter 2, argues for a higher level of village-city interaction in the sixth century, but evidence for this remains inferential.

ous domains, who could be counted upon and in what circumstances, whose advice was valuable on what topics. Social norms of reciprocity and propriety were clear and dictated who shared what sort of information and knowledge with which others and under what circumstances. Since network ties were strong both in the ordinary sense of the word (i.e., dependable), and in the network-theory sense that a person's friends were likely to be friends with one another, social norms were correspondingly strong. Commitments made in this context were credible because people knew a lot about one another's business, and, when necessary, sanctions might be levied on free-riders. The environment was a "safe" one in that cooperation was socially mandatory and defection was difficult.

Given this (very partial) description, it is easy enough to imagine Prasiai as the home village of an Athenian named Tellus; in a story recounted by Herodotus, Tellus was described by the traveling Athenian lawgiver and sage, Solon, as the "happiest man ever to live." Tellus' exemplary happiness is manifest in ties of kinship (his flourishing children and grandchildren), modest prosperity, and honors he received after being killed in battle against Athens' invading neighbors. As in the story of Tellus, the strong ties binding the Prasieis were based, in the first instance, on kinship and locality. Like Tellus, they shared a clear sense of which behaviors were valued and which censured. Happiness, in this context, is predicated on good luck and on acting in accord with one's own accurate inductive knowledge of a traditional and commonly held set of values and practices. Strong common values, based on the intimate knowledge of one another's abilities, character, and day-to-day behavior are typical of strong-tie networks and can help to explain the workings and some of the attractions of traditional face-to-face communities.[21]

Ideal-type Prasiai-like villages (and Tellus-like lives) are celebrated by some historians of ancient Greece and communitarian political theorists. Liberal theorists (e.g., Waldron 1992; Kateb 1992) respond that strong values are not necessarily good values; prejudice and intolerance toward outsiders may be among the attitudes promoted by highly cohesive local communities (Putnam 2000; 2007). But for our present purposes, weighing the relative moral value of individual freedom against social

---

[21] According to Herodotus' Solon, Tellus of Athens, "was from a prosperous city, and his children were good and noble. He saw children born to them all, and all of these survived. His life was prosperous by our standards, and his death was most glorious: when the Athenians were fighting their neighbors at Eleusis [an Athenian town], he came to help, routed the enemy, and died very finely. The Athenians buried him at public expense on the spot where he fell and gave him much honor" (1.30.4–5). The traditionalism of this portrait, and its implied contrast with the conditions of late-fifth century Athens are emphasized in Ober 2006 and in progress. Nevett 2005: 93–96 argues for close ties among residents of rural demes, based on a study of house architecture.

cohesion is not the main issue. The key thing, from the point of view of organizational performance, is that small-scale networks based primarily on strong ties are very good at distributing information internally, but they are poor conduits for importing or disseminating useful knowledge *outside the local network itself*. As a consequence, closed strong-tie networks tend to be relatively unproductive as elements of a larger social system. The problem is a lack of "bridging ties."

In a classic article, the sociologist Mark Granovetter (1973) demonstrated that small-scale networks based on strong ties among individuals promote intensive interaction but do not allow for extensive "bridging" from one network to another. In the limit case, in which each of my friends is also each other's friend, there is no space for bridging at all—every new tie I form must necessarily be a tie shared by all of my existing friends. Thus there is no feasible way of bridging to another network of persons— nor is there any possibility for bridging over to me from a network that is similarly strongly tied. Strong-tie networks tend to operate as small and closed cliques. Lacking bridges to other networks, these cliques are resistant to the free flow of information outside the local network. Cliques render large-scale cooperation more difficult and impede coordination across an extended social network. As a result, it is harder to aggregate knowledge or align action at larger scales. The gains potentially reaped from extensive cooperation remain limited—and the problem of scale looms as unsolvable.[22]

If we imagine late-sixth-century Prasiai as characterized primarily by strong ties (either as a single strong-tie network or as a collection of such networks), the residents of Prasiai would have had relatively few bridging ties outside their local community, few connections with other towns or neighborhoods in Attica. Of course, the hypothetical limit case in which *all* a person's friends were one another's friends is unlikely ever to have existed in practice. But to the extent that strong-tie networks were a general social norm in the many villages scattered across Athenian territory, overall Athenian capacity for effective joint action was likewise limited. Relatively low Athenian state capacity in the areas of military, building,

[22] Granovetter 1973. See further, Granovetter 1983, 1985; Krackhardt 1992; Gargulio and Benassi 2000; Diani and McAdam 2003. Padgett and Ansell 1993 and Gould 1995 are notable examples of how social network theory can be used to explain an actual historical situation (the rise of the Medici in fifteenth-century Florence and social movements in Paris in the later nineteenth century). M. T. Hansen 2002 explores knowledge networks in multiunit firms, an organizational situation with striking analogies to Athens and its constituent demes. Chang and Harrington 2005 emphasize the need for persistent diversity within networks and quality of ties for effective network performance based on both innovation and learning. My thanks to Paul Edwards for sharing unpublished work on the "weakness of strong ties," which focuses on the tendency of cronyism to lead to mediocre performance.

and domestic policy in the pre-democratic period (chapter 2: eras I and II) is consistent with the hypothesis that sixth-century Prasiai (and other Athenian villages and neighborhoods) were characterized by strong-tie networks.[23]

It seems very likely that, with a degree of local variation, this hypothetical "Prasiai situation" was replicated many times over in the predemocratic era, and throughout much of the territory of Athens. Some Athenian villages were smaller than Prasiai; others were considerably larger. Some Athenians living on isolated farms might have had very small and cliquish networks approaching the perfectly closed limit case; others in urban neighborhoods and villages near the city might have had more extensive networks with more bridging ties. It certainly cannot be true that all sixth-century Athenians were living out their lives entirely within local strong-tie networks; we know, for example, that some Athenians were involved in regional and overseas trade. But overall, it seems safe to say that something like the Prasiai model sketched out above was the seventh- and sixth-century Athenian norm—just as it was the norm throughout most of Greece. That "world of Tellus" social norm was the central problem faced by Cleisthenes in the months after the Athenian Revolution of 508 B.C.

At the moment of the revolution, the people of Athens demonstrated a capacity for at least short-term collective action at a moment of extreme national danger: Confronted by the double specter of foreign domination and a return to the pre-tyrannical oligarchic rule of a handful of "big men," many of the ordinary people of Athens gathered in the city and forced the surrender of a Spartan-led army after a three day siege of the Acropolis. They recalled Cleisthenes, who had been exiled by the would-be oligarchic rulers of the city after having "taken the people as his comrades" and proposing popular institutional changes. Back in Athens, with expectations running high, Cleisthenes took on the task of rapidly creating a new government.[24] Whatever else it accomplished, Cleisthenes' new order had to be able to put a large and highly motivated military force into the field—and had to do so very quickly. This was no mean feat, given that in all probability Athens had never had an organized "national army." Earlier Athenian military actions, such as the battle in

---

[23] Purcell 1990 rightly warns against overstating the insularity of archaic Greek villages. It is surely the case that *some* Prasieis will have had extra-Prasiai bridging ties, perhaps through the fictive kinship of the old Ionian tribe system, through cult, or through marriage ties perhaps, especially in nearby villages. The point is that, in comparison with later Athenian history, Prasiai of the late sixth century is likely to be relatively lacking in bridging ties.

[24] Athenian revolution: Ober 1996, chapter 5; 1998; Forsdyke 2005; Pritchard 2005. Kleisthenes: Raaflaub, Ober, and Wallace 2007.

which Tellus heroically died, had depended on ad hoc cooperation among the relevant local big men, but after the revolution, their authority was thrown into doubt.[25]

Cleisthenes' comrade-constituents, the demos that had recalled him from exile, expected a system of government suited to their newly expressed identity as participating members of a political community. Oligarchy and tyranny, the familiar modes of archaic Greek political organization, had been discredited by the events leading up to the uprising. Although other Greek poleis experienced political upheavals in the sixth century and there was much experimentation with institutional forms (Robinson 1997), there was no "off the shelf" organizational model for Cleisthenes to follow. The "Prasiai situation," the cliquish strong-tie local networks that characterized ordinary Athenian social life, rendered it difficult to achieve the large-scale joint action necessary to defeat the expected Spartan attack—and then to sustain a flourishing community so that Athens's great potential (relative to its rivals) in terms of human and natural resources would be realized in fact.

If "Prasiai" was the problem, the revolutionary uprising itself pointed to the solution. Cleisthenes had been recalled to Athens after the demos had demonstrated its potential for large-scale joint action in the three-day siege of the Acropolis. Athenians clearly now thought of themselves as sharing an Athenian identity, which could potentially come to mean belonging to an extended network that included the entire polis. The design opportunity for Cleisthenes was building on a capacity revealed in a moment of crisis and based on a shared Athenian identity. The challenge was creating institutional conditions for a productive equilibrium that would enable the Athenians to reap the individual and collective benefits of social cooperation. Although Cleisthenes lacked the theoretical apparatus of modern social science, the solution he devised makes sense when it is described in terms of social network theory. Cleisthenes created institutions that employed the principles of incentives for knowledge sharing, lowering communication costs, and context-sensitive information sorting. A key to the new system (although probably an unintended consequence of institutional design) was the emergence of many bridging "weak ties" between members of local strong-tie networks.

Granovetter (1973) showed that by contrast to strong ties, weak ties (i.e., the case in which my friends are unlikely to be friends with one another) *do* promote bridging across extended networks. Weak ties break down the claustrophobic environment of cliques by efficiently transferring information across an extended network. Weak ties are therefore an

---

[25] No Athenian regular army before 508: Frost 1984; see further, Siewert 1982.

essential complement to strong-tie networks for social mobilization and for overall organizational cohesion. Granovetter's key conclusion (1973: 1376): was that "the more local bridges . . . in a community and the greater their degree, the more cohesive the community and the more capable of acting in concert." In the terminology used by ancient commentators on his reforms, Cleisthenes "sought to intermix" ([Aristotle] *Ath. Pol.* 21.2–3) the residents of Athenian territory.[26]

Cleisthenes accomplished this intermixing by bypassing the four traditional Ionian tribes (*phulai*) to which the Athenians (like other ethnically/ linguistically Ionian Greeks) traditionally belonged, and inaugurating ten new and blatantly artificial tribes. These new tribes would play important roles in the new political system. They would also become key markers of Athenian identity. Each of the ten new tribes was named after an Athenian mythical hero; according to Athenian memory, the ten heroes were chosen by Apollo's priestess at Delphi from a much more extensive list. Notably, the new tribes would not be territorially contiguous; each tribe drew about a third of its membership from communities located in coastal, inland, and urbanized regions of Athenian territory.[27]

As a result of Cleisthenes' tribal reform, Prasiai now became one of the eleven demes—that is, towns, villages, or urban neighborhoods—constituting the newly created tribe of Pandionis. Prasiai was designated a *coastal deme*, as were three other, nearby villages, each located near the eastern coast of Attica. These four coastal demes of the tribe Pandionis made up the coastal "third" (*trittys*) of the tribe. They were administratively joined to four inland demes to the west (the inland trittys), and to three city demes—neighborhoods in or near the main city of Athens (the city trittys). The citizens of the eleven demes, grouped in these three "thirds," were now officially the tribe Pandionis. The same organizational principles were used in constituting the other nine tribes. The new system is represented schematically in figure 4.2.

Cleisthenes' organizational design was at once radical and practical. It was predicated on integrating long-standing, familiar "natural" units—

---

[26] The value of social networks in building "communities of practice," and thus to organizational performance, is well attested in business literature: Wenger 1998; Davenport and Prusak 1998: 37–39, 65–67; Brown and Duguid 2000: 142–43, 157–59; Benkler 2006.

[27] Anderson 2003 offers a detailed review of Cleisthenes' program, with bibliography. In practice, the new tribal system required a good deal of tinkering; not all "coastal" demes, for example, were located right on the coast: see Traill 1975, 1986. It is sometimes argued that the tinkering was part of a conscious plan that meant to allow Cleisthenes' family (the Alcmaeonids) to dominate Athenian politics: Lewis 1963; Stanton 1984. If there ever was such a plan, it failed in that the Alcmaeonids did not come to dominate Athenian politics. Contrast the *absence* of active planning in the "robust action" model of network formation that in fact allowed the Medici family to dominate Florentine politics after 1433: Padgett and Ansell 1993.

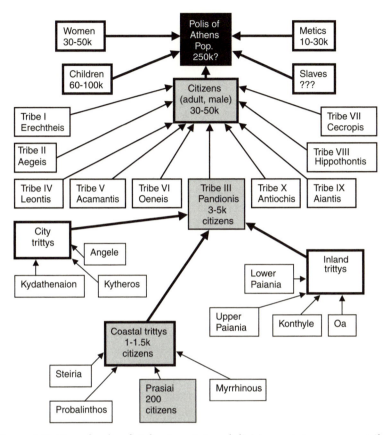

Figure 4.2. Four levels of Athenian civic subdivisions: status groups, tribes, trittyes, demes.

the existing villages and neighborhoods of Athens—into new, unfamiliar, and highly artificial units: the ten new tribes. The tribes and their constituent "thirds" were the institutional bridges by which a stable local identity ("resident of Prasiai") was linked to a desired national identity ("participatory citizen of Athens").

Tribes would now be the basis for mustering a national army. The core of the army was heavy-armed infantrymen (hoplites). Roughly speaking, these were the wealthiest one-third of the Athenian population. In the aftermath of Cleisthenes' reforms, some sixty or seventy men of Prasiai might be expected periodically to march into battle as hoplites along with hoplite villagers from the three nearby towns in the coastal district. This would not be anything new; we can assume that the big men of the central Athenian coast had been mustering their heavy-armed supporters against pirates and other local threats for generations. But now the men of Prasiai would also muster alongside members of tribe Pandionis who hailed from faraway inland and city demes (Siewert 1982; Christ 2001).

Likewise, much of Athenian ritual life was now restructured on a tribal basis. The Prasieis would make sacrifices and eat ritual meals, march in parades, and dance in ritual contests with their fellow tribesmen, the Pandioneis.[28] As a result, people with very different life histories and different sets of social and technical knowledge frequently found themselves in close social proximity to people they never would have otherwise known. The system very literally "intermixed" Athenians from different geographic/economic zones in a variety of psychologically powerful activities. The experience of marching, fighting, sacrificing, eating, and dancing, together in this newly "intermixed" grouping, would, according to Cleisthenes' plan, lead to a strengthened collective identity at the level of the polis. As we shall see, the system also promoted extensive bridge building across the existing strong-tie networks, and these bridges were essential to the process of knowledge aggregation.

THE COUNCIL OF 500: STRUCTURAL HOLES AND BRIDGING TIES

Among key political institutions introduced or restructured in conjunction with the new deme/tribe system was a new Council of 500, a linchpin institution that was given control of the vital agenda-setting function. The Council was charged with the key task of, deciding what matters should be discussed in the full Assembly of Athenian citizens. The Assembly, which all Athenian citizens in good standing were entitled to attend whenever they pleased, was a potentially chaotic legislative body. In the democratic era thousands of citizens attended its frequent meetings (forty per year in the fourth century). The Assembly was the embodied citizenry—the demos—and as such decided all important matters of state policy, including finance and matters of diplomacy, war, and peace. The Council met very regularly in Athens, eventually in a purpose-built architectural complex (see, further, chapter 5). In addition to its vital function of setting the Assembly's agenda, the Council had responsibility for the day-to-day administration of state affairs, including meeting foreign delegations and reviewing the performance of outgoing Athenian magistrates. As we have

---

[28] On the intertwining of ritual, financial, and civic life in the Athenian tribe, see Osborne 1994. Sacrificing and eating: Schmitt-Pantel 1992. Marching: Maurizio 1998. Dancing: Wilson 2000: esp. 56–57, 75–76; *contra*: Pritchard 2004, who argues that tribal choruses were limited to the elite; but the inferential argument undervalues native talent at the expense of opportunity—any tribe that limited its recruitment to elite dancers would be disadvantaged in the competition. Tribal networks were also helpful, especially for non-elite Athenians, in legal disputes: Rubinstein 2000.

seen, in the "dispatching decree," the Council also played an important executive role in ensuring that policy dictated by the Assembly was properly carried out.[29]

According to Cleisthenes' plan, the new Council of 500 was to be made up of ten fifty-man delegations—one delegation from each of the ten newly created tribes.[30] The members of each tribal delegation were in turn selected at deme level. Each year every deme sent forward a certain number of councilors, based on the deme's citizen population.[31] Prasiai annually sent three councilors as part of Pandionis' fifty-man delegation. Meanwhile, the large inland deme of Lower Paiania and the city deme of Kydathenaion each sent eleven men, while tiny Upper Paiania and Konthyle each sent only one. Tribe Pandionis' annual delegation to the Council of 500 is represented schematically in figure 4.3.

What choices, made by an individual member of the Council, might either promote or hinder the Council's overall capacity for joint action? Lacking any detailed first-person narrative from antiquity, a thought experiment must suffice. So imagine a councilor (*bouleutēs*) from Prasiai—let us call him Poseidippos (at least one man of that name did later live in Prasiai)—embarking upon a year's service on the Council in the first year after it was founded.[32] Poseidippos was probably selected by lot for service; this

[29] Rhodes 1985 is the fundamental and indispensable description of the Council of 500, its origins, and its role in Athenian government; see esp. chapter 3 for an analysis of the Council's main areas of responsibility: finance, army and navy, public works, and religion.

[30] Rhodes 1985: 17–18 favors a later date (ca. 462 B.C.) for the introduction of the tribal delegations serving in rotation as "presidents" of the Council, but he notes that the scholarly *communis opinio* is that the tribal teams were a Cleisthenic innovation. The argument for a later date is from the silence of our sources on the matter; yet given the scantiness of our sources for the early democracy, this silence is hardly surprising. Rhodes also believes that lower-class Athenians (*thetes*) were excluded from the Council through the fifth century, but were admitted in the fourth century when demographic constraints made it impossible to fill the quota otherwise. Given that there is no compelling evidence for exclusion of thetes in the earlier Council, I have assumed that they were potentially present from the beginning, although in practice it may have taken some time and the provision of adequate pay for service for thetes to have in fact served on the Council.

[31] Quotas are based on fourth-century evidence. The problems of whether there was ever a change in quotas, based on population change, and whether new demes were added in the post-Cleisthenic era (and how this might have affected the deme quotas) are vexed; no scholarly consensus has yet emerged. Here I assume that the system was put into place in the immediate post-revolutionary period, and (with Traill 1975: 101–3) remained essentially unchanged through 322 B.C. The main lines of the argument I develop here would not be much affected by the kinds of changes that have been proposed to date, e.g., by M. H. Hansen et al. 1990.

[32] I am assuming here that the Council, along with the deme/tribe system, was put into existence in the immediate aftermath of the Revolution of 508; an alternative view holds that the system was not fully functional until 501/0: Rhodes 1985: 1, 191–93; Badian 2000.

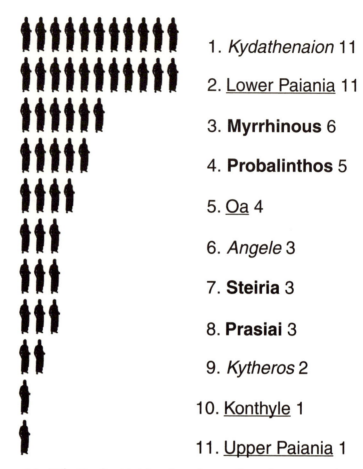

1. *Kydathenaion* 11

2. Lower Paiania 11

3. **Myrrhinous** 6

4. **Probalinthos** 5

5. Oa 4

6. *Angele* 3

7. **Steiria** 3

8. **Prasiai** 3

9. *Kytheros* 2

10. Konthyle 1

11. Upper Paiania 1

Figure 4.3. Tribe Pandionis' delegation of councilmen for one year (quotas by deme). City demes = *italics*, inland = underlined, coastal = **bold**.

was, in any event, the later selection procedure. He took up temporary quarters in the city, rightly expecting to spend a great deal of time serving on the Council; in later years, at least, the Council met some three hundred days each year (Rhodes 1985: 30). Let us stipulate, on the basis of our description of late sixth-century Prasiai, that among the forty-nine other members of the tribal team, Poseidippos had strong ties with his two fellow Prasieis but no bridging ties to any of his other fellow councilors. The point is that when the year's new group of councilors first took up their office, many of the deme delegations that made up each tribal delegation of fifty were already likely to be strong-tie networked, but there were relatively few bridging "weak ties" between the strongly tied local deme networks. This is a microcosm, at the level of fifty men, of the large-

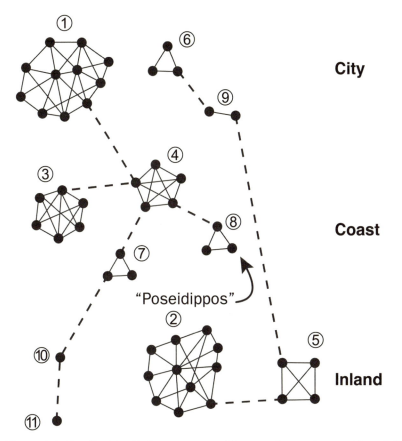

Figure 4.4. Pandionis' tribal team as a social network: starting position. Solid lines within deme networks (numbered 1–11) are hypothetical strong ties. Dashed lines between deme networks are hypothetical weak ties. Prasiai is deme 8.

scale problem Cleisthenes faced as he embarked upon his reform plan. The hypothetical "starting point" situation of the fifty members of the Pandionis team as they entered upon their year of service on the Council in 507 B.C. is represented in figure 4.4.

As he takes up his office, Poseidippos is friends only with his two fellow Prasieis among his fellow councilors from tribe Pandionis, but he knows that he must work closely with forty-seven men with whom he has no current ties, weak or strong, and then with the other 450 councilors from the nine other tribes. According to Cleisthenes' plan, the fifty-man tribal teams were responsible for much of the work of the Council—each tribe would take a leading role in directing the Council's business for a tenth of the year in rotation with the other nine teams. During the period when a tribe-team was exercising its presidency, a third of its delegate-members were on twenty-four-hour duty. In later generations, in the fifth and fourth centuries, they would eat together (using vessels carefully labeled as "public property") and sleep in a distinctive round building (a *prutanikon*) called the Tholos, located in a central position on the west side of the Agora, Athens' public square.[33]

If Poseidippos had known the terminology of contemporary network theory, he would have described the Pandionis team as a network riddled with "structural holes." That is to say, there were many substantial gaps, bridged by few or no weak ties, between the eleven deme networks, each of which featured a dense matrix of strong ties. The holes are evident on figure 4.4: there are no existing ties, for example, between demes 1 and demes 6 and 9 or between deme 8 and demes 7, 2, and 5. In one sense, these holes are an institutional design problem, in that, as we have seen, they represent the absence of the sort of dense networking via weak ties that Granovetter identified as a prerequisite for effective joint action. And so we may say that the holes are a problem that Cleisthenes needed to solve by his new organizational design. Yet, paradoxically, these same structural holes also represent real opportunities—both for the individual willing to take the effort to bridge them and for the organization as a whole. The presence of so many structural holes offered a key incentive to an ambitious and entrepreneurial councilman.

As Ron Burt demonstrated in a series of influential studies (esp. Burt 1992, 1997), in a networked structure, the holes between densely linked subnetworks are points of entrepreneurial opportunity because the individuals who bridge those holes gain social capital. They do so simply by taking up a strategic position in respect to the flow of useful information and social knowledge: they become the conduits through which information passes, and they reap rewards accordingly. Burt showed that, in modern business firms, the social capital accumulated by diligent bridgers of structural holes translates into material gain (e.g., higher salaries), and thus individuals have strong incentives to identify structural holes and to establish bridging ties across them. The social capital that accumulates from bridging holes potentially benefits all members of the network, although the original bridge builders do especially well. Among Burt's important general points is that networked organizations with many structural holes also present many opportunities for entrepreneurial gain by individuals willing and capable of occupying bridge positions. There is, therefore, a correlation between being "full of holes" and the develop-

---

[33] On the Tholos as the headquarters of the presiding tribal delegatio, see Rhodes 1985: 16. Cf. Camp 2001: 69–70, and the studies cited below, n. 40.

ment and maintenance of an entrepreneurial, innovation-prone, organiza-tional culture.[34]

Much of Burt's work builds on insights that are intuitively obvious—one need not have mastered network theory to recognize that advantages accrue to those willing to build bridges between cliquish subnetworks within a larger body that must undertake a common enterprise. The dili-gently "networking" social entrepreneur is a common feature of institu-tions of all kinds. The principle is the same whether it is a secondary school, a business firm, a professional association—or a Greek council.

Because a given Athenian councilor's term was limited to a year, the value of networking on the Council was likewise limited when it is com-pared to institutions (e.g., the U.S. Senate) in which continuous member-ship may span decades. The wealthiest and most socially prominent coun-cilors might regard network building under these conditions as unlikely to reward the effort. Let us stipulate, therefore, that Poseidippos is among the poorest and least well-connected councilors on his tribal team. Like other Athenian fathers, Poseidippos seeks good marriages for his sons and daughters, but he cannot offer large dowries to suitors.[35] The hope of advancing his family's position gives Poseidippos a strong incentive to try to build social capital, which might stand in lieu of larger cash settlements. Stipulate further that Poseidippos is the sort of individual who intuitively recognizes the social capital gains (and the associated utility gains over time) available to a bridge builder. As such he will use opportunities of-fered by the frequent meetings of Pandionis' tribal team of fifty to build bridges to men from other demes, starting perhaps on the basis of shared occupational interests, distant kinship relations, or common cult member-ship. The personal interactions within the tribal delegation are intense, as its members struggle to accomplish their duties—and thereby, since the assumed context is 507 B.C., to save their polis and themselves from de-struction at the hands of the angry Spartans. That intensity facilitates rapid tie formation, and thus makes it easier for Poseidippos to form friendship ties with strangers. The result is illustrated in figure 4.5.

As the year goes on, Poseidippos becomes an increasingly well-re-spected and highly valued member of his tribal team because of his bridg-ing position. He has a handle on more and more useful information—that is, he learns what people in other demes know. He learns something, for example, about pottery manufacture from his city-deme contacts and something about upland olive farming from his inland contacts. He also

---

[34] On structural holes, see Burt 1992, 1997, 2004; Gargiulo and Benassi 2000.

[35] Dowries were very substantial expenses even for relatively wealthy families; many of the fourth-century "non-productive" Athenian loans recorded on the "Attic *horoi*" involve borrowing for dowries: Finley 1953; cf. Cox 1998.

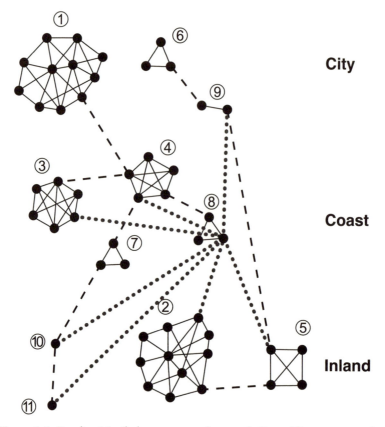

Figure 4.5. Pandionis' tribal team network, stage 2. Dotted lines represent hypothetical new weak ties established by "Poseidippos."

accumulates more and more social knowledge. He knows who among the members of his Pandionis team is trustworthy and on what topics, who is friends and enemies with whom, and so on. He is therefore in a position to *aggregate* important items of information: to bring disparate knowledge pieces together for problem solving. The social capital he stands to gain is a strong incentive to reveal his own latent knowledge—that is, the expertise and experience he has gained in the course of his life—and to share his newly aggregated knowledge with others. The intimate conditions of service on the Council reduce the costs of communication. Meanwhile, Poseidippos's growing social knowledge promotes greater discrimination in respect to information sorting. As a source and a conduit of useful aggregated knowledge, Poseidippos assumes the role of informed leader in deliberations. He thereby accrues advantages for himself and he enables his tribal team to get its job done.

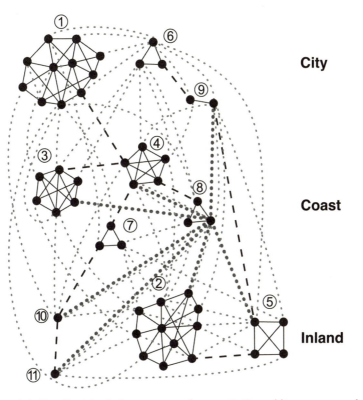

Figure 4.6. Pandionis' tribal team network, stage 3. Dotted lines represent hypothetical new weak ties established by various team members.

Poseidippos is not the only one to see the advantages of building bridging links across local networks. Others on his team imitate his example. As a consequence, the Pandionis delegation is soon densely networked by weak links, as illustrated in figure 4.6.

Pandionis is not special, of course: according to Cleisthenes' design, each of the tribes features similar demographic diversity. Thus, structural hole opportunities exist in each tribal team, and on the Council as a whole. As a result, the bridge building we have hypothesized for Pandionis went on within each of the ten tribal teams. Moreover, the same process went on at an extensive network level *between* tribal teams of the Council. If the social capital for being a tribal team-level bridger of local networks and aggregator of knowledge was considerable, it was that much greater at the level of an intertribal bridge builder. And so, we can postulate that over the course of the year the membership of the Council as a whole becomes linked by weak ties and came to function as a single, extended network. The upshot is that the 500 members of the Council become more capable of working cooperatively, both at the level of the tribal delegations of fifty and as a committee of the whole.

The networking process I have hypothesized, above, based on the social composition and governmental responsibilities of the Council of 500, directly addressees the public action problems affecting knowledge aggregation. As weak-tie bridges link existing strong-tie local networks across regions, across kinship groups, across occupational groups, and across social classes, useful knowledge flows across the extended network with increasing ease. As the network becomes more dense and social capital grows, social knowledge is exchanged ever more freely. As they witness and experience the social capital gains that come with communication, experts in various technical domains are more willing to share their "proprietary" information. Others realize that their tacit knowledge of people and processes, formerly simply taken for granted as a sort of obvious "common sense" among the members of a strong-tie network, is valuable when brought to the surface and made explicit within a diverse group of people possessing very different sorts of tacit knowledge.

As the year goes on, both the latent specialized technical knowledge and the generalized tacit knowledge necessary to making good decisions, which had formerly been isolated inside individual minds and in closed networks, becomes increasingly accessible to the deliberations of the group as a whole. As councilors become clearer about who is good at what, and whom to go to for what sort of information, they can be more discriminating about their recommendations and as a result the whole council becomes increasingly capable of doing its difficult job well.

Moreover, as the Council overcomes its public-action problems and learns to work cooperatively toward its common goal, it can potentially access external knowledge resources distributed through the entire population of Athens—and beyond. Because each councilor has a network of contacts *outside* the Council, each councilor is a bridge between the Council and a local subset of the larger population. As a result, the Council, as a body, can access, at fairly low cost, a good deal of the total knowledge available to the extended Athenian community. As a result, at least potentially, "Athens knows what the Athenians know."

Finally, because councilors ordinarily serve only for a year and are judged, and potentially rewarded, on the basis of how well they serve the public purposes of the polis, the Council as an institution never developed a self-serving identity or corporate culture.[36] The rules of order remained

---

[36] This key insight was developed by Gomme 1951. Doug McAdam suggests to me that it might be counterproductive to enforce a rule against consecutive terms of service in the first few years of the Council's existence, since the new Council would thereby be deprived of all the knowledge accumulated in the previous year. On the other hand, Peter Rhodes

sufficiently simple and transparent, to be learned by each year's incoming class. Because each year's turnover is complete, all councilors enter upon their year on something approaching equal footing; there is no in-group of "old Council hands" controlling the agenda. As councilors build their extended networks and work together over the course of the year on problems of polis governance, they come to better grasp the larger governmental system of which they are (for a year) one part. Government ceases to be regarded as a black box, and councilors can quite quickly become fairly expert at the work of politics.

Their growing system-level expertise conjoins with the councilors' growing social knowledge based information-sorting capacity, and so they are better able to judge the value of available knowledge to the larger purposes of the polis—and thus better able to make good decisions in the exercise of their office. As a result, better agendas are set, the government is better run day-to-day, and so Athens does better overall. We can thereby begin to understand how participatory democratic institutions could help promote growth in productive capacity and overall organizational success.

Organizational and Individual Learning

So far we have focused on the first year after Cleisthenes' establishment of the Council of 500, and so we have been assuming that Poseidippos and his 499 fellow bouleutai entered their first tribal team meetings and first full Council sessions innocent of what to expect. We have postulated that they were motivated by fear that a failure to make good on the promise of the revolutionary uprising would lead to Athenian defeat in an impending war, and that some councilors had strong incentives to build bridges across social networks. As we have seen (chapter 2, era III), the new democratic system worked in that the Athenians were able to field a substantial army in 506 B.C. The Spartans withdrew their forces when their Corinthian allies balked. Perhaps they had expected to confront only a small "traditional" Athenian force led by the local big men of western Attica, yet found themselves confronted with a full levy of the new national army. Athens also won signal victories over its northern and eastern neighbors. The victories of 506 gave the Athenians some breathing room, and the new system was well established within a generation—in time to confront the very serious threat of a Persian invasion in

(personal communication) notes that it might have been thought important to get the notion of non-repetition embedded from the start.

480 (chapter 2, era IV). Meanwhile, the Athenians' experience with self-government was growing.

Let us next imagine Poseidippos' son, call him Poseidippos II (in violation of ordinary Greek naming habits, but for simplicity's sake), as he enters upon a year's service on the Council sometime in the mid 470s, shortly after the victory over Persia. Like his father, Poseidippos II lives in Prasiai. He had been formally voted upon by his father's demesmen when he reached age eighteen. Because he had been accepted by them as a legitimate son of an Athenian man the vote was positive, and thus Poseidippos II became at once a demesman of Prasiai and a citizen of Athens. Like his father, as a councilor, Poseidippos II is confronted with a new challenge—the city had been sacked by the Persians and many of the villages were looted. Rebuilding would be expensive. It would be more difficult because Sparta had opposed Athens' plan to refortify and would be of no help in building and maintaining the long-term anti-Persian alliance that most Athenians saw as essential to Athens' long-term security and return to prosperity.

Unlike his father, Poseidippos II had a sense of what to expect on the Council—he knew in advance many of the rules (written and unwritten) governing work on the Council. He had his father's recalled experience to draw upon, but also the experience of a full generation of Prasieis who had served, three each year, and brought back home much of what they had learned to the village. Over time, every Athenian citizen who cared to avail himself of it had easy and redundant access to men who had served on the Council and had faced a variety of crises and impasses. Both their successes and their failures became part of the general lore passed on across local social networks. Former councilors' accounts of their experience served as an incentive to future councilors. Because he had observed men upon their return from government service over the years, Poseidippos II knew that increased status and recognition could come with a year on the Council. He recognized that the work would be hard and at times frustrating and that he would be taken away from the pleasures and opportunities offered by his ordinary life. Yet these negative considerations were overbalanced by the anticipation of gaining honors and social capital by playing a bridge-building role and by the substantial and long-term benefits associated with that gain.[37]

---

[37] There is no obvious way to test whether the explanatory variable of Council service led to a rise in the dependent variable of individual or family utility (measured by wealth or otherwise). It has sometimes been asserted, on the basis of sketchy evidence, that known councilmen were wealthier, on the average, than ordinary Athenians; see Rhodes 1985: 4–6 and Ober 1989: 139–41 for a review of the question. Those who make the "wealthy councilors" argument invariably assume that the relationship must be "well off *ex ante*, therefore councilor" rather than "councilor, therefore better off *ex post*." Yet if there actu-

Within Poseidippos II's own lifetime, the growing aggregate experience of Council service will have changed the structure of local and cross-polis social networks. Poseidippos II had grown up in a Prasiai in which social conditions were deviating from the tightly bounded "world of Tellus" into which his father had been born. If we stipulate that Poseidippos I's gain in social capital had enabled him to marry one of his daughters to a somewhat wealthier man from an urban deme to whom he had "bridged" in the course of his Council service, Poseidippos II would have kinship ties to a different social stratum and in a different region of the polis as a result of his father's Council year.[38] The point here is that the "weak-tie" friendships that were forged in a year's service ramified through the lives of many individual Athenians and thereby across the polis as a whole. As a result, local strong-tie networks were supplemented at a polis level by an increasingly rich and complex network of strong and weak links.

As an extensive social network of weak *and* strong ties, the polis as an organization had an enhanced opportunity to build a store of collective social capital and thus gained the ability to work more cooperatively and more effectively in addressing public action problems. At the same time, the Athenian population was large, and (at least in the early to mid-fifth century) growing quite rapidly. As a result, even as the density of bridges across the extended network grew, there were always structural holes opening up and thus always new opportunities for entrepreneurial "bridge builders"—the relatively great size of Athens and its constant exposure to demographic change (a function of, inter alia, war casualties, disease, immigration, and emigration) meant that there was no meaningful risk of network ossification. The ties within the extended polis network never became so dense and overlapping as to threaten the entrepreneurial culture Poseidippos I first experienced in the late sixth century.

We can now jump ahead to the time period described at the beginning of this chapter: to 325/4 B.C. and the Council that managed the naval station support expedition, as proposed by Cephisophon of the deme Cholargos. Assuming the family line of Poseidippos I has continued, his great-great-great-great grandson, Poseidippos VI, might have served on that Council. Perhaps, like many Athenians over the generations, he has moved away from his home deme, and now lives in the city. But he still

---

ally *is* a measurable correlation, the direction of influence might be the latter. The entire question deserves further study; see further, Taylor 2008 (discussed below, this chapter).

[38] On interdeme marriages, see Osborne 1985a: 27–38 (documenting 32 intrademe and 131 extrademe marriages), and Cox 1998: 38–67. Jones (2004: 16, 65) seeks to minimize the significance of what was evidently a common practice. Athenian literature is rich with examples of marriages across social lines, and such "mixed marriages" were regarded as characteristic of democratic culture: Lape 2004. More research is needed on the question of how public service might have affected marriage patterns.

attends deme meetings (some of which are held in the city) and he literally wears his deme identity around his neck—as a bronze citizen's identification tag used (inter alia) in lotteries for service on boards of magistrates (Kroll 1972).

Poseidippos VI still feels the pull of the network incentives that had motivated his ancestors. But over the generations the material incentives for Council service had been formalized. He was paid a daily wage for his service, and the Pandionis tribal team competed for a prize offered by the demos, honoring the year's best team.[39] When serving as the Council's presidents, Pandionis' tribal delegation (and the other nine in rotation) still met in the Tholos that was being planned during Poseidippos II's term of service. But when he attended meetings of the full Council, Poseidippos VI usually sat in a New Bouleuterion (see, further, chapter 5). As before, most Council meetings were open to the Athenian public. The Old Bouleuterion, in which Poseidippos II had deliberated over the rebuilding of the city, was now dedicated to the Mother of the Gods and being used to house the state archives (see, further, chapter 6). Here, councilors and other Athenians could consult the record of Athenian laws and decrees. A small staff of public slaves and citizen-clerks was available to help with archives and technical matters, yet this staff never amounted to anything like a professionalized bureaucracy; the main work of the Council was still done by the councilors themselves.[40]

By 325 B.C., the accumulated and transmitted knowledge of 180 years of institutional experience and policy experiments and the results of 180

---

[39] Pay: 5 obols/day for ordinary service, 6 obols (1 drachma)/day for service while the members of the tribal team were serving as presidents; see Rhodes 1985: 16–17. Annual prize for best tribal delegation, offered by the Council in the early fourth century and by the demos by the mid-fourth century (*IG* II² 1142): Rhodes 1985: 8, 22–23.

[40] The Old and New Bouleuteria: Rhodes 1985: 31–33; Camp 2001: 44, 127. The early construction date (ca. 500) and original function of the building identified as the Old Bouleuterion, preferred by, for example, Rhodes and Camp, have been much debated; I think that the evidence favors the early date. See Shear 1995; Raaflaub 1998: 93–95 with bibliography; Papadopoulos 2003: 260–97; Pritchard 2005: 146–47 with bibliography. Meetings of the Council were occasionally held elsewhere (Rhodes 1985: 35–36): on Salamis, on the Acropolis, at Piraeus, at Eleusis (during the Mysteries), in the Theseion, and in the stadium. Meetings open to public: Rhodes 1985: 40–43. Before the 360s a principal "secretary to the Council" and, after the 360s three other citizen-secretaries (an *anagrapheus*, an *antigrapheus*, and an *epi ta psēphismata*) were annually assigned to the Council, but their tenure (like that of all Athenian citizen-clerks) was annual. Secretaries: [Aristotle] *Ath. Pol.* 54.3–5 and Rhodes 1985: 16, 134–42; M. H. Hansen 1999: 123–24, 244–45; Henry 2002. Public slaves (*huperetai*) looked after records in the Metroon and the records of the *poletai*; perhaps a half-dozen other public slaves were available to assist the Council (*SEG* 24.13). Rhodes 1985: 142–43 emphasizes the modest size of the Council's staff: there is no warrant for imagining a substantial professionalized bureaucracy, comparable to that typical of parliamentary democracies, working in the background.

years of networking among Athenians were potentially available, orally or in written form. The councilors charged in the "dispatching decree" with sitting on the dock at Piraeus, and ensuring that the right ships were sent out in a timely fashion to the new colony in the Adriatic, had this store of knowledge to draw upon, which helps to explain how five hundred amateurs could come up with recommendations that were so very detailed and specific. The Council had learned, for example, that the right level (in terms of an equilibrium between incentive value and costs to the state) for setting the first, second, and third prizes for "first trireme to the dock" was 500, 300, and 200 drachmas; that two days were adequate for dealing with legal appeals by trierarchs, and that a 10,000-drachma fine would generally suffice to discourage malfeasance, even among those officials handling major accounts.[41]

In sum, because of a structured capacity for passing on what was learned, the Athenian Council had developed the character of a learning organization. As valuable experience accumulated over time, a formal archival system was developed, and many of the work routines for accomplishing the Council's work were codified (chapter 6).[42] Yet the regular turnover of Council membership and the diversity of experiences new Councilors brought to the table ensured that the socialization of the members of the Council never approached the level at which innovative solutions were likely to be suppressed in favor of ossified routinization. The Council was manned by amateurs, in that their experience as councilors was limited to two terms. In practice and perhaps, therefore, in principle, terms were always non-consecutive. Yet the apparent seamlessness with which knowledge, both innovative and routinized, could be aggregated and made available to decision makers on the Council enabled them to manifest some of the characteristics associated with experts who have thousands of hours of personal experience to call upon. The decision-making process of the Council itself had, over time, evolved into a sort of "expert system," capable of addressing a wide variety of problems.[43]

[41] The dispatching decree was passed on a motion from the floor of the Assembly (and thus employed the enactment formula *edoxe tōi dēmōi* (rather than *edoxe tēi boulēi kai tōi dēmōi*), but the Council had overall supervisory responsibility for the expedition. I am assuming that accumulated Council-service experience stands (at whatever remove) behind Cephisophon's decree. About half of known Athenian decrees were ratifications of recommendations (*probouleumata*) of the Council; the other half were amended recommendations or proposals from the Assembly floor; see M. H. Hansen 1999: 140, with literature cited.

[42] The formulaic language of enactment and disclosure typical of Athenian decrees (Hedrick 1999) is one piece of evidence for routinization.

[43] The term "expert system" ordinarily refers to electronic computing techniques that seek to simulate (and thereby regularize and make easily accessible to end users) the decision-making processes of experts, see Jackson 1999.

BOARDS OF MAGISTRATES AS REAL TEAMS

The Council of 500 was an extremely important Athenian government institution, and one that Greek historians know a lot about, which justifies the extended treatment of it in this chapter. But the Council was never "Athens' real government" and showed no tendency to become the dominant institution of government.[44] If we are to understand the role of knowledge aggregation in Athenian performance, we must recognize that the Council was only one institution among many others. Many Athenian governing bodies had to work together in close coordination in order to address major policy issues and to produce generally successful outcomes. This is evident when we consider the 14 formal institutions mentioned in the dispatching decree.[45]

By the mid- to later fourth century, the age of Aristotle, Demosthenes, and our imaginary Poseidippos VI, the Athenians annually selected some seven hundred magistrates *in addition to* the five hundred members of the Council. About one hundred of these were elected in the Assembly. The other six hundred were, like the councilors, chosen by lot. Most of them served on collegial boards, typically composed of ten citizens and supported, like the Council, by a small staff of clerks (public slaves or working citizens). In some cases (e.g., the ten generals, elected annually by the Assembly), boards were composed of one member from each tribe. In other cases, for example the Dispatchers (see above, this chapter), the board's members were selected from the citizenry at large.[46]

Boards had no formally preassigned internal leadership roles; the members of each board were expected to work as a team to accomplish specific outcomes that were specified in the board's constitutional charter (the law or decree by which the board was established—for example, the Dispatchers in the "dispatching decree"). These magisterial boards handled a great deal of public business—from leading armies and navies in the field, to oversight of public festivals, to disbursing welfare payments to handicapped citizens and orphans of citizens who died in battle (chapter 6). Accountability procedures were strict. No magistrate could enter upon

[44] The thesis of De Laix 1973, that the Council was indeed the senior institution of Athenian government and the Assembly little more than a rubber stamp, has not found much acceptance among Greek historians.

[45] Rhodes 1985: 137 notes that nowhere in the considerable surviving political literature of the fourth century is there any hint that the Council had to be watched lest it become too powerful; in chapter 3 he discusses the close interaction of the Council with other Athenian government bodies.

[46] Athenian magistrates, their numbers, duties, and accountability procedures: M. H. Hansen 1999: 225–45.

his year of service without passing an initial scrutiny (*dokimasia*)— a screening that concerned reputation for character and conduct of life, rather than competence. And no magistrate could leave office without undergoing a formal review (*euthuna*) of how he and the other members of his board had acquitted themselves in office, especially in respect to any public funds under their control. Sanctions for malfeasance could fall upon individuals or upon the entire collegial board (Roberts 1982; D. Harris 1994).

Like the fifty-man tribal teams on the Council, the members of a ten-man magisterial board had to figure out how to work together in order to achieve an outcome that could only be gained by cooperative joint action. The opportunities for intrainstitutional networking were obviously somewhat limited on magisterial boards, but there were abundant chances for cross-institutional networking as boards worked together on projects like the naval station. Moreover, the relatively small size of most Athenian boards offered important organizational advantages.

In terms of solving public-action problems, increasing personal job satisfaction, and balancing the advantages of diversity of perspective with shared identity, the Athenian institutional environment appears close to ideal for the formation of what J. R. Katzenbach and D. K. Smith (1993, revised edition of 2003 cited here) describe as "real teams." In their influential study Katzenbach and Smith describe and advocate structuring the work of organizations around teams—small groups of workers with complementary skills, a common purpose, a common set of performance goals, a commonly agreed-upon approach to their work, who hold each other mutually accountable for their collective performance (2003: xvii). The result, as they claim on the basis of detailed case studies, is both substantially enhanced overall organizational performance and enhanced individual job satisfaction.[47]

In Katzenbach and Smith's model, instead of the familiar resort to command-and-control "single-leader-driven" initiatives, true teams are given considerable yet clearly defined responsibility for various domains of problem-solving. By reference to a series of real-world case-based examples (mostly for-profit business firms, but including some not-for-profit organizations), Katzenbach and Smith seek to demonstrate why and how

---

[47] Business literature building on Katzenbach and Smith's work includes Manz and Sims 1995; Purser and Cabana 1998. For scholarship on the social and psychological underpinning of team-based work processes, see Cohen and Bacdayan 1994; Hargadon and Fanelli 2002; Mannix and Neale 2005. J. Roberts 2004: 123–25 notes the potential motivational problems of teamwork arising from moral hazard due to incomplete observation of activities and free-riding; he notes, however, that reputation effects (highly relevant among the members of small teams working intensely together on a single problem) may offer a solution.

employing teams can improve an organization's competitive perfor-mance. They emphasize the importance to team performance (and thus to overall organizational performance) of accountability, setting specific performance challenges and goals that are "outcome based" and measur-able. The size and composition of teams are important: Katzenbach and Smith recommend a fairly narrow size range (four to twelve persons) and warn against changing team membership frequently or arbitrarily. They note that building effective teams does not typically require a great deal of prior training, and emphasize that much of the necessary learning will be gained "on the job."

Research on teams shows that in order to perform well, teams must avoid various common small-group deliberative pathologies: strategic be-havior predicated on long-term individual gains can lead to knowledge hoarding that compromises shorter-term outcomes. Conformist group-think and information cascades (chapter 5) can emerge when team mem-bers are either too similar in their perspectives, or too diverse in their perceived identities. If deliberation leads people to more extreme posi-tions, polarization can warp individual judgments and may lead to sup-pression of useful information.[48]

At Athens, service on most teams was intense for its duration, but the duration was ordinarily limited to a single year. Intense ongoing interac-tion over the year allowed members to learn a good deal about one anoth-er's real strengths and weaknesses, whereas the limited term lowered the incentives for harmful strategic behavior based on hoped-for long-term gains. Shared tribal identities and citizen status created a groundwork of cultural similarity, while the selection process virtually guaranteed that team members would come to the table with different personal perspec-tives. These features, along with a background culture that emphasized formal equality in respect to public speech (isēgoria) and legitimized vocal dissent, arguably promoted conditions that maximized the chance for val-uable unique information to be presented, heard, and incorporated in group decisions.[49]

Although Katzenbach and Smith were certainly not thinking in terms of Greek poleis, their description of an ideal-type, team-based organiza-tional environment is reminiscent of the conditions under which Athenian magisterial boards operated: Athenian boards of ten fall within the recom-mended size range and had a fixed (yearly) membership. They had clear

---

[48] On deliberative pathologies, see Gigone and Hastie 1993; Sunstein 2000, 2002, 2007; Mutz and Martin 2001; Mendelberg 2002; Delli Carpini et al. 2004; Ryfe 2005; Stasavage 2007.

[49] Detailed studies of ancient Greek deliberative practices: Ruzé 1997; Farenga 2006. My thanks to Margaret Neale for discussion of these issues.

objectives and success was measured in formal reviews. Because they faced the possibility of both individual and common sanctions in the case of malfeasance, members were individually and mutually accountable. Katzenbach and Smith's conclusion is that teams are effective "whenever a specific performance objective requires collective work, shared leadership, and real time integration of multiple skills, perspectives or experiences" (2003: 269). This could serve as a succinct description of the democratic Athenian approach to administration by magisterial boards. Overall, Athenian organizational success may be attributed in part to a "team-based" institutional design that avoided common deliberative pathologies—at least much of the time.

If we imagine Athenian boards as teams, as manifesting the effectiveness characteristics of "real teams" (as opposed to being ill-defined groups of the sort that Katzenbach and Smith call "pseudo teams"), and if we suppose further that small magisterial collegial boards (like the much larger Council) were capable of sustained and aggregated "institutional learning" over time through a mix of innovation and routinization of past experience, it becomes easier to see how the various magisterial bodies responsible for the naval-station support expedition were able to coordinate and accomplish their various duties in a timely and effective manner.

If we further suppose that the members of the various teams were linked by strong and weak ties, both with one another and with members of the Council, and thus undertook their work within an assumed context of an extended social network that also functioned as a knowledge network, the capacity for coordination between the work of the magisterial boards and the Council becomes less mysterious. Moreover, in any given year, some Council members would have served on various collegial boards and some board members had served a year on the Council. Because of incentives for knowledge sharing, cross-institutional experience of men with prior experience in other bodies of government was available to their colleagues. Movement of people across institutions enhanced opportunities for innovative cross-appropriation of practices and techniques. The process of annual rotation, while impeding the development of deep individual expertise (and long-term strategic behavior) *within* a single institutional domain, facilitated knowledge exchange *across* institutions and thus potentially enhanced both innovation and coordination throughout the system of Athenian government.[50]

---

[50] The Athenian system thus captured the value of transfer of useful knowledge across institutional boundaries, thereby allowing individuals to adapt what they have seen previously "into what they now know as possible" (Hargadon and Fanelli 2002: quote 297). Some globally distributed firms very self-consciously move people across geographically dispersed units on a regular basis and at considerable expense, in part in order to capture the value of innovative cross-appropriation, but also because they recognize the general

Ostracism, Assembly, and People's Courts

Many features of Athenian institutions can be illuminated by reference to the role of incentives and sanctions, communication costs, and sorting within a knowledge-based system.[51] Ostracism, the famous (and perhaps unique) mechanism by which Athenians annually had the opportunity to vote a single man into exile, is a case in point.

Each year, at a designated meeting of the Assembly, the Athenians voted on whether an ostracism was called for. If the vote was yes, a special sort of "election" was held in the Agora: each Athenian then had the opportunity to cast a ballot, in the form of a pottery sherd (*ostrakon*) inscribed with a name, against anyone he pleased. The "winner" (whoever received a plurality of votes) was exiled for ten years. Recent scholarship has clarified the original political purposes and the symbolic meaning of this puzzling institution. Symbolic meaning is unquestionably central to how the Athenians understood the practice of ostracism. Yet in terms of public action and dispersed knowledge, ostracism can also be seen as an elegant way to aggregate Athenian social knowledge on two questions. At the preliminary meeting of the citizen Assembly, the Athenians answered the first question, "Is there anyone in the polis sufficiently dangerous to warrant expulsion from the polis without a trial?" If the majority answer was yes, the count of *ostraka* subsequently cast in the Agora answered the second question: "Who is he?"[52]

Two features of ostracism are particularly striking. First is the absence of any necessary assumption of past misconduct; an ostracism was not a legal trial (although ostracized men could be tried in absentia, see chapter 5); no charges were filed. Next is the lack of publicly provided information or deliberation: there were no public speeches of prosecution or defense. Once the decision was made to hold an ostracism, each individual citizen made up his mind about whom to vote against on the basis of whatever knowledge he happened to have or sought to gain. These fea-

---

value of building internal social networks: Orlikowsky 2002. As Hargadon and Fanelli (2002: 300) point out, "The process of knowing in organizations exists as a social phenomenon in the recursive social interactions between individuals."

[51] Lyttkens 1992, 1994, 2006 (taxation); Quillin 2002 (amnesty); Schwartzberg 2004, 2007 (law and diplomacy); Fleck and Hanssen 2006 (agricultural economy); Kaiser 2007 (trierarchies); and Teegarden 2007 (anti-tyranny legislation) are notable examples of explanatory approaches to various aspects of Athenian institutions, which emphasize rational action and incentives, although they do not focus in the first instance on dispersed knowledge.

[52] Ostracism as ritual, and its origins in the sixth-century "crisis of exile": Forsdyke 2000, 2005, which reviews and supplants earlier literature. The evidence for ostracism outside of Athens is exiguous: Forsdyke 2005, appendix 2.

tures suggest that the institution was designed to focus voters' attention on a calculation of expected public gains and losses, rather than on justice or retribution for a malefactor's past actions. So we might imagine the "Who is he?" question as taking the form, "Who among of the current leaders will cause the greatest net harm if he remains in the city over the next ten years?" Viewed in this light, ostracism takes on some of the characteristics of the modern "prediction market," a remarkably accurate non-deliberative means of aggregating opinions about the likely course of future events (Sunstein 2007).

There was no way (then or now) to know whether the "right answer" emerged from a given ostracism, but Athens certainly did not suffer from a lack of innovative and successful leaders during the half-century (480s–440s) during which almost all recorded ostracisms were held. After an ostracism in ca. 417 (Rhodes 1994) returned an anomalous "winner" (perhaps due to collusion among the two most obvious candidates), the Athenians never again answered "yes" to the first question about whether to hold an ostracism in a given year.

The citizen Assembly and the People's Courts are generally regarded as signature institutions of the Athenian democracy, and their effective functioning is certainly among the most mysterious aspects of Athenian political organization.[53] In both cases, mass audiences (6000–8000 in the case of the Assembly, 200–500 or more in the case of the courts) were responsible for making vitally important decisions under severe time constraints on the basis of having heard public speeches on different sides of an issue. Assemblymen ordinarily had to make a number of decisions by the end of the day (and often in a half day); every Athenian jury had to arrive at its judgment by day's end. In both legislative and judicial (especially public/criminal court) venues, highly skilled speakers, advocating different and mutually incompatible courses of action, addressed the mass audience on complex and important matters. In each case the audience, having listened, expressed its decision by a simple-majority voting mechanism: ordinarily a raised-hand vote in the Assembly and always a secret ballot in the courts.[54]

Some historians have argued that the decision-making context of Assembly and courtroom must have mandated an increasingly powerful role for highly expert public speakers, and that these political experts domi-

[53] For detailed assessments, see M. H. Hansen 1987 (Assembly) and Lanni 2006 (People's Courts).

[54] For details of voting, see M. H. Hansen 1999: 125–60, with literature cited. The timely closure of discussion is often underappreciated, although it is among the key design principles of Athenian institutions; see Manville and Ober 2003: 133–35.

nated governmental processes by exercise of their superior mastery of both rhetoric and technical matters. How, these scholars have asked, could the simple folk who attended the Assembly or sat on the juries hope to make reasoned judgments about complex issues concerning, for example, public finance? Surely, they suggest, the supposedly deliberative decision-making bodies were little more than rubber-stamp mechanisms. The prior assumptions of elite-domination arguments are that open deliberations would not add value to decisions and that aggregating diverse public knowledge would not yield good answers. Athenian government, according to the theory, must, therefore, have been mostly in the hands of experts with many years of experience. Since Athenian government did not provide leaders with positions of continuous executive authority, the elite-domination thesis relies on assumptions about the power asymmetry inherent in the rhetorical situation and the inevitability of voting cascades. Because prominent Athenian public speakers (the model is often Pericles) were typically expert in aspects of government and highly trained in rhetorical technique, the ordinary citizens were easily controlled while an illusion of government by the people was maintained.[55]

If the argument developed in this chapter is correct, this elite-domination argument is fundamentally flawed in its assumption of radical informational asymmetry between elite speaker and mass audience. The domination argument regards the 200–500 jurors who gathered to try a given case, and the 6000–8000 Athenians who gathered for a given Assembly meeting, as a mob—heterogeneous in its preferences but homogeneous in its ignorance. This mob was, the argument goes, in thrall to experts who held a monopolistic control of the knowledge relevant to policy decisions. As I have sought to show, the ignorant-mob assumption is false, and we must pay attention to the resources for rational choice making possessed by individual Athenians. Each juryman and assemblyman should be understood as both an individual agent capable of learning and as a node in an extensive social network that was also a network of knowledge.

Because of various opportunities for joint action on a tribal basis, networks were especially dense within tribes. In the case of juries, the lottery mechanism (at least that used in the fourth century) assured that an equal

[55] Kallet-Marx 1994 and Moreno 2008 argue that elite politicians dominated the Assembly through their rhetorical finesse and a monopoly of expertise in matters of public finance and the grain trade. Kagan 1991 and G. Anderson 2003 offer "great leader" driven accounts of late sixth- and fifth-century Athenian politics; see the critique of Pritchard 2005. Rhodes 2000 focuses on the importance of leadership but is attentive to the institutionalized difficulties of achieving any sort of dominant political role. Rhodes, forthcoming, focuses on the Assembly and rejects the notion that expert orators dominated a passive audience. Much of my earlier work, notably Ober 1989, 1996, challenges "inevitability of elite-domination" arguments. On cascades, see, further, chapter 5.

number of men would be chosen from each tribe, and thus each juryman could count on the presence of a "fair share" of men with whom he was likely to share ties. In the case of the Assembly, every assemblyman knew that the matters to be discussed had been worked through in advance and the agenda had been set by a tribal team and then by the full Council. The members of the Council had learned the value of social and knowledge networks, and became better informed on a variety of substantive matters, as they worked to identify and to aggregate the information and social knowledge relevant to the Assembly's decision.

It is a demographic certainty that every jury and every Assembly included a high percentage (exactly how high depends on how one models Athenian life expectancy: Hansen 1986) of men who had been members of the Council and/or of various magisterial boards, and who had become in the process reasonably expert at various aspects of Athenian governance. Although a given Athenian, sitting on a jury or in the Assembly, might well be inexpert regarding the matters under discussion, he was likely to know many men among those in attendance who were considerably more knowledgeable and more experienced in the matter at hand.

Imagine, for example, the Assembly deliberations that led to the passing of the dispatching decree. Let us suppose that a young and inexperienced member of tribe Pandionis was struggling to understand the implications of Cephisophon's proposal. Scanning the crowd, he spots Poseidippos VI, who (as we stipulated above) was a member of the Council that year, but whose tribe was not in presidency and thus he was attending the Assembly as an ordinary citizen. Our naïve tribesman from Pandionis now had a lead to follow in judging the debate. He could assume (on the basis of his own experience of networks linked by both weak and strong ties and their social-capital building reward/sanction processes) that highly experienced Poseidippos shared his own preference for outcomes that would benefit the polis. And so he could follow Poseidippos' lead in response to the recommendations suggested by public speakers without much fear that he was setting himself up for a sucker's payoff in this complex "public policy game." Poseidippos' lead would not be particularly subtle—Athenian assemblymen (and jurors) were famous for their *thorubos*, meaning vociferous and emphatic responses to public speakers.[56] Poseidippos' response was in turn conditioned by his own monitoring of the reactions of those in his extensive network whom he knew to be particularly expert on the tactical advantages associated with certain ship types, incentives for trierarchs, and so on. Similar aggregation processes were going on throughout the assembly place, as the less experienced followed the lead

[56] Bers 1985 (courts); Tacon 2001 (Assembly).

of the more experienced, and as the more experienced monitored those whose expertise they trusted. This is, as I argued earlier (chapter 3), just the sort of process that Aristotle alludes to in his well-known passage illustrating the "summation argument."

As the Assembly engaged in debate on the dispatching decree, only a relatively few men, possessing some expert knowledge of both the matter at hand and rhetorical technique, would be likely to speak up. After all, if even one percent of the eight thousand men in attendance had attempted to address the Assembly, the result would be chaos. But although only a small number spoke from the *bēma* (speaker's platform), a great deal of expert knowledge dispersed across the Assembly was leveraged by the members of the audience. Those who did take the platform on the matter could not hope to "control" the decision because they had no monopoly on specialized knowledge. The huge decision-making group knew, in the aggregate, much more than *any* individual speaker, no matter how expert he might be. Many within the group had considerable experience in the process of institutional knowledge collection, while others were still in the process of mastering the process through participating in it. Because every public speaker's recommendations were judged and tested against the aggregated knowledge of the polis, speakers remained advisers—granted a hearing if their advice squared with what the demos collectively knew, quickly booed from the speaker's platform if it did not. While the final vote might take the form of an informational cascade (chapter 5), the cascade could not gain momentum if a speaker's argument contradicted the collective "wisdom of the crowd."[57]

The "inevitable expert-elite domination" argument gains a spurious common-sense credibility because of the limited experience most modern individuals have with participatory processes of self-governance. The networked epistemic process I described above depends on the development of considerable tacit knowledge (chapter 3) of political processes. Like riding a bicycle or swimming, the tacit knowledge that constituted effective democratic citizenship could be learned from experienced others and through personal experience, but it could not easily be documented in a "user's manual." This may be at least part of why the Athenians retained a performance advantage into the late classical period. While specific

---

[57] Contemporary critiques of large-scale participatory democracy (notably Dahl and Tufte 1973: 66–88) overemphasize the time commitment by introducing the notion that participation demands that each participant in an Assembly must speak (perhaps for an equal time) on each matter. The network approach discussed above suggests that it is possible to scale participatory democracy well beyond the face-to-face level; whether it is practicable at the modern nation-state level is another question.

Athenian institutions could be, and were, profitably adopted by other poleis, the full package of democracy in the Athenian style was not easy for other states to mimic because complex bodies of tacit knowledge do not travel well.

Most of us today lack the tacit knowledge that would be necessary for aggregating knowledge in deliberative assemblies. Because experimental work reveals the tendency for the emergence of pathologies in modern deliberative bodies (juries and small groups), some modern scholars have supposed that deliberation at scale is an impossibility. The Athenian case suggests this assumption is wrong. Athenian political history appears to show that the capacity to collect the knowledge necessary for rational decision making on complex policy matters through processes of open public debate is not an arcane accomplishment, but a skill that can be learned by ordinary people.[58] It seems likely (although this remains a hypothesis to be tested) that, because it involves so much tacit knowledge, the sort of "on the fly" collection of social and technical knowledge that I have argued was typical of Athenian large-scale decision-making bodies should be regarded as a skill that cannot be mastered *except* through practical experience.[59]

I have concentrated on the Assembly since the People's Courts are treated in more detail in chapter 5. Briefly: because jurors had no formal opportunity for deliberation among themselves and the vote was by secret ballot, the epistemic process of the jury courts incorporated aspects of ostracism's "prediction market" approach, in which the (relatively) independent knowledge of individuals is aggregated, and the Assembly, with its deliberative features of multiple viewpoints and non-secret voting. In the courtroom, many of the facts at issue were contested by the litigants and unknowable in the face of contradictory testimony. As a consequence, a juror's decision would often turn on social knowledge—on what he knew *ex ante* or learned in the course of the trial about the litigants' characters and ways of life. The jury's vote thus represented an aggregation of new and existing social knowledge.

[58] Jon Krosnik points out to me that this proposition could be tested. A large-scale deliberative poll (Fishkin 1991) could employ the standard methods of experimental social and political psychology to test the performance of a large deliberative group that met frequently over an extended period of time, and made decisions of genuine consequence. It would be a costly experiment to undertake, but the cost could surely be justified in light of the great importance, to democratic theorists and practitioners alike, of the question, "Does deliberation work?"

[59] The irreplaceable educational value of personal participation in public affairs stands at the center of all modern theories of participatory democracy. See, for example, Pateman 1970; Mansbridge 1983; Fung and Wright 2003: esp. 27–29; Freitag 2006. Similar considerations were raised by democratic Athenian writers: Ober 2001 (= 2005, chapter 6).

The approaches to aggregating knowledge in Assembly and court-room were therefore different in some important particulars, but they were sufficiently similar for extensive experience gained in one large-scale institutional setting to be readily transferred to another. As we will see in the next two chapters, the general principle of "low-cost cross-appropriation of institutional expertise" is a persistent feature of Athenian democracy. Along with the development of standard practices and archived experience, the institutionalized capacity for innovative cross-appropriation was a key part of individual and organizational learning, and helps to explain the comparatively strong performance of the democratic polis.

The Athenian system of government both encouraged (through incentives) and required (in order to broaden the range of available knowledge) participation from a diverse population. As we have seen (chapter 3), equality of opportunity for public participation was a cherished Athenian value. The institutional design model developed in this chapter is based on offering substantial incentives (honorary and material) for political service. These incentives made public service possible and desirable across class lines. Formerly inexperienced men had the chance to become experienced in political affairs, indeed, to become in some ways expert at the work of democratic politics. By gaining experience and therefore confidence in their own capacities, they *lost* a substantial *disincentive* to political activity. Substantial power inequalities remained between elite and non-elite social strata. But opportunities for political activity were to some degree equalized across Athenian class lines by the use of the lot (Taylor 2007) and, across the mid-fifth and fourth centuries, by pay for service.

The model I have presented here predicts that, over the course of time (i.e., between T1 and T2 in figure 4.1), the population of "politically active citizens" should be increasingly representative of, and indeed functionally coextensive with, the citizen population as a whole. The obvious advantages enjoyed by wealthy citizens, and by those with easy geographical access to the city center, should lessen. The degree of over representation of wealthy and city-local citizens among the population of the politically active should decline. This prediction is borne out by Clare Taylor's demographic analysis of nearly 2200 politically active Athenians in the fifth and fourth centuries. In the fifth century, 19 percent of identifiable politically active citizens were wealthy (i.e., from the liturgy-paying class: ca. 4 percent of the total population) and 58 percent came from near-city demes (aggregate bouleutic quota 123/500: ca. 25 percent of the total population). In the fourth century, by contrast, only 11 percent of citizens known to be politically active were wealthy and 31 percent were from near-city demes. Taylor's numbers do not prove that citizens' growing experience with government processes (or any other candidate variable) *caused* the trend to equalization. Her results are, however, consistent with the model offered here. The opposite result (growing inequality of access) would, by contrast, falsify it.[60]

The value of aggregated knowledge helps to explain how costly participatory decision-making institutions might improve Athenian performance—even though, like all decision-making processes, Athenian processes were fallible and sometimes produced bad policy. The social context of aggregation processes explains how Athenian institutional design promoted learning—both organizational learning, so that the system as a whole became more expert, and individual learning by citizens engaged in a lifelong civic education. Collection of knowledge was, however, only one part of Athens' epistemic democracy. To explain how aggregated knowledge was put into action, we now turn to the second epistemic process, the alignment of knowledge commonly held across a diverse population.

---

[60] Taylor 2008, arguing persuasively that exogenous factors (e.g., demographic changes due to disease, war, rural migration to the city) are inadequate to explain the growth in participation. Taylor's figures fit well with the conclusions of Morris 1998a: 235–36, who notes that in comparative terms, and especially in comparison with the pre-democratic period, the pattern of landholding in fourth-century Athens was "*extremely* egalitarian" (Morris' emphasis: Gini coefficient of 0.382–0.386).

Chapter 5

ALIGNMENT: COMMON KNOWLEDGE,
COMMITMENT, AND COORDINATION

ONCE AN ACTION has been planned and a decision made, the question is how to carry it out. Implementing group decisions demands that individual efforts be aligned. Like aggregation, alignment is an epistemic process, predicated on the right people having and using the right information in the right context. The fourth and final step in Pettit and List's account of joint action (chapter 1) is that the beliefs and intentions of the relevant parties in regard to the salient plan are commonly known by them. Common knowledge can degrade decision making if epistemic diversity is suppressed. Yet *after* a decision has been made, *lack* of common knowledge results in uncoordinated follow-through, higher implementation costs, and reduced organizational performance.

Just as making plans democratically requires institutions for collecting dispersed knowledge, so too carrying out plans in the absence of command-and-control mechanisms requires institutional support for aligning common knowledge. In the Athenian democracy, disparate governmental bodies and individuals proved capable of coordinating their actions to implement decisions: armies were mustered and dispatched, fleets were gathered and launched, taxes were collected, and public funds were distributed—all with less executive control and regulatory apparatus than modern states tend to regard as essential.[1]

Athenian public decrees (chapter 4) and laws (chapter 6) often took the form of work orders, setting out the responsibilities of various institutionalized groups and individual officeholders for accomplishing a

---

[1] Examples of effective Athenian coordination include the web of institutions involved in the dispatching decree discussed in chapter 4, the building of the Athenian navy and Athenian planning in the face of Persian invasion in the 480s, the response to military crises in the Peloponnesian War, and the legal reforms of the late fifth century (see chapter 2). Each of these legislated plans for major new undertakings called for the involvement of a different and novel mix of institutional and individual actors. Mader 2006 shows that Demosthenes' well known complaint that the Athenian Assembly was all talk and no action (i.e., passed decrees without follow-through) was a rhetorical tactic, and does not describe actual Athenian practice. Lack of knowledge essential for coordinated action is a recurrent

specific end.[2] Many provisions of the orders are quite detailed, especially in respect to rewards and punishments. Yet the orders remained only outlines: exactly *how* each body was to achieve its role is unspecified. There were no formal administrative protocols mandating how Athenian magistrates were to carry out their work. This would be unremarkable if Athens had been organized as a centralized hierarchy, so that each public actor knew to look up a chain of command for direction. The puzzle is how a decentralized participatory democracy could have coordinated its many working parts in the absence of formal command and control and without elaborate protocols.[3] As in the case of decision making, the puzzle can be solved by analyzing Athenian processes for organizing useful knowledge at scale. Like aggregation, alignment depended on balancing an ongoing commitment to institutional innovation with the productive routines characteristic of social learning.

ALIGNMENT AND HIERARCHY

Behind every Athenian statute lay the implicit assumption that coordination could be achieved in the absence of a unitary executive, through dispersed choice making and self-regulation. With no central authority responsible for imposing order, we might expect that each governmental body would act strategically, seeking to exploit ambiguities in outline-form work orders to enhance its own resources and power. Yet Athenian legislators assumed that institutional and individual actors, once presented with a menu of incentives and sanctions, would cooperate in carrying out common goals. Given Athenian performance over time (chapter 2), the assumption appears valid.

This chapter examines the epistemic process of alignment that underwrote the Athenians' capacity to carry out joint actions, so that imaginative work plans, presented in outline form in public decrees and laws, sufficed to attain public goals.[4] Coordination without formalized proto-

---

theme in critical discussions of modern public policy, e.g. international aid and development efforts: Bannerjee et al. 2006.

[2] In this sense, decrees of the Assembly and laws to do with taxation and trade passed in the fourth century by *nomothetai* are similar in form.

[3] The question can be framed in the terms discussed by Stinchcombe 2001: Athenian laws and decrees are "formalities" that appear to have worked well. Yet Athenian formalities worked well because they were undergirded, not only by other legal formalities, but by a set of informal but predictable social behaviors. See, further, chapter 7.

[4] Modern political science literature on institutional interaction in stable representative democracies tends to focus on strategic action by institutional actors; see chapter 3. The

cols was possible because the diverse individuals who manned government offices shared a substantial body of relevant social knowledge. Athenian legal, political, and religious institutions effectively publicized shared commitments, shared social values, and simple procedural rules.

Coordinating the behavior of multiple actors, so that each acts cooperatively in order to arrive at a commonly intended goal, has been a problem for human communities across scales and across time. Coordination among the members of a cooperating group was highly valued but difficult to achieve in the competitive culture of the Greek polis. In a famous poem (F 16 West) Sappho describes a debate over "the most beautiful thing":

> Some say a host of horsemen is the most beautiful thing
> on the black earth, some say a host of foot-soldiers,
> some, a fleet of ships; but I say it is
> whatever one loves.

Each of Sappho's imagined interlocutors proposes a military formation as a candidate for "the most beautiful"—a body of men and equipment whose extraordinary beauty inheres in their coordinated movement. But military movements typically require command and control. Hierarchical forms of coordination depend on the multiplication of formal protocols, which in turn rewards specialized expertise in protocol management, promotes the growth of bureaucracy, and leads inevitably to Michels' conclusion that democracy is impossible in the face of the demands of organization. In this chapter we trace the problem of aligning the knowledge on which individual choices were made by reference to several mechanisms promoting accurate following. In each case, individuals have rational reasons to cooperate; they share a preference for certain mutually beneficial outcomes. None of these mechanisms requires formal authority for the players to achieve their jointly intended goal.

In the simplest mechanism, *first-choice following*, perfect coordination requires only that someone make a first move and that all others follow her lead in an alignment cascade. Imagine a round table, seating several diners. In front of each diner is a dinner plate. Equidistant between the dinner plates is a bread plate. Should each diner use the bread plate to his right or left? The diners are ignorant of the etiquette governing bread plate choice. Each wants use of a bread plate, but no one has *an ex ante* preference for the plate on his right or left. The problem is solved as soon as one diner (L) leads off by choosing the plate on her left. Observing her

---

absence of a developed "institutional identity" within Athenian bodies featuring short terms of service and high turnover was rightly emphasized by Gomme 1951.

choice, another diner (F^1) follows her lead by using the plate on his left, as do all other diners ($F^2 \ldots F^x$), who observe either the original leader or another diner's subsequent choice. This alignment cascade of accurate following provides each diner with a bread plate, and so the coordination problem is solved. Alignment is "once and for all" (at this party), and it works equally well at any scale.

Straightforward first-choice following assumes no special information on the part of the leader or knowledge held in common by the diners, and it demands no precommitments from them. First-choice following may contribute to common knowledge when, for example, "use the plate to your left" becomes established as a rule of social etiquette. But first-choice following is quite limited in its application because it can solve only fairly simple coordination problems.[5]

More complex forms of coordination, considered below, require one or more of the added features of informed leaders, common knowledge, and credible precommitments. In the *leader-following* mechanism employed by animal groups on the move, individuals accurately follow the lead of specially informed leaders of the moment, enabling the group to make better choices about direction of movement. In the *rule-following* mechanism that facilitates traffic flow, coordinated individual movements toward diverse goals follow from common knowledge of simple procedural rules. The *commitment-following* mechanism for mustering before battle requires credible precommitments from participants because the cost to each individual of cooperating, if others do not, is high.

Coordination of institutional action in the complex participatory democracy of Athens assimilated elements from each of these mechanisms. Once a policy decision had been made, members of the community (individuals, social groups, and formal institutions) acted so as to implement it. Coordinating their actions required formulating mutually compatible individual plans based on their knowledge of others' likely behavior. They coordinated their behavior by learning a substantial body of common knowledge, following informed leaders, mastering a set of simple procedural rules, and accepting the credibility of others' precommitments. Publicity made relevant knowledge commonly available for uptake by the socially diverse community; Athenian media included public monuments and communal rituals. The architectural form of public buildings and spaces allowed for public gatherings at multiple scales. Intervisibility

---

[5] It also allows for strategic planning which might favor those whose turn to move comes later in a series. This may be one reason that the order of tribal teams on the Council was determined by nine separate lotteries, rather than one "first chance following" lottery at the beginning of the year. See Rhodes 1985: 19–20.

among participants fostered the growth of politically relevant common knowledge. The relationships among the coordination mechanisms and media discussed in this chapter are schematically illustrated in figure 5.1.

Following Leaders, Rules, and Commitments

Following Informed Leaders

In the simple case of first-choice following, the leader need not be specially informed, because the menu of choices is binary, and either choice results in an equally good once-and-for-all outcome. When the choice of possible directions of movement is large and subject to change, and when different movement choices will result in better or worse outcomes, following an uninformed leader is likely to turn out badly. By contrast, following an informed leader allows for good outcomes. It is commonly taken for granted that centralized command is the prerequisite for this sort of "complex informed-leader following," and thus the well-coordinated organization is often assumed to require a dominance hierarchy. Accurate following by followers of the leader's commands in an established hierarchy with a clear authority structure undoubtedly explains many sorts of organized human activity. As we saw in chapter 3, economists and organizational theorists have emphasized the productivity advantages that hierarchies seem to enjoy because of their capacity to coordinate activity of many individuals over time and space, through processes of command and control. Yet, as F. A. Hayek points out (chapter 1), central control can, under the right conditions, be trumped by free-choice mechanisms that efficiently capture widely dispersed knowledge.[6]

In Athens there was no identifiable command structure, no clear dominance hierarchy among citizens, and no one individual was designated as overall leader. In the case of coordination as accurately following a leader in a given direction, who should Athenian F^1 (and thus $F^2 \ldots F^x$) choose to follow? As we have seen (chapter 4), the success of the Athenian system of democratic governance was predicated upon a process of knowledge aggregation, and that process frequently focused on group deliberations, for example by tribal teams of fifty on the Council of 500 and by magisterial boards of ten. Deliberative aggregation processes allowed for "informed leaders of the moment" to take an important role in the decision-making process. The next question is: How, without resort to command and control, dominance hierarchy, or authoritative leaders, did the Athe-

---

[6] I owe thanks for discussion of the phenomenon of coordination of accurate following to Julio Rotemberg, who studies the phenomenon of price leadership among firms under conditions of asymmetrical information.

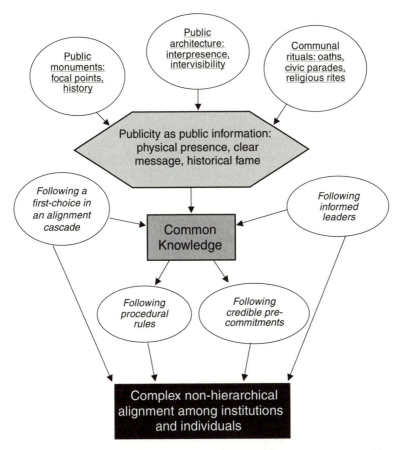

Figure 5.1. Schematic representation of Athenian alignment process: <u>publicity media</u> for building common knowledge and *alignment mechanisms*.

nians move from decision to implementation, from approving plans to carrying them out? Experimental work concerning "animal groups on the move" helps to provide an answer.

The general problem of how the actions of a large group of individuals could be closely coordinated in the absence of dominant leaders long bedeviled students of animal behavior; obvious examples include flocks of birds and schools of fish. The problem was solved by a simple algorithm: each of the group's members has an inherent preference for maintaining a certain proximity to other members of the group (e.g., "no less than one body length and no more than two"), has no background preference for moving in any given direction, and will follow the lead of individuals who manifest behaviors associated with being specially informed. The algorithm makes possible large-scale alignment cascades of accurate and complex following: the seemingly magical effect of a school of fish or flock of birds quickly changing direction en masse. Each movement of the school is determined by the actions of a few individuals who have formed movement preferences on the basis of happening to be informed, for example by noticing the presence of food or predators, or having prior experience in migration. The larger the group, the smaller is the percentage of its numbers required to generate a coordinated movement of the whole.[7]

Like most buyers and sellers in a market, most fish in the school remain ignorant about *who* in the group has special information and *why* those near them in the school are suddenly headed one way rather than the other—they simply follow accurately and they are likely to benefit accordingly. Leadership shifts readily, depending on which individuals happen to "know" something useful. In cases where the actions of multiple sets of informed individuals simultaneously present the group with different movement options, consensus follows from plurality: the largest subset of informed subjects "wins" in that the school follows them. If the number of informed individuals headed in different directions is similar, the consensus decision of the group (and thus its direction of movement) is based on *quality* of information. In this case the informed subset that determines the group's movement is the one exhibiting the least error in its directional movement—that is, manifesting the best internal coordination.[8]

[7] Couzin et al. 2005, and Klarreich 2006. For example, a few fish, randomly finding themselves at the outer edge of the school, happen to detect the presence of either food or a predator. Those individuals develop preferences on the basis of that information and act accordingly—swimming toward food or away from predators. The other members of the school act on their algorithmic preference for maintaining a standard proximity to one another. And so the entire group accurately follows the lead of individuals who have indicated, by their change of direction, that they have formed a movement preference. Folk theories of coordination among large groups of animals assume "group mindedness," seeing schools of fish, etc., as quasi-organisms; the folk theory is charmingly set out by Steinbeck and Ricketts 1976 [1941]. In fact, all genetically unique (i.e., not clones) group-dwelling animals face coordination problems. The group is composed of multiple individuals, each seeking its own good (at least in terms of its reproductive chances). Yet each individual's chances for success depends directly on its membership in a group capable of accurately coordinating its actions.

[8] Couzin et al. 2005: 515 conclude: "Efficient transfer of information, and decision-making, can occur within animal groups in the absence of explicit signals or complex mechanisms for information transfer. This means that informed and naïve individuals do not have to be able to recognize each other and that leadership can emerge as a function of information differences among members of a population, and [leadership] is therefore transferable. No inherent differences between individuals (such as dominance due to large body size) need be invoked to explain leadership, although these properties can also influence group motion. Furthermore, the mechanism of coordination . . . requires only limited cognitive ability, and demonstrates that individuals can respond spontaneously to those that have information."

The algorithm governing animal group movements obviously cannot be applied mechanically to choice making in human groups. Yet it does have implications for democratic coordination in that it demonstrates that complex leader-following can be based on leaders possessing useful information rather than positions of dominance. It refutes the notion that complex following requires *established* leaders.

FOLLOWING PROCEDURAL RULES

Driving on the right (or the left) side of the road is a familiar example of rational cooperation. As in the leader-following case, there is relatively little concern about defection. If a driver violates the procedural right-side driving rule, it is likely to be the result of a mistake rather than an attempt to cheat; other drivers point out the error by honking and shouting. Each driver has a rational interest in cooperating with the right-side rule because coordinated collective action optimizes the chance of a positive outcome for each driver: getting where each is headed as quickly as possible and with a minimum chance of traffic accidents. The right-hand driving rule is an example of first-choice following, but driving in traffic is a great deal more complex than using a bread plate. The complex coordination demanded by driving in traffic is achieved by adding other procedural rules, and by establishing common knowledge of those rules among drivers. Unlike the leader-following case, each individual can pursue the goal of arriving at a unique destination because the essential "following" function is rule based, not leader based.

Driving in traffic does not require dominant leaders or the steady intervention of command authority, but it does require that the road system be rationally planned and that drivers all master a standard set of procedural rules about allowable speeds of movement, conditions for yielding right of way, and so on. Traffic rules are relatively simple, so most competent adults can learn them quickly and their use becomes second nature through practice and habit: driving in traffic demands no special expertise.[9] Driving rules produce coordination because they are a matter of common knowledge among drivers. The steady flow of traffic (merging, exiting, lane-changing, and so on) assumes not only that each driver knows the rules, and that each (mostly) follows the rules in the absence of external policing, but also that each driver knows that others also know the rules. When drivers share common knowledge of the rules, the behavior of drivers is predictable (up to a point), and traffic can flow relatively smoothly. If all do share common knowledge of the rules, and if the road

---

[9] In ordinary English usage we signal our attachment to a norm of cooperation among drivers by generically designating crashes as "traffic accidents": the unintended result of error rather than a result of someone's deliberate defection from the rules.

system is well designed, we each get where we are going with minimum of bother. Athenian institutions were characterized by clear and simple procedural rules. Those rules became a matter of common knowledge among Athenians through mechanisms of publicity that we will explore in more detail below.

FOLLOWING PRECOMMITMENTS

In the case of driving in traffic, rule following is obviously mutually advantageous and serious defections are relatively rare because the benefits to individuals of obeying the rules are high and the costs are low. In choice-making situations where the costs are potentially much higher, mechanisms to ensure credibility in respect to precommitment are required. This is especially the case in situations in which cooperative behavior entails risks that are inversely proportional to the number of expected participants. Suppose that polis A(ttacker) invades polis D(e-fender).[10] If only a few hoplites from D muster, each man's chances of being killed increase dramatically. Each D hoplite will muster *only* if he supposes that enough others will muster too. Adequate numbers will muster if D's hoplites share certain knowledge in common: each hoplite believes that it is important to oppose the enemy and therefore is willing to muster if others will, too. But a successful muster requires more than a widely held belief that the enemy should be opposed. It also requires that *the fact that the belief is widely held is also widely known.* That is to say, the successful muster will take place if and only if each hoplite knows that the others believe the enemy must be opposed and so intend to muster—and if he in turn knows that they all know the same thing about him, and so on.[11]

If each of D's hoplites held the same belief (the enemy should be opposed) but there was no common knowledge regarding that belief, each hoplite would have no reason to suppose that there would be a large-scale muster. As a result, each would imagine that he would face greatly increased personal risks should he choose to muster. The outcome is that relatively few would be rationally willing to assume the risk. As a result, the muster would fail and polis A's invasion force would not be opposed—even though all of D's hoplites privately believed that the enemy

---

[10] Stipulate that A and D are roughly equivalent in potential military capacity. A is attacking with a large force that will require a similarly large force to repel. Given the defender's advantages in hoplite warfare (shorter lines of communication and supply, knowledge of terrain), if D fields a force equivalent to that of A, there is a high probability that the invading force will be repelled.

[11] On the role of common knowledge in solving this kind of problem, see, further, Chwe 2001, with discussion below. On precommitment, see Elster 1985, 2000.

should be opposed. The *lack* of common knowledge, resulting from a failure of publicity in respect to preferences and commitments, can therefore be fatal to the capacity of a community to act in a coordinated fashion to gain ends that all believe to be desirable and that are in fact achievable. This phenomenon helps to explain, for example, the survival of widely despised autocrats, just as the sudden emergence of common knowledge can help explain their sudden overthrow.[12]

Polis A will be more likely to invade if A believes that the residents of D are not committed to opposing an invasion. If D is not committed to resist, the benefits of invasion will come to A at a low cost. But if D is committed to resistance, and if A knows that the costs of invasion will be high and its chances of success will be low, then A's decision makers are less likely to regard invasion as feasible. D may therefore achieve the desired outcome of deterring an invasion by committing to resistance: by effectively publicizing the preferences and commitments of the hoplites of D. That commitment must, however, be credible to A. As in the case of the internal coordination problem of the muster, coordination between states based on credible commitment requires *publicity* of that commitment: D must find a way to publicize its commitment to resist to the decision makers of A.[13] Suppose A is an Athenian-type democracy, and thus that A's decision-making body is a large and diverse citizenry. The publicity by which D advertises its commitment must in this case be of a sort that can gain the attention of that large and diverse citizenry. Limiting publicity to private communication among a handful of elite foreign policy experts is more likely to fail in achieving interstate coordination if one or more of the states involved is a participatory democracy.

In sum, D must find a way to build common knowledge among its hoplites and then publicize the fact of that knowledge. If A and D are both democracies, the citizens of A must come to share the knowledge common to the citizens of D. When the A citizens know that the D citizens share common knowledge that D's soldiers are committed to fight, and D's citizens know that A's citizens know, and A's citizens know that D's citizens know, and so on—then D's commitment is genuinely credible. Under these circumstances, A and D may find that they are able to coordinate their foreign policies so that disastrous conflicts are avoided. Al-

---

[12] Kuran 1991: example of the East European revolutions of 1989.

[13] This point is memorably captured in Stanley Kubrick's black comedy masterpiece, *Dr. Strangelove*. The Soviet government has bound itself to massive nuclear retaliation by creating a Doomsday Machine that automatically launches missiles in response to an American first strike. The title character addresses the Soviet ambassador, "Of course, the whole point of a Doomsday Machine is lost, if you keep it a secret! Why didn't you tell the world, *eh*?" The embarrassed answer: "It was to be announced at the Party Congress on Monday. As you know, the Premier loves surprises."

though, in practice, this sort of interstate coordination sometimes failed (e.g., in the case of the Athenian invasion of Sicily in 415), postulating an interstate "publicity regime" may help to explain why, especially in the era before the Peloponnesian War, inter-polis conflict, while frequent, was often limited to contesting marginal borderlands. Postulating an inter-polis publicity regime would help to explain why Greek warfare was not even more destructive than it was and how the approximately one thousand state equilibrium of the extended Greek city-state culture was maintained.[14]

The continued prevalence of Greek inter-polis warfare, along with the forms of military organization that had crystallized by the sixth century B.C., rewarded high levels of cooperation among a state's inhabitants, effective coordination of their efforts, and publicity rendering their commitments credible to one another and to residents of other states. Sparta's superiority in hoplite engagements was long predicated on the Spartans' superior capacity to bring a large body of highly trained men to the field of battle. It is not coincidental that Spartan culture was profoundly devoted to two goals. The first was to instill such deep common knowledge among its soldiers about proper behavior that non-compliance was not a viable option for individual Spartans. Next was publicizing abroad, throughout the Greek world and beyond, the Spartan commitment to military effort. The well-known epigrams commemorating the three hundred Spartans who died at Thermopylae in obedience to their law (Herodotus 7.227) exemplify both goals.[15] Sparta was an extreme, but not a unique case. Archaic and classical Greek social norms—sustained by public rituals (e.g., parades), incentives (pay, honors), and sanctions (disesteem, formal loss of status)—publicized the propriety of mustering for men of the hoplite class as a matter of common knowledge. Individual poleis actively publicized their commitment to fight—for example, by setting up victory monuments, by publicly honoring heroic warriors, and by sponsoring public rituals in which young men were inducted into the warrior's life.[16]

The military oath, sworn (at least in the later fourth century, and probably much earlier) by the Athenian *ephebes* (youngest year-classes of

[14] For the limited destructiveness and limited goals of much traditional Greek warfare, see Connor 1988; Ober 1996, chapter 5. Krentz 2002 argues for higher rates of casualties but focuses on the well-documented major conflicts that I suppose limited coordination among poleis ordinarily prevented.

[15] On the Spartan system of military education and Spartan publicity of its own prowess, see Tigerstedt 1965; Cartledge 2001:79–90; Ducat 2006.

[16] On Greek rituals and rhetoric associated with *andreia* (manly courage), see Rosen and Sluiter 2003; Balot 2004; Roisman 2005. On the conflict in democratic Athens between those social values and the rational desire to survive, see Christ 2006, chapters 2 and 3.

Athenian soldiers), is a publicity medium that neatly catches the spirit of "if I know you all will fight, then I will too." Each young soldier swore a sacred oath (witnessed by various divinities) that he would fight for his homeland, "as far as is in my own power and together with all my comrades." The public act of oath taking helped to make each young soldier's commitment to fight a matter of common knowledge. At the same time, the willful act of binding himself to a particular course of future action by the act of oath taking helped to render credible the commitment to fight of each soldier—and thus of the Athenian youth as a body. Even in the face of the high risks and potentially high costs associated with Greek hoplite battle, the ephebes themselves, the rest of the Athenians, and Athens' rivals, were all given reason to believe that the ephebes' commitment was credible. Participation in the ritual of oath taking, along with its explicit commitment guarantee, built common knowledge among the ephebes that made each ephebe's decision to muster when called up a more rational one. Common knowledge and credible precommitments are thus central and intertwined aspects of oath taking, which was a common feature of Greek, and especially democratic Athenian, public culture.[17]

CASCADING AND SOCIAL EQUILIBRIUM

Designers of Greek political institutions confronted the question of how to promote alignment in political as well as military practices. Command and control by a dominant central authority (as in Persia, under the Great King), and strong forms of ideology (as in Sparta, under the "Laws of Lycurgus"), were two possible approaches. But those solutions were not available to a participatory democracy. Thucydides' Pericles claimed (2.35–46) that Athens rejected Spartan-style hypersocialization and relied instead on choices freely made by free citizens to gain its public ends. The Athenians were able to achieve high levels of coordination among individuals and institutions by intermixing the four mechanisms discussed above for facilitating accurate following: first-choice, informed leader, procedural rules, and credible commitments. While all Athenian formal institutions (including the Council and Assembly) relied on an array of mechanisms for sustaining complex coordination, the Athenian People's Courts provide a particularly good example.

[17] Oath of the ephebes: RO 88. Date: Siewert 1977. Civic psychology: Farenga 2006. Prevalence of public oath taking in Athens: Mirhady 1991; Cole 1996. Survey of uses of oaths in Greek culture: Sommerstein 2007. Lysias (2.62) and Sophocles Fragment 144 (and Christ 2001: 407) underline the essential value of military oaths. For attempts by modern

Jurors and presiding magistrates were assigned to courts by lottery, eventually through the use of a sophisticated allotment machine (*klērōtē-rion*) that sped up the selection process through a variation on the first-choice mechanism. Jurors were publicly precommitted by their juror's oath to follow the procedural rules of Athenian law. Athenian litigants often portrayed themselves as specially informed and made frequent reference to items of common knowledge in building their arguments. Speeches were heard by large audiences, and subsequently publicized through the circulation of written texts. Athens' repertoire of common knowledge was, therefore, extended and deepened through legal practice. Athenian legal rhetoric demanded constant innovation in the invention and presentation of arguments. It depended upon speakers and audiences alike having learned an extensive body of technical and social knowledge. As such, legal rhetoric exemplifies the innovation/learning dynamic that, so I have argued, was the motor driving democratic Athenian performance. Finally, trade-offs between alignment and resistance to alignment, in the people's courts as in other decision-making assemblies, contributed to Athens' non-hierarchical epistemic equilibrium while sustaining its social equilibrium.[18]

Athenian popular government was sustained by the facility with which the community aligned itself in cascades of accurate following at appropriate times. For example, the Athenian Assembly annually passed a great number of decrees, many of them concerning routine matters. Given the limited time available for meetings, many decrees were necessarily passed by consensus; the members of the Assembly must frequently have accurately followed the lead of informed individuals by allowing recommendations (*probouleumata*) of the Council to pass without dissent. Cascading on non-controversial matters allowed for the time-consuming process of aggregating diverse information before making hard decisions.[19]

American educators to employ variants of the Athenian ephebic oath for nationalistic common-knowledge building, see Hedrick 2004.

[18] Allotment machine (*klērōtērion*): [Aristotle] *Ath. Pol.* 64.1–3, 66.1 with commentary of Rhodes 1981. Changing mechanisms of allotment of jurors to courts: Kroll 1972. Jurors' oath: below, note 30. Litigants' self-portrayal: Hall 1995. Proceduralism of Athenian law: Todd 1993, and comments of Carey 1998. For a fuller discussion of how Athenian public rhetoric exemplifies temporary leadership, and employs innovation and learning, see Ober 1989. On Athenian trial procedure and practice, see further, Christ 1990; Johnstone 1999; Lanni 2006.

[19] M. H. Hansen 1999: 139–40, 149 discusses concrete motions proposed by the Council as *probouleumata* and passed by consensus in the Assembly through *procheirontonia*. Bikchandani, Hirshleifer, and Welch 1992 develop a general theory of informational cascades and their social effects; Kuran 1991, 1995 discusses cascades in political contexts; Lohmann 2000 reviews the literature on informational cascades and common knowledge. These studies do not address the possibility of formal institutions designed to promote and control cascades.

Cascading at the wrong time was counterproductive. Common knowledge, in the form of "groupthink," would corrupt the decision-making process if it prevented diverse perspectives from being considered *during* deliberations on difficult matters. But *following* the policy decision, common knowledge was a valuable epistemic asset because it offered individuals reasons to act cooperatively on a shared commitment to a chosen course of action. Common knowledge of simple procedural rules and historical precedents, along with the credible commitments that emerged when key actors willingly bound themselves to a future course of possibly costly action, allowed each Athenian to cooperate in the implementation of innovative plans of action in the reasonable expectation that others' actions would be in accord with their own.

In classical Athens, credible precommitments and a repertoire of common knowledge facilitated complex coordination. The process was, however, complicated by the fact of social diversity. Although Athenians shared some core preferences in respect to outcomes, substantial differences remained. This meant that some alignment cascades not only would block access to useful knowledge, but would be socially disruptive. A popular leader might, for example, seek to precipitate a cascade of accurate following among the poorer majority of Athenians in the direction of overturning established rules regarding property rights. Alternatively, he might seek an alignment cascade of the propertied majority in the direction of excluding the poorest Athenians from participation rights. This is, of course, the "tyranny of the majority" problem that so concerned Tocqueville and other critics of participatory democracy.

Resistance to cascading in Athenian law courts protected the Athenian social equilibrium. The individual juror's stubborn unwillingness to follow the lead of even very prominent litigants was an essential epistemic bastion of the Athenian social order. Athenian courtroom procedure, which ensured the equal number of jurors from each of the ten tribes and protected the secrecy of individual votes, made alignment cascades more difficult to produce in legal settings, especially when fundamental values were in conflict.[20]

Athenians were intensely aware of the endemic tension between ordinary citizens and elites. Social elites (i.e., persons distinguished for their education, wealth, and status) tended to seek positions of political domi-

---

[20] Unlike Assembly voting, which was ordinarily by show of hands, voting in the People's Courts was by secret ballot. Had judicial cascades been common in actual Athenian legal (as opposed to legislative) practice, prosecutors would frequently have been subject to the penalties associated with failing to secure 20 percent of the votes. Yet arguably the fear of a cascade discouraged weak prosecutions and led defendants with weak cases to settle out of court or, like Hipparchus (below, this chapter), leave the city before trial.

nance. While some elites favored the establishment of a hierarchical social and political order in which dominant positions would be permanent and exclusive, resisting local elite dominance was a settled preference of most non-elite Athenian citizens. Plato's characters Thrasymachus (in the *Republic*) and Callicles (in the *Gorgias*) express sophisticated versions of commonly held Athenian views when they describe democracy as a coordinated response of the individually weak "many" aimed at preventing the dominance of a few would-be rulers. Meanwhile, at least some non-elite Athenians would have preferred to appropriate the property of the wealthy by employing the legal and legislative apparatus of democratic government to fine them heavily for petty infractions and to tax them at a high level. If elite Athenians acted on their desire for domination, or if the majority of Athenians acted on their desire to appropriate the property of the elite minority, the Athenian socioeconomic equilibrium would be destabilized.[21]

The emergence and persistence of a dynamic equilibrium in which elite and non-elite preferences were balanced, such that the regime was stable and Athenian productive capacity was sustained, underwrote the success of Athenian government by the people. Within that equilibrium position, informed individuals—for example, Assembly speakers like Themistocles in the debates leading to the Athenian decision to fight at Salamis in 480 (chapter 2, era IV)—were able to assume leadership roles by advocating and carrying through innovative policies. Meanwhile, new procedural rules and mechanisms for making individual and institutional commitments credible were devised and implemented. The legal system played a key role in building useful social knowledge and publicizing commitments, but also in regulating the system by offering reasonable safeguards against socially disruptive cascades of accurate following. Those safeguards were strengthened in the fourth century B.C.

The crisis of the late fifth century (era VIII) saw a short-term collapse of democratic institutions, disruption of the Athenian social equilibrium, and a corresponding decline in productive capacity. In the aftermath of the crisis, new and reaffirmed institutional mechanisms—the distinction between law and decree, an amnesty oath, the oath of magistrates to respect private property, and a series of legislative initiatives aimed at rendering the tax burdens on wealthy Athenians more equitable—buttressed the credibility of the commitment of diverse social groups to a cooperative order in which the interests of both elites and non-elite Athenians would be protected and advanced. Meanwhile, Athenian democratic institutions multiplied opportunities for each citizen to learn, over the course of his

---

[21] This line of argument is developed in detail in Ober 1989, 1998.

lifetime, a substantial and complex body of socially valuable common knowledge and to make and to accept binding social commitments.

Close reading of a legal case illustrates the role of Athenian institutions in building and publicizing credible commitments and common knowledge. It also reveals the dynamic tension between the goals of aligning knowledge in order to promote state security and committing to rules that sustained the social equilibrium.

A Trial for Treason, 330 b.c.

In 330 b.c. the Athenian statesman Lycurgus unsuccessfully prosecuted an Athenian trader named Leocrates on charges of treasonously leaving Athens when he ought to have remained to help defend the city. Lycurgus was a prominent Athenian politician, an expert in public finance, holder of important electoral offices, sponsor of major public buildings, and subsequently honored by his compatriots for his services to the polis. Leocrates is otherwise unknown; he was certainly not politically prominent. Litigants in major Athenian trials spoke at length before large audiences. Athenian legal conventions offered them considerable, although not infinite, scope for developing lines of argument that may appear tangential to the case. Lycurgus' only surviving courtroom speech is rhetorically distinctive in a number of ways (Allen 2000a). For our purposes it is valuable in its detailed exploration of democratic joint action and its focus on the material and ideological resources that the democratic polis made available to its citizens for identifying and addressing public-action problems.[22]

Lycurgus' speech concentrates on two commitment equilibria, each of which depended on alignment based on common knowledge. The first is the commitment of the citizenry to undertake the sacrifices necessary to secure polis security as evidenced by their actions in the immediate aftermath of Athens' military defeat at Chaeronea. Lycurgus characterizes the security of polis in the period after the battle of Chaeronea as a common pool resource—a valued possession, collectively owned by the citizenry. As such it was vulnerable to a commons tragedy if self-interested individuals took more from the pool than they gave back to it. The second equilibrium is the citizens' commitment to enforcing legal sanctions against individuals whose behavior threatened the first equilibrium. These two equilibria are linked: Lycurgus argues that each citizen's commitment to saving the state must be credible to Athenians and outsiders alike, and

---

[22] Lycurgus and his speech (1 *Against Leocrates*): Humphreys 1985 (political biography); Hintzen-Bohlen 1997 (cultural and building programs); Mossé 2007 [1989]: 181–88 (policies realistically address the present environment as well as being nostalgic); Allen 2000a

that the community must make its commitment to sanction deviant behavior credible to internal and external audiences in order for security to
be preserved.[23]

Because the legal issue of whether Leocrates had actually broken the
law by leaving Athens in 338 remained in doubt, Lycurgus' strategy in
the speech was to seek a cascade of following based on these two equilibria. He emphasizes that the jurors' decision would signal their belief
in one of two states of affairs. If they overwhelmingly found Leocrates
guilty, this would signal that security was a commonly held Athenian preference, and that the legal sanctions that sustained it were (like driving in
traffic) based on rational coordination around shared interests. In this
case, the jurors would show that they regarded Leocrates, like a willful
left-side driver in a right-side driving system, as dangerously aberrant.
Acquitting Leocrates, he implies, would, by contrast, signal that the jurors
regarded Leocrates' choice to leave the city as rational and comprehensi-
ble, and so would reveal Athens as endemically vulnerable to collective-
action problems.

At the end of the day, a third equilibrium, the jurors' oath-bound commitment to judge on the basis of the law, evidently trumped Lycurgus'
rhetorical gambit for precipitating a cascade among the jurors. After the
speeches of prosecution and defense, when the jurors cast their ballots the
count was evenly split: 250 each for prosecutor and defendant. Leocrates
was therefore acquitted (Aeschines 3.252).

Lycurgus' failure to gain a conviction points to a rule-following aspect
of Athenian joint action: if the social equilibrium that underpinned the
democracy were to be sustained, the jurors, each of whom had sworn an
oath to judge according to the law and according to justice when the
law was silent, must appear to be committed to taking the established
laws seriously (Johnstone 1999). Athenian jurors had very considerable
discretion in respect to judgment (Lanni 2006). Emotion, equity, and the
reputations of litigants were relevant aspects of Athenian legal judgment
(Allen 2000b). Yet if juries manifested no commitment to the law as a
limit on the scope of judicial discretion, elite defendants, faced with politically ambitious prosecutors and juries dominated by non-elite citizens,
would have little incentive to continue playing the game. Although we

---

(rhetorical analysis of the speech). For a recent translation of the speech (with a brief introduction), see Worthington, Cooper, and Harris 2001.

[23] Credible commitment issues in Athenian lawmaking: Schwartzberg 2004, 2007. The
historical importance of credible commitments for democracies: North and Weingast 1989;
Bates et al. 1998; Schultz and Weingast 2003; Haber, Mauer, and Razo 2003; Stasavage
2003. Gürerk, Irlenbusch, and Rockenbach 2006 emphasize the essential role of sanctioning
institutions in the evolution of viable societies.

obviously cannot know the motives of those jurors who voted guilty and not-guilty in the trial of Leocrates, both the *content* of Lycurgus' speech and the *outcome* of the trial underline the delicate balance between the competing social goods of enhanced coordination and the preservation of a social equilibrium that was predicated upon a credible commitment to legal rules.

Lycurgus claimed that Leocrates had chosen to abandon the city at a historical moment, some eight years before, when coordinated cooperation among the residents of Athens had been imperative. Leocrates was charged with having disobeyed a law against abandoning Athens immediately following Athens' defeat at the battle of Chaeronea in 338. In response to the battlefield defeat, according to Lycurgus (1.16), "all of you [citizens] quickly foregathered in Assembly," and passed emergency legislation for the defense of the polis. That legislation included a decree forbidding Athenians to leave the territory of Attica; the wording of the decree apparently extended the definition of treason to include the act of "fleeing from risk on behalf of [one's] country."[24] The key question remained: Had Leocrates left Athens before the decree was passed? Lycurgus' inability to demonstrate that fact is the key weakness of his case. Leocrates seems not to have been enrolled as a hoplite, serving as a magistrate, or otherwise under oath to perform a specific public service. Under ordinary conditions (i.e., before the emergency decree requiring all Athenians to remain) he would be free to come and go from Athenian territory as he pleased. Lycurgus' argumentative strategy centered on the publicity value of punishing a defector, even if Leocrates' defection had been a lapse of moral responsibility rather than a breach of his legal duty.

Throughout his speech, Lycurgus emphasizes the vital importance of voluntarily cooperative effort on the part of the citizenry. He claims that the moment of crisis, after the battle had been lost and the Macedonians appeared poised to invade Athenian territory, "every citizen" experienced terrible personal misfortunes (1.41). Yet the response of the residents of the polis was an alignment cascade of coordinated action for the common good (1.44): men of every age volunteered for service. "Some charged themselves (*epemelountō*) with the task of building walls, others of making trenches and palisades. No one in the polis was idle." In Lycurgus' rhetoric, even inanimate objects become willful and cooperative agents (1.44): the land gave up its trees for palisades; the dead gave up their tombstones for walls; and the temples gave up arms and armor dedicated to the gods. Surrounded by this intense yet orderly flow of cooperative activity, Leocrates nonetheless chose to ignore both the commands of the

---

[24] See MacDowell 1978: 178–79, 185, citing a fragment of Theophrastus' *Laws* (= Pollux 8.52; *Lexicon Rhetoricum Cantabrigiense* s.v. *eisangelia*).

elected generals and the lead of his fellow citizens. He gathered his possessions, quietly slipped out a postern gate, and sailed away to Rhodes
(1.17). According to Lycurgus, Leocrates' actions did not go unob-
served—his choice to leave the city was noted at the time by his neighbors
(1.19) and his abandonment of Athens became notorious throughout
Greece—especially because they contrasted so strikingly with the reputation of the Athenians' ancestors for ambitious patriotism (1.14).

Throughout the speech of prosecution, Lycurgus contrasts Leocrates'
defection with the coordinated efforts and sacrifices cooperatively undertaken by all other Athenians. He emphasizes the importance of each citizen's personal choices to polis security as a common pool resource: Athens' overall safety had rested with Leocrates because "the polis is a
possession secured (*oikeitai*) through each person's individual share (*idia
moira*) in guarding it" (1.64). Leocrates rests his case for the necessity of
severely punishing (death or exile according to Aeschines 3.252) a mis-
deed some eight years past squarely on the value of credible commitments.
In order for the treason law to be an effective deterrent against the other-
wise-favored choice of defection in the face of great risk, there must be a
commitment on the part of the entire polis to punish those who defected
from the cooperative regime of shared risk taking in a time of common
danger. In order for that commitment to be credible, it must be a matter
of common knowledge among the citizens. Leocrates' departure further
endangered the city because it undermined common knowledge among
other Greeks regarding the patriotic Athenian commitment to defending
their territory.

The core of Lycurgus' argument for punishing Leocrates is that the
habit of cooperation was the foundation of Athens' military security.
Maintaining that habit as an equilibrium required punishment of defectors. If the Athenian commitment to severely sanctioning acts of defection
is not credible, other individual Athenians might choose the obvious
course of ensuring their own safety in times of crisis, leading quickly to a
commons tragedy. Moreover, absent a credible Athenian commitment to
punishing defectors, rival powers would not regard Athenian military
preparations as a credible deterrent to aggression. Notably, Lycurgus emphasizes that punishment of Leocrates would serve to educate the youth
of Athens in proper behavior (1.9–10) *and* that the trial is being closely
watched by other Greeks (1.14–15).

The necessity of preserving credible commitments to preserve a common pool resource is closely entwined in Lycurgus' speech with an argument for the instrumental value of common knowledge. The role of publicity in maintaining the capacity of the democratic constitutional order
to achieve coordinated action among an extensive citizenry and the reciprocal role of Athenian institutions in publicizing relevant information are

recurrent themes in Lycurgus' speech. As part of a series of historical digressions, meant to show that punishing Leocrates would be consistent with the polis' honorable traditions, Lycurgus (1.117–19) tells the following story about a prominent Athenian of the early fifth century B.C. who fled the city rather than face trial:

> When Hipparchus, the son of Charmus, did not stand his trial for treason before the people but let the case go by default, they [the Athenians] sentenced him to death. Then, as they did not secure his person to answer for the crime, they took down his statue from the Acropolis and, melting it down, made a stele of it, on which they decreed that the names of wrongdoers and traitors should be inscribed. Hipparchus himself has his name recorded on this stele and all other traitors too.

Lycurgus then directs the clerk of the court to read, first, "the public decree (*psēphisma*) which authorized the statue of Hipparchus to be taken down from the Acropolis and then [read] the inscription at the base of the stele and the names of the traitors later engraved upon it." After the documents had been read in court, Lycurgus poses a hypothetical question of the jurors: "What is your impression of them [the Athenians who punished Hipparchus], gentlemen? Had they the same [presumptively overlenient] attitude as yourselves towards wrongdoers? Or did they, by obliterating the memorial (*mnēmeion*) of the traitor, since they could not command his person, punish him with all the means at their disposal?" Lycurgus concludes this section of his speech with an explanation of public intention: "The simple fact of melting down the bronze statue was not enough for them; they wished to leave to their successors a lasting example (*paradeigma*) of their attitude to traitors." That is to say, they sought to publicize the matter, both at the time and for the benefit of future generations.

Lycurgus is our only source for this story about Hipparchus, who was, however, famous as the first man to be ostracized. The trial on charges of treason must have been held some time after Hipparchus' ostracism in 488/7 B.C. Assuming Lycurgus has got his history right, it should date to around the time of the Persian wars. Lycurgus' account of the origins of the traitors' stele points to the importance of prominent monuments in the democratic state's "public economy of esteem" and highlights the Athenian demos' role in authorizing public monuments.[25]

---

[25] Hipparchus, a relation of the Pisistratids, was the first Athenian to be ostracized: [Aristotle] *Ath. Pol.* 22 and Plutarch *Nicias*. 11. On ostracism, see Forsdyke 2005 and above, chapter 4. Economy of esteem: Brennan and Pettit 2004.

The assemblymen, sitting as a treason court, condemned Hipparchus to death in absentia. Lycurgus emphasizes that they added to this unenforceable capital penalty a striking act of public dishonoring by taking down a bronze statue that Hipparchus had dedicated on the Acropolis, melting it, and recasting it as an inscribed stele. The entire process may have been carried out publicly in the Agora. The newly cast bronze stele was then set up at public expense with an inscription on its base explaining the nature of the list. At the head of the stele's roll call of infamy—as, presumably, upon the base of the original statue—Hipparchus' name appeared prominently. But now, rather than recording an honorable individual act of piety, his name headed up a group of wrongdoers and traitors. Anyone doubting the credibility of the Athenian commitment to punishing traitors would immediately have his doubts put to rest by a visit to the traitors' stele.[26]

The Athenian process of public dishonoring as described by Lycurgus is reminiscent of the well-known Roman practice of *damnatio memoriae*. Yet in the Athenian case the destruction of a statue of a condemned individual does not entail the *erasure* of the miscreant's name on public monuments, but the *erection* of a monument intended to keep his name in public memory. The traitors' stele is not an aberration: the "Attic stelai," famous in classical antiquity, were set up in the Agora to publicize the sale of the confiscated property of Alcibiades and others who had profaned the Eleusinian mysteries in 415 B.C. Lycurgus' reference to the traitors' stele in his speech was not an erudite allusion to an archaic practice, but calls out a well-established punitive use of publicity by the democratic state.[27]

Lycurgus claims that the assemblymen specifically intended the reconfigured monument to be a model (*paradeigma*) for future generations: a public record of wrong individual action (treasonous defection), right joint action (punishment of a traitor), and essential political principle (credible commitment). In Lycurgus' account it is a concern with creating and sustaining common knowledge regarding credible commitment to sanction that is the thread that ties together the choices of two chronologically distinct speakers in the public interest: the anonymous prosecutor

[26] On the legal process of *eisangelia*, see M. H. Hansen 1975. On archaic bronze statuary, see Mattusch 1988; Osborne 1998. The stele, a rectangular inscribed slab which may be either of bronze (e.g., [Aristotle] *Ath. Pol.* 53.4, and Christ 2001: 410) or marble, was the standard medium for public inscriptions. There is evidence of bronze-casting operations on the slopes below the site of the Temple of Hephaistos, who was at once the mythical divine ancestor of the Athenians and the god of metallurgy and technological innovation. Mattusch 1982.

[27] For an enlightening treatment of *damnatio memoriae* in the later Roman empire, and its relationship to public memory, see Hedrick 2000. Attic stelai: Pritchett 1953, 1956; Furley 1996: 45–48.

of Hipparchus in the early fifth century B.C. and Lycurgus himself some 150 years later. The same concern ties together the Assembly's act of authorizing a private monument to be replaced with a public one, and the monument itself. Finally, common knowledge ties together various Athenian audiences, across time and space. The jurors listening to Lycurgus in an Athenian courtroom in 330 B.C., their ancestors sitting in the Assembly place a century and a half earlier, and the many visitors to the Acropolis who had noticed the stele in the years in between were imaginatively brought together, through Lycurgus' words, into a unified community of knowing. That imagined community shared knowledge about the iniquity of treason and the Athenian commitment to punishing traitors.

The result of calling to mind a unified diachronic community and its unifying common knowledge would be, Lycurgus hoped, the crystallization of a common conviction among the present jurors on the subject of how to respond to a wrongful act. He sought to take the role of informed leader of the moment who reminds the community of what it already tacitly knows, and thereby invites all to follow his lead in judging Leocrates' actions as requiring punishment. When it came time to vote on the defendant, each juror was meant to think and act on the basis of his common knowledge of the unflinching standard of righteous punishment set by the ancestral body that had condemned Hipparchus and set up the monument, and in concert with the many subsequent visitors to the monument, each of whom had, we are to suppose, been properly instructed by the ancestral model on the topic of right collective action in the face of the threat of defection.

Through his historical allusion to the traitors' stele and other public monuments and communal rituals, Lycurgus sought to establish the preconditions for an alignment cascade of accurate following on the part of the jurors. In this particular end, he failed. Yet, as suggested by the posthumous honors the Athenians later offered him for his role in promoting the prosperity of the polis (Hedrick 2000, noting the emphasis on accountability in the honoring decree), Lycurgus was generally successful as a democratic politician. The outcome of the trial of Leocrates demonstrates the salutary institutional limits on the power of Athenian leaders to persuade popular audiences that enforcing the law was a matter of solving a coordination problem, just as the content of Lycurgus' speech points to the role of informed leaders and their involvement with publicity mechanisms and media in making knowledge alignment a means of democratic policy implementation.

In the trial of Leocrates, despite their shared preference for maintaining the security of the state and their recognition of how sanctioning defection helped to maintain security, many of the jurors apparently remained unconvinced that Leocrates was actually guilty of breaking the law. If Leocrates had not broken the law, the cascade of accurate following sought by Lycurgus would have signaled a lack of commitment on the part of the jurors to the law and to their oath to judge according to the law. Multiplication of such violations would threaten the Athenian social equilibrium, which depended upon the credible commitment of non-elite jurors (who were invariably in the majority) to follow the established rules when casting their votes. Lycurgus' failure to precipitate a cascade points to the role of legal institutions in maintaining a robust social equilibrium, just as his appeal to the value of common knowledge and credible commitment to punish defection points to the role of legal speech in building a useful body of common knowledge that allowed for coordinated cascades in other public domains.[28]

COMMON KNOWLEDGE AND PUBLICITY

If the only goal of a legal system is determining the right answer to the question "Is X guilty or liable before the law?" alignment cascades and common knowledge must be regarded as unqualifiedly bad.[29] But, whereas some Athenian laws were very specific (chapter 6), other laws left much to the jurors' discretion (Lanni 2006). The Athenian juror swore his oath to follow the law where it was clear and to seek justice where it was not; there were no legal experts available to draw a bright line between clarity and its absence.[30] The goal of getting right answers to clear legal questions was an important role of the People's Courts, but they also served political functions. Ordinary courts decided on "constitutional" issues and could overturn legislation passed in the Assembly if it was considered to be in violation of the standing laws. Athenian courts were directly involved in time-sensitive implementation of policy (as in the dispatching decree) and had to render judgments promptly. From the perspective of overall organizational performance, arbitrary, unpredictable legal judgments were potentially more harmful than judgments that predictably aligned on shared values and common knowledge.

[28] On the equation of justice with procedural fairness in Greek culture and Athenian legal practice, see Ober 2005c. Tom R. Tyler and his collaborators emphasize the social and psychological value of procedural justice in contemporary organizations: Lind and Tyler 1988; Tyler et al. 1998; Darley, Messick, and Tyler 2001. On the education of jurors in Athenian courtrooms, see Too 2001.

[29] This is the burden of Cass Sunstein's recent work on deliberative pathologies among American juries: Sunstein 2000, 2006, 2007.

[30] The juror's oath has plausibly been restored to read as follows: "I will cast my vote in consonance with the laws and decrees passed by the Assembly and by the Council, but, if there is no law, in consonance with my sense of what is most just, without favor or enmity.

The Leocrates case shows that legally determined right answers were regarded as important, and their importance limited the tendency to judgment by alignment. Yet when the law offered no clear guidance or the facts of the case remained obscure, the jurors were required by their oath to seek the most just outcome. A shared repertoire of common knowledge, along with a common commitment to democratic values, meant that in these circumstances jurors would often align in more or less predictable ways. This predictability allowed elite and ordinary individuals to plan their lives, and helped to sustain the social equilibrium between them. Yet, because the common-knowledge repertoire was constantly being augmented, legal predictability did not degenerate into ossified routines. Athenian legal judgments, in the aggregate, remained responsive to the ever-changing environment without devolving into a mere barometer of change. The trials of Socrates (399 B.C.) and Phokion (318 B.C.: Mossé 2007 [1998]: 203–207) are reminders that the system was not always equal to the task of either legal correctness or justice, but fallibility is a fixed cost of democracy. The basic point is that it is a mistake to equate appeals to common knowledge in Athenian courtrooms with malfunctions in the democratic machine.

Building common knowledge in public institutions addresses the "carry through" problem faced by people with shared goals, but who will not individually act to achieve them unless each believes that others will act likewise. In game theory, common knowledge is conventionally assumed to be perfectly accurate and infinitely deep, an assumption that is, in practical terms, "ridiculously implausible" (Gintis 2000, 13–14). In the real world, the common knowledge shared among the members of a community remains imperfect. Before the trial of Leocrates, for example, some of the jurors probably had never heard the story of Hipparchus and were unsure how much others knew about it. Even after Lycurgus gave his speech, no one could be sure that each and every juror had taken it all in. But imperfect common knowledge can help to address coordination problems. In a given group, coordinated activity can occur if a critical mass of people know x, have good reason to believe that enough others know x, that enough others know they know, and so on. The actual size of that mass depends on cultural variables and the anticipated individual costs of cooperation.[31]

I will vote only on the matters raised in the charge, and I will listen impartially to the accusers and defenders alike"; see M. H. Hansen 1999: 182–83; Mirhady 2007.

[31] Common knowledge may be said to be perfectly accurate when x is precisely the same for all participants. Common knowledge can be described as infinitely deep when it moves through an infinite number of levels of mutual knowing, i.e., per above, Level 1 = when A knows x, Level 2 = A knows that B knows x. Level 3 = B knows that A knows that B knows x , Level 4 = A knows that B knows that A knows that B know x, and so on, ad infinitum.

Publicity can be defined as the "public presence" of information. Along with formal government institutions (courts, Assembly, Council, teams of magistrates), Athenian monuments, religious rituals, and public architecture served as media for publicity. The traitors'-list stele mentioned by Lycurgus was, for example, a highly visible monument set up in a public place. Each Athenian could reasonably assume that many (if not all) other Athenians had seen it. The monument's message, "Athenian traitors are punished," was clear in that it was easily understood by the viewer. Moreover, the stele was famously enmeshed in Athenian history. As Lycurgus understood, history—past events and stories that become known—is itself a medium for common knowledge. A similar "publicity triad" of prominent physical presence, clarity of message, and historical fame recurs in other Athenian monuments and rituals.[32]

Common knowledge is not just a matter of passively "taking up" a particular message; it is an active social experience. Personal *interpresence* and especially *intervisibility* among interpresent individuals create a particularly effective environment for building common knowledge because each participant can personally observe not only *that* others know some piece of information in common, but *how others respond to* that information. Because they were jointly present in the court, the jurors shared the experience of the litigants' presentations. Moreover, they could observe other jurors and learn from what they observed, paying attention to facial expressions and exclamations: Athenian juries were notoriously vocal in their response to litigants. Through picking up an array of visual and audible cues, experienced jurors could accurately gauge one another's response to each part of each litigant's presentation.[33]

References to past events by litigants added to the repertoire of Athenian common knowledge. Publicly announced at the conclusion of the

---

Kuran 1991 demonstrates how difficult it is to determine in advance how much common knowledge is enough to produce a history-changing alignment cascade. See Chwe 2001: 76–79 on the cognitive problems involved with common knowledge in practice, and how they might be solved.

[32] Publicity: Chwe 2001: 13–16 and passim; Brennan and Pettit 2004: 141–94, with reference to the roles of recognition, reputation, and fame: "publicity understood as audience size is the fuel of the economy of esteem." Chwe 2001: 87–91 treats history as like publicity in its relationship to common knowledge. Here, I consider history to fall under the general category of publicity, but I do not suppose that this points to any meaningful difference in approach.

[33] On the importance of eye contact: Chwe 2001: 30–36; on vocal Athenian juries: Bers 1985. There has been some debate over whether Athenian public forums were designed to encourage "one-way" (speaker to audience) or "two-way" (speaker to audience and audience to speaker) communication although there is no doubt that two-way communication was in fact standard practice; see Ober 1996, chapter 8, with references cited. A focus on common knowledge suggests, however, that the communication *among* the members of the audience (and among "bystanders": Lanni 1997) was equally important.

trial, the verdict itself became an item of common knowledge. The Leo-crates trial verdict was, for example, cited by an Athenian prosecutor in a major trial tried later in 330 B.C. (Aeschines 3.252). The knowledge made public in the course of a trial might, as we have seen, concern monu-ments and their messages, political history, personal reputations of liti-gants, jurors' responses to arguments and rhetorical ploys—as well as laws and judgments. All this was shared in the first instance by the partici-pants and bystanders; it was subsequently more widely publicized through gossip and the circulation of texts of speeches.[34]

The Athenian legal system employed the coordination mechanisms of accurate following, procedural rules, and credible commitment. An Athenian jury's judgment in a criminal trial was publicly announced in the form of an x number voting guilty and y voting for acquittal. The vote can be understood as a public expression of an informed subset of the citizenry and an invitation with a specific weight (the size of the majority) to the rest of the citizens to follow a particular lead.[35] Innovative legal arguments and the jurors' interpretive discretion ensured that the system of justice remained flexible and adaptive to a changing environment, while the clear procedural rules (formal and informal) of the Athenian legal system allowed individuals to make rational individual choices, plan for the future, and coordinate their actions with those of others.

People's Courts were steadily in session in Athens, and the relatively long speeches of litigants offered a particularly good opportunity for mak-ing knowledge public. But the courts were only one of many public fo-rums in which common knowledge was used and developed. The same citizens served on juries, on the Council of 500, and on teams of magis-trates; along with their younger fellow citizens they also attended the As-sembly and fought in the armed forces. The reiterated and overlapping experience of participation in public institutions had the effect of giving the Athenian citizen a great deal of practice at assimilating new informa-tion and judging the response of his fellows to it—thus adding to an exten-

---

[34] Citations of history by litigants: Pearson 1941; Nouhaud 1982; Worthington 1994, chapter 6. For use of arguments from precedent in Athenian trials, see Lanni 2004; Rubin-stein 2007. Gossip: Hunter 1994: 96–119. Circulation of texts of speeches: Worthington 1996. S. Lewis 1996 offers a general survey of how news was disseminated in the Greek world (and especially Athens), emphasizing its informality and the role of social class.

[35] In the trial of Leocrates, for example, the vote was evidently 250 to 250 (with one juror perhaps failing to vote); at the trial of Socrates in 399 the vote was approximately 280 for Meletus the prosecutor, 220 for Socrates as defendant. In a private (civil) case it was x for litigant A and y for litigant B. Likewise, Pettit and List, forthcoming, point out that the value of the Condorcet voting process (in which votes are, however, strictly independent) is to send a signal with a particular strength (the size of the majority) regarding the likelihood of the decision's correctness.

sive repertoire of what was commonly known. The upshot was a growing capacity of individuals and institutional bodies to coordinate their actions in the implementation of policy.

RATIONAL RITUALS AND PUBLIC MONUMENTS

Michael Chwe (2001) has drawn attention to the role of "rational rituals" in building common knowledge and thus furthering coordination in complex societies. Greek poleis featured a wide array of public rituals that combined religious, commemorative, celebratory, and civic functions. Major Athenian rituals included cross-town (Panathenaic) and cross-country (Eleusinian) parades, ceremonies commemorating soldiers fallen in war (the Athenian "ancestral custom": *patrios nomos*), and dramatic festivals—as well as public sacrifices, communal feasts, dances, and political rituals (e.g., ostracism). Rituals were performed at multiple scales—some by demes, by tribes, by the citizenry, by women, or by the polis as a whole. Meanwhile, local associations (phratries, cult groups, kinship groups) performed a wide variety of rituals on a smaller scale (Jones 1999). Right to participate and level of participation in particular ceremonies were often limited or regulated—e.g., by residence, kinship, initiation, gender, or civic standing—but virtually all members of the Athenian community, including resident foreigners and slaves, were drawn into public and private ritual activity. Rituals were typically repeated on a regular rotation (daily, monthly, annually) and are strongly associated with social learning (Osborne 1994). Yet the Athenians were constantly innovating in this, as in other domains: new state and local rituals were introduced, new gods were recognized by the state, new public monuments and sacred spaces were regularly added to the existing repertoire. Not coincidentally, Lycurgus was famous, not only as a prosecutor and financial expert, but also for his efforts to increase the prominence of publicly performed Athenian rituals.[36]

While all Greek poleis performed public rituals, the Athenians of the classical era were renowned for their extraordinarily dense ritual calendar. Athens was not only recognized in classical antiquity as a highly successful democratic community, but also as an intensely *festive* community, remarkably committed to the public performance of ritual. Table 5.1 gives a sense of the crowded Athenian ritual calendar, but the table is radically incomplete in that it lists only state festivals. All Athenian months except Maimakterion (October/November) are also attested as having multiple

---

[36] Good introductions to Athenian state religion and ritual practice include: Garland 1992; Parker 1996, 2006. See, further, Mikalson 1983; Schmitt-Pantel 1992 ; Wilson 2000; Cole 2004; Goff 2004. Many aspects of civic life were also highly ritualized: Bers 2000

TABLE 5.1
The annual Athenian calendar of ritual events (simplified)

Athenian Month	Gregorian Month	Major Ritual Events Sponsored Annually by the Athenian State
Hekatombion	June/July	Hekatombaia, Kronia, Synoikia,* Panathenaia,* Aphrodisia?
Metageitnion	July/August	Metageitnia?, Eleusinia*
Boedromion	August/September	Niketeria, celebration of victory at Plataea, Genesia, celebration of victory at Marathon (Charisteria), Boedromia?, celebration of the return from Phyle (Demokratia?), Eleusinian (Great) Mysteries,* Epidauria, Plemoxoai
Pyanopsion	September/October	Pyanopsia, Theseia*?, Kybernesia? Thesmophoria (women only),* Chalkeia, Apatouria,* Oschophoria, Stenia (women only)
Maimakterion	October/November	Pompaia? (no deme sacrifices, rituals are recorded for this month)
Posideon	November/December	Posidea?, Rural Dionysia,* Haloa
Gamelion	December/January	Theogamia, Lenaia,* Patrios nomos?
Anthesterion	January/February	Anthesteria,* Diasia, Lesser Mysteries (at Agrai)*
Elaphebolion	February/March	City Dionysia,* Pandia
Mounychion	March/April	Delphinia, Mounychia, Hephaisteia?, Hiketeria, Olympieia
Thargelion	April/May	Thargelia,* Bendideia, Plynteria, Kallynteria?
Skirophorion	May/June	Skira (women only),* Dipolieia (Bouphonia), Diisoteria? Arrhephoria, sacrifice to Zeus Soter

Sources: Mikalson 1975; Simon 1983.

Notes: Months are 29 or 30 days. * = multiple day festival. ? = month is uncertain. Intercalation is at the discretion of archons, and done somewhat randomly (typically a "second Posideon"), so the correspondence of Athenian and Gregorian calendar is only approximate. The Athenian civic calendar has ten subdivisions (according to the rotation of tribal presidencies) and is not easily coordinated with the festival calendar, giving modern scholars a great deal of trouble (see Mikalson 1975; Pritchett 2001 for discussion of this highly technical and controversial field), but seems not to have bothered the Athenians. Each ritual calendar month would be likely to include three or four meetings of the Assembly. Annual festivals for which the month is not known include the Brauronia, Arkteia, and Herakleia.

deme sacrifices and other regular ritual events. Monthly rituals to various gods and heroes were also celebrated on the first eight days of each month. All told, at least 120 days each year, and perhaps as many as 170, featured some Athenian state-sponsored religious ritual.[37]

In light of the relative lack of regimentation in Athenian private life (at least compared to Sparta), the social diversity of the population, and the class-sensitive costs and benefits of participation, an individual might choose a higher or lower level of ritual participation. Yet standard convic-

---

draws attention to the ritualized aspects of the almost daily procession of jurors to their courts. Lycurgus' religious "program": Humphreys 1985; Hintzen-Bohlen 1997.

[37] Athenian reputation for the most densely packed ritual calendar in Greece: [Xenophon] *Ath. Pol.* 3.2, 3.8. Deme festivals: Jones 2004: 88.

tions about piety and patriotism clearly held it as appropriate for each
Athenian to participate in the ritual life of the polis.[38] Although we cannot
say how many ritual events each year the median Athenian experienced
at state or local levels, the number would be high by modern standards—
and, more relevantly for our comparative purposes, higher than if he had
lived in some other Greek polis. If we accept Chwe's argument that rituals
serve a rational function of promoting coordination through building
common knowledge (in addition to structuring social meanings and
thereby helping participants to make better sense of their lives), then Athens would appear to be extraordinarily well equipped relative to later
democracies and relative to its polis rivals.

In contrast to the more familiar meaning-centered anthropological approach to ritual, Chwe's approach is not in the first instance concerned
with thick description of social meaning. While meanings are acknowledged as fundamentally important, the primary concern is with rituals as
publicity media. In addition to the deeper meanings that emerge in the
performance of a given ritual, each participant also learns, through his or
her participation, the simple fact that others are witnessing just what he
or she was witnessing. As in other publicity media, if A and B are interpresent at a cultic performance and observe, say, a ritual epiphany, A
knows that B knows that the epiphany has occurred, and knows that B
knows that A knows and so on. A and B share common knowledge of
the epiphany—irrespective of the diverse social meanings they may each
take away from it.[39]

All Athenian rituals (like rituals elsewhere) featured a certain amount
of basic informational content. Things were done, said, and shown, and
participants shared common knowledge of that basic informational content. Moreover, many Athenian rituals (again, like rituals elsewhere) were
reperformed on a regular schedule. Repetition builds common knowledge. Rather than having to grasp the informational content of a ritual
and others' response to it in a one-time event, the participant revisits content and responses, perhaps in the company of the same participants, over
and over again. That which is commonly known becomes more extensive
and more accurately known.

All public rituals may be said to involve common knowledge, but rituals with civic content (e.g., the oath of the ephebes, the public funeral

[38] Socrates' failure to participate in state rituals has been plausibly suggested as among
the factors that made him vulnerable to charges of impiety in 399 B.C. See Brickhouse and
Smith 1989 for discussion.

[39] Meaning-centered anthropological approach to ritual: Geertz 1973, 1983; Sewell
1999; Ortner 1999; Inglis 2000. Influential "Geertzian" readings of Athenian ritual include
Connor 1987 and a number of the essays collected in Dougherty and Kurke 1993.

for the war dead) are particularly relevant to solving the coordination problems associated with government by the people. Grasping that civic content *as common knowledge* relevant to coordination of action *in a democratic community* was part of what the ritual was "about" for the Athenian participants. It is notable for our purposes that explicitly civic informational content was *added* to major public rituals featuring pre-democratic histories, citizen- and non-citizen participants, and thickly lay-ered extrapolitical meanings—for example, the Eleusinian Mysteries, the Panathenaic festival, and the City Dionysia.[40]

Along with communal rituals, public monuments function as publicity media for conveying civic informational content. Prominent public monu-ments can help to solve everyday coordination problems by providing commonly referenced physical "focal points" that allow similarly well-informed persons to coordinate their movements without detailed com-munication. In an oft-cited example, two very well known monuments, Grand Central Station and the Empire State Building, serve as focal points enabling, respectively, natives and visitors to New York City to coordinate plans for meeting one another. As focal points, monuments are themselves part of a repertoire of spatial common knowledge, and as such they help people to navigate their way through the landscapes they jointly inhabit, and to do so in a coordinated manner.[41]

Some monuments serve an additional alignment function. As carriers of readily accessible informational content, public monuments may present spectators with a commonly available, relatively clear, and therefore "uni-tary" account of some aspect of shared culture or history. As we have seen, Lycurgus cited the bronze traitors' stele as a paradigmatic message-bearing Athenian monument. In Lycurgus' speech the stele was taken as exemplifying, through its history and its inscribed text, the salutary civic role of publicity.

We must keep in mind that in light of the human capacity to attach new, and potentially subversive, meanings to existing objects, the unity and clarity of the message attached to a public monument are necessarily limited. For example, Martin Luther King Jr.'s 1963 "I have a dream" speech, delivered from the steps of the Lincoln Memorial in Washington, D.C., used the setting of a very prominent public monument to contest then-prevalent American assumptions about race and politics. Yet King's highly self-conscious appropriation of Lincoln's monument (and citation

[40] For a sample of recent work on the civic content of Athenian rituals, see Strauss 1985; Winkler and Zeitlin 1990; Boegehold and Scafuro 1994; Alcock and Osborne 1994; Os-borne and Hornblower 1994; Mossé 1995; Maurizio 1998; Goldhill and Osborne 1999; Wilson 2000.

[41] Schelling 1980; Chwe 2001: 88–89, 96–97.

of Lincoln's Emancipation Proclamation of 1863) also points to the enduring power of the Lincoln Memorial to publicize a particular history (the enslavement and subsequent liberation of African Americans) and particular values (liberty and equality as exemplified by "government of, by, and for the people"). King's strategic choice of a location for his speech suggests that public monuments may facilitate socially valuable coordination, not only in periods of stability and consensus, but in and through eras of social turmoil and civil conflict.[42]

The polis of Athens boasted a great many monuments erected by or with the permission of the democratic state. The Acropolis was packed with monuments: temples, altars, statues, dedications, and public records (Hurwit 1999). Other prominent monuments were located in the lower city, especially in the Agora (see below). Yet others were scattered throughout the countryside (e.g., the Soros, the monumental grave of the 192 Athenian soldiers who fell at Marathon in 490 B.C.). Of course, as the Roman-era travel writer, Pausanias, richly documents, other Greek poleis and sanctuaries also boasted prominent monuments. There is nothing democratic about monuments as such. Some important Athenian "focal point" monuments were constructed by the tyrants before democracy, notably the Altar of the Twelve Gods in the Agora, which served as a central "point zero" for measuring distances across Athenian territory. The informational content, in terms of shared history and values, that was publicized by many well-known Athenian monuments—the Parthenon temple, the great statues of Athena Parthenos and Athena Polias on the Acropolis, or the Athenian Tribute Lists—concerned empire and "polis nationalism" (Hedrick 1994, 2006). While significant as high-value products of a highly successful community, these monuments are not particularly helpful in specifying what is distinctive about the role of common knowledge in a participatory democracy.

Nonetheless, certain prominent and distinctive Athenian monuments, strategically located in or near the Agora, stand out as highly "democratic" focal points carrying very specific civic informational content about the democratic history of the community. Well-known examples of monuments that featured prominently in the coordination of action by democratic citizens include the "tyrant killers" statue group sculpted by Kritios and Nesiotes and dedicated in ca. 477 B.C., and the Eponymous Heroes monument erected originally sometime in the fifth century and rebuilt on a new foundation in the fourth. The tyrant-killer monument served as a rallying point for Athenian democrats in times of political crisis. The Eponymous Heroes monument was the site at which public

---

[42] See, further, Ober 2005b, chapter 3.

announcements, for example lists of hoplites summoned for military service, were posted. It was here that members of each tribe could find tribe-specific information. These very self-consciously democratic monuments served both as focal points for coordinating the movements of citizens through public space, and as history lessons, recalling the revolutionary origins of democracy and the establishment of the new democratic institutional era that followed it. Each publicized a clear and unitary body of information relevant to governance by the people, and did so by appealing to particular histories and values. The point is that (unlike many other monuments in Athens and elsewhere in Greece) these particular monuments, and some others like them, were distinctively concerned with making democratic content public—and thereby with building a distinctively democratic body of common knowledge.[43]

ARCHITECTURE AND INTERVISIBILITY

Chwe emphasizes the value of "inward-facing circles" of interpresent persons in building common knowledge: "An inward-facing circle allows maximum eye-contact; each person knows that other people know because each person can visually verify that others are paying attention."[44] Imagine that a group of spectators is arranged in a line such that each can observe an "event" (say a speech or a ritual) at which new information is presented (fig. 5.2a). They will each have knowledge of the event, but the extent of their common knowledge is limited by their difficulty in observing one another's reactions to the event. If the same group is rearranged in a circle, each spectator can simultaneously observe the event and the reactions of the other spectators, as they commonly observe the event (fig. 5.2b).

Chwe points out that that some modern meeting spaces are self-consciously designed to allow meetings to take the form of inward-facing circles in which attendees are able to maximize eye-contact verification of others' attention. The Fort Worth (Texas) city hall meeting room, for example, takes the form of a modified "theater in the round," with banked rows of inward-facing seats arranged in a three-quarter circle; in the remaining quarter-circle are seats for city officials and a speaker's podium. The addition of multiple rows of spectators means that intervisi-

---

[43] Hedrick 2000: 330–31 emphasizes the informational content of Athenian democratic inscriptions. Tyrannicides monument as democratic focal point: Ober 2005b, chapter 10; Teegarden 2007. Eponymous Heroes monument and its history: Shear 1970; Camp 2001: 157–59.

[44] Chwe 2001: 4–5, 30–35, quote on 5.

a.

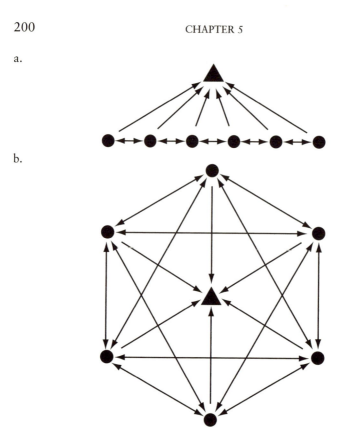

b.

Figure 5.2. Spectators observing event, in line (a) and in circle (b).

bility will not be complete (I cannot meet the eyes of those sitting directly in front or in back of me), but banking the rows makes it possible for many more people to be accommodated in the same circular area and to remain intervisible with a high percentage of those present (fig. 5.3). Direct visual and aural access to the center is maximized for a larger number, as is intervisibility among the interpresent participants. This is, of course, the approach to space taken by Greek theaters—an architectural form that originated in Athens. Audiences in theatrical spaces develop common knowledge that is accurate, because all witness the same performance, albeit from somewhat different perspectives. Their knowledge is also extensive in that all are continuously aware of the presence of many other observers and able to monitor other participants' reactions to the performance.

The common knowledge communicated in the inward-facing circle need have nothing to do with democratic participation or the civic realm. The knowledge shared among the participants in the kiva ritual of native peoples in the American Southwest or the audiences in the Roman colia.

b.

c.

Figure. 5.3. Inward-facing circular spaces: simple circle (a) and Greek theater (b and c).

seum need not have been civic in content. Yet the inward-facing circle is well suited to the deliberative and learning processes of democratic self-governance. Edward Durrell Stone, the architect of the Fort Worth city hall, sought to re-create the intervisibility experience of a traditional American town meeting (see chapter 2) by enhancing each participant's ability to "observe feelings and responses" of others.[45] If a participatory democracy on the Athenian model requires common knowledge, and if

[45] Chwe 2001: 30–31, citing Goodsell 1988: 166. Cf. Bryan 2004 for detailed analysis of the town meeting experience Stone sought to re-create.

Stone's and Chwe's intuition about inward-facing circles and knowledge were shared by ancient Greek architects, then we might expect Athens to construct inward-facing civic spaces. That expectation is amply fulfilled—at multiple architectural scales.

Democratic Athens stands out among Greek poleis in its efforts to construct and improve inward-facing public spaces. These spaces were built in different scales for participant-audiences of 50 to 17,000 persons. They were erected especially in the central city, but also in larger demes throughout Attica. The buildings are either round in ground plan or incorporate inward-facing seating within a rectilinear building plan. We have seen (chapter 4) that many Athenians spent a very substantial amount of time conducting public business. Because much of an Athenian's "public business time" (e.g., as a councilman) as well as much of his "political culture time" (as a theater goer) was spent in inward-facing spatial contexts, the costs of public service and political culture produced a substantial public benefit, not only by efficiently aggregating knowledge for better decision making, but also by efficiently building common knowledge and thereby facilitating complex coordination across Athens' large and socially diverse population.[46]

Monumental inward-facing public buildings were constructed only during the democratic period of Athenian history (i.e., eras III–XI). The Mycenaean Greeks had constructed monumental round *tholos* tombs in the Late Bronze Age (1600–1200 B.C.), and houses with inward-facing seating may have been common in the ensuing Dark Age (1100–750 B.C.).[47] But there are no examples of monumental inward-facing structures, identifiable as public buildings, anywhere in Greece before the late sixth century. There was considerable monumental building sponsored by the tyrants of pre-democratic sixth-century Athens (era II), but none of the tyrants' buildings appear to be designed as inward-facing spaces. The construction and improvement of monumental inward-facing public buildings in Athens begins with the emergence of democracy in era III,

---

[46] Here I focus primarily on the function of public spaces as publicity media, rather than the civic *content* of the information presented in each space, but I have argued elsewhere (as have other scholars in detail) that the scripts of dramatic performances witnessed by audiences in Athenian theaters had considerable civic content as, quite obviously, did the speeches and discussions carried out in buildings and spaces designed specifically for the conduct of government business. See Euben 1986; Winkler and Zeitlin 1990; Wallace 1997; Goldhill and Osborne 1999; Wilson 2000. Content of public speeches: Ober 1989; Yunis 1996; Johnstone 1999; Hesk 2000.

[47] Tholos tombs include the famous "tomb of Agamemnon" at Mycenae, but they are a standard architectural form throughout Bronze Age Greece. A modest rounded building with bench seating from a Dark Age site in south Attica is identified by Lauter 1985 as a public building; but the form was common in Dark Age private houses: Morris 1998b.

continues through the period of democratic flourishing (eras IV–XI), and ends abruptly with the end of the democracy's continuous existence. In the post-democratic third century there was a hiatus in major public building of all kinds. When monumental building resumed in the second century (late era XII), major new public buildings, typically sponsored by Hellenistic kings as gifts to the city of Athens, were in the form of stoas or temples; they were not designed as inward-facing structures for civic purposes.[48]

According to the most convincing analysis of the archaeological evidence, it was very soon after the foundation of democracy in 508 B.C. that Athens began to construct major new inward-facing public buildings. In ca. 500 B.C. the Athenians erected a purpose-built Bouleuterion (Council House) on the western side of the Agora for the meetings of the Council of 500. Meanwhile, they created a theatral (large, semi-circular with banked, curved seating) area called the Pnyx for the exclusive use of the citizen Assembly. At about the same time, the Agora was formally designated as open public space by the establishment of boundary markers at its entrances. Here the Athenians gathered for various public purposes, probably including attending dramatic performances of tragedy. At least two demes had been provided with actual theaters by the late sixth century (see, further, below, this chapter).[49]

About a generation after the construction of the Bouleuterion, in ca. 470, the round building known as the Tholos was constructed just south of the Bouleuterion as a purpose-built *prutanikon* ("office for the *prutaneis*"). Here the fifty members of each tribal team, serving their intense one-tenth year of "presidency," met and ate (and a third of them slept) in relative comfort. In the same general period, the Athenians constructed the first purpose-built version of the Theater of Dionysus on the south slope of the Acropolis. This post–Persian War burst of architectural activity was followed by the great building program of the imperial mid-fifth century. Athenian imperial-era architecture focused (as had the pre-democratic building program of the tyrants) on constructing imposing temples on the Acropolis and in rural sanctuaries. Yet the imperial-era program included a spectacular inward-facing building: the Odeion a new and per-

---

[48] History of public building in Athens: Camp 2001. It is notable that inward-facing public spaces (theaters and Assembly buildings) become common in Greek cities in Asia Minor in the fourth century; many design elements of both institutions and architecture seem to be borrowed (perhaps at some remove) from democratic Athens. We know relatively little about the physical arrangements of Athenian law courts (Boegehold 1995); Carey 1994 notes the lack of formal distinction between legal and other public space in Athens.

[49] Old Bouleuterion: see, chapter 4, note 40. Pnyx I: Forsén and Stanton 1996. Agora *horoi*: Ober 2005b: 185–88.

haps roofed public performance space directly adjacent to the Theater of Dionysus.[50]

In the late fifth century, in the last phase of the Peloponnesian War, the Old Bouleuterion was transformed into an archives building and dedicated to the Mother of the Gods as the Metroon. Meanwhile, a New Bouleuterion was erected directly behind the old one. Immediately after the war the Pnyx was rebuilt on a new orientation. Some fifty years later, in the third quarter of the fourth century, the Pnyx was once again reconstructed. At about the same time, the Theater of Dionysus was completely rebuilt in a major building program associated with the leadership of Lycurgus, the prosecutor of Leocrates. The fourth century also seems to be a particularly active period for constructing inward-facing spaces outside the city proper. We have scattered fourth-century evidence for the existence of fourteen deme theaters in the Attic countryside; other deme theaters, for which we lack evidence, were probably built in this era as well (see, further, below, this chapter).[51]

By the third quarter of the fourth century (era XI, the age of both Lycurgus and Aristotle), Athens was amply provided with an impressive array of inward-facing spaces for public purposes. The spaces in the city varied considerably in seating capacity depending on their function: Tholos, 50; Bouleuterion II, 500; Odeion, 3000?; Pnyx III, 8000+; Theater of Dionysus II, 17,000. The Tholos and Odeion remained structurally and functionally substantially as they had been in the fifth century. But other inward-facing buildings underwent changes in architectural design. In the New Bouleuterion of the late fifth century, what appears to have been a "squared U" rectilinear seating plan in the Old Bouleuterion was replaced with a new seating plan, the details of which are, unfortunately, obscure and much debated. The rebuilt Theater of Dionysus was both more architecturally ambitious and probably much larger than its fifth-century predecessor (Csapo 2007). When the Pnyx was first rebuilt, at the end of the fifth century (Pnyx II), the orientation of the meeting space was reversed, which allowed access to the auditorium to be much more carefully monitored and controlled. The third phase of the Pnyx was enhanced architecturally and, like the Theater of Dionysus, featured expanded seating capacity.

The architectural revisions to the Bouleuterion, the Theater of Dionysus, and the Pnyx appear, on the face of it, to be driven in large part by what contemporary architects refer to as "program design issues"—that is, the practical purposes of the people using the space rather than the

---

[50] Tholos, Odeion, Theater of Dionysus: Camp 2001: 69–70, 100–101, 144–46.

[51] New Bouleuterion: Camp 2001: 127. Pnyx II and III: Forsén and Stanton 1996; Camp 2001: 132, 153–54, 266.

aesthetics of "buildings as large-scale public sculpture." There is no reason to believe that the inward-facing buildings had to be rebuilt due to
damage or to changing aesthetic notions of what counted as good architecture.[52] There is no comparable pattern of democratic-era rebuilding of
undamaged public buildings that were not used for public meetings (for
example, the Acropolis temples, or the Agora stoas used as magistrates'
offices). It is possible, then, although it remains to be proven, that the
Athenians chose to spend resources in rebuilding existing government
structures in a conscious effort to improve inward-facing space at different scales. The cost would have been justified if the changes resulted in
substantial net gains in common knowledge.

Scaling Common Knowledge

Chapter 4 argued that the institutional organization of government at the
multiple scales of deme, tribe, and polis offered opportunities for expanded social networks and thereby facilitated knowledge aggregation.
Public gatherings at the same three scales offered opportunities for gaining common knowledge, and thereby facilitated alignment. We have already noted the role of the Eponymous Heroes monument for publicly
disseminating tribe-level information, and the dense local ritual calendars
of individual demes. Indirect evidence for deme/tribe/polis scaling of common knowledge emerges from the history of local deme theaters.

The pattern of sequential reconstruction of major urban inward-facing
public spaces is recapitulated in the architectural history of the best-
preserved theater in Athenian territory outside the city—at the deme of
Thorikos in the silver mining region of southern Attica. The theater at
Thorikos was originally constructed in the late sixth century, either
shortly before the reforms of 508 (like the theater at Ikaria, which is usually dated to ca. 520 B.C.) or immediately after the reforms. The Thorikos
theater was subsequently rebuilt in the fifth century, and was rebuilt again
in the mid-fourth century. In its final phase the Thorikos theater could
hold about 3200 persons.[53]

Deme theaters were almost certainly used for presenting tragedy, comedy, and dithyrambic choruses at the festival of the "rural Dionysia."
Presumably (although we lack direct evidence of this) they were also used

---

[52] Contrast, for example, Athenian temples destroyed or damaged in the course of the
Persian wars: Camp 2001: 57–58.

[53] Thorikos theater: Camp 2001: 312–13; Csapo 2007: 99–100 (with revised seating estimate and bibliography).

for meetings of the local deme Assembly.[54] Thorikos had a bouleutic quota of five or six (variable from year to year, as in a number of demes) and thus an adult male citizen membership of perhaps 300–400 persons. In constructing a theater with a seating capacity of 3200, the fourth-century theater builders at Thorikos certainly expected much larger audiences. It might be thought (e.g., Camp 2001: 313) that the large capacity of the Thorikos theater is an anomaly, to be explained by the (presumably) exceptionally large population of the southern Attica mining region. Yet a substantial part of the district's population would have been mine slaves, who seem unlikely theatergoers.

An alternative hypothesis is that the theater in Thorikos was sometimes used for public purposes that transcended those of the deme itself. The most obvious candidate for a suprademe body that might have gathered in Thorikos' theater is tribe V: Acamantis, of which Thorikos was a constituent deme. The hypothesis that local deme theaters could have served tribal functions receives indirect support from recent seating-capacity estimates for a theater discovered by archaeologists in the territory of Euonymon, a large (bouleutic quota 10) "city" deme of tribe I: Erechtheis. The Euonymon theater, as rebuilt in circa 350–325 B.C., is estimated to have seated in the range of 2500–3750 spectators. Since, in the later fourth century, each tribe had a citizen population of about 3000, it appears that the Thorikos and Euonymon theaters each could have accommodated the citizen membership of one tribe.[55]

The geographic distribution of known deme theaters supports the hypothesis that they were sometimes employed for inclusive gatherings that exceeded the local deme population. More inclusive gatherings would build more extensive common knowledge, and would further the desirable end of sustaining interaction and solidarity across strong-tie local networks. A total of fourteen deme theaters are directly or indirectly attested in the fragmentary literary, epigraphic, and archaeological evidence.[56] Given the exiguous state of the empirical data, it is very likely that other deme theaters existed as well.

[54] Demes could stage tragedy, comedy, and dithyramb, as they wished and were able. Deme assemblies: Whitehead 1986: 86–90; Jones 2004: 86–87. Known and hypothesized uses of deme theaters: Whitehead 1986, 212–22; Jones 2004: 87, 140–42.

[55] Euonymon theater: Camp 2001: 315; Csapo 2007: 99–100; Moreno 2008: 44–45, 60, who assumes, without argument, that the theater's capacity could not have exceeded the deme's total population. Analysis of the partially preserved theaters at Ikaria and Rhamnous (Gebhard 1974: 434–36; Camp 2001: 289–91, 301–5) might yield estimates of their audience capacity.

[56] Evidence for deme theaters: Whitehead 1986: 212–22. There is direct evidence (archaeological or epigraphic) for theaters at seven Attic demes (Roman numeral = tribe; Arabic number = bouleutic quota): Euonymon I-10, Ikarian II-5, Thorikos V-6, Archarnai VI-22, Aixone VII-8, Piraeus VIII-9, Rhamnous IX-8,). There is credible indirect evidence for seven

Thirteen of the fourteen attested deme theaters were located in relatively large demes—that is, in one of the thirty-eight demes with an annual bouleutic quota of 4/5 to 22; only Kollytos (quota of 3), one of the five "intramural" demes located within the walls of the city, is among the 101 smaller demes (quota 4 or below) attested to have had a theater.[57] None of the seventy-six demes with a quota under 3 has a recorded theater. Given that only about a quarter of Athens' demes was relatively large, this distribution pattern is unlikely to be happenstance—it seems probable that relatively large demes were considerably more likely to have had theaters than relatively small demes, and that few, if any, very small demes ever had theaters. Thus, to the extent that extraurban dramatic and choral performance was both "theater-centered" and an integral part of Athenian life (as the annual festival of the Rural Dionysia attests), we can suppose that residents of small demes attended the theater in larger demes—that is, that there was considerable interdeme theatergoing.

In the current state of our literary, epigraphic, and archaeological evidence it cannot be positively demonstrated that interdeme theatergoing was organized by tribes. But the remarkably equitable distribution of known theaters among tribes suggests that it was. The fourteen attested deme theaters are spread among nine of the ten tribes—only tribe IV (Leontis) is so far without an attested theater. Five tribes (V, VI, VII, IX, X) are attested as having one deme with a theater. Three tribes (I, III, VIII) are known to have had two demes with theaters, and one (II) had three. That distribution is very close to an optimally equitable distribution of fourteen theaters across ten tribes. The probability of such an equitable distribution occurring randomly appears to be low.[58] It therefore seems likely that theaters were distributed among demes in some way that took distribution by tribe into account. The distribution mechanism, assuming there was one, might have involved central polis-level planning, but it might just as well have emerged from competitive emulation among

others: Anagyrous I-6, Myrrhinous III-6, Paiania III-11, Halai Araphenides VII-6, Eleusis VIII-11, Aigilia X-6).

[57] The 38 largest demes represent only about 27 percent of the 139 demes, but just over 60 percent of the total bouleutic quota—and thus, presumably, a roughly similar percentage of the total citizen population. The urban deme of Kollytos is located just south of the theater of Dionysos; it is conceivable that the comedies (Aeschines 1.157) and tragedies (Demosthenes 18.180, 262) attested as having been held there (presumably at a celebration of the rural Dionysia) were staged in the theater of Dionysos, borrowed by the deme for the purpose.

[58] Actual distribution (of fourteen theaters among ten tribes) = 3 2 2 2 1 1 1 1 1 0. Optimally equitable distribution = 2 2 2 2 1 1 1 1 1 1. Thus only one "move" (from 3 to 0) is needed to achieve optimal equity. Working out the actual probability of such an equitable distribution occurring by chance proves to be a remarkably difficult statistical problem. My thanks to Lynn Gale and Christopher Achen for help on this gnarly issue.

tribes. For our purposes, the distribution mechanism is less relevant than the likelihood of tribe-sensitive distribution.[59]

In sum, it appears likely that by the fourth century B.C. each of the ten tribes had at least one theater in one of its major demes and that deme theaters were somehow associated with the activity of the ten tribes. In light of the equitable distribution of attested deme theaters across tribes and the capacities of the theaters at Thorikos and Euonymon, it is quite possible to suppose that some, if not all, deme theaters were regularly used for tribal events as well as for local deme events. Tribal events held in theaters might have included meetings of tribal assemblies, tribal festivals, or dress rehearsals of tribal dithyrambic choruses to be presented in the city.[60] If this general hypothesis is correct, the education in the process of knowledge aggregation that citizens received at the ascending civic scale levels of deme, tribe, and polis was recapitulated, at the same three scale levels, in common-knowledge-building, inward-facing public spaces. Through engagement in aggregation and alignment at multiple scales, the citizens' experience of socially valuable epistemic processes grew, as the democratic community developed more sophisticated institutional and architectural practices.

Inward-facing seating, and thus intervisibility among participants, is a consistent architectural feature of buildings designed for Athenian public meetings and erected by the democratic state. The central Agora itself, with its officially defined and strictly enforced open space in which citizens could gather to speak with and see one another, can be regarded as the original Greek model for the structuring of space so that interpresent individuals would be both intervisible and interaudible.[61]

It is important to keep in mind that the organization of space for interpresence and intervisibility was not an Athenian innovation. As J.–P. Vernant (among others) has emphasized, the existence of the Agora as an open and publicly shared space "in the middle" (*es meson*) of the Greek polis is characteristic of citizen-based egalitarian political organization in late archaic and classical Greece.[62] Moreover, inward-facing buildings

---

[59] If we assume that the "larger demes more likely to have theaters" rule holds, and we assume that "every tribe has at least one deme theater," then we can guess that deme Phrearrhioi had a theater that is as yet unattested: with a bouleutic quota of nine, it is the only large deme among the twenty demes of tribe Leontis. The conjoined tribal and deme-size distribution of deme theaters hypotheses presented here could be tested by archaeological investigation of the deme site of Phrearrhioi, which was in the "coastal" trittys of Leontis and located in southwestern Attica.

[60] Tribal assemblies: Hopper 1957: 14–16; Jones 1999, 161–69.

[61] On the ideal polis as being *eusunoptos*, that is, easy to take in at a glance by citizens who know one another's character, see [Aristotle] *Politics* 1326b22–25, 1327a1–3.

[62] On interpresence in the Agora and its political importance for the emergence of a distinctive Greek approach to political organization, see Vernant 1982.

are not unique to Athens. In the fourth century a number of other poleis and Panhellenic sanctuaries built their own theaters, and some poleis are known to have had at least one or two government buildings designed for large meetings. In the Roman era, as generically republican (democratic or wide-franchise oligarchic) forms of self-governance were replaced with narrow oligarchies, the original open-space Agora of a number of Greek cities, including Athens, was filled in with very large stoas and with temples—buildings that were not well suited to inward-facing public meetings.[63]

The Athenian architectural history surveyed above can, therefore, be set in a Panhellenic historical and political context. Yet the wider Greek context does not adequately explain exceptional features of classical Athenian architectural development. No other classical Greek polis is known to have constructed a built environment with Athens' rich array of large urban and extraurban inward-facing buildings.[64] There is a historical association between democracy in Athens and architecture promoting intervisibility. Like the Greek theater, the *ekklēsiastērion* (theater-like public meeting place for gatherings of a citizen assembly; in Athens, the Pnyx), the *bouleutērion* (large-scale roofed public building for a large probouleutic council), and the *prutanikon* (public building intended for public gatherings of several dozen magistrates; in Athens, the Tholos) may be Athenian architectural innovations. It appears quite possible (although the evidence is debated) that each of these architectural forms was first realized in Athens in the early decades of the democracy. When these architectural forms were adopted by cities beyond Athens, they are often associated with democratic governments.[65]

The ritual event, the monument, and architectural space can each be understood as a medium for publicity. Exposure to and experience with these media builds more extensive and more accurate common knowledge and can thereby facilitate the alignment of efforts across a diverse population. Public investment in public rituals, monuments, and architecture is cost effective if it enables a community to address what would otherwise be intractable coordination problems. The advantages of building common *civic* knowledge are, I have argued, considerable in a participatory

[63] Wycherley 1962 makes this point. The sequential Agora plans offered in H. Thompson and Wycherley 1972 (cf. updates in Camp 1992) demonstrate this process graphically.

[64] If we base the "inward-facing public building" count on M. H. Hansen and Nielsen 2004, *Inventory* record of the relevant forms of public building (scoring 2 for plurals, thus underreporting) Athens' score is 6. Its nearest competitors, Syracuse and Olynthos, score 3. These numbers give only a subjective sense of Athens' preeminence, but there can be little doubt that Athens did, in fact, construct more inward-facing buildings than any other Greek polis in the classical era.

[65] McDonald 1943; a useful survey, but in need of updating.

democracy without command and control mechanisms for imposing order. Common knowledge is not inherently political, much less inherently democratic. But it is readily employed for the political purpose of democratic governance. The proliferation of inward-facing meeting spaces, along with the development of explicitly civic rituals and the erection of focal-point monuments to commemorate democratic history, expanded the Athenians' common knowledge of rules, commitments, and leaders' reputations. Because Athenian publicity media built common civic knowledge and made public commitments more credible, they fostered epistemic alignment. Alignment has negative effects if it leads to context-inappropriate cascading. But in the right social context, alignment is extraordinarily valuable. Coordinated efforts, made possible by aligned knowledge, facilitated policy implementation and thereby enhanced Athenian state performance.

Chapter 6

CODIFICATION: ACCESS, IMPARTIALITY, AND

TRANSACTION COSTS

A DECISION MADE by aggregating dispersed knowledge, and implemented by aligning common knowledge, gains greater purchase on future behavior when it becomes codified knowledge. In the epistemic process of codification, a decision is incorporated into the action-guiding "rules of the game," with potentially substantial effects on the distribution of social rewards and punishments.[1] When rules are very hard to change and resistant to reinterpretation, they will stifle productive innovation. When rules are very fluid, the returns to social learning will be low. In an ideally productive epistemic equilibrium, rules are significantly action guiding but remain revisable and interpretable. At Athens, the dynamic forms of knowledge that were employed in the processes of aggregation and alignment were captured, through the act of codification, in a text—a written law (*nomos*) or decree (*psēphisma*). In many cases that text was inscribed on a marble stele—literally "written in stone"—and publicly displayed. The constitutional process for legal amendment (especially as revised at the end of the fifth century; see chapter 5) along with the legal and social contexts in which the codified rules were used, pushed back against the tendency to ossification. Athenian rules were clear and stable enough to return substantial benefit to political participation and civic education. Codified knowledge allowed Athenians to lay plans for the future with some confidence, and at the same time encouraged them to think about ways in which their individual and collective circumstances might be improved if the rules were changed.

INTENTION AND INTERPRETATION

In a participatory democracy, codified knowledge is not static; it is returned to the realm of action and change through the choices made by

---

[1] Rules of the game (in regard to economic payoffs): North 1990; Baumol 1993, 2004. See discussion in Greif 2006, and above, chapter 1. Survey of codification practices in antiquity: Lévy 2000.

those affected by the new rule. The Athenian law code allowed for a legal dispute to be heard under a wide variety of procedures and venues, depending on the choices of disputants (Osborne 1985b; Todd 1993). Democratically produced Athenian rules were, moreover, ordinarily subject to revision through established constitutional rules of legal amendment. In the fourth century, rules were hierarchically sorted into decrees (*psēphismata*), which could be changed by a single vote of a deliberative body (ordinarily the Assembly), and laws (*nomoi*), which could only be changed after a series of decisions by constitutionally distinct bodies.[2] Revisability was a general principle of Athenian rule making, but not a universal one. In rare cases, especially in legislation concerning foreign policy, entrenchment clauses deterred amendment by imposing sanctions on anyone proposing to change the rule.[3]

Codification promotes joint action by projecting the intentions of rule makers into the future. Intentions are of primary importance in the epistemic processes of aggregation and alignment. Michael Bratman's (1999) philosophical model of joint action and Pettit and List's (in progress) model of corporate agency center on the shared intentions of group members to promote a goal, their intention to pursue that goal, and their commonly held belief that others in the group had formed similar intentions (see chapter 1). The relationship between intention and action changes, however, as shared intentions are projected into the future.

The choices made by the individuals originally engaged in decision making and implementation bear some relation to choices subsequently made by those subject to the rule. The relationship is not, however, reducible to accurate following—to learning the original policy makers' intentions through (for example) reading a text, and then acting accordingly. The information contained in a codified rule must be interpreted by those subject to it. Interpretations change with context. As the debate in American constitutional law over the Founders' "original intent" shows, decision makers' past intentions are not transparent and certainly cannot be determined by a simple backwards induction from the downstream effects of their decisions.[4]

---

[2] The formal distinction between *nomos* and *psēphisma* was an innovation of the legal reforms of the late fifth century. See M. H. Hansen 1999: 161–64, with literature cited.

[3] On the vocabulary of entrenchment, see Boegehold 1996. Schwartzberg 2004 and 2007 connects the practice of entrenchment in Athenian legislation to the need for the democracy to make its foreign policy commitments credible, but she also notes its rarity and the Athenian concern with maintaining "mutability" and thereby retaining potential for innovation and avoiding legal ossification.

[4] Cavanaugh 2001 helpfully discusses modern intentionalist constitutional doctrine with reference to Aristotle. On the lawgivers' intentions in Athenian legal rhetoric, see Yunis 2005.

Interpretation allows for productive innovations to emerge over time without changes in the formal rules. Interpretation is a socially desirable antidote to ossification. Yet at some point innovations arising from unfettered interpretive scope may negate the rule's value as a guide to action. Codified Athenian legislation helped individual Athenians, and others subject to Athenian rules, to weigh the likely costs and benefits of any given action and to be more confident in assessing the risks entailed by their own choices. When the rules of the game are specified and known, the game's players are in a position to make better choices. Yet when those rules become ossified, or are exploited by strategic actors for socially unproductive purposes, organizational performance suffers. As with the related epistemic processes of aggregation and alignment, a learning/innovation equilibrium determines the impact of the codification process on outcomes.

It is no simple matter for modern historians of ancient Athens to specify the precise intentions of the original authors of codified legislation or of those who first carried it out. The naval station dispatching decree (chapter 4), for example, announces that the new station was meant to protect Athenian and foreign shipping. That statement of legislative purpose surely reflects, but cannot fully specify, the complex intentions of the men who (like Cephisophon of Cholargos) proposed specific legislative language or who (like the imaginary Poseidippos VI) applied their social and technical knowledge to the decree's drafting and subsequently voted for it. Our incapacity fully to specify intentions is not reason to abandon intentionality in our analysis of Athenian institutions. The intentions of Athenians like Cephisophon and Poseidippos were formed in the specifiable context of the institutionalized processes of knowledge aggregation and alignment. I have suggested, in the previous two chapters, that if we understand the relevant processes, we can go some way in reverse engineering the system: beginning with codified inscribed texts (the dispatching decree) of policy decisions and descriptions of how policy was implemented (Lycurgus' speech), we can construct a narrative to explain the kinds of knowledge that went into and subsequently flowed from a codified rule.[5]

Athenian speakers in legal trials (like Lycurgus) often attribute particular intentions to long-dead lawgivers, claiming that Solon, for example, hoped to produce certain effects with his laws.[6] In this way courtroom

---

[5] The contextual method I am advocating here is analogous to that employed by "Cambridge School" intellectual historians of political thought, who argue that one can better understand a major text (e.g., Hobbes' *Leviathan*) by analyzing the argumentative context in which it was written. See Tully 1988 and further discussion in Ober 1998, chapter 1.

[6] This practice has something in common with contemporary "originalist" interpretations of the American Constitution; as in the case of the American Founders, Solon was regarded by later generations as an exceptionally wise lawgiver. Solon's intentions were inferred from his writings (in this case poems, or poems attributed to him) and from a body of stories that grew up around him (Croesus narrative: Herodotus 1.30–33). Of course

speakers can claim that those salutary and originally intended effects would be promoted if the jurors made the right decision in the current trial. Athenian forensic claims regarding lawmakers' intentions are not independent evidence for original legislative intent. But forensic claims do have something to tell us about how *later* Athenians interpreted and employed the laws by which they governed themselves—which helps us to specify some of the material effects of codified knowledge upon those who were subject to it.

Among the questions that can be asked of a state's policy is whether, over time and in comparison with rivals facing similar opportunities and constraints, it hindered or promoted the state's performance. This chapter will argue that Athenian legislative intentions that we can specify and the effects we can measure were leading in the same relatively productive direction. Of course not all policy—of Athens or any other state—is concerned with increasing productivity. The primary aim of a given initiative may be, for example, the promotion of social justice or social security (below, this chapter). Yet it is axiomatic that when competitive failure can result in elimination, policy cannot long remain so depressing in its effect on productive capacity as to render the state incapable of competing with its rivals.

A good deal of legislation in modern states is specifically concerned with enhancing productivity through economic incentives and financial instruments. While the ancient Athenians had a much less elaborate apparatus to draw upon in designing policy, at least some Athenian legislative enactments appear to be self-consciously aimed at increasing productivity through lowering transaction costs. Below, we will consider a particular example, a law regulating silver coinage.

OPEN ENTRY, FAIR PROCEDURE, AND TRANSACTION COSTS

One determinant of the effect a new policy will have on productivity is whether it serves to raise or to lower transaction costs—that is (per chapter 3), the expected *ex ante* and *ex post* costs to individuals of making potentially profitable contracts or bargains. When transaction costs are lowered, productivity is raised (at least potentially) because the increased profit from low-cost bargains increases the value and the frequency of transactions. Here our concern is to understand how the policies made by Athens, as a state, affected the transaction costs incurred by the members of the extended Athenian community—understood as those persons

---

"what Solon intended" invariably turns out to suit the speaker's forensic purposes. See Mossé 1979 (now translated into English in Rhodes 2004) and the essays collected in Blok and Lardinois 2006.

doing business and making their living within Athenian territory. I have argued (chapter 2) that at various points in Athenian history Athens was extremely productive in comparison with rival poleis. For much of the fifth century (eras V–VIII), Athenian productivity is at least in part a function of coercive imperialism and violent (or at least potentially violent) resource extraction. But in the early democracy that preceded the imperial period (eras III–IV) and in the post-imperial fourth century (eras IX–XI), Athens had no substantial empire from which to extract major resources. During these pre- and post-imperial eras, Athenian economic performance depended primarily on domestic production and exchange.[7]

Knowledge is a central element in the transaction-cost/productivity equation: if both parties to an exchange share full and transparent access to all the information relevant to the exchange, their transaction costs drop accordingly. But under conditions of incomplete information—and especially of asymmetrical access to important information—transaction costs increase. Suppose, for example that B(uyer) and S(eller) seek to exchange B's silver ingots for S's grain. If B is an expert dealer in grain, a careful examination of S's goods may bring their information into something approximating symmetry.[8] But the other side of the equation remains cryptic: B knows the silver content of the ingots he is offering, but S does not. S incurs costs in gaining that information and will need to cover those costs in the price of his grain.[9] Similarly, if S offers his grain in measures that are unknown to B, B will need to cover the cost of measuring out the grain for himself before he can conclude the bargain. Likewise, exchanges will be more costly if B and S must spend a lot of time

[7] It is wrong to imagine that Athens had *no* imperialistic ambitions or tendencies before or after the era 478–404: cf. the expropriation of land from Chalcis in 506. Athens also engaged in foreign policy that has been interpreted as imperialist in the first and second quarters of the fourth century: see Buckler 2003 for detailed discussion. But in any event, with the exception of the control of three Aegean islands, Lemnos, Imbros, and Skyros, which were regular sources of revenue from a grain tax (Stroud 1998, and below, this chapter), Athenian imperial enterprises after the period of the fifth-century "high empire" are unlikely to have produced net revenue gains. See further, Griffith 1978. Karayiannis and Hatis offer a transaction cost analysis of the imperial era economy, focusing on the role of trust and social capital among citizens rather than on rent extraction.

[8] Levitt and Dubner 2005: 55–85 offer a clear account of the economic problems associated with information asymmetries. The general absence of state-sponsored standards for certifying the value of commodities (e.g., grain or meat) in classical Greek antiquity, along with problems in standardized measures (especially at the high-volume, wholesale level), is the subject of ongoing research by Steven Johnstone.

[9] Van Alfen 2004/5 offers a case study of the transition from a bullion-currency transaction standard, to a coin-currency standard in Saite Egypt (era of Persian control: late sixth through late fourth century). Attempts to determine and indicate silver purity led to elaborate systems of cutting and counterpunching—operations that obviously drove up the costs of transactions. Cuts and counterpunches remain common on coins (as well as ingots) in Egypt and the Levant, but are rare on coins found in Aegean hoards: van Alfen 2002: 2–7.

and effort in finding each other in the first place (an *ex ante* cost). If either B or S is uncertain as to how any dispute arising between them will be arbitrated (an *ex post* cost), or has reason to distrust the arbitration procedure, his risk factor increases. In each case, overall costs of doing business go up. As transaction costs mount, the chance that a mutually beneficial transaction will successfully be concluded declines.

If B and S were both employees of a single firm, subject to the same command and control hierarchy, each of the information uncertainties considered above would be lessened—which is the heart of Coase's (1988 [1937]) argument about the origins of the firm and a key point in Williamson's (1975, 1981, 1985) transaction-cost economics. Within the framework of an organization, the ground is leveled by hierarchy (S is ordered to deliver a certain amount of grain to B at a certain time) and by internal accounting mechanisms (both the price of the grain and the amount are measured in standard units specified in advance by the organization). Transaction costs are thus kept low. Alternatively, if B and S are carrying out their private-party exchanges in a state-established regulatory framework, they may have access to state-issued coins of fixed purity and weight, and to standardized grain measures. The state's authority for issuing standard currency, establishing standard weights and measures, and maintaining a legal apparatus to settle disputes serves, like the command and control apparatus of a firm, to lower transaction costs.

Transaction-cost economics also helps to explain why firms seek to grow larger by adding seemingly peripheral operations to their core processes: vertical integration brings more aspects of production under the low transaction-cost regime. This in turn promises to extend the zone of efficient exchange and thus to increase overall profitability margins. A similar story can be told about hierarchical states, which also employ extensive command and control mechanisms and standardized accounting practices. Yet as the hierarchical organization (firm or state) extends command and control, the requirement for routinization of processes can overwhelm its capacity for innovation. As a result, flexibility and entrepreneurial enterprise may be eroded—especially as systems grow very large and complex. Profitability drops and the organization becomes increasingly vulnerable to more innovative and nimble rivals.

Modern firms, concerned to regain flexibility and entrepreneurial advantage, sometimes seek to create internal competitive markets that nonetheless remain governed by standard firmwide rules and accounting mechanisms.[10] This arrangement in some ways resembles the economic governance policies of a modern democratic state committed to promoting a market economy. In both cases, the organization is seeking to cap-

---

[10] See J. Roberts 2004, who discusses a variety of intraorganizational incentive structures designed to maintain innovation while retaining the advantages of low transaction costs.

ture some of the benefits associated with hierarchy while avoiding hierarchy's depressing constraints, that is, seeking conditions in which the rules
provide a level playing ground for productive exchanges on the basis of
"symmetrical information" about the conditions governing those exchanges. The goal is a knowledge regime that secures the transaction cost
advantages associated with equal access to relevant information and yet
promotes innovation and entrepreneurial enterprise by allowing individual choices to drive transactions. The question before us is how a participatory democracy might do something similar in gaining the advantages
of symmetrical information and competitive markets, yet without having
developed an elaborate command and control hierarchy in the first place.

I hypothesized above (chapter 3) that Athenian material flourishing
should be explained in part by the state's success in lowering transaction
costs. This could have been accomplished, I suggested, through standardizing and publicizing rules and practices that in turn helped build and
maintain a relatively reliable and secure exchange environment. We can
test this hypothesis by, first, specifying how various instruments available
to a participatory democracy *should* operate if the state's goal were optimizing (i.e., driving down and keeping down) transaction costs; and then
asking how far Athens conformed to or diverged from that optimal position (see table 6.1). We should keep in mind, however, that in light of the
various non-material ends sought by the democratic polis (chapter 1), low
transaction costs should be thought of as a satisficing condition (that is,
an attempt to meet criteria for adequacy in respect to conditions of exchange) rather than as a unitary goal subject to true optimization.

Among the instruments available to participatory democracies (as well
as to more hierarchical organizations) are clear and accessible codes of
formal rules (laws, customs, administrative protocols) designed to protect
persons and their property; standardized and easy-to-use dispute-resolu-
tion procedures (mandatory or optional modes of binding or non-binding
arbitration, courts of law); and dependable state-imposed sanctions for
punishing delinquents. A second set of instruments includes established
standards for weights and measures; standardized exchange media (gov-
ernment-issued and guaranteed currency, standard forms of contract);
convenient facilities, such as centralized market places, well-designed
transport and communication networks; and effective policing. Finally,
the state can keep transaction costs low by keeping down the rents it
extracts (directly or indirectly) on exchanges, or that it allows others to
extract.[11]

---

[11] Xenophon's *Poroi* (*Revenues*), an essay written sometime in the mid-fourth century
B.C. with the explicit aim of improving Athenian state revenue through the encouragement
of industry (especially silver mining) and trade (by promoting immigration by metics) advocates a number of these measures. See discussion by Gauthier 1976; Doty 2003; and below,
this chapter.

TABLE 6.1
State-determined conditions for low-transaction-cost bargain making

Instrument	Openness: Access	Fairness: Impartiality
1a. Formal rules (laws, decrees, customs)	Publicly posted or common knowledge, stable, archived, legible, simple, non-contradictory, comprehensive, relevant to current conditions.	Apply impartially to all parties; protect bodily integrity, property, dignity of all. *Bodily integrity and dignity of citizens favored.*
1b. Dispute procedures (litigation, arbitration)	Swift, reliable, easy to use, difficult to abuse, available to all. *Non-citizens without standing in some legal procedures.*	Treat similar cases and similar disputants similarly.
1c. Sanctions (punishments, limitations)	All delinquents are liable to punishments that are standardized, appropriate to the infraction, widely publicized.	Applied similarly to similar infractions. *Intentional murder of citizen punished more severely. Slaves liable to beating as additional or replacement penalty.*
2a. Exchange media (coinage, weights, measures, contracts, sureties)	Readily obtainable, comprehensive, stable, recognizable, reliable, standardized.	Impersonal, used by all. *Only citizens (with some exceptions) may own real estate.*
2b. Facilities (marketplaces, communications, transport, storage, security)	Centralized open-access markets, low-cost communication and transport systems, reliable and secure storage. Housing, religious apparatus readily available.	Available for use by all on similar terms.
3. Third-party rents (taxes, bribes, protection)	Taxes on exchanges low, simple, centralized, returned to productive system. Restraints on corruption, violence, rent seeking, misuse of government apparatus.	Applied similarly to similar cases. *Most metics pay special taxes. Athenian settlements abroad and tax-farming favor citizens.*

Note: Italics = substantial and systematic Athenian deviations from optimal conditions.

Each of these various instruments must manifest two general properties if it is to work effectively to lower transaction costs: it must be open, and it must be fair. By open, I mean that that the instrument is accessible in respect to entry (as opposed to restricting entry according to extraneous criteria) and clear in respect to interpretation (as opposed, for example, to being interpretable only by insiders "in the know"). By fair, I mean that the instrument is impartial in its effects in that it distributes goods and bads according to criteria that are evenhanded (as opposed to criteria that are arbitrary or "loaded" in favor of insiders) and impersonal in that it does not identify and preselect particular categories of individuals for special treatment (good or bad) on the basis of extraneous criteria. These various optimizing criteria are laid out schematically in table 6.1.

Table 6.1[12] is meant to specify the ways that government intervention in a market would render bargaining in that market as close to frictionless as possible—thus as close to the ideal conditions imagined in what has become known as the Coase Theorem. As Coase himself (1988: 174–75) emphatically pointed out, the ideal conditions of the Coase Theorem do not and could not exist in the real world, and thus, even with the best possible will, no government could *eliminate* transaction costs. A government, to exist and thereby facilitate the low transaction-cost regime, must have some way to maintain itself, which makes it very likely that it will need to levy taxes of some sort on at least some kinds of exchange (row 3).

Every real-world government falls short of achieving perfect access and impartiality. This shortfall occurs at least in part (per above) because governments attempt to achieve a variety of ends in legislation. Lowering transaction costs is balanced against other goals of state policy. In modern governments, for example, the principle of openness, in terms of both entry and clarity, is compromised not only by security considerations but by rules created by legislative enactment and by administrative protocols developed and administered by professional bureaucrats. These rules are intended to fulfill important public purposes; they are meant (inter alia) to protect consumers from fraud or safety risks. The complexity of modern rules, and the technical legal language in which they are cast, tend to raise transaction costs. Complex rules require (inter alia) that those making bargains employ legal specialists to design contracts and to defend the principals to exchanges against charges of having violated rules that are far from transparent (at least to those non-experts lacking the necessary technical training).[13] This in turn bars entry to those who cannot afford to purchase the requisite legal expertise.

Athenian legislative processes produced government rules and other instruments that, in comparison to modern legislation, were publicly accessible, simple, and clear. Athenian laws and decrees, for example, were relatively brief and composed in ordinary language, posted in public places, and available for consultation in standard forms.[14] Nor, as noted in chapter 3, is there any reason to suppose that there were complex administrative protocols working in the background. Athenian government

[12] Athenian violations of openness and fairness: M. H. Hansen 1999: 87–88, 97–99, 116–22.

[13] Huber and Shipan 2002 offer a comparative analysis of the choice of modern legislators to draft detailed legislation or to leave the details to administrative rules drafted by unelected civil servants. In either case, the result is that the end users are subject to rules that require expert interpretation.

[14] See, for example, Thomas 1989: 60–93, 2005; D. Harris 1994; Hedrick 1999, 2000; Richardson 2000; Davies 2003.

instruments were not, however, completely open and impartial. Various Athenian instruments discriminated according to the status of the individual in question.

We will briefly consider, below, some aspects of Athenian rules (notably the development of commercial law), facilities for exchange (including standards of measurement), and attitudes toward third-party rents. The goal is to answer the question of how well Athens conformed to or diverged from the optimal transaction-cost regime laid out in table 6.1. But first we will consider in detail a particular piece of Athenian legislation, one that reveals a good deal about both the state's rational concern for lowering transaction costs and ideological commitment to unfair discriminatory practices. Looking at a particular policy in detail gives a better feel for how the process of codification worked in practice and how it affected the willed actions of people subject to Athenian law. Moreover, focusing on a legislative initiative of the 370s helps us to resist the error of misconstruing the rationalization of the fourth-century Athenian economy as entirely a product of the fiscal reforms that were enacted after Athenian losses in the Aegean War of 357–355 B.C.[15]

A LAW ON SILVER COINAGE, 375/4 B.C.

At a meeting held some time between July of 375 and July of 374 B.C., the Athenian Assembly decided, on a motion by a certain Nikophon, that the polis should consider a revision in the standing laws governing the exchange of silver currency in the city.[16] That decision may have been made under provisions of the "Review Law"—that is, at the annual meeting at which the Assembly took up a standing agenda item mandating that each section of the Athenian law code be reviewed and voted upon by the Assembly. Alternatively, Nikophon's motion to consider a change in the law may have been made at an ordinary meeting of the Assembly by invoking the "Repeal Law" that allowed any specific law in the existing code to be challenged. In this case, the Council of 500 must have actively considered the matter in advance of the meeting, and must have

[15] On the war (conventionally, but confusingly called the Social War), see Buckler 2003: 337–84. On the financial reforms associated with Eubulus (and then Lycurgus) and the development of new commercial laws (*dikai emporikai*), see below. Note that if several substantial owl series sometimes thought to be Egyptian imitations are in fact Athenian state issues of the earlier fourth century (as suggested by Kroll 2006), this would be further evidence for Athenian economic activity in era X.

[16] RO 25 with citation of some of the earlier scholarship. *Editio princeps* with commentary: Stroud 1974. See also Figueira 1998: 536–47; Engen 2005 (with detailed literature review). The best analytic treatment is van Alfen 2005.

decided to place "considering changes to the laws on coinage" on the agenda of the relevant Assembly meeting. In either case, following the vote that allowed the laws governing coinage to be reconsidered, the Assembly was legally required to name five Athenians as advocates for the existing law. These five men would be responsible for defending the current laws against Nikophon's challenge when it came time to decide whether to change the law or not.[17]

His motion to consider revision having passed the Assembly, Nikophon was now legally required to write up his proposed new law on a whitened board, and also to indicate which, if any, laws currently in force must be repealed in order to accommodate his proposed new legislation. The board was to be prominently posted in front of the monument of the Eponymous Heroes in the Agora (chapter 5), so that any Athenian who so desired could consider the exact wording of Nikophon's proposal and discuss it with others. Some time later, at a second meeting of the Assembly, the demos voted to empanel (on a particular day) and to provide pay for the necessary number of "lawmakers" (nomothetai). These would have numbered 501–1,501, possibly more, depending on how important the Assembly considered the proposed changes. The nomothetai were selected by lot from the ranks of the approximately six thousand registered jurors—men over age thirty who had that year taken the juror's oath and so were available for service on the People's courts.[18]

On the appointed day, Nikophon presented his case for changing the laws to the nomothetai, in what amounted to a prosecutor's brief. The five advocates, previously chosen by the Assembly to oppose the change, served as defenders of the existing laws. Having heard both sides in this

[17] Athenian nomothesia procedure: M. H. Hansen 1999: 168–69, with notes. We do not know how the five advocates were chosen, or whether they would have been expected to have some special expertise in Athenian law. In any event, we can suppose that following their appointment they were expected to study the existing laws carefully, as well as analyzing the alternative proposed by Nikophon: if they were not experts coming into the Assembly, they were expected to develop the requisite expertise in short order.

[18] The whitened board rule (Davies 2003: 325) allowed the Athenians to decide whether there was a prima facie case for allowing the process for potential revision to go forward. If Athenian opinion found Nikophon's proposed change to be without merit, a vote not to empanel nomothetai or provide their pay would end his challenge. The procedure is conservative in that it requires that momentum for change be sustained across time (two assemblies and a meeting of the nomothetai) and across institutional bodies (Council, Assembly, nomothetai); Harrison 1955 gets it right when he describes the process as a sort of democratic brake on the otherwise remarkably quick legislative process. Presumably the Council could stop the proposal from going forward by refusing to put "empanelling and paying nomothetai" on the agenda of the second meeting, but (per chapter 4) there is no reason to suppose that would happen in the face of Athenian public opinion that favored going forward.

quasi trial, the *nomothetai* voted, apparently by show of hands; a simple majority decided the matter. Because Nikophon's motion passed, his proposed law came to be written into the Athenian law code and inscribed on a marble stele.[19]

Nikophon's law concerned the process by which coinage circulating in the city was approved as legal tender or removed from circulation. It specifies the duties of a preexisting state-appointed Approver of silver coins (*dokimastês*). It establishes a second Approver in Piraeus with identical duties. It lists the various magisterial boards that will be involved with setting up the Piraeus Approver and indicates penalties for lawbreaking. As it happens, a marble stele inscribed with this law was discovered in 1970 by archaeologists in the Agora, and so we have an almost complete copy of Nikophon's law. The law reveals much about the design of Athenian legal institutions, suggesting that the Athenians explicitly sought to facilitate market exchanges by using government institutions to lower transaction costs. The translated text of Nikophon's law follows, arranged for convenience of citation into outline form.

> Resolved by the *nomothetai* in the archonship of Hippodamas [375/ 4 B.C.]; Nikophon made the proposal:
>
> 1. Athenian [*Attikon*] silver [coin] shall be accepted [by all sellers of goods] when
>   a. it is found [by the Approver] to be [solid] silver and
>   b. has the public stamp [*dēmosios charaktēr*: obverse: bust of Athena; reverse: owl and letters ΑΘΕ = "Athena"].
> 2. The public Approver [*dokimastēs*: a public slave; see below] shall sit between the [bankers'] tables [in the Agora] and approve [coins] on these terms every day except when there is a deposit of money [state revenue payment], in which case [he sits] in the Council-building [*bouleutērion*].
>   a. If anyone brings forward [to the Approver] foreign [*xenikon*] silver [coin] having the same stamp as Attic [coin], <if it

---

[19] It is not clear how the proceedings would go if there were multiple proposals for mutually incompatible new laws. Depending on how long a given case took to decide, it might have been possible for the panel to consider several motions on a single day (M. H. Hansen 1999: 169), but once the *nomothetai* had voted for a change, the new law would be in place. The five advocates, who had prepared to defend the former law, would hardly be in a position to mount a case in defense of the new law that they had just finished opposing! So we must assume that either (by convention or by law) it never happened that multiple mutually incompatible proposals came before a given panel of *nomothetai*, or that there was some sort of sorting device (a lottery?) determining the order of presentation and that the first challenge to pass ended the proceedings. In this case, alternative proposals could, of course, be reintroduced in subsequent meetings of the Assembly.

is good>,[20] he [the Approver] shall give it back to the man who brought it forward [for review];[21]

b. but if it has a bronze core or lead core or is fraudulent [*kibdēlos*: i.e., an impure alloy rather than near-pure silver], he [the Approver] shall cut through it immediately and it shall be [confiscated as] sacred property of the Mother of the Gods and he shall deposit it with the Council [of 500].

3. If the Approver does not sit, or does not approve in accordance with the law, he shall be beaten by the Conveners of the People [*syllogeis tou dēmou* = 30 sitting members of the Council, three from each tribe] with 50 lashes of the whip [i.e., punished as a slave].

4. If anyone does not accept the silver which the Approver approves, he shall be deprived of what he is selling that day.

5. Exposures [*phaseis*: a legal process by which concerned persons "outed" illegal actions of others: here, sellers refusing to accept approved coin] shall be made [by individuals, to magistrates, as follows]

a. For matters in the grain-market to the Grain-guardians [*sitophulakes*: lotteried magistrates]

b. For matters in the Agora and the rest of the city to the Conveners of the People

c. For matters in the import market [*emporion*] and in [the rest of] the Piraeus to the Overseers of the Import-market [*epimelētai tou emporiou*: lotteried magistrates]—except for matters in the grain-market, since [*phaseis* about matters] in the grain-market are [to be made] to the Grain-guardians [per 5a, above].

6. For matters exposed [by the legal process described in 5], those that [concern sums that] are up to 10 drachmas the relevant magistrates [listed in 5] shall have the power to decide. Those that are beyond 10 drachmas they [the magistrates] shall introduce to the People's court [*dikastērion*].

7. The *thesmothetai* [a board of 6 lotteried archons: senior magistrates] shall provide and allot a People's court for [the magistrates named in 5 a–c] whenever they request, or shall be fined 1000? drachmas.

---

[20] Stroud's proposed restoration (Stroud 1974) of this lacuna as *e[an kalon]*, "if it is good," is accepted here. Alternate restorations: RO 25, p. 114.

[21] The question of whether the "foreign issue/Athenian-type good coin" that the Approver handed back to the buyer is returned *as approved* (and thus must be accepted by the seller), or whether it is handed back as "not produced by the Athenian state, but evidently good coin" (leaving the decision of whether or not to accept it to the seller) is a matter of controversy. I argue below for the "good by not approved" reading.

8. For the man who exposes [wrongdoing, per 5], there shall be a share of a half [of the assessed penalty] if he [serving as legal prosecutor] convicts the man whom he exposes.

9. If the [exposed and convicted] seller is a slave-man or slave-woman, he/she shall be beaten with 50 lashes of the whip by the magistrates [in 5a–c] with responsibility in the matter.

10. If any of the magistrates does not act in accordance with what is written [here], he shall be legally denounced [*eisangellein*] to the Council of 500 by whoever so wishes [*ho boulomenos*] of the Athenians who have the legal right to do so [*exestin*: i.e., the denunciation of a magistrate to the Council must be by a citizen in good standing];

    a. if he [the accused magistrate] is convicted he shall be dismissed from his office

    b. and the Council of 500 may levy an additional fine up to 500 drachmas.

11. So that there shall also be in the Piraeus an Approver for the ship-owners [*nauklēroi*] and the traders [*emporoi*] and all the others [involved in exchange], the Council of 500 shall [either]

    a. appoint [an Approver] from the [existing] public slaves if available

    b. or shall buy [a slave in which case] the Receivers [*apodektai*: lotteried magistrates] shall allocate funds [for his purchase].

12. The Overseers of the Import-market [see 5c, above] shall see that he [the Approver in Piraeus] sits in front of the stele of Poseidon, and they [the Approver in the Piraeus and responsible magistrates] shall use the law in the same way as has been stated [above] concerning the Approver in the city.

13. Write up this law on a stone stele and set it up [*katatheinai*]

    a. in the city between the [bankers'] tables [i.e., where the city Approver sits]

    b. and [set up a copy] in Piraeus in front of the stele of Poseidon [i.e., where the Piraeus Approver sits].

    c. The secretary of the Council of 500 shall commission the contract [for inscribing and erecting the two stelai] from the Sellers [*pōlētai*: lotteried magistrates], and the Sellers shall introduce [the contract] into the Council.

14. The salary payment [*misthophoria*] for the Approver in the Import-market [in Piraeus] shall be [in the current year, prorated] from when he is appointed; and the Receivers shall allocate as much [salary for him] as for the Approver in the city.

a. [after the current year] the salary payment [of both Approvers] shall be from the same source as for the mint-workers [i.e., a specific budget controlled by some board of magistrates, not specified here but presumably ascertainable by Athenians].

15. If there is any decree [*psēphisma*] written on a stele contrary to this law [*nomos*], the secretary of the Council of 500 shall demolish [*katheletō*] it.

(Translation Stroud 1974, slightly emended)

As in the case of the naval-station dispatching decree considered in chapter 4, this law on silver coinage reveals how Athenian institutional design addressed public-action problems. It is immediately apparent that the general intent of the law is to facilitate mercantile exchange in the two key market zones of Athens: the central Agora and the port town (deme) of Piraeus, some 5 miles to the south. The new Piraeus Approver is explicitly (§11) established for the convenience of shipowners, traders, and "others." The law's apparent goal is ensuring that silver coinage remains a reliable and low-transaction-cost exchange mechanism. Both in the Agora (as before) and (now) in Piraeus an expert state official will be available to guarantee that the coinage in circulation in Athens is of proper quality. The law generally mandates that those trading in Athens accept Athens-produced silver coins bearing the standard "stamp": bust of Athena obverse/owl reverse (§1). It specifically requires the acceptance of coins that have been approved by the Approvers (§5), thereby rendering approved Athenian silver coins "legal tender." It provides for the tacit certification of certain silver foreign coins as good, and for the confiscation of bad coins. Finally, it provides appropriate incentives and sanctions so that all Athenian officials involved in the process are motivated to fulfill their duties. The intended result is that all persons involved in exchange in Athenian markets are provided in common with an essential item of information: that the currency in circulation in Athens is trustworthy in regard to its silver content.

The law assumes that exchange is taking place primarily in the form of coined silver money, which was a standard means of exchange throughout much of Greece in the classical period. Many, although not all, classical Greek poleis issued their own very high quality silver coinage in state-run mints (see chapter 2); typically each city's coins featured distinctive types on the obverse and reverse. In the fourth century a number of poleis (including, by midcentury, Athens) also issued bronze coins; a few issued gold or electrum coins as well (Mackil and van Alfen 2006). Athens had issued gold coins and silver-plated bronze coins during an emergency near the end of the Peloponnesian War. But the state-issued silver-plated bronze coins were officially withdrawn by the mid-390s; coined silver remained the primary exchange medium in Athens and other Mediterranean markets. A short digression into the conditions under which Athenian silver coinage was produced will help to clarify what is going on in the law.[22]

SILVER OWLS, ATHENIAN AND IMITATION

Athens was able to mint exceptionally large issues of silver coinage at least in part because of the rich silver mines of south Attica. We do not know much about state law governing silver mining before the fourth century, although the mines must have been state regulated by the early fifth century. We have seen (chapter 2, era IV) that the Athenians decided in 483 to use an initial windfall of revenue from the silver mines to support the public purpose of navy building, rather than distributing the windfall revenue to the citizenry. By the mid-fourth century B.C. a detailed set of rules regulated the leasing of mineral rights, as well as the relations between leaseholders and local landowners. The goal of this legislation was to protect the property rights and capital investments of various parties involved in a mixed agricultural/industrial regional economy in which there would inevitably be conflicts over labor (slaves were used in large numbers in the mines and sometimes ran away), water (needed both to wash out the silver ore and for agriculture), and negative externalities incidental to the production of silver: acrid smoke from refineries, dumps of mining tailings, and so on.[23]

The Athenian state took over the refined silver from individual entrepreneurs. These individuals (at least by 367 B.C. and probably before)

---

[22] Introduction to ancient coinage: Howgego 1995. History of Athenian coinage: Flament 2007. Athenian wartime gold and plated coins: Head 1911: 373; Grandjean 2006. Plated coins officially withdrawn: Aristophanes, *Assemblywomen* 819. Of the 198 poleis for which some constitutional data are available (see appendix 1): 34 minted no coinage, 17 produced only bronze coins, 44 produced only silver, and 107 minted silver and some other metal (usually, from the fourth century onwards, bronze but sometimes gold or electrum). From the time of their first appearance in the fourth century onwards, bronze "small change" coins were very popular; bronze coins are much more common than are precious-metal coins in archaeological contexts: Callataÿ 2006. Silver currency remained, however, the primary form of exchange for larger transactions.

[23] Athenian state production of coinage was high through much of the fifth century, especially after 449 B.C. (excepting the immediate aftermath of the Persian Wars [Starr 1970], and a crisis period at the end of the Peloponnesian War), and very high in the second half of the fourth century (*pi* style series: van Alfen 2000: 21); there remains considerable controversy over early-fourth-century issues: see Kroll 2006 and Flament 2007: 55–58. History of Athenian coinage policy: Figueira 1998; Grandjean 2006. Mine slaves: Lauffer 1979. Mining region and methods: Kounas et al. 1972; Mussche et al. 1975. Relations between mining

leased from the state on an annual basis the rights to extract silver ore from mines that often lay beneath privately held land. The contractors also produced near-pure silver bullion from the mined ore, employing a complex industrial infrastructure of washeries and furnaces. The state was the only seller of mine leases and (apparently) the only buyer of bullion, and so had a monopoly at both ends of the supply chain. But Athens kept the individual lessor's incentives relatively high and the state's own profit margins relatively low. In the fourth century, leases were calibrated according to risk, with lease rates of proven mines set much higher than speculative "new shafts." The state evidently bought bullion from producers at a rate that approximated the value of coined silver less minting costs. Although there is reason to believe that mines were being leased in the first quarter of the fourth century (our earliest surviving list of leases, from 367/6, mentions an "older stele"), it may have taken some time to get the incentives set right after the disruption of the Peloponnesian War. The epigraphic evidence of mining leases suggests that the mining district may not have fully rebounded from the Peloponnesian War–era decline until the 340s. By that time the state leasing of mines may have been bringing in as much as 160 talents each year, an amount roughly equivalent to 25 percent of imperial tribute in the mid-fifth century.[24]

Athenian coinage was conservative in terms of its types: obverse (bust of Athena) and reverse (owl, olive branch, AΘE); the standard coin used in trade was the tetradrachm (four-drachma piece). Although stylistic differences allow expert numismatists to date Athenian coin series, the untrained observer may initially find it difficult to distinguish a late-fifth-century tetradrachm from an early-fourth-century Athenian tetradrachm (figure 6.1, nos. 1–2). The "brand" of Athenian silver coinage was thus (like, say, the Nike swoosh or the Coca-Cola script) very well established.[25] The brand stood for solid quality: Athenian tetradrachms were nearly pure silver and standardized in weight (17 g ±. 15 g for post–Persian War coins). A genuine "owl" (as the coins were called, after the image of Athena's owl stamped on the reverse) was thus dependable as an ex-

---

lessees and landowners: Osborne 1985a, chapter 6. Mining cases in Athenian law: MacDowell 2006.

[24] Athenian mining operations: Conophagos 1980. Leasing: Hopper 1953; Ober 1985: 28–30; Shipton 2001; RO pp. 180–82.

[25] Through most of the fifth century, owl series are very monotonous. There are noticeable stylistic changes in the fourth century especially with the *pi* style owls (Athena's bust now features a profile eye, for example) that begin in the mid-century. Notably, these mid-century changes in the coinage coincide with the development of the maritime courts and the creation of new offices for magistrates responsible for some aspects of economic policy: Kroll 1993: 8; van Alfen 2000: 21; see below, this chapter and note 35. Weight and purity of Athenian coins remain constant throughout. Head 1911 remains a helpful survey.

Figure 6.1. Athenian state-issued owls (left column: 1–3) and imitation silver owls (right column: 4–6). **1.** Athens, late 5th c. AR tetradrachm (bona fide owl) 17.15 g (ANS 1997.9.196, John D. Leggett, Jr. bequest). **2.** Athens, early 4th c. AR tetradrachm (bona fide owl). 17.15 g (ANS 1959.137.1). **3.** Athens, c. 405 B.C. AR/AE drachm (official plated issue; note that the cut in this coin was likely applied in Athens to demonetize it). 3.65 g (ANS 1966.232.1). **4.** Egypt?, early 4th c. AR double shekel? (anonymous imitation; note that countermarking, such as appears on the obverse, was primarily a Near Eastern and Egyptian practice) 16.82 g (ANS 1944.100.24208, E. T. Newell bequest). **5.** Palestine, late 5th/early 4th c. AR double shekel? (marked imitation; note Aramaic *shin* on the cheek).16.52 g (ANS 1971.196.2). **6.** Babylonia?, 4th c. AR double shekel? (perfunctory imitation; note cut on reverse, perhaps to check purity)16.97 g (ANS 1974.274.2). Key: AR = silver. AE = bronze. g = gram. Photographic images courtesy of © American Numismatic Society. My thanks to Peter van Alfen, ANS curator of Greek coins, for selecting the six coins for this figure, for photography, and documentation. J. Kroll (per litt.) suggests no. 4 is state-issued.

change medium, a dependability that in and of itself served to lower transaction costs. Exchanging goods for silver owls eliminated the steps of assaying the purity of silver (a difficult, time-consuming, and destructive process) and weighing bulk silver. Although Athenian owls, like all Greek silver coins, were exchanged primarily on the basis of their commodity value (the worth of the silver itself), they also possessed a "fiduciary value added" in the Athenian state's guarantee of precious metal content and standard weight.

In the latter part of the fifth century, the Athenians had mandated the use of Athenian coinage throughout their empire.[26] By the fourth century, the great empire was just a memory, but Athenian owls remained among the most common coins in circulation in the eastern Mediterranean region.[27] A market favoring Athenian coinage was beneficial to Athens in a number of ways: the state probably made a small profit on each coin it produced (the exchange value of the coin minus cost of bullion plus minting cost). Mining enriched many individual Athenians. It supported local deme economies, like that of Thorikos, in south Attica (cf. the big, well-built Thorikos theater, chapter 5). Perhaps most importantly it helped attract traders and their business to Athens, where they knew that they would be contracting their bargains in a reliable exchange medium.[28]

The great esteem in which owls were held throughout the eastern Mediterranean led to the production of "owl-like" coins outside of Athens. By the mid-370s substantial numbers of *imitation owls*—that is, coins with the "Athenian stamp" but not issued by the Athenian state—were circulating in eastern Mediterranean markets, including Athens. The phenomenon of "pseudo-owls" has been well documented by numismatists; imitations of owls began to appear in the fifth century, but became very common only in the early fourth century. Many imitation owls were produced by foreign states, especially in Egypt and the Levant. Others were in all probability minted by individuals. Some pseudo-owls were good coins, in that they were comparable in silver content to Athenian-produced owls; other pseudo-owls were bad coins in that they looked like

[26] Coinage decree: Meiggs and Lewis 1988, no. 45. Figueira 1998 is the fullest discussion, although his interpretation is controversial on many points. For our present purposes the much-discussed problem of the decree's date is not of great moment.

[27] The wide extent of the circulation of Athenian owls, especially in the fourth century, is evident in even a superficial perusal of the coin hoard evidence collected in Thompson et al. 1973. See, in detail, Flament 2007 (catalog of hoards that include Athenian owls), and further discussion of the hoard evidence in chapter 2 and table 6.3, below.

[28] Xenophon, *Revenues*, written in the mid-fourth century, makes a point of the desirability of silver as a medium of trade. Cf. Aristotle, *Nicomachean Ethics* 1133a.

real owls but had a much lower silver content. An important part of the Approver's job was discriminating between good and bad pseudo-owls and treating them accordingly (§2). Examples of imitation owls circulating in the Aegean region at the time of Nikophon's law are illustrated in figure 6.1, nos. 4–6.[29]

In economies where the value of money is fiduciary, it is natural to think of *all* imitation money as counterfeit, produced with the intention to deceive and thereby defraud. Yet clearly Athenian law did not treat all imitation owls as counterfeits in this sense. Peter van Alfen has recently brought greater terminological precision to the numismatic discussion of imitation by distinguishing between seven categories of ancient coins:

1. Prototypes (state-issued originals: in this case real silver owls: fig. 6.1, nos. 1–2).
2. Artistic imitations (e.g., medallions that are clearly distinguishable from prototypes and may have had different functions).
3. Anonymous imitations (close copies, that may, at the margin, be indistinguishable from the prototype: fig. 6.1, no. 4).
4. Marked imitations (relatively close copies of prototypes that are clearly distinguished by their producers from prototypes, for example, by the addition of a special symbol, and therefore unlikely to be confused with prototypes by experienced traders: fig. 6.1, no. 5).
5. Perfunctory imitations (not close copies of the prototype in any sense: fig. 6.1, no. 6).
6. Official plated and debased coins (e.g., the emergency Athenian War issues of plated bronze owls: fig. 6.1, no. 3).
7. Counterfeit plated and debased coins (privately manufactured for the purpose of deception).[30]

---

[29] The imitation owl phenomenon: Thompson et al. 1973: 154, cf. 200. Stroud 1974: 175–78 with plate 25d–f; Figueira 1998: 528–35; van Alfen 2000: 2002: 32–48, and especially 2005. Stewart and Martin 2005 note that the jump in imitation owls ca. 400–375 B.C. coincides with a massive increase of imports of Athenian-made pottery into Egypt. Kroll 1993: 4–5 reports that 22 percent of the 129 Greek silver coins found in the Athenian Agora excavations were "unofficial" (not prototypes, in van Alfen's typology, below); 22 of these were clads ("plated"), and between 5 and 7 were high-silver-content imitations. Van Alfen 2005: 344 notes that of 791 Athenian coin types in the American Numismatic Society collection, some 19 percent are high-silver-content imitations and 8 percent are plated. These are noisy statistics, as van Alfen points out, especially because one expert's real owl may be another expert's imitation, but they certainly show that pseudo-owls were circulating in Athens, and that the Approvers would have had some work to do.

[30] Van Alfen 2005, with excellent discussion of Nikophon's law in the context of the problem of imitation coinages. Athenian law specified death for producing van Alfen's category 7 counterfeits: Demosthenes 20.167.

Approval, Certification, Confiscation

Nikophon's law seeks in the first instance (§1) to ensure that prototypes (Athenian state-produced silver owls: van Alfen category 1) are accepted in Athens. The law then refers to two primary categories of imitations. Section 2.a of Nikophon's law mentions foreign silver coins that possess the two bona fide characteristics possessed by prototypes: the public stamp and (apparently—there is a lacuna in the text of the law, due to damage to the stone) the right silver content. These coins, which we may call "good fakes," are to be returned by the Approver to the individual who brought them forward. Van Alfen's category 3 and 4 (anonymous and marked imitations) are presumably the primary categories involved, although coins in categories 2 and 5 might also fall into this category. The good fake owls are contrasted with bad coins: counterfeits of van Alfen's category 7 and perhaps still-circulating state-produced plated coins from category 6.[31] The law (§2.b) mentions clads (lead- and bronze-core coins) and "fraudulent" coins, presumably referring especially to counterfeits made from alloys of silver and base metal. These low silver content coins were presumably being passed off as solid silver owls, with the intension of defrauding naïve traders. In contrast to the good fakes, these bad coins were to be confiscated by the Approver.

The danger of being deceived by counterfeit coins had long been a matter of concern among the Greeks: the "fraudulent coin" was quickly adopted as a metaphor for human insincerity in archaic Greek poetry.[32] It is therefore a particularly notable feature of Nikophon's law that it does not lump all pseudo-owls into a single homogeneous category of bad (because it is "non-prototype") coinage. Good fakes, that is, coins that look like owls and are presumed by the Approver to have silver content similar to real owls, are to be "handed back" to the individual who presented them for approval. There has been considerable debate over the question of whether the good fakes were handed back to their owners *as approved*. Although the wording of the law is not decisive on this point and scholarly opinion differs, I think that there is very good reason

[31] The law does not mention category 6 coins explicitly, and a strict interpretation of the grammar of the key sentence in section 2 of the law would mean that all plated and fraudulent coins are regarded as *xenikon* (i.e., not Athenian state produced). Yet the fact that section 1 of the law specifies Attic *silver* coins with the public stamp as the coins that must be accepted makes room for a category of Attic *non-silver* coins with the public stamp that are not approved. In any event, any war-issue coins still in circulation were clearly to be treated by the Approver *as if* they were foreign frauds.

[32] Kurke 1999; Seaford 2004.

to believe that pseudo-owls that were handed back were not "approved," and thus their acceptance by sellers was not mandatory.[33] Yet it is very clear that good fakes are not being pulled out of circulation by the Athenian state, nor are their owners in any way penalized. Indeed, by returning it to its owner, the Approver may be said to have "certified" a given pseudo-owl by issuing his expert opinion that it was good (*kalon*). The bad fakes (clads and counterfeits: §2.b) and presumably also Athenian-produced plated coins (the emergency issue of the late Peloponnesian War, now no longer regarded as legal tender: fig. 6.1, no. 3) are not only to be confiscated by the Approver, they are to be cut through (as has the plated coin in fig. 6.1, no. 3), and then dedicated by the Council of 500 to the Mother of the Gods. This apparently meant storing them in the Metroon—the Old Bouleuterion, now being used as the state archives building.[34]

Table 6.2 lays out a schematic judgment grid for the Approvers, on the dimensions of origin (Athenian or foreign: column) and quality (good or bad: row). Upon making his expert judgment regarding the "box" into which the coin should fall, the Approver takes a mandatory action. That action results in the coin remaining in circulation or being removed from circulation. In the case of good coins (left column), the buyer is either legally required to accept the coin in payment for goods (if it is certified as good *and* approved as Athenian), or, according the most likely interpretation, he is left free to accept or not (if it is certified as good, but *not* approved as Athenian).

Box 1 is straightforward: the law's explicit intent is to protect the value of Athenian-produced silver by guaranteeing its quality and mandating

---

[33] Stroud 1974: esp. 169 and 186 makes the argument for mandatory acceptance of good fakes—i.e., that being handed back means "approved." This interpretation was vigorously challenged by (*inter alios*) Buttrey 1981 and 1982, who regarded it as impossible that any Greek polis would *mandate* the acceptance of imitations. The *phasis* dispute procedure might seem to favor Stroud's interpretation: Assuming that approved coins and unapproved good fakes are both handed back by the Approver to the buyer, there is potential for post-approval dispute about which was which. But in Buttrey's favor is the fact that mandatory acceptance of non-state produced coins opens a dangerous possibility for fraud: if *mala fide* counterfeiters produced 85–95 percent silver fakes perceptually indistinguishable from near-pure silver coins, the state could find itself in the untenable position of mandating the use of bad counterfeits. My thanks to Peter van Alfen for clarification of this point and other issues having to do with Nikophon's law and Athenian coinage.

[34] Stroud 1974: 177–78 discusses two plated coins found by excavators near the Metroon-Bouleuterion complex, and plausibly concludes that these had been confiscated by an Approver and subsequently cut through and dedicated to the Mother of the Gods, as called for in Nikophon's law. It is particularly notable that confiscated coins are deposited in a building used to house state archives. It is tempting to suppose that these bad coins were kept as a study collection that the Approvers could refer to when preparing themselves to deal with potentially suspect coin series; see below.

TABLE 6.2
Approvers' judgment matrix, mandatory actions taken (**bold**), and consequences for
subsequent circulation and use as legal tender (***bold italic***)

1. Athenian (*Attikon*)
    Good (silver)
    Certify and approve (as *dokimon*)
    Remains in circulation
    Mandatory acceptance
	3. Athenian (*Attikon*)
	    Bad (plated bronze = w/drawn war issue)
	    Cut, confiscate, dedicate
	    Removed from circulation
	    Unacceptable

2. Foreign (*xenikon*)
    Good (silver)
    Certify (as *kalon*), return to owner
    Remains in circulation
    Optional acceptance
	4. Foreign (*xenikon*)
	    Bad (plated bronze or lead, fraudulent)
	    Cut, confiscate, dedicate
	    Removed from circulation
	    Unacceptable

its acceptance in trade. Box 4 is equally unproblematic given that counterfeits posed an obvious threat to the Athenian owl brand. Likewise, box
3: it was essential to distinguish between the state-produced but now
withdrawn emergency war series and silver owls. If coins that looked like
owls and were passed off as owls but did not have the silver content of
owls proliferated in the polis and were allowed to circulate freely, traders
would lose faith in owls as a means of exchange and in Athens as a market. If the state ignored fraud based on the passing of counterfeits, the
danger arose that, according to Gresham's Law, bad money would drive
out good. This would in turn drive up the transaction costs that had been
lowered by the reputation of owls for purity because traders would be
hesitant to accept genuine owls on the chance that they were counterfeit.
The state absorbed the costs of an official no-fee approval process in order
to combat that deleterious outcome.

Ordering the Approver to confiscate bad fakes without reimbursement
to their owners imposed a cost on their owners—who can be roughly
divided into cheats (those who knew the coins were bad) and naïves (those
who had taken counterfeit coins from others, believing them to be good
coins). Given the sanction entailed by confiscation (at minimum, the loss
of the residual silver content) and the likelihood that bad coins would be
identified and confiscated by the expert Approver, cautious cheaters were
likely to be discouraged from trading *ex ante*. Bolder cheaters would be
weeded out *ex post*. In either case, their removal helped to optimize the
market. Naïves for their part were penalized for their folly by the state
rather than by opportunistic and better-informed traders. Given the existence of the Approvers, naïve traders in Athens always had recourse to
the services of an expert and so had only themselves to blame if they
ended up in possession of counterfeits. Any injustice associated with

penalizing the innocent naïve whose coins were confiscated was apparently countered by the gains associated with quickly removing bad fakes from the system and efficiently punishing cheaters.

Box 2 of table 6.2 is initially puzzling. It is not immediately obvious why the law should have allowed coins (like those in fig 6.1, nos. 4–5) that might be confused with real owls (nos. 1–2) to remain in circulation. A "handed-back" pseudo-owl was, in effect, given expert certification as "good" (*kalon*)—that is, pronounced by a state-appointed currency expert to be "neither clad, nor fraudulent." And thus the production of "sincere imitations" of Athenian coinage was not discouraged by the Athenian state, nor was trade in pseudo-owls banned. Indeed, the fact that the law makes a point of stating that good pseudo-owls were exempt from confiscation may be regarded as an explicit guarantee to the trading community that Athens will protect the property rights of those in possession of good fakes. All of this would be inexplicable if we were to think of pseudo-owls simply as counterfeits.

As we have seen, the owl "brand" was important to the Athenian trading environment, and the gains to the Athenian community from the production of silver coins were considerable. Why allow "generic" owls to circulate in the city without penalty? Why not protect the brand by confiscating pseudo-owls outright, or by marking them as dubious (e.g., ordering the Approver to "cut before returning"), or by charging their owners a reminting fee? I would suggest that the law's framers realized that penalizing "good fakes" would drive up transaction costs, by putting an unnecessary burden on legitimate transactions. The Athenians tacitly permitted imitations of their owl brand because doing so facilitated trade.[35]

Suppose, counterfactually, that the Athenians had chosen to confiscate all coins regarded as fakes, good and bad, without reimbursement. This would impose very high costs on honest traders who were in possession of good fakes and were offering their trading partners silver value similar to that of real owls. Many good fakes are indistinguishable from real

---

[35] On the likely negative impact of cutting a coin on its subsequence acceptance, see van Alfen 2002: 6, 2004/5: 18. A modern analogy might be generic drugs, which lack the "brand" of the original but are chemically identical. Negotiations between drug makers eager to defend their profits and their brand, and public agencies eager to provide inexpensive health care, are, in their turn, productive of complex rules. It is possible, based on the relatively few legible lines of an as-yet-unpublished Athenian law from 354/3 (Agora Inventory no. 7495), that there was a general recall and reminting of owls two decades after Nikophon's law; this may be connected to the *pi* series, see Kroll 2006. The law is explicitly attentive to the needs of private individuals and to the necessity of accomplishing its goals quickly. My thanks to Molly Richardson for allowing me to consult her in-progress transcript of this important inscription.

owls, except by experts, and even modern experts disagree on whether a given coin or coin series is Athenian prototype or sincere imitation. If honest traders, who were presumably no more expert than modern Greek numismatists at distinguishing real owls from "good fakes," were at risk of losing good silver coins to confiscation every time they sought to make a bargain, it would be a severe damper to trade in Athens. Alternatively, suppose the state had demanded that when good fakes were presented to the Approver and identified as such, they must be exchanged for genuine Athenian coins. In this case, the Athenians would have to decide who should pay reminting costs—that is, the labor costs associated with gathering and transporting the good fakes, melting down the silver, recasting new blank flans, and restamping the blanks with official Athenian dies.

The state could run this (counterfactual) reminting operation at a profit—as did, later, the Ptolemaic state monopoly in Hellenistic Egypt.[36] Depending on the state's profit margin this would have imposed fairly high costs on traders. Or the state could exchange real owls for good fakes at par, thereby eliminating costs to traders, but running a deficit-producing operation that could prove prohibitively costly to the state, given the large number of pseudo-owls in circulation. Finally, the state could charge just enough for exchanging good fakes for real owls to cover its reminting costs. This last option would impose moderate costs on traders.

A hypothetical decision tree (fig. 6.2) for the law's framers shows that the choices Nikophon's law actually makes—confiscating bad fakes and allowing good fakes to remain in circulation—optimizes the trading environment by keeping transaction costs low for well-informed and honest traders, while discouraging cheats and fools. Comparing the actual (in bold) and counterfactual branches of the decision tree strongly suggests that Athenian interest in protecting the state "brand," and/or reaping profits by gathering rents from traders in the form of mandatory reminting costs, was trumped by a concern for keeping transaction costs low.[37]

[36] Egyptian monopoly on coinage: Emmons 1954; Le Rider and Callataÿ 2006: 140–44. Reden 2007b provides the context. A mid-fourth-century decree of Olbia (Dubois 1996, no. 15 = Austin and Vidal-Naquet 1977, no. 103) that is modeled on the Nikophon law (a copy of which was found in Olbia) stakes out a middle ground: mandatory use of Olbian gold and silver coinage, but restrictions on rents from reminting. At about the same time, two Athenians (along with their kinsmen and slaves) were granted special traders' privileges in Olbia (Dubois 1996, no. 21), suggesting that the dissemination of institutions (in this case, an adapted law) and close trade relations may be related.

[37] Robert Keohane points out to me that maintaining currency liquidity (i.e., ready availability of coins) is another (in this case, macroeconomic) public good that is supported by the official Athenian tolerance of the pseudo-owls. Currency liquidity is especially important for trading states and difficult to maintain in specie-standard currencies (cf. the practice of hoarding). It is implausible that the Athenians could have clearly understood the economic

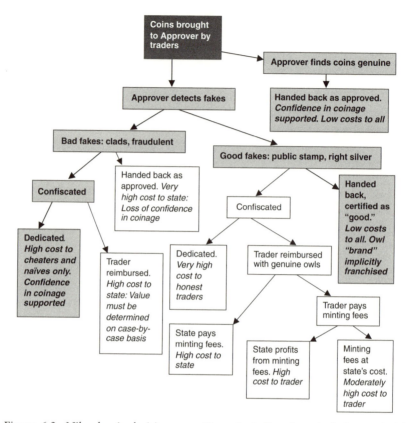

Figure 6.2. Nikophon's decision tree. Costs in *italics*. Actual choices in **bold** (gray boxes).

The law recognizes three distinct classes of coins: prototypes (van Alfen category 1), good fakes (van Alfen categories 2, 3, 4, 5), and bad coins (van Alfen category 6 and 7). The box matrix (table 6.2) indicates that each class was treated differently. But what of coins that are at the margin—say, a good fake that was a bit off-color, possibly indicating a lower than standard silver content but equally possibly indicating some innocent environmental condition? Or what if a coin so accurately imitated a

---

reasons *why* loss of liquidity would have deflationary effects (depressing production of goods, and potentially precipitating economic depression, as in Europe 1873–96). But the Athenians could certainly have noted the empirical fact that markets flourished when silver currency (even if not Athens-produced) was readily available, and they must have recognized that taxing "good fakes" would discourage the import of foreign silver to the Athenian market.

real owl that even an expert could not quickly decide whether or not it was a state-produced prototype? Some cases could not be objectively decided without resort to laborious tests. Yet the speed and clarity of the approval process was intrinsic to its economic value: a slow and uncertain approval process would be worse than none. All of this suggests that the expert Approver should not be regarded merely as a sort of automaton, ordered to do a technically demanding but merely mechanical job. Rather, he was an umpire, empowered to make quick and absolute judgment calls (confiscate vs. return; certify and approve vs. certify without approval) on inherently ambiguous cases. Just as a pitch in baseball is a strike if and when the umpire has called it a strike, a foreign silver pseudo-owl circulating in Athens was good if and when the Approver called it good; a coin was a real owl if and when the Approver declared it real. In essence, then, by adding an expert to the system of exchange, the Athenian state added a marginal fiduciary value to coins about which there was always some inherent ambiguity.[38]

In order for this quasi-fiduciary system to work properly, both Approvers must judge consistently on similar cases. If the two umpires did not make their calls on the basis of very similar standards, the "spread" between them might be manipulated by more sophisticated traders to the disadvantage of the less sophisticated. This would in turn obviate the intended goal of equalizing information among traders. These considerations point to the need for expertise on the part of the Approvers and for close coordination between them. We can now begin to understand at least part of the reason why the Approvers were public slaves. The choice

---

[38] On the means that a *dokimastēs* could use for quick judgment, see Bogaert 1976, citing [Arrian], *Discourses of Epictetus* 1.20.7–9, who notes that a silver tester (*agurognōmōn*) used sight, touch, smell, and hearing to test coins. It is tempting (although completely speculative) to guess that when they were not on duty at their tables, the dokimastai engaged in tests (by cupellation, a destructive method that allows for accurate determination of silver content) when examples came their way of new series of pseudo-owls. Once a few examples from a series had been tested "in the lab," the dokimastai would be able to deal efficiently with all coins from that series through visual inspection in their daily practice "at the table." A concern with standardizing assaying practices is not a uniquely ancient concern. In 1856, a British parliamentary committee found "that the laws regulating the assaying of gold and silver are in a most confused state, and that almost every office is established and regulated by Statutes or Charters exclusively applicable to itself. The practice of assaying is to afford protection to the public against fraud, and the Committee believe that it ought to be maintained, and since it is a convenient mode of collecting the revenue. They suggest that several statutes should be repealed, to remove the anomalies and confusion on assaying, and the consolidation of the laws into one statute for the establishment and regulation of Assay Offices throughout the UK" (HMSO 1856, paper 190: Select Committee on Silver and Gold Wares).

of public slaves for this vital office meant that Approvers could become
true experts (see chapter 3). Men who had engaged in the same demanding task for thousands of hours, who had looked carefully at tens
of thousands of coins, could be expected to develop a high level of profes-
sionalism and consistency of judgment. That would have been impossible
had the Approvers been lotteried citizen amateurs who held office only
for a year. Moreover, as we shall see, the fact that the Approvers were
slaves allowed for frightful sanctions if an Approver did not properly
fulfill his duties.

With these considerations in mind, we can better imagine how the system worked in practice. Suppose that S(eller) is offered 100 drachmas by
B(uyer) for a certain quantity of wheat. Because, if S demands an approval, any bad fakes detected by the Approver among B's coins would
be confiscated, B had a strong incentive not to offer S bad fakes in the
first place (i.e., to be neither a dishonest nor a naïve possessor of bad
money). S wants to make the deal but is concerned about the quality of
B's coins. Because they are trading grain in the Piraeus, B (or his agent),
accompanied by S (or his agent), takes the coins to the Piraeus Approver.
S and B can be quite sure that they will find the Approver sitting at his
table in front of the stele of Poseidon, because they know he can be punished if he is not. The Approver examines the coins offered by B. Prototypes are certified and approved. Pseudo-owls that turn up in the process
are returned to B unapproved. B may choose to offer them to S nonetheless, perhaps at a discount. S is within his rights to demand prototypes in
payment and can walk away from the deal if they are not forthcoming.
But S may not choose to exercise this legal option because S has received
a tacit guarantee that he will in any case be receiving "good coins": B and
S now share symmetrical information about the quality of the coins and
may be able to agree on a fair discount rate for good fakes.

Once enough coins have been reviewed to complete the sale, B proffers
them to S. But suppose S now refuses to make the deal. Assuming all the
coins involved in the sale had been approved, B (in person or via a third
party) can "expose" S to the relevant magistrate (§5a–c). Because the
amount of the transaction is over 10 drachmas, the magistrate refers the
matter to a People's Court. If the court sides with B, then S loses all the
grain he offered for sale that day. The state takes half of S's grain, and B
(or the third party) takes the other half of it. S therefore, has a very high
incentive to accept approved coins without demur. The requirement that
S accept the approved coins removes any incentive on S's part to use the
official apparatus of the approval process as a delaying device—to tie up
B's capital while S seeks a higher price for his goods. Thus B is protected
from S's use of the referral to the Approver merely as a way to keep B's

offer alive while seeking a better price from some other buyer. Because he understands S's incentives, and because his ownership of the coins is at risk only if they are bad, B need not fear that the transaction cost involved in bringing his coins before the Approver will be increased by the risk of losing either his bargain or his honestly held property.

The mandatory acceptance provision means that S will not challenge B's coins unless he really doubts the coins' quality while sincerely wanting to make the deal. The transaction cost incurred by the resort to the Approver is not, therefore, built into every exchange. The office of Approver remains a state-provided third-party guarantee that works in the background to lower the information asymmetry that exists because B might know something about the quality of his coins that S does not. It does not become a burdensome mandatory bureaucratic step that must be factored into the cost of doing business in Athens.

An incidental benefit to equalizing valuable information is the common-knowledge gain that comes with the resort to the Approver: S and B (or their agents) are interpresent before the Approver, and so they have common knowledge of the value of the coins and the bona fides of those offering and accepting them. That common knowledge extends to any interested bystanders because the process is carried out in a public place: B's incentive not to offer bad fakes is increased because he stands to lose his reputation for honesty if the Approver confiscates his coins. Likewise, S stands to lose reputation if he seeks to welch on a deal after the approval process has been completed.

In sum, the Approver system protected both sellers and buyers. If we suppose that S and B had a choice of polis markets in which to do business, and if we assume that Athens was (at least initially) unique in its provision of expert Approvers, we can see why S and B would choose to trade in Athens. Thus we can begin to see how the democratic legal system provided Athens with differential advantages over its polis rivals.

The legal system of Athens provided traders with an incentive to trade in Athenian state-minted owls. By doing his business in approved prototypes in Athens, B is offered a sort of state-funded business insurance in the form of easy access to the legal apparatus of Athenian magistrates and courts. Traders' use of prototype owls is voluntary, in that there is no Athenian sanction against the use of good pseudo-owls or, for that matter, the coinage of other states. Yet, given the choice, traders who knew that they might do business in Athens are likely to *prefer* prototype owls that would, therefore, have circulated in the Greek world at a premium. The fifth-century command-and-control imperial *requirement* that traders employ Athenian owls was thus replaced with an *incentive* that seems to have achieved very much the same end.

TABLE 6.3.

Comparison of polis coins found in datable coin hoards from across the Greek world,
fifth and fourth centuries B.C., top ten poleis (ranking is by total number of hoards
in which one or more coins of that polis appears).

Polis	Hoards 5th		Hoards 4th		Coins 5th		Coins 4th	
	Count	%	Count	%	Count	%	Count	%
Athens	45	18.9	56	9.9	1,284	3.7	7,152	6.5
Syracuse	48	20.2	33	5.9	963	2.8	793	0.7
Aigina	24	10.1	25	4.4	960	2.8	535	0.5
Akragas	35	14.7	8	1.4	698	2.0	22	0.0
Taras	20	8.4	23	4.1	593	1.7	1,426	1.3
Kroton	21	8.8	18	3.2	466	1.4	155	0.1
Metapontion	19	8.0	20	3.5	1,017	3.0	226	0.2
Gela	30	12.6	9	1.6	565	1.6	72	0.1
Olbia	11	4.6	21	3.7	456	1.3	813	0.7
Corinth	10	4.2	19	3.4	197	0.6	1,145	1.0
All hoards	238		564		34,385		109,433	
10-polis %						20.9		11.3

Notes: Hoards count = number of dated hoards in which at least one coin of the polis occurs. Hoards
% = percentage of total dated hoards in which at least one coin of the polis occurs. Coins count = number
of the polis' coins in dated hoards. Coins % = percentage of the polis' coins in all coins in dated hoards.
Total (all hoards) count = total dated hoards, total coins in dated hoards (from all mints, both polis and
non-polis). 10-polis % = aggregate percentage of coins from ten top polis coins in all dated hoards. Data
derived from Thompson et al., 1973; see further, chapter 2 and appendix B. This data is noisy, because,
inter alia, some of the coins described as owls in the inventory may be pseudo-owls.

Table 6.3 shows that in the fourth century, as in the fifth, more Athenian
coins appear in more Greek coin hoards than do coins of any other Greek
polis. Athenian coins were *more* heavily favored, relative to coins of other
poleis, by hoarders of coins in the fourth century than had been the case
in the fifth century. The percentage totals suggest that the growth of non-
polis mints in the fourth century (especially under Philip of Macedon,
Alexander, and the early Hellenistic dynasts) limited the "market share"
of the polis mints, with the aggregate share of the ten top poleis in the
total number of hoarded coins dropping from about 21 percent in the
fifth century to about 11 percent in the fourth. One or more Athenian
coins appears in about 10 percent of fourth-century hoards, down from
19 percent of hoards in the fifth century; all rival poleis also experienced
declines in this measure. Meanwhile, however, the percentage of Athenian
coins in all hoards *grew* from 3.7 to 6.5 percent; among rival mints, only
Corinth similarly exhibits growth. This is noisy data, but the conclusion
that Athenian coins remained very much in demand in the Mediterranean
world long after the end of the imperial era is not in doubt.

LEGAL STANDING AND SOCIAL STATUS

Among the notable aspects of Nikophon's law is the way in which it takes account of the legal status of those whose behavior it regulates, even as it creates the conditions for impersonal, "status-blind" exchanges in the Athenian market. As we have seen, the Approvers were public slaves. This is made explicit in the provision (§11) for establishing a new Piraeus Approver. He is either to be selected from the existing body of state-owned slaves (presumably from among those working currently in the mint or as clerks in the magistracies), or to be purchased on the open market if there is no suitable candidate (i.e., no one with the necessary expertise) among the state's current human inventory. We have already seen that the requirement for both expertise and consistency in the office of Approver made it preferable not to use lotteried annual citizen-magistrates for this job.

Unlike free persons, the slave Approvers can be whipped if they are derelict in their duties; the "parallel" legal penalty for free persons would be a monetary fine.[39] Likewise, if a slave-seller of merchandise is exposed as refusing approved coinage and convicted, whipping is added to the confiscation of goods (§9). There is a glaring asymmetry here: the sanctions are much more severe for slaves than for free persons. And yet slaves are otherwise assumed to be full parties to transactions. The public slave Approvers are, for example, to be paid a regular salary. Section 14 of the law is devoted exclusively to the issue of paying the salary of the two Approvers, and to ensuring that the new Piraeus Approver is properly compensated for the partial-year service that is anticipated. How, then, is the asymmetry to be explained in a system that seems to be so concerned with creating symmetry in the conditions of exchange?

A seller-slave (§9) might well be using his or her own capital, and acting as an independent agent. Slaves who "lived apart" from their masters and paid over a portion of the earnings of their own privately owned businesses are well documented in Athens.[40] In this case, the function of the additional punishment would be expressive: whipping the slave reminds all parties of the yawning gulf between slaves and the free. In other cases, however, the slave seller might be acting as an agent for his or her owner. In this latter circumstance, in addition to maintaining the expressive purpose of enforcing status distinction, the legal threat of beating has a rational purpose.

---

[39] Corporal punishment of slaves at Athens: Hunter 1994: 154–84. Hypothesis that a drachma is regarded as the equivalent of a stroke of the whip: M. H. Hansen 1999: 121.

[40] Slaves living apart from the masters: E. Cohen 2000, with literature cited.

A slave acting entirely as an agent for a master might choose to engage in fraudulent (and thus transaction-cost-increasing) business practices. Given that the goods confiscated by the state were not his or her own, the slave's material incentive not to defect from ordinary and honest business practices depended on the unpredictable monitoring and response of a master. Recognizing this, the state adds a severe physical sanction, one that would operate irrespective of any sanction that the slave's owner might or might not choose to impose.

Alternatively, a slave owner, as an "invisible" third party and thereby insulated from suffering reputation losses, having calculated the risks of losing goods to confiscation, might seek to coerce his slave into fraudulent market practices by the threat of punishment. The state matches that (potential) threat with its own coercive threat while also (in other legislation) limiting the absoluteness of the coercive authority exercised by masters over slaves.[41] Nikophon's law thus creates a "rational choice" situation for the seller-slave: choose between being punished by the state or by his or her masters. The obvious fact that both choices are fundamentally bad (even if not *equally* bad) vividly illustrates Terry Moe's argument for why rational-choice theory must take structural power asymmetries into account. The Athenian system of slavery allowed choice making by slaves, but treating a slave's choice between his torturers simply as a subset of choice about economic risk would obviously obscure essential moral as well as functional features of the system.[42]

Nikophon's legislation is a particularly good illustration of certain general principles of Athenian law, notably enforcement, jurisdiction, accountability, and transparency. The law is provided with substantial enforcement provisions aimed at those in the trading community who might break the law by refusing to accept approved coins. Because Athens did not have an elaborate police apparatus (Hunter 1994), initiative for enforcement was left in the hands of private individuals who observed wrongdoing; these might be victims or concerned third-party bystanders. Section 5 of the law calls for the "exposure" (*phasis*) of wrongdoers. Potential exposers are motivated to serve as "voluntary" enforcers of the law by being rewarded with a half-share in the confiscated goods of those convicted, whether the conviction is obtained by relatively quick magisterial decision when the exposure concerns an exchange of under 10 drachmas, or by court action for larger sums.[43]

---

[41] Discussion of the law on *hubris*: Ober 2000 (= Ober 2005b, chapter 5); the establishment of the Theseion as an official slave refuge: K. Christensen 1984.

[42] Moe 2005. J. Cohen 1997 offers a deeply insightful analysis of slavery along these lines.

[43] Note that a *phasis* might concern only one exchange (a seller's refusal to accept approved coins from one buyer), but the successful exposer's half-share is of all the goods the

By contrast with §10, which restricts denunciations of magistrates to "Athenian citizens with standing," §5 does not refer to the status of potential exposers; the implication is that anyone who so wishes can expose anyone else who illegally refuses to accept approved coins. We cannot say exactly how this would have worked in practice across the multiple status categories (free/slave, male/female, resident/visitor, citizen/non-citizen) that structured Athenian social relations. But on the face of it, there are no status restrictions on those who would take the role of exposer, and the apparent care with which the law is framed makes it unlikely that this was merely an oversight on Nikophon's part. The openness of access to the enforcement mechanism is an important "field of play leveling" feature, given that those involved in money transactions crossed the full spectrum of Athenian status groups. As we have seen, the law does not treat free persons and slaves identically in terms of punishment, but neither does the key enforcement mechanism build in a legal advantage for citizen males as "privileged insiders." That sort of formal asymmetry would obviously increase transaction costs, in that "outsiders" would be without legal recourse in the case of being cheated, and would have somehow to compensate for that asymmetry in the bargains they struck.[44]

Jurisdiction is closely related to enforcement: The law not only specifies the geographic jurisdiction of the two Approvers, but exactly which magistrates will have what jurisdictional responsibility in terms of enforcement of the law (§5a–c). Magisterial jurisdiction is organized according to geography and commodity. The basic division of enforcing magistrates' legal duties is according to a geographic principle—between the Conveners who deal with matters in the city (especially the Agora §5b) and the Overseers who deal with matters in Piraeus (especially the Import Market, §5c). But there is a notable exception to this general division of jurisdictional authority. Exposures of infractions in the grain market are to be referred to the Grain-guardians (§5a, c). In contrast to trade in all other commodities, which remain unspecified, the law is especially concerned that issues arising in the grain market be dealt with by a particular board of magistrates with special responsibility for grain. This exceptional legal status accorded to the grain market is indicative of the great

---

seller is offering that day. The gain to the exposer from a magistrate's summary judgment could, therefore, potentially be considerably more than 5 drachmas. The legal sanctions against dishonest magistrates must, consequently, be severe enough to discourage potentially profitable collusion.

[44] Slaves living outside of Athens are specifically foreseen as engaging in "exposures" (*phaseis*) and "indications" (*endeixeis*) of violators of export rules that set up an Athenian monopoly on ruddle in three of the four small poleis of Keos (RO 40, lines 19–20: mid-fourth century B.C.): here slaves are offered freedom as well as a part-share of the proceeds of a successful prosecution.

and enduring importance of grain imports to the city. Not only was imported grain a major revenue source for Athens (from harbor dues), but it was a strategic necessity because the Athenian grain crop was at least periodically inadequate to feed the population of the city.[45]

As in the case of the dispatching decree (chapter 4), provisions concerning magisterial accountability take up a very substantial amount of space in the coinage law. The public-slave Approvers, as we have seen, are subject to whipping for failing to fulfill their duties (§3). But other magistrates are likewise called to account. The six *thesmothetai* are threatened with an apparently collective fine of 1000 drachmas if they fail to call courts into session for trying serious cases brought to them by magistrates who receive "exposures" from concerned individuals (§7). By contrast to that provision, which is aimed at a particular body of officials, §10 empowers any Athenian with legal standing (that is, any male citizen who has not been disenfranchised as a result of legal action) to denounce any derelict magistrate to the Council of 500. This is an explicit statement of a general principle of Athenian law that allows citizens to serve as prosecutors for "public" crimes—that is, for delicts that have a directly adverse effect on the community at large. In the case of denunciations under Nikophon's silver law, the five hundred members of the Council are evidently to serve as the jurors in a formal legal proceeding in which the voluntary "denouncer" would serve as prosecutor and the accused magistrate(s) as defendant. The law limits the punishment in the case of conviction to dismissal from office with an option additional fine of up to 500 drachmas.

Unlike the dispatching decree, the Council, as a body, does not have an overall managerial role to play in the operation of the silver law, but the Council and some of its constituent members are involved in setting the new bureaucratic apparatus in place—appointing the new Piraeus Approver (§11), commissioning the contract for the two stelai in the Agora and the Import Market (§13), and destroying existing stelai recording decrees that contradict the current law (§15). After the apparatus is up and running, the Council or its members are responsible for receiving bad fakes for deposit in the Metroon (§2b), for whipping derelict Approvers (§3), and for accepting exposures in the Agora (§5b).

Presumably, it could come to pass, then, that the Council could be asked to try itself, although in practice it appears that the Council would be responsible for disciplining those of its members assigned to undertake the specific responsibilities laid out in the law. Nikophon's law, like other Athenian laws, seems to seek a middle ground between two desired ends:

---

[45] Special status of grain: Garnsey 1988; Whitby 1998; Oliver 2007, chapter 1; Moreno 2008. Special legal restrictions meant to ensure that maritime loans contracted in Athens resulted in grain coming to the Athenian markets: Lanni 2006: 151–52, and discussion below.

on the one hand, there is the goal of separating accountable agents from the institutions enforcing accountability; on the other hand, there is the administrative efficiency inherent in allowing a body with substantial aggregate experience and knowledge of a process to take a primary role in disciplining those who fail to fulfill their role in that process. Likewise, assigning summary power of judgment to magistrates in small transactions, but requiring judgment by a People's Court in matters over 10 drachmas, stakes out a middle ground. In this case the two desired ends are speedy, thus low-cost, summary judgments and adherence to the democratic principle that heavy punishments should be levied by large bodies, rather than individual magistrates.[46]

Transparency is a final jurisprudential principle that is manifest in Nikophon's law. The exact wording of the law is made immediately available to those who might have recourse to it. The law itself calls for its own public promulgation in the form of two copies inscribed on stone stelai. One was erected in the city Agora; the surviving stele on which the law is preserved is evidently this Agora copy. The other was set up in the Piraeus. Both copies of the law are displayed at the places where the Approvers sit and carry out their work.

We must imagine each Approver as taking up his post in the immediate vicinity of a prominently displayed copy of the law that specifies the duties of his office, mandates his own punishment for dereliction of duty, yet also details the procedure for punishing those who refuse to accept as final his expert and umpire-like judgments. With its double publication, the new law quickly became common knowledge among those who made use of the approval process. Anyone who felt that proper procedure was not followed in an approval could quickly refresh his or her memory of what recourse was available. Moreover, the Approver's personal vulnerability, as a possession of the state, and the power vested in him, as an expert and an agent of the state, are both prominently on view. Nikophon could hardly have made the conjoined rational and expressive purposes of his law clearer.

RULES AND RENTS: HISTORICAL SURVEY

The overall trend of Athenian institutional history, from the early sixth to the mid-fourth centuries B.C. was toward greater access, by more people, to increasingly valuable public information and processes, and toward reduced public partiality in the sense of codified advantages held by members of one group in favor of others. These trends were not linear

---

[46] An exception is made for certain categories of malefactors who were "caught in the act": M. H. Hansen 1976a.

and they remained radically incomplete from the points of view of both optimization and justice. Formal rules and cultural habits ensured that native males retained substantial and economically significant legal, political, and social privileges. The distinction between free and slave remained fundamental. In comparison with other ancient societies and with rival Greek poleis, Athens in the fourth century B.C. appears to have moved a long way toward open entry and impartiality. Yet when measured against the standards of an ideal-type open access society Athens fell far short. The following historical survey draws on the narrative and the studies cited in chapter 2. It may also be read in conjunction with the more detailed constitutional history offered in Ober 1989, chapter 2.

In the early archaic period (era I) the rules governing Athenian society appear characteristic of fragile natural states. Formal institutions were weak and unstable; coalitions among elite families were fluid. Solon's (era II) appointment as archon with the powers of lawgiver in 594 was a turning point for Athenian openness and fairness, as in other ways. Solon's laws were publicly displayed in written form, and thus were, in principle at least, accessible to any literate person.[47] The principles on which they were based were clearly stated and publicized through Solon's lyric poetry. Substantively, Solon's reforms made basic immunities accessible to the entire native population: Athenians need no longer live in fear that economic failure would lead to the ultimate status degradation: becoming another Athenian's chattel or being sold abroad. New legal procedures rendered magistrates liable to prosecution, and every Athenian gained the right to prosecute criminal behavior on another's behalf. Access to high public office was still limited to an elite, but the limitation was now based on the relatively impartial test of assessed wealth rather than bloodline.

The Athenians later attributed a great deal of legislation to Solon, including the law on *hubris* which criminalized the (legally undefined) act of "treating with disrespect" any resident of Athenian territory, including slaves; sanctions for breaking the new laws ranged from fines to execution. A half-century later, Solon's laws had evidently gained currency; the tyrant Peisistratus retained them, at least in name. Peisistratus' interest in dissolving patronage networks he could not control led him to sponsor traveling judges and make capital loans for agricultural projects; this offered rural Athenians something closer to parity with urban citizens and an alternative to partial local elites in resolving disputes.

---

[47] The extent of functional literacy in Solonian, or for that matter, classical, Athens is a matter of conjecture; scholarly estimates vary considerably. See, for example, Harvey 1966; Thomas 1989, 1992; W. Harris 1989; Hedrick 1999, 2000; Richardson 2000. Thomas 2005 notes the importance of written law in Greek perceptions of justice as fairness.

Athens saw considerable immigration during the era of the tyranny; in the immediate aftermath of the Revolution of 508 these immigrants became citizens (Badian 2000: 452). The new democracy was founded on a unique (and perhaps desperate) act of inclusivity, and from this moment on the active citizenry would include elites and non-elites on a relatively even legal footing. The first third of the fifth century (eras III–V) saw a series of institutional reforms that cumulatively stripped the old elite families of many of their traditional privileges in respect to access. Access to public office was made more realistically available to a broad spectrum of citizens with the introduction of pay for office and jury service in the middle decades of the fifth century (era VI). With the rapid growth of a self-consciously capable and socially diverse citizenry, one that was collectively familiar with the rules governing the People's Courts, Council, and Assembly, Athenian institutions became increasingly resistant to elite capture.

By the second third of the fifth century, the institutions of the young democracy were being put to the service of imperial management, and disputes within Athenian-controlled territories were legally remanded to Athenian courts. Jurors came to be regarded by critics of democracy (Ps-Xenophon 1.16–18) as a collective patron, eager to extract rents from imperial subjects by restricting access to legal redress, and offering favorable judgment only to those who played the game. With its relatively stable institutions and a vibrant (by ancient standards, at least) civil society; with a citizenry capable of performing the tasks (and reaping the rents) of imperial management; with the same citizens simultaneously serving as an extensive and highly skilled body of military specialists, Athens was emerging as a new organizational form: a mature and democratic natural state. The unexpected successes of that form of organization, across a wide range of domains, provoked the wonder of contemporaries and has fascinated observers ever since.

Whether the fifth-century democratic natural state could have stabilized in its imperial form remains a question for counterfactual history (Morris 2005b); as it happened, the disaster in Sicily fatally upset the equilibrium between elite and non-elite citizens. After democracy was restored following the oligarchic interlude of 411 B.C., the Athenians recognized a need for regularizing the formal rules; a commission was formed to collect the laws of Athens. Around the same time, the Old Bouleuterion was dedicated to the Mother of the Gods; the Metroon, as it now came to be called, served, among other functions, as the repository of official state archives, including the written laws.[48]

---

[48] The establishment of the archives: Boegehold 1972 (dating to 409–406 B.C.); Sickinger 1999; Davies 2003: 328–29. Thomas 1989: 66–83 argues that there was relatively little

The last phase of the Peloponnesian War saw a serious violation of established Athenian legal procedures when, in 406, most of the year's elected generals were tried en masse in the Assembly and sentenced to death. This break with democratic self-restraint in the use of majority rule was soon followed by the violent rule of the Thirty. The leaders of the oligarchic junta limited access to legal immunity to those whose names appeared on a list of three thousand citizens, and they struck names from the list at will. New laws were announced but never published. Established judicial process was abandoned. Defendants had no hope of acquittal if the leadership sought their conviction; voting on verdicts was not secret, and jurors feared retaliation if they challenged the will of the junta. Sanctions were arbitrary. Property was confiscated from the wealthy (especially from *metics*—resident foreigners) at the whim of the leadership; thousands were expelled from their homes and hundreds summarily executed or disappeared.

The restored democracy reacted forcefully in response to this catastrophic breakdown of the ordinary rules of the Athenian game. The recently collected laws were publicly displayed and stored in the Metroon. In a major constitutional shift, decrees of the Assembly were made subject to the authority of the established laws. New laws would be made by large boards of *nomothetai*, rather than by direct vote in the Assembly (chapter 5). Legal processes (*graphai*) that allowed proposers of illegal decrees or inappropriate laws to be prosecuted in court gave teeth to this hierarchical ordering of rules. As a democratic brake on policy making by majorities in the Assembly, the new legal regime reduced the danger of majoritarian tyranny. An amnesty, proclaimed and enforced in the courts, prevented devolution into a cycle of vengeance and retribution. The Athenian social equilibrium was restored.

Shortly after the restoration, a new dispute resolution procedure was put into place: citizens who reached age sixty would serve as public arbitrators. Litigants in "civil" disputes (*dikai*) were now required to undergo a relatively quick (in principle) legal arbitration before pursuing grievances in court. The concern that amateur arbitrators would be more concerned with equity than justice and might fail the test of impartiality was addressed by the right of dissatisfied litigants to appeal their case to the People's Courts. Over the course of the century, the Assembly relinquished (*de facto* or *de iure*) legal authority over treason trials; major infractions of public order would now be consistently tried in the People's Courts, with their provision for secret ballot and greater institutional re-

---

actual consultation of written documents, whether inscribed or archived, in Athens; but her argument is against those who have imagined that there was a complete shift from an oral to a written culture in the classical period; see further, Hedrick 1999.

sistance to cascading (chapter 5). Written evidence became more prevalent in some, although not all, Athenian legal contexts. The number of preserved Athenian public inscriptions (as well as private epitaphs) rose dramatically from the fifth to the fourth century (Hedrick 1999).

EXPANDING ACCESS

A striking change in legal access and impartiality was introduced in the mid-fourth century, with the establishment of new procedures for trying cases involving merchants. The "maritime suits" (*dikai emporikai*) were distinguished by two innovative features. First, male non-citizens, certainly including metics and short-term visitors, and most probably including slaves, were offered the same legal standing in these commercial cases as citizens. All now had the right to initiate a case, to serve as witnesses, as well as to defend themselves against charges in their own name. Next, the judicial discretion of the jury was limited by the requirement that charges be filed, and the case be decided, by reference to a written contract.[49]

The responsibility of the jury in a maritime case was to decide whether the terms of a specific contract had or had not been fulfilled. While this still entailed judging the veracity of narratives offered by the litigants, the interpretive scope of the jury was considerably restricted. As a result, the decisions of juries in maritime cases were said to be "carried out according to the rule" or "by the book" (*akribeis*: Demosthenes 7.12, and Lanni 2006: 149 n. 4), rather than made on the basis of jurors' all-things-considered judgment, which included the past behavior and estimated future social value of those engaged in the dispute. The motivation for the new procedure is not stated in the five extant speeches on which our knowledge of the legal innovation primarily rests. Yet it is widely, and surely correctly, assumed to be the state's desire to attract foreign traders to the Athenian market, by offering them free access to dispute resolution procedures on equal footing with Athenians. Moreover, the provision that the new suits be judged "monthly" (Demosthenes 33.23)—while somewhat obscure in precise meaning—was explicitly intended to guarantee swift legal action, thereby removing the incentive of locals to drag out proceedings to the disadvantage of temporary visitors.

---

[49] Lanni 2006: 149–74 offers a concise description of the maritime cases and cites a wealth of earlier scholarship. E. Cohen 1973 reopened interest in the maritime suits and remains the most detailed analysis, but Cohen's belief that maritime cases were tried by special juries of experts in commercial law rests on dubious evidential grounds and appears incorrect; see Todd 1993: 334–37. On the other hand, the doubts raised by Todd (1994)

Adriaan Lanni (2006: 166) suggests that "litigants in *dikai emporikai* appear to have focused their arguments on the terms of the contract, whereas speakers in non-maritime cases involving written contracts or wills include a more contextualized account, basing their claims on what they perceive to be the fair result as well as the proper contractual interpretation." The "fairness" Lanni refers to concerns just distribution of goods, with fair shares determined by the relative social worth of the parties, rather than the "fairness as impartiality" I have emphasized above. Lanni rightly argues that the procedural innovations employed in maritime cases do not point to a revolution in standard Athenian legal doctrine. Continued attention to social context, and the relatively broad view of what counted as a relevant argument in non-maritime cases, is, she suggests, indicative of a sustained and fundamental Athenian commitment to legal procedures that gave the jury broad interpretive scope. As I have argued elsewhere (Ober 1989), interpretive scope on the part of jurors was an important safeguard against elite capture of the democratic court system.

The dikai emporikai ought not, however, to be regarded simply as anomalous, or as driven entirely by the particular needs of the mid-fourth century. Rather, the two senses of fairness—as *procedural* justice and as *substantive* justice—represent two facets of Athenian democratic values. The first, procedural sense of fairness, centers on the value of impartiality in respect to judgment, an aspect of equality in respect to opportunity. The second sense of fairness centers on getting the best, most equitable outcome. If, when they came into court, litigants had no way of guessing which value would be to the fore, the simultaneous presence of the two senses of fairness might have led to confusion, arbitrary judgments, and widespread opting-out of the legal system. During the crisis of the late fifth century, this dysfunctional devolution appeared to be well advanced. But in the codified legal environment of the fourth century, the system regained its legitimacy and therefore its salutary role in stabilizing the democratic equilibrium. With the inauguration of the maritime suits, the two distinct dispute resolution domains were clearly distinguished, and potential disputants could therefore be reasonably clear about the values and rules that would apply in a given case.

Shortly before the new procedure for maritime suits was introduced in the mid-350s B.C., the prolific and generically innovative Athenian writer, Xenophon, circulated a pamphlet on the subject of *Revenues*, in which

---

regarding the access of non-citizens to courts trying maritime cases are unconvincing. E. Cohen 2005 offers a succinct survey of Athenian commercial law.

he made a number of suggestions for increasing Athenian state income.[50]
He recommended a mix of rent-seeking and access-expanding measures.
His most retrograde suggestion was to have the Athenians acquire a large
body of state-owned slaves who could be leased out to private parties,
especially as laborers in the silver mines. The right analogy, Xenophon
argued, is tax farming, but slave farming would be more lucrative, he
claimed, because it is less liable to manipulation. The slaves could be controlled, even in time of war, he urged, by tattooing them as public property
and establishing strategic garrisons in the mining district. The shadow of
classical Sparta, where Xenophon had lived as an exile, and its state-
owned population of helot serfs looms large in these passages.

On the other hand, whereas Sparta was famous for its periodic mass
expulsions of foreigners (Rebenich 1998), Xenophon proposed institutional changes intended to make Athens more attractive to foreigners.
The goal was economic growth: "The rise in the number of residents and
visitors would of course lead to a corresponding expansion of our imports
and exports, of sales, opportunities for wages, and custom-taxes" (3.5).
The means Xenophon advocated was opening entry and assuring quick
and fair dispute procedures. Xenophon suggests offering prizes to state
market officials who most justly and quickly resolved disputes, arguing
that, as a result, a "far larger number of merchants would trade with us
and with much greater satisfaction" (3.3). Xenophon proposed freeing
metics from mandatory military service, but allowing them the honorable
role of serving as voluntary cavalrymen. He also suggested granting foreigners rights in respect to real estate ownership (*enktēsis*: 2.5). He points
out that all of this was simply a matter of changing the rules: "These
[measures] need cost us nothing whatever beyond benevolent public decisions (*psēphismata*) and proper implementation" (*epimeleiai*: 3.6).

Other measures, including building new hostels for shipowners and
visitors and improving the market facilities for merchants, would, Xenophon acknowledged, require substantial capital inputs by the state. But
Xenophon believed that it would be possible for Athens to borrow the
necessary capital from private sources. The state could offer high rates
of interest and, at least as important, loans would be guaranteed by the
credibility of the state itself, "which is to all appearances the safest and
most durable of human institutions" (*ho dokei tōn anthrōpinōn asphale-
staton te kai poluchroniōtaton einai*: 3.10). Although Xenophon does not
say so explicitly, the established reputation of the restored democracy for
repaying its loans (favorably noted by [Aristotle] *Ath. Pol.* 40.3) is the

---

[50] For scholarship on Xenophon's *Revenues*, see above, note 11.

relevant background condition. Xenophon's assumption that the democracy could borrow its way out of a financial/military hole on the basis of its credible commitment to repay loans anticipates contemporary arguments for the political-economic roots of the "democratic advantage" (Schultz and Weingast 2003, and above, chapter 3).

It is tempting to imagine a mid-fourth-century tribal team of the Council considering Xenophon's ideas, rejecting his plan for seeking rents by acquiring and farming public slaves, but fastening on the genuine value of offering greater legal access to non-Athenians engaged in trade. While it remains unknown whether this, or any of Xenophon's other proposals, was directly taken up by Athenian decision makers, the similarity between certain of his recommendations in the *Revenues* and the reformed procedure for maritime suits is strong (cf. Lanni 2006: 151). The similarity suggests that at least some of Xenophon's notions were aligned with the political realities of the mid-fourth century.

The Athenians granted major honors to foreigners, including citizenship, more readily in the fourth century than they had in the past (Henry 1983), and these grants were much more than empty gestures. As wealthy and generous foreigners gained access to the Athenian public economy of esteem, honor, and reciprocal gratitude, they also gained the valuable assurance of secure refuge in a powerful polis should things go wrong at home (K. Allen 2003). In some cases, Athens-resident communities of foreigners were granted *enktēsis*—public permission to acquire real estate—with the express purpose of establishing the religious cult practices of their homelands. In 333/2 B.C., for example, the Assembly granted a group of Athens-resident merchants from Citium on Cyprus *enktēsis* for a sanctuary dedicated to Aphrodite, "just as also the Egyptians have built the sanctuary of Isis."[51]

Access to property rights and to preferred forms of religious worship are conjoined in this decree, and the conjunction obviously would have lowered the psychic costs to worshippers of Citian Aphrodite and Egyptian Isis of long-term residence in Athens. While the decree does not say why the grants were given, it does mention that the grant was to a group of *merchants*. It seems likely on the face of it that the legislative intent was to make Athens more attractive to foreign (including non-Greek) traders.

There were many other attractions to trading in Athens, and at least some of these can be ascribed to the democratic state's self-conscious employment of the principles of open access and impartiality as incentives to merchants. Like other poleis, Athens protected retail traders and their

---

[51] RO 91, and Simms 1989 on dating and legislative intent.

customers by mandating standard weights and measures (Lang and Crosby 1964; Figueira 1998: 296–315). The state provided market officials of various sorts (*agoranomoi, sitophulakes, epimelētai tou emporiou*) as well as the Approvers of silver currency (above) to enforce fair trade practices ([Aristotle] *Ath. Pol.* 51; E. Cohen 2005; Bresson 2000, chapter 8). The harbor facilities at Piraeus were improved in the fourth century, and facilities were provided for storage of grain (see below). Attention to the value of time, evident in Xenophon's proposals and the *dikai emporikai*, was manifest in the public provision, in the Agora, of a prominent and technologically sophisticated water clock, capable of measuring the hours according to the change in seasons.[52] Measuring value by counting enables impartial exchanges. Reviel Netz (2002: 334–40) has documented the distinctiveness of classical Athens' "counting culture," notes that most known examples of the "western abacus" come from Athenian territory, and associates Athenian numeracy with both economic development and democratic institutions.

Certain Athenian rules constrained the freedom of traders living in Athens to buy and sell just as they pleased. Laws aimed at ensuring that there would always be an adequate supply of grain in the polis required Athens-resident traders to ship grain only to the Athenian harbor, forbade loans on grain shipments that would not come to Athens, and limited the amount of grain that could be exported once it had arrived in Athens. But substantial amounts of grain were legally reexported (Whitby 1998; Oliver 2007, chapter 1). With its large population Athens was a big market, and these regulations do not seem to have dampened interest in large-scale trade in bulk commodities. As a leading center of Mediterranean trade, Athens saw the development of new and sophisticated forms of banking and credit, which were used by citizens and foreigners alike and regulated, at least to a degree, by state law. In the aggregate, these various developments help to explain the steep rise in state revenues and state capacity in the third quarter of the fourth century.[53]

[52] Agora water clock and changing ideas about time: Allen 1996; cf. Camp 2001: 159. Reed 2003, chapter 5, and Oliver 2007, chapter 1, survey the classical Athenian state's interest in encouraging trade, and measures taken. Oliver 2007, chapter 3, demonstrates that the Athenian concern for attracting traders through honors, religious accommodation, and tax breaks continued into the third century B.C.

[53] Restrictions on grain trade: Lanni 2006: 151–52. Banking and credit: E. Cohen 1992. Epigraphically attested records of distinctive Athenian forms of hypothecation (*horoi*): Finley 1953; Millett 1991. Millett and Finley regarded these new (or at least newly recorded in archaeologically visible form) fourth-century means of raising money from the ownership of land to be "non-productive" because the funds were often raised for social purposes (e.g., dowries) rather than for example, investment in, say, better farm equipment, but this unnecessarily discounts the potential economic value of social capital; see chapter 4. Lead

Democracy and Social Security

Democracy is strongly correlated with Athens' movement toward more open entry and greater impartiality. The Athenian version of the elite coalitions that have historically produced rents by limiting access in natural states (North, Wallis, and Weingast, in progress) was broken down by the emergence and consolidation of Athenian democratic institutions.[54] Democracy's successful challenge to standard forms of elite domination is especially clear in the decades following the Revolution of 508 and again in the fourth century, after the oligarchic interludes of the late fifth century. In each case, democracy was brought about (created or restored) in opposition to *increased* elite exclusivity. Both Isagoras in 508 and the Thirty in 404 sought to sharply restrict access to political rights and legal immunities and used their power in arbitrary and violent ways. In post-revolutionary and post-counterrevolutionary Athens (as, perhaps, elsewhere) fairness and openness (at least among free males) were especially highly valued by the many because a level of access to which people had grown accustomed had suddenly been rolled back. Partiality had been bluntly used to further the interests of an elite few at the expense of all others. Because the rollback was sudden and violent, the ugly face of elite domination was revealed; its ideological mask, the guise of elite legitimacy (based in claims of special birth, education, wisdom, inherent goodness, etc.) was let slip. When the centrality to elite coalition rule of access-limiting mechanisms was made so starkly visible, a democratic counter-strategy of opposition by *increasing* access must have become that much more obvious.

Opening access through institutional reform helped to stabilize democracy, in both post-revolutionary periods, because it undermined the basis for elite coordination and made it more difficult for elites to gain the resources necessary to reestablish domination (Ps-Xenophon 2.19, 3.12–13; Teegarden 2007). As democratic Athens moved in the direction of more open access, some parts of Athenian society and law came to appear strikingly modern. Significant parts of the Athenian economy were,

---

tablets with hypothecation records concerning houses, workshops, and land from Camarina, Morgantina, Chalcidice, and the Cyclades from the fourth to second centuries B.C. are being studied by C. Grotta and M. Manganaro. When fully published, these may give us a better sense of the dissemination of standard forms of credit and contract across the Greek world.

[54] De Ste. Croix 1983: 96–97, 283–300 is a helpful summary of the ways in which democracy, as practiced at Athens, limited exploitation (in Marx's sense) of the poor by the wealthy. Cf. Shaw 1991. Loraux 1986 and Wohl 1996, 1998 argue for continued aristocratic ideological domination but acknowledge substantial change in material conditions.

however, still based on rules and conditions of exchange that favored the extraction of rents by a supercoalition of elite and non-elite native males.[55] As a result, contracts entered into freely by appropriately informed parties defined only part of the Athenian economy. The sharp divergence among modern assessments of Athenian economy and society (surveyed in Morris 1994; Cartledge 2002) is, to some degree, a function of attending to different sides of this Janus-faced, natural/open, traditional/modern community.

The limitations that the Athenian democracy placed on the extractive power of traditional elites was socially significant and produced historically unusual conditions: Athenian agricultural small-holders exchanged the produce of their lands under conditions that were very different from those experienced by most peasants throughout history. The key difference was that Athenian agriculturalists were neither sharecroppers, forced to pay large rents to landowners, nor were they heavily taxed by the state. The Athenian taxation system was progressive in that only relatively wealthy Athenians paid the *eisphora* tax based on their self-reported property, and only the very wealthy were subject to liturgies (Christ 2006: 146–70). Because small-holders were able to profit from surpluses they produced, they had incentives to invest in their land and had more time to devote to public business—time that repaid them by maintaining the conditions that protected them from the imposition of burdensome taxes (Wood 1988). Athenian elites likewise failed to maintain robust informal systems of personal patronage, which could have returned rents to the elite through asymmetric provision of "favors" and services. Athens was remarkably lacking in the structures of patronage that are common in other pre-modern societies.[56]

Public service was valuable to many Athenians, economically as well as in other ways, but Athenian government never devolved to a political spoils system. The use of the lottery and limitations on iteration in most offices, along with strict accountability procedures (the mandatory *eu-*

---

[55] This point has been argued in detail by studies emphasizing native-male domination, the "cup half empty" of Athenian democracy. See, for example, Jameson 1978, 1997; Mactoux 1980; Loraux 1993; Johnstone 1998; Morris 1998b; Katz 1999; Rosivach 1999; Thompson 2003. While my emphasis here has tended to be on the "cup half full," because it better explains the Athenian exceptionalism that is the primary subject of this book, the shortcomings of Athens in respect to justice, when measured against contemporary standards of equality and fairness, are profound.

[56] Some, but not all, of the advantages enjoyed by Athenian small-holders would have been evident in non-democratic but republican Greek poleis: Hanson 1995. General absence of strong forms of private patronage in Athens: Millett 1989. Mossé 2007 [1994/95]: 189–95, and Zelnick-Abramowitz 2000 offer nuances, but Millett's main thesis stands. Patronage in other ancient Mediterranean societies: Veyne 1992 [1976]; Saller 1982; Wallace-Hadrill 1989; Domingo Gygax 2006a, 2006b.

thuna after each year's service) made it difficult for an Athenian magistrate to use the power of his office to extract rents from those needing access to government services. Despite persistent Athenian fears that public speakers and diplomats were taking bribes, there is no evidence pointing to a pervasive practice of bribe taking among ordinary magistrates.[57]

Rather than a source of rents for a few well-connected insiders, the codified rules of Athenian government returned tax revenues to the society in the form of security of various kinds. Military security is the most obvious, and was certainly by far the most expensive. As we have seen (chapter 4) the continuous need to provide adequate military security against various external threats (including pirates) demanded a great deal of governmental attention. Athenian citizens were, however, also relatively secure in other ways. They did not have to worry much about organized violent crime. While we do hear of house break-ins and cloak stealing, and while there certainly was some violent crime resulting in bodily injury and death, Athens seems nevertheless to have been remarkably unviolent when compared with other premodern communities. This was not the result of diligent policing. Athens had no organized police force in the modern sense; the relatively peaceful social order emerged, rather, from the cultural norms that developed along with codified rules of legal order. The internalization of the law code in respect to day-to-day behavior resulted over time in less violence and more security for each resident.[58]

The democratic government also provided various kinds of social and economic security. Orphans of men who fell in battle were raised by the state; daughters were given dowries (Jones 2004: 52). Handicapped citizens were provided with a basic daily stipend (Lysias 24; [Aristotle] *Ath. Pol.* 49.4). Able but indigent citizens could find work rowing the warships. Older citizens, no longer able to do hard manual labor, often served on juries and did other forms of paid government service. The laws governing the import of grain were designed to ensure an adequate supply of food to the populace, and at affordable prices (M. H. Hansen 1999: 98–99). By the mid-fourth century, if not before, the Theoric Fund underwrote citizen attendance at public festivals (Hansen 1976, 1999: 98). The general point is that Athenians, especially those without deep pockets, were able to plan more ambitious lives than would otherwise have been feasible. They could take potentially lucrative short-term risks, and could seek new opportunities that offered long-term payoffs by investing time and effort in acquiring technical and social knowledge. All of this was possible only because the government returned a substantial part of its

---

[57] Accusations of bribery: Taylor 2001a, 2001b.

[58] Policing in Athens, by public officials and self-help: Hunter 1994: 120–53; Christ 1998. Low levels of violent crime in Athens: Herman 1994, 2006; Riess 2006.

revenues to society in the form of basic social insurance. Athenians were, if only to a degree, buffered against certain forms of hardship and catastrophe that remain all too familiar even in the contemporary world, and as a result the entire community did better over time.[59]

Codified democratic rules that predictably redistributed wealth to provide military and social security ultimately benefited elite as well as ordinary Athenians. Democracy proved not to be a zero-sum game in which the masses turned the tables on the elite by seeking big rents from the rich. While traditional elite practices of rent extraction were overthrown by the democracy, and wealthy citizens shouldered the primary tax burden, the democratic regime protected private property. Elite families found that they had many opportunities to benefit from the robust and diversified Athenian economy. Politically ambitious elites could no longer simply assume positions of authority as a matter of established privilege. Yet members of old and wealthy families learned that the new democratic regime offered leadership opportunities. Democratic leadership required accommodation to the principles and practices of democratic institutions and discourse. On the other hand, as Athens grew richer and more powerful, the psychic and material rewards of leadership expanded accordingly. The success of democracy, before and after the Peloponnesian War, made accommodation to the democratic rules sufficiently attractive to a sufficiently large portion of the elite strata of Athenian society to enable the emergence and subsequent restoration of a productive social equilibrium between mass and elite.[60]

The consolidation of a mass/elite social equilibrium meant some reduction in the risks associated with endemic hostility among social classes. As we have seen (chapter 3), civil conflict, exacerbated even if not caused by class divisions, was common in the Greek cities of the classical period and extremely destructive of life, property, and state capacity. To the extent that democracy provided a social environment in which open civil strife was less likely, it thereby provided a fundamental form of social

---

[59] State provision of social security: Burke 2005. Allows lucrative risk taking: Ober 2005b: 83–88. Democratic Athenian concern for ensuring things necessary for living a decent life is consistent with Amartya Sen's (1993, 1999) analysis of the relationship between democracy and provision of "capabilities."

[60] Mass-elite relations and the conditions of elite flourishing under Athenian democracy: Davies 1981; Ober 1989; Rhodes 2000; Forsdyke 2005. Incorporation of "middling," hoplites into the equilibrium: Hanson 1995: 351–84. The mid-fourth-century epitaph of a certain "Archippos of the deme Skambonidai" (*IG* II² 7393) offers a snapshot of the ideology sustaining the equilibrium: the epitaph contains strong echoes of the "world of Tellus" in noting that Archippos was blessed (*eudaimōn*) both in having left children who had children of their own and in having received a gold crown from the Athenian polis. Weingast 1997 offers a formal model for how democracy can create a robust mass-elite equilibrium.

and political security. The aggregate value of democracy as a guarantor of military and social security is impossible to measure, but was clearly very high.

The widespread recognition that security was valuable, provided by democracy, and unlikely to be as readily available under non-democratic regimes, helps to explain apparent peculiarities of Athenian history. Elite Athenians, metics, and slaves risked their lives fighting alongside ordinary citizens in the resistance to the Thirty in 404. Likewise, many elite Athenians took considerable risks on behalf of pro-democracy movements in the years after 322 B.C. These choices on the part of those who might appear, on the face of it, to be disadvantaged by the democratic rules of the game can in part be explained by the rational expectation that democratic security was better than the available alternatives. This certainly does not mean that metics, slaves, or elites regarded the rules of the democratic game as substantively just in respect to the distribution of goods, or that they would choose Athenian-style democracy over a utopian alternative. Yet when the choice was democracy or a relatively narrow oligarchy, some of them evidently believed that democracy was far more likely to further their interests—far enough, anyway, to justify taking extraordinary personal risks to preserve or regain it.

Horizons of Fairness

Perhaps some of those non-citizens who fought for democracy in 404 did so in the expectation that democratic restoration would lead to a historic breakthrough in political access and a corresponding reduction in native-citizen partiality. That might have happened: a block grant of citizenship to those who had aided the democrats was passed by the Assembly, only to be slapped down in the People's Court. Meanwhile, some elite Athenians had the opposite hope, that the new democracy would choose to limit participation rights to property owners with estates of a certain size. Reducing the citizen body may never have been put to a vote, but it was a live issue in the immediate postwar years. In the end, the rules that had governed citizenship between 451 and 413 were reasserted: no property requirement for citizenship, but no large-scale enfranchisement of non-natives, either. The substantial changes in legal procedure made at the end of the fifth century were not paralleled by new criteria for naturalization.[61]

---

[61] Pro-democratic choices of non-citizens in 404 and postwar settlement: Strauss 1986; Ostwald 1986: 503–9; Loening 1987; Wolpert 2002; Ober 2005b: 89–91. The pro-democ-

In retrospect, and in comparison to the liberation of African slaves in the course of the American Civil War, the Athenian failure to extend access in the course of the post–Peloponnesian War democratic restoration seems a missed opportunity—morally deplorable and otherwise indefensible. That missed opportunity points to the stickiness of the status distinctions that sustained the democracy—distinctions that, in some cases, were buttressed by legal rules specifying the source of legally relevant information. In light of the Athenians' recognition of the value of freely shared information, and the richness of Athenian incentives for motivating free persons to share what they knew, the maintenance of the Athenian restriction of slave testimony in most legal contexts to statements obtained under torture is particularly egregious, and seems especially likely to have been counterproductive.[62]

The supercoalition between elite and non-elite native males was predicated on maintaining rent-producing restrictions on non-natives and slaves. The Athenian democracy was committed to the protection of private property, and that would continue to include chattel slaves (Mossé 2007 [1981]: 85–91). Athenians remained ideologically unwilling to place their slaves' interest in personal freedom, dignity, and equal treatment in the scales of justice, despite the fact that freedom, dignity, and equality were highly valued by citizens. That unwillingness was, perhaps, motivated by a recognition that, if given proper weight, the interests of slaves in freedom would outweigh the property interests of slave owners. A similar recognition of the likely effect of taking others' interests seriously, as a matter of justice, may account for the sustained restriction on political participation rights for Athenian women despite publicly performed thought experiments (such as Aristophanes' *Lysistrata* and *Assemblywomen*) premised upon women's capacity and interest in working actively for public (as well as private) goods. Athens' well-being as a community arguably suffered because the rents collected and superior status asserted by the supercoalition of native males blocked the possibility of developing a democratic decision-making process that would have given

racy choice was far from universal: compare the more than 20,000 slaves who, according to Thucydides (7.27.5), escaped from Athens to Spartan-held Decelea after 413.

[62] Athenian torture of slaves for obtaining legal testimony: Thür 1977; Carey 1988; Du-Bois 1991; Gagarin 1996; Mirhady 1996, 2000. Whether this practice was common or not, and how the evidence of torture testimony (the subject of much of the scholarly debate on the subject) was employed, is of less moment, for our purposes, than the simple fact that the practice remained on the books and was frequently alluded to by litigants. The Athenian public response to a series of events in 415 b.c. (smashing of Herms and mocking of sacred mysteries), spun out of control at least in part because much the relevant information was possessed by slaves; see detailed account in Furley 1996.

real weight to considerations of justice for women and slaves, and to the value of the knowledge uniquely held by them.[63]

The natives' near-monopoly on ownership of private real estate was a substantial rule-protected privilege. The rise in special grants of rights to own real estate (*enktēsis*) around the middle of the fourth century (Pecírka 1966) showed that the citizen monopoly could be breached, but it nevertheless remained the norm. The near-monopoly ensured citizens an advantage in credit markets, where loans typically required land as collateral. Likewise, the limitation of legitimate marriage and legal inheritance by citizens to unions between citizens artificially restricted the marriage market. After 451/0 B.C. Athenian fathers did not compete with foreigners when seeking suitable matches for their daughters. It is very likely that the median dowry would have increased if the market were opened. This might have been good for the Athenian economy in the long run, but native Athenian fathers, facing the prospect of unmarried daughters, were unwilling to trade off their own, certain, short-term advantage for uncertain and general long-term social benefits.[64]

The ample imperial rents that had flowed to the state and to individual Athenians, rich and poor (Finley 1978), largely dried up with Athens' loss of the Peloponnesian War. Many Athenians must have realized that there could be no return to the imperial era. Their successful turn to forms of wealth seeking that depended on free exchange rather than coerced extraction is, as I have argued above, the key to explaining the revival of Athenian capacity in the fourth century. But, despite the best efforts of Athenian writers (Aristophanes, *Assemblywomen*; Xenophon, *Revenues*; Isocrates, *Peace*) to lay it to rest, the "ghost of empire" (Badian 1995; Buckler 2003: 221–25, 383) continued to haunt Athenian dreams. The residual habits of imperial-era rent seeking may be detected, for example, in heavy-handed mid-fourth-century attempts to impose a trade monopoly on the export of ochre (a coloring agent) on three of the island-poleis of Keos (RO 40) as well as in state-supported Athenian settlements outside Attica, notably on Samos (Cargill 1995; Hallof and Habicht 1995; Salomon 1997). The farming of grain taxes on three Aegean islands (Lemnos, Imbros, and Skyros) still directly controlled by Athens is a case in point.

The tax-farming system, by which the right to collect one-twelfth of the total grain production of each of the three islands was annually auc-

---

[63] The argument here is based on J. Cohen 1997.

[64] Periclean Law of 451/0 requiring "double endogamy" and Athenian marriage system: Humphreys 1993; Patterson 1981, 1998, 2005; Lape 2002–3, 2003. Hoepfner and Schwander 1994 survey the relationship between the Greek polis and real estate. Nevett 2000 describes real estate markets in classical Greece, emphasizing the value of urban land.

tioned off to a single bidder or syndicate, offers insight into Athens' hybrid fourth-century economy. A tax of one-twelfth was not extortionate by ancient standards, but the tax underlined the fact that the agricultural land of the three islands was under the control of the Athenian state. The agriculturalists upon whom the grain tax was levied were either native islanders subject to Athenian authority, or Athenian rentier-settlers (cleruchs) if we assume the natives had been permanently expelled by Athenian imperial fiat in the fifth century B.C. According to the expulsion hypothesis (Moreno 2003, 2008) Athenian proceeds from the islands were rents in the most basic sense. But even if we assume that natives were in possession of the land, and that the taxes for which they were liable paid in part for their own military security, the Athenian approach to tax farming nonetheless asymmetrically distributed risks in favor of the residents of Athens.[65]

New rules for tax farming on the three subject islands were established in a law proposed by the veteran democratic leader Agyrrhios in 374, just a year after Nikophon's law on silver coins, considered above.[66] By seeking both rents and public security, by employing market- and non-market mechanisms, Agyrrhios' law succinctly brought together seemingly incongruous elements of the fourth-century Athenian public economy. The law was explicitly intended to provide public goods for Athenians in the form of enhanced social and military security: the taxes, to be paid in grain rather than coin, were to be farmed "in order that the people may have grain publicly available" (lines 5–6). Once transported to Athens, the tax grain was to be sold, by a board of ten annually elected officials, at a price set by the Assembly, when (after a certain date) the Assembly decided that the time was right. The money raised by the grain sale was to go into the military budget (lines 36–54). By setting the *date* of sale, the Assembly chose when to intervene in the grain market. Timing the grain sale right would promote the goal of stabilizing the cost of grain, which

Leiwo and Remes 1999 point out that partnerships between metics and citizens might effectively circumvent the restrictions of the law.

[65] One-twelfth was a conventional rate for the leasing of land, one that recurs (expressed in monetary terms) in private contracts. Rules of land tenure and leasing: Millett 1991. Contrast, the conditions of helots in Sparta: Ducat 1990; Luraghi and Alcock 2003. Practice of public auctions at Athens: Langdon 1994.

[66] Agyrrhios' law: Stroud 1998; RO 26, with detailed commentary; Moreno 2003, 2008. The suggestion of Harris 1999, that the law describes a transit tax rather than a tax on grain grown on the three islands, cannot be right; see RO commentary pp. 123–24. Agyrrhios was famous for having sponsored the introduction and increase in Assembly pay in the years immediately following the restoration of democracy: [Aristotle] *Ath. Pol.* 41.3; a concern for the social security of the citizens may be the thread that connects these two legislative initiatives.

was the staple food of Athenians, as of other Greeks.[67] By setting the *price* at which the grain would be put onto the market, the Assembly could calibrate, very precisely and on an annual basis, the relative needs of social and military security. Setting a higher price for the tax grain would increase the military budget at the expense of subsidizing food, and vice versa.

The tax farmers themselves assumed the risk for transport, sales taxes, and auctioneer's fees, but once the grain was in port, the state stepped in to provide facilities for secure storage (15–16). The concern for standard measurement is patent in the grain law: the taxes of the islands were farmed in an auction in which each participant (individual or syndicate) bid volumes of grain, rather than money. Each island was annually auctioned on the basis of shares; each contract share was for 500 *medimnoi* (units of capacity measurement) of grain. At the auction, the would-be tax farmer who bid the highest number of shares won the right to collect taxes on the island that was being auctioned off. Once the amount of grain he had bid was finally delivered to the Athenian market, the tax farmer was required to *weigh out* the total volume of grain he had bid. The law mandated that the tax farmer deliver the grain dry and clean, "arranging the standard weight on the balance, just as the other merchants" (8–36, translation: Rhodes and Osborne). The public-good *goal* of specifying delivery of grain in the form "x volume at y weight" is clearly to control quality; the *method* is to require the use of standard weights and measures, and standard mercantile practices in employing them.

A successful tax farmer would need to have considerable technical expertise, a tolerance for risk, and a clear understanding of how the rules worked. The actual amount of grain represented by a twelfth of a given island's production (the amount the successful bidder was legally entitled to collect) would vary from year to year, and bids for each island were taken from tax farmers before the harvest was in. The tax farmer would make a legal profit on the transaction only if his successful bid (the amount of grain he agreed to deliver to Athens) turned out to be lower than the amount he subsequently collected. The intent of the law was to provide Athenians with a predictable annual supply of standard-quality grain and with monetary revenue from the sale of grain. That intent was pursued by a competitive auction and by quality-control provisions that made it difficult for tax farmers to cheat the state.

Given the state's power to sanction, a profit-maximizing tax farmer was strongly discouraged from seeking to cheat the Athenian people. Agyrrhios' law is silent, however, on the subject of tax farmers who

---

[67] Garnsey 1998. A modern analogy is a state reserve bank that can choose when to buy or sell money in an attempt to stabilize the value of a national currency.

cheated the islands' grain producers by taking more than one-twelfth of their grain. If we suppose that some producers were natives who continued to possess and farm their own land, that silence is ominous in that it leaves native producers vulnerable to collusion between Athenian tax farmers and military governors. The silence is even more ominous if it means that the natives had been permanently expelled by force and their land appropriated. In this case, the producers being taxed were elite Athenians, and so Agyrrhios' law (like the *antidosis* law regulating annual liturgical duties) pitted Athenian elites against one another, with disputes to be settled in the People's Courts. In either case, state power was involved in the systematic extraction of valuable resources. The codification of that power relation in a law that focuses exclusively on the interests of Athenians defines the limited horizon of Athenian legal fairness.

In his work on entrepreneurs, the economist William Baumol (1990, 1993, 2004) contrasts the high-productivity economic strategy of continuous innovation with the historically common strategy of rent seeking. Baumol points out that the established cultural and institutional rules prevalent in a given society may encourage entrepreneurs to focus either on innovation or rent seeking. In Athenian law we see both. Baumol's argument suggests that to the extent that the codified rules protected citizens from competition, Athenian economic performance underachieved its full productive potential. How much further *could* Athens have gone toward an open, fair, and innovation-driven economy, without losing the benefits of state-sponsored social insurance and without precipitating an ideological crisis? That question can only be approached counter-factually, but certainly deserves further thought. In Agyrrhios' law, use of the constitutional process by an entrepreneurial politician yielded an innovative administrative rule that outsourced the state's rent collection to entrepreneurial tax farmers.

Chapter 7

CONCLUSIONS: GOVERNMENT BY THE PEOPLE

THE PREVIOUS CHAPTERS have sketched a portrait of classical Athens as a participatory and deliberative democracy, as a state that outperformed its rivals in part because of its superior capacity to make use of dispersed knowledge. Of course, no historical account can claim to have captured the past in all of its complexity, "as it really was" (Novick 1988). Some historical portraits, like some artistic portraits, may not be overly concerned with accuracy in the sense of representing past reality; such portraits do not realistically depict particular features of their subjects but may nevertheless be valuable in that they reveal some truth about the human condition. Other portraits, while sharing the ambition to reveal general truth about humanity, can also be said to capture the likeness and thereby to represent some particular truths (if never the whole truth) about their subject. I hope to have written a historical portrait of this latter sort.[1]

My portrait has focused on epistemic processes because the role of useful knowledge has been relatively neglected both in previous historical portraits of Athens and in recent social-scientific attempts to explain the performance advantage enjoyed by democracies in competitive environments. The goal has been to supplement these other approaches, by highlighting the relationship among knowledge, performance, and democratic institutions.

KNOWLEDGE IN ACTION

The first figure in this book (1.1) offered a static picture of the relationship between knowledge processes and democratic organizational design. Figure 7.1 illustrates the dynamic flows of the system and thereby sums up the account of Athenian government by the people that has been developed in the previous chapters.

---

[1] Hannah Arendt's (1958) depiction of the Greek polis is an example of a "historical portrait" that does not accurately represent any real polis but captures important truths nonetheless. See, further, Kateb 2000; Euben 2000.

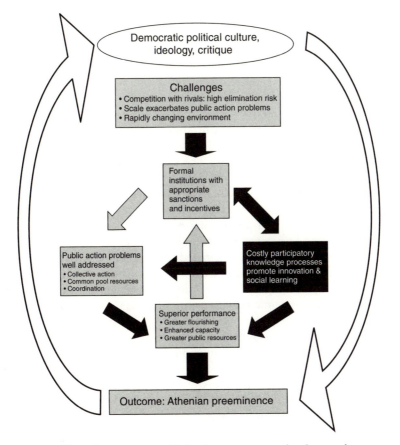

Figure 7.1. Flow-chart portrait of Athenian government by the people.

The "costly participatory knowledge processes" box is highlighted in the figure because this book's emphasis has been on the underappreciated contribution of social, technical, and latent knowledge to the flourishing of democratic organizations. The black arrows indicate the primary flow of the book's argument: challenges arising from a competitive environment, along with the exacerbation of public action problems that come with increased scale, helped to stimulate the development of formal institutions with incentives and sanctions appropriate to encouraging individual choices that furthered public purposes. Athenians could count on the state's commitment to individual rights in respect to private property, citizenship, and legal process. That commitment grew more credible over time. While commitment mechanisms were employed by other Greek republican states, the Athenian panoply of epistemic institutions appears to have been unique. Athenian institutions addressed key public-action problems in the areas of collective action, common pool resources, and coordination. Those problems were addressed, in part, by a distinctive array of democratic knowledge processes. These epistemic processes, rather than being a drag on the system, contributed substantially to Athens' advantage over its republican rivals.

Addressing public action problems via participatory processes of knowledge aggregation, alignment, and codification (as opposed to the more familiar coercive approach of command-and-control) introduced substantial costs. Paying for participation in government by non-elite citizens was a major public expense. The expense was more than covered because costly participative processes had the beneficial effect of promoting a dynamically productive relationship between knowledge and governance. Public rewards encouraged experimentation. Innovators responded by devising and advocating new policies and adjustments in policy making and executive institutions. As a result, Athenian policies responded more readily to unanticipated challenges, and Athenian institutions adapted more quickly to the changing environment than did those of Athens' major competitors. Evolving knowledge processes in turn helped to address endemic public-action dilemmas, for example by lowering transaction costs through lessening information asymmetries. Meanwhile, enhanced levels of social cooperation accompanied the social learning that arose from many individuals gaining political experience through "working the machine" of self-government.

Athens encouraged private investments in social learning, which in turn yielded public goods. Individual investment in learning was rational because ongoing institutional innovations were built on a foundation of stable democratic principles. Athenian institutions were reliably grounded in practices of accountability, transparency, and legitimate dissent. Stable principles ensured that effort expended in learning how the system worked was not wasted, whereas ongoing innovations ensured that governmental routines avoided ossification. The organizational design thus allowed innovation and social learning to be reciprocally self-regulating, while rewarding innovators and learners alike.

Because fundamental Athenian principles of government remained quite stable, individuals could lay their future plans with relative confidence. Because new formal institutions were devised and old ones evolved readily in response to new challenges, social entrepreneurs were constantly provided with new opportunities. The system offered a menu of incentives (public honors, material rewards) for those who successfully learned and innovated, and sanctions (social opprobrium, fines) for those who failed to learn. A productive "epistemic equilibrium" thereby emerged and was dynamically sustained over time by the willing activity of many well-motivated participants. With innovation and learning in dynamic equilibrium, the Athenian economy did well under changing conditions; overall material flourishing and state capacity were robustly supported. The result is that Athens was able to take fuller advantage of its relatively great size, natural resources, and human capital, and so achieved (in the fifth century) and then regained (in the fourth century) a position of preeminence among its city-state rivals.

The system was more complicated in its actual workings than the black arrows alone would suggest. The gray arrows indicate secondary (for the purposes of this study) effects of the system. Superior Athenian performance was certainly not entirely a matter of superior epistemic processes; institutional solutions to public-action problems had positive impacts on performance through building confidence, morale, and a sense of solidarity among residents. Meanwhile, as Athens became more productive and public revenues increased, institutions were better funded and functioned more effectively. Participation widened as the system became more capable of rewarding public service (e.g. through pay and honors) and deepened in that each individual was able to participate more fully on the basis of his accumulating store of useful knowledge.

Finally, as indicated by the white arrows, there was a steady and reciprocal interchange between culture, challenges, outcomes, and the institutionalized processes that have been the primary subject of this book. Athenian democratic culture promoted an ideology grounded in values of freedom, equality, and dignity. It also promoted the critique of democratic failings, thus pushing back against the tendency to ideological rigidity and conformist groupthink. The culture built and sustained a background commitment to democratic values; that background commitment allowed the democracy to survive periods of infrastructure destruction, demographic catastrophe, policy failure, civil conflict, and institutional collapse. Culture served as a sort of "flywheel" capable of storing social energy and making it available when the system was temporarily incapable of fully repaying the costs to individuals of their participation. The relationship between civic culture and formal institutions of government was reciprocal because the working of the system also energized democratic culture. The institutionalized processes of self-government, along with the flourishing economy and burgeoning state capacity they supported, extended and deepened democratic culture by embedding culture in practices: as sharers in a democratic culture, Athenians rationally chose to participate in the productive work of citizenship. Their choices in turn constantly re-created and sustained their culture.

These conclusions, if correct, have implications for thinking about democracy today. If management of knowledge, distributed among a diverse population through the operation of participatory institutions, helped to promote high performance in the competitive world of classical Greece, there is less reason to assume that the role of the citizen in a modern democracy need be limited to occasionally choosing among competing elites on the basis of their party affiliation. The Athenian case suggests that, contrary to the standard arguments of technocrats and "democratic elitists," a democratic community need not imitate the centralized command-and-control systems typical of oligarchic and autocratic organizations in order to perform well. A participatory democracy on the Athenian model can potentially equal, or perhaps even surpass, authoritarian rivals by doing the very things that command-and-control apparatus is often supposed to do uniquely well: make good decisions on the basis of the best available information, coordinate effort among individuals and groups, and increase the return to cooperation by internalizing transaction costs.

The issue of scale remains (chapter 3). Yet the difference in scale between city-states and nation-states does not vitiate the potential value of the Athenian case for thinking about modernity. Most obviously, most modern non-state organizations and many sub-state political units are no larger than Athens was. Even at the level of the nation-state, it is possible to imagine extending the Athenian approach of reproducing epistemic processes and democratic principles at multiple institutional scales. The full potential of modern information technology for facilitating knowledge aggregation and public action in democratic contexts remains to be explored (Sunstein 2006).

THE DEMOCRACY/KNOWLEDGE HYPOTHESIS REVISITED

The central chapters of this book tested the hypothesis set out at the end of chapter 1:

> *Democratic Athens was able to take advantage of its size and resources, and therefore competed successfully over time against hierarchical rivals, because the costs of participatory political practices were overbalanced by superior returns to social cooperation resulting from useful knowledge as it was organized and deployed in the simultaneously innovation-promoting and learning-based context of democratic institutions and culture.*

That hypothesis could be invalidated by demonstrating that its premises were false: by proving, for example, that Athens did not perform well relative to its rivals; that the environment of the city-states was not particularly competitive; that Athens was not strongly democratic or did not confront serious public-action problems; that political participation rates were relatively low or were limited to a socially homogeneous body of persons; that Athenian epistemic institutions were not distinctive. The hypothesis could be falsified by showing that Athenian institutions served to aggregate preferences but not knowledge; that Athens was characterized by low rates of institutional innovation; that Athenian institutions and culture manifested low rates of social learning; that epistemic processes played no significant role in increasing returns to social cooperation; or that some exogenous factor adequately accounts for Athenian exceptionalism. Although I cannot claim to have answered each and every one of these invalidation and falsification conditions in a systematic way, each has been addressed in some detail in the preceding pages.

My argument in favor of the hypothesis began with a series of general premises: First, that the information and expertise essential to making good policy decisions will be widely dispersed in a socially diverse population. Second, that a knowledge regime that effectively collected, coordinated and codified knowledge while properly balancing innovation with social learning will promote state capacity. Third, that endemic public-action problems must be addressed by well-designed institutions in order to achieve the necessary level of voluntary cooperation in respect to information exchange and innovation. Finally, that addressing public-action problems requires motivating individuals through a mix of incentives, sanctions, and learned social norms. I then sought to demonstrate, empirically, that Athens did in fact outperform its peer-rivals (other Greek poleis) in respect to flourishing and capacity (chapter 2).

Given the empirical fact of a flourishing democratic community, and in the absence of any good candidate for an exogenous cause of flourishing, the argument's premises predict certain features of institutional design: institutionalized forums for participatory and deliberative decision making at multiple scales, including but not limited to face-to-face; systematic development of extensive social networks featuring both strong and weak ties; managing state business through "real teams"; procedures for rendering social commitments credible; extensive publicity media for building common knowledge; public architecture maximizing intervisibility among participants; instruments and rules to drive down transaction costs by reducing information asymmetries among parties to exchanges; incentives at various levels for productive innovations; sanctions against free-riding; an abiding concern for rotation, transparency, and accountability; a cultural commitment to civic education that stopped well short of totalizing social indoctrination.

Each of these predicted features of institutional design (among others) is well attested in classical Athens. These institutional features were not typical of the predemocratic era; they emerged from and were integral parts of democratic processes and practices of participation and deliberation. Moreover, the development of Athenian capacity in foreign, domestic, and building policy correlates to and is led by the development of institutions with distinctive epistemic features. It therefore seems fair to conclude that Athenian flourishing can indeed be attributed, at least in part, to the creation and maintenance of a system of democracy in which the costs of participation were, over time and in the aggregate, outweighed by the value of its participatory knowledge regime.

The absence of falsification conditions, the presence of the predicted institutional features, and the apparent correlation between capacity and democracy do not yield an irrefutable proof of the democracy/knowledge hypothesis. But they do, I submit, add up to a strong case in its favor. A refutation of the democracy/knowledge hypothesis would need to offer a different explanation for the empirical evidence for Athenian flourishing and for the apparent historical correlation of Athenian democracy and capacity, and would have to account for the historical development and persistence of the relevant features of Athenian institutions.

To the extent to which the hypothesis holds, it is a refutation of Robert Michels's influential "iron law of oligarchy": viz., that participatory democracy could not contribute to a group's success in the long-term, because participatory democracy is unsustainable given the demands of organization. Michels' theory may still hold under most conditions, but it is not universally applicable and therefore should no longer be regarded as an iron law of political organization. Furthermore, Athens, especially in the later fourth century, appears to be an early example of a system that in some salient respects resembles what North, Wallis, and Weingast (in progress) call the "modern open-access order." This in turn suggests that, in the domain of social science, "modernity" may be more useful as an analytic concept than as a description of a unique chronological era.

A next step would be to seek to generalize the Athenian case as a formal and positive, and thus systematically testable, theory of participatory democracy and knowledge organization. That undertaking is outside the scope of this book, but the empirical and theoretical work undertaken here points to its feasibility and potential value.

FORMALITY AND EXPERIMENTATION

I have left unresolved the question of how much of the observable phenomenon of Athenian flourishing was the result of formality (that is, a well thought-out blueprint for state governance dating back, originally, to the late sixth century) and how much of the system emerged through an informal and experimental process of trial and error over time.[2] The answer is, no doubt, "some formality, some experimentalism," but it seems impossible to determine just how much weight to give to each side of the equation. The earlier chapters offer considerable evidence for ongoing trial-and-error experimentation. Yet it remains the case that at key moments in the late sixth century, in the late fifth century, and in the mid-fourth century, an unruly body of prior experimental development was both formalized and transformed by what are reasonably construed as comprehensive governmental blueprints. The detailed rules for the approval of silver coinage discussed in chapter 6 exemplify the Athenian capacity to employ formalities when necessary, just as the lack of detailed administrative rules for interinstitutional coordination in the naval-station dispatching decree (chapter 4) points to Athenian experimentalism. A similar, and similarly dynamic, tension is manifest in the practice of Athenian law, where, by the mid-fourth century, extensive judicial discretion in most areas of criminal and civil law (chapter 5) coexisted with detailed and specific regulations in commercial law (chapter 6). Judicial discretion sustained democratic experimentalism, whereas legal specificity provided higher levels of predictability for traders in Athenian markets.

The question of formality is related to the problem of relating observable effects of popular government to legislators' original intentions. Given the state of our evidence, those intentions are largely unrecoverable. Yet the coherence and robustness of the system, in its parts and as a whole, point to a recognition of and thoughtful concern for problems of public action. The conclusion that Athenian institutional designers were attentive to public action is consistent with the evidence of classical Greek literature: Aristophanes, Herodotus, Thucydides, Plato, and Aristotle (among other Athenian-resident writers) were well aware of public-action problems, and aware of the potential of epistemic processes for addressing them (Ober, in progress).

The innovative design of Athenian institutions, especially in respect to the organization of knowledge, should not be attributed to a single genius or even to a series of geniuses. But the system itself, as manifest in Athenian democratic ideology, culture, and government institutions, displays an inner logic of design that may be traced back to the revolutionary era in which Athenian democracy first crystallized. Innovations introduced in response to new challenges by subsequent generations of Athenians adapted to changing conditions and extended the scope of the

[2] The formality/experimentation distinction is helpfully addressed, with reference to modern organizations, by Stinchcombe 2001.

system, while retaining its fundamental deliberative and participatory logic. That logic can be expressed, by slightly emending Abraham Lincoln's resonant phrase, as "government of and for, and therefore *necessarily by* the people."

INSTITUTIONS AND IDEOLOGY

The previous chapters have focused on Athenian institutions and how they were conjoined into a complex and effective system of governance. Yet formal institutions, in Athens as elsewhere, necessarily operate within a cultural milieu. Institutions are accepted as legitimate (or rejected as illegitimate) on the basis of ideological dispositions.[3] At the same time, however, people's experience of formal institutions is a *source* of ideology and can strengthen or undermine ideological commitments. Some degree of institutional/ideological reciprocity will be present in any working political system. The ideological dispositions of persons who live out their lives as subjects of institutional authority are inevitably influenced by the experience of being subject to the authority of those institutions. A primary purpose of social and political criticism, from Plato onward, has been to expose the operations of institutionalized authority, especially its role in promoting the development of dispositions that might not otherwise be chosen by the individuals in question.[4]

The situation in respect to the reciprocity of institutions and ideology in a democracy is in some ways distinctive. Democracies are more likely than oligarchies or autocracies to regard criticism as legitimate. Democratic public discourse and institutional authority are likely to respond (if only at some remove) to criticisms that identify genuine problems and point to feasible solutions.[5] Reciprocity between institutions and ideological dispositions is to the fore in a participatory democracy on the Athenian model, because a relatively high percentage of the community's residents have had the distinctive experience of serving as an *agent of* institutionalized authority, as well as the ordinary human experience of being its subject.

By the early fifth century, no Athenian who was chosen for a magistracy, for example the Council of 500, would have taken up office in a

---

[3] North 1981: 45–58 emphasizes the essential role of a dominant ideology in sustaining legitimacy, and the impossibility of high performance in its absence. Greif 2006 includes ideology and culture in his expansive definition of "institutions."

[4] This point is variously developed by Althusser 1990 [1966]; Gramsci 1971; Butler 1997, and in other strains of Marxist and post-modern political and social theory.

[5] Ober 1998, chapter 7. See, further, Allen 2000b, 2004; Balot 2006.

condition of tabula rasa. He had already been conditioned by growing up in an ideology and a culture defined in part by democratic institutions. As a product of his interactions with other Athenians he knew a good deal about the government and its workings. He had been socialized as an Athenian citizen by participating in public rituals and organized practices of governance—for example, deliberating according to the principle of equal right to public speech (*isēgoria*) and voting on policy proposals as an equal among equals in the citizen Assembly. He expected to bring his own social knowledge, and whatever technical expertise he might possess, to bear in Council discussions. Yet he also expected to learn a great deal, in terms of both technical and social knowledge, from the experience of being a councilor. After his year of service, the knowledge he had gained as a councilor was returned to the culture through his everyday social interactions.

Athenian governmental practices manifested formal political principles, such as transparency and accountability, that are now widely recognized as characteristics of good government. The practices of Athenian government also manifested less formal but nonetheless familiar governance principles. These included a respect for local jurisdiction, rotation of office and turn taking in respect to assuming positions of authority, attending to the merits of arguments, and the necessity of achieving closure in a timely manner.[6] The practices and principles learned by each Athenian magistrate were generalized across the Athenian government system. Moreover, these standard practices and principles pertained across a range of scales. As we have seen, the work of Athenian governance was organized across groups of 10 (boards of *archontes*), 50 (tribe-teams of *prutaneis*), 200 (*dikastēria*), 500 (*boulē* and *dikastēria* for public cases), 1500 (*nomothetai*), 6000 or more (*ekklēsia* and ostracism). Likewise, much of Athenian ritual and political activity was organized across the ascending scales of deme, tribe, and polis. The consistency of practice and principle between institutions and across scales reinforced the socialization of the Athenian citizen into the central ideological presuppositions that sustained democracy.

The Athenian system was effective in part because it worked as a practical form of civic education. By participating in "working the machine" of democracy, the individual Athenian was both encouraged to share his own useful knowledge, and given the chance to develop and deepen various sorts of politically relevant expertise.[7] This civic-education-as-politi-

---

[6] The practices and process principles of Athenian democracy are laid out in more detail in Manville and Ober 2003: 119–50.

[7] On Athenian civic education, see further, Ober 2001 (= Ober 2005b, chapter 6), with literature cited.

cal-socialization can be generalized as a sort of organizational learning. As such it served two primary functions. First, by building common experience via reference to standard ways of doing things, it lent a relatively high degree of predictability and efficiency to institutional functions carried out by amateurs and enabled amateurs to become relatively expert in their jobs. Because organizational learning was consistent (in terms of practices and principles) across Athenian institutions and across scales, the efficiency gains associated with standardization of processes were readily captured across the Athenian government as a whole. Next, learning as socialization helped to sustain democracy by granting it ideological legitimacy in the eyes of the citizenry. Predictability, standardization, and legitimacy all lowered transaction costs and thereby reduced the friction inherent within every complex system.

The opportunity for amateurs to develop something comparable to expertise in the public realm, through many hours of practice across the course of a lifetime, distinguishes the experience of ancient Athenian citizenship from its modern analogs. This has obvious implications for thinking about how the system's epistemic features produced practical results. The presence on deliberating boards (e.g., the tribal teams of the Council) of many persons, from diverse walks of life, with deep public policy experience, inevitably affected the conditions of public deliberation. Modern experiments have produced decidedly mixed performance results for deliberating groups (chapter 4). Some negative and positive features of deliberation may be context-independent. But modern deliberating groups lack features of analogous Athenian groups that seem likely to be highly relevant to performance: the rewards and sanctions for each modern deliberator are nugatory; the opportunity for social networking over time is limited; the relevance of prior political experience to the deliberative process is questionable. The Athenian case suggests that in order to measure the true potential of deliberating groups, experiments will need to model key aspects of Athenian-style political socialization, including participatory expertise, potential for long-term social interactions, high stakes, and deliberative experience at multiple scales.

If socialization to ideological norms had been the only, or even the primary function of the Athenian citizen's experience of institutional life, it is unlikely that Athens could have sustained strong performance across a long history featuring periodic and substantial environmental change. As I have repeatedly emphasized (with reference to the work of James March and his collaborators), there is an inherent tension between learning as socialization and the redeployment of knowledge for innovation. This tension has been the subject of empirical research; there are many well-studied test cases in which too little or too much socialization led to poor organizational performance. Theoretical models point to positive and negative tipping points (chapter 3). There is no simple formula for getting the learning/innovation balance right, but overall and over time, the Athenians appear to have found a balance point that yielded high returns to both learning and innovation.

Athenians were well known in Greek antiquity for their innovative experimentalism. Thucydides (e.g., 1.70.2–71) makes a point of contrasting Athenian innovation with Spartan conservatism in the imperial era of the fifth century. The habit of innovation continued into the post-imperial fourth century. One form of innovation was the creation of new government offices, including Lawmakers, Dispatchers, Approvers, and financial magistrates. The capacity for innovation *within* existing institutions was equally important to Athenian success over time. Fourth-century examples include the emendation of the law code; recruitment and selection of jurors; new responsibilities for the Council of 500 and Areopagus Council; revisions to systems of taxation; military mobilization and the duties of generals. Examples of both new institutions and changes within institutions could readily be multiplied.[8]

Athenian institutions addressed a constantly changing menu of challenges by encouraging the cross-appropriation of expert knowledge from one domain to another, by mixing social knowledge with technical knowledge, and by bringing latent knowledge into view. Innovation was encouraged by the Athenian ideology of civic identity: Athenians thought of themselves as particularly experimental and innovative people, just as Spartans, for example, evidently thought of themselves as particularly conservative. Athenians valued innovation as a good in itself because it was a manifestation of their communal identity, of what they supposed was special and excellent about themselves as a people—as well as valuing innovation as an instrument for gaining other goods. Neither formal institutions nor ideology can be isolated as the driver of the will to innovate and to reward innovation. Rather, the democratic system was produced and sustained by the recursive, reciprocal relationship between ideology and innovation. That relationship fed a productive cycle that maintained relatively high levels of governmental predictability and reliability while allowing adequate space for dynamic adaptation to an ever-changing environment.[9]

---

[8] The distinctive and self-conscious Athenian focus on innovation is likewise evident in other cultural domains, for example, in styles of vase painting (Neer 2002) and choral performance (Wilson 2000: 297).

[9] The Athenian pride in innovation is notable, for example, in Aristophanes' comedies. Aristophanes, taking the comic poet's expected critical role (Ober 1998, chapter 3), often points out that innovation can lead to trouble and reminds the Athenian audience of the value of consistency and stability. The counterfactual thought experiment of imagining Aristophanes' comedies being translated into a Spartan milieu, with the Athenian characters

Exceptionalism and Exemplarity

This book has been primarily concerned with explaining the phenomenon of Athenian preeminence in the competitive world of the Greek city-states, and thus it has focused on Athenian exceptionalism. Athens was regarded by contemporary Greek observers as a remarkable polis, but not as existing outside the general category "polis." Aristotle, for example, mixed examples drawn from Athenian political history and contemporary practice with the history and practices of other poleis in writing his *Politics*. If no other known polis was as productive as Athens, this does not mean that the other poleis were inefficient when measured against other premodern states. As noted above, other Greek republican states featured commitment mechanisms that promoted private choices favorable to public outcomes. While the full array of Athenian epistemic institutions seems to have been unique (at least in classical period), other classical Greek states employed deliberative councils, rotating boards of magistrates, sound currency, and publicity media—all features that were important to Athens' performance.

The innovation/learning dynamic that drives performance within organizations is also operative across ecologies of organizations (Levitt and March 1988: 329–32). Democratic Athenian institutions were based on principles well known in the Greek world (Robinson 1997 and forthcoming). Moreover, specific Athenian institutions and practices were widely imitated, especially in the fourth and third centuries. Examples, which could be multiplied, include political and festival architecture; currency rules (e.g., at Olbia); laws on tyrannicide (Teegarden 2007); allotment tokens (*pinakia*) and machines (*klērōtēria*: Kroll 1972: 268). Athens ought, therefore, to be regarded as exemplary as well as exceptional—as a model for what the Greek polis, as a form of political organization, could accomplish with the proper organization of substantial material and human resources. Without resorting to fallacious teleological explanations (it is certainly *not* true that all Greek poleis were purposefully striving to achieve the end of becoming more Athens-like), we can think of Athens as a particularly successful, highly developed, and well-studied exemplar of the general type "republican/democratic polis."

Coming to a better understanding of why Athens performed especially well should shed light on the performance of other city-states and, by extrapolation, on the Greek city-state culture as a whole. To the extent that other city-states were like Athens in their political culture and institu-

---

cast as Spartans, points to the ideological differences between the two communities: it is almost impossible to imagine "innovation-besotted (male) Spartans" as stock characters.

tions, we might expect them to manifest some of the performance characteristics of Athens. At a higher level of abstraction, if we might even think of the Greek world as in certain respects a macrocosm of the Athenian microcosm: the Greek city-state culture, taken as a whole, more closely resembles Athens' dispersed authority structure than it does, for example, the more centralized systems of imperial Rome or China.

Approached from the perspective of exemplarity rather than exceptionalism, the uniquely well-documented Athenian case can help us to understand a puzzle that has lurked in the background of each of the previous chapters, that is, the impressive aggregate performance of the thousand-plus state Greek city-state culture. As noted in chapters 2 and 3, recent research suggests that the Greek world was more densely populated than might be expected of a pre-modern society, and that its people were generally healthier and wealthier on a per capita basis. According to various measures, at least some of the regions inhabited by Greek city-states appear to have been better off during the Classical/Hellenistic era than they would be again until the twentieth century.[10] This historically remarkable fact is even more striking in that the city-states featured, on the whole, governments that were not based on strict command-and-control, and economies that were not dependent on continual territorial expansion.

If we suppose—following the lead of Douglass North (1981), Margaret Levi (1981), and Charles Tilly (1990)—that a predatory impetus to rent seeking by power holders drives early state formation, then we would expect the emergence of expansionist states featuring exploitative systems of patronage, command-and-control systems of internal governance, and dominated by a monopolistic elite. The logic of coercive state building indeed seems to result in the standard ancient pattern of kingdom and empire. As I noted in chapter 3, ancient Rome provides a model that conforms quite closely to the early-modern European experience of state building in a "coercion-intensive region" (Eich and Eich 2005, quote p. 32). From this interpretive perspective, the large (perhaps 7 million persons) and long-lived Greek city-state culture would appear to be a historical anomaly—the exception that proves the rule.

If the Greek city-state culture had been poor and sparsely populated, the apparent anomaly would not be of general interest. Polis culture has indeed been described as an "evolutionary dead end," doomed from the beginning to extinction at the hands of better-organized imperial powers. According to this line of argument, the Greek poleis were fatally ill-organized: citizens lacked the proper sense of deference necessary to support a proper hierarchy, and the poleis "were all, without exception, far too

---

[10] Key studies include Morris 2004, 2005a; Kron 2005; M. H. Hansen 2006b.

democratic" (Runciman 1990, quote p. 364). But given what we now
know about the demographic and economic performance of that culture,
it is less easy to brush the Greek city-states aside as historical ephemera,
unworthy of serious attention when compared to the great and glorious
empires of the past. It is worth asking how much the economic success of
the Macedonian and Roman empires owed to the foundation of an extensive city-state culture.

Credible commitment mechanisms associated with republicanism must
be an important part of the explanation for the overall high performance
of the Greek city-state ecology. Yet a partial explanation for the flourishing of the polis culture as a whole might be extrapolated from my
epistemic explanation for exceptional Athenian performance. The Greek
city-state ecology is historically exceptional in terms of its size and duration, but there are other examples of city-state ecologies from throughout
human history (M. H. Hansen 2000, 2002b). The late-medieval north-
Italian ecology is especially well documented and has remarkably "modern" features (Greif 2006; Molho and Raaflaub 1991). When exceptions
begin to multiply, the rule must be rethought. If we take the contemporary
world of nation-states as normative, the centrally controlled empires of
antiquity, with their "expand or collapse" state-building dynamic, may
come to seem less overwhelming in their relative analytic importance. The
"dead end" of the dispersed-authority city-state culture deserves further
analytic attention.

In contrast with imperial Rome or China, the multistate Greek world
of the mid-fourth century B.C. seems in certain ways a miniature-scale
version of the post-1989 contemporary world: in both cases we find several hundred states of various sizes engaged in interstate economic and
military competition. Borders are, on the whole, fairly stable, and systematic border violations by aggressor-states typically trigger vigorous military response. Many of the most successful states feature republican/
democratic constitutions and relatively open-access economies. These
successful states are capable of sustaining economic growth over time.
There is a good deal of successful experimentation with multistate federations. Despite endemic competition, there is considerable international
cooperation among the states, promoted by interstate institutions, yet
there is no authoritative central "world government."[11]

There are, of course, serious limitations to the Greek world/contempo-
rary world analogy, even if we ignore differences in scale. In an epistemic
revolution beginning in the eighteenth century and continuing to the pres-

---

[11] For the conception of the modern world as a multistate system, and the importance of
cooperation as well as competition in controlling transaction costs and allowing for overall
growth within that system, see Keohane 1984, 2002.

ent, science, technology, education, and business have been thoroughly institutionalized, allowing for vastly denser populations and much higher rates of economic growth. Monotheistic religions are powerful ideological forces. There is today no great exogenous threat on the horizon in the form of command-and-control empires to compare with ancient Persia, Macedon, or Rome. Nonetheless, the comparative historical case of the world of the Greek city-states permits the radical thought that our own modernity may not be in every sense unparalleled.

Perhaps modernity need not be predicated entirely on features that are unique to the last few hundred years of human history. Modernity may, in some sense, have ancient Greek (among other) precedents, and this need not be a matter of direct influence. Just as the processes of state building in early modern Europe and ancient Rome seem structurally similar, it may be the case that the contemporary world's nation-state culture is sustained by an organizational environment somewhat similar to that which sustained Athens as a state and the ancient Greek city-state culture as an ecology. That environment is, as I have suggested in the previous chapters, characterized by diversity rather than homogenization, distributed knowledge rather than centralized expertise, democracy and choice rather than command and control.

The posited structural analogy between our modernity and ancient Greece ought to be a hopeful thought for proponents of democracy. It suggests that political organization predicated on dispersed, common, and codified knowledge is not a contingent feature of a unique historical era. The extensive multistate culture, featuring self-governing democratic states, may offer a robust alternative to more centralized and less democratic imperial systems. Moreover, if participatory and deliberative epistemic democracies can compete successfully in a multistate ecology, then democracy need not be reduced to a choice between an occasional competition among elite leaders and a fleeting political moment, structurally fated to be overwhelmed by iron laws of organization.

The history of Athens and the Greek city-states shows that stabilizing democracy at scale demands good institutional design, and that getting the design right is not easy. The emergence of an extensive culture featuring democratic open-access states was not historically inevitable. Ancient Greek history offers no reason to assume, complacently, that the coercive and predatory command-and-control empire is now a relic of the past. But if a multistate system featuring successful democracies is not a one-time event, arising from unique conditions, then getting the design right ought not be just a matter of chance.

Throughout this study I have emphasized that human beings seek individual utility, while also pursuing other goods. For some people, utility includes gaining power over others by achieving a position of superiority. Because, like other social animals, humans tend to establish social hierarchies, democratic equality may seem contrary to human nature. Yet humans are also, as Aristotle (*Politics* 1253a) realized, in some ways different from other social creatures. We are *especially* political animals: not only rational, but uniquely capable of sophisticated communication. We are willing, under the right circumstances, to share what we know and eager to seek meaning in our collective lives. Classical Athenian history shows that participatory and deliberative democracy is a realistic, as well as a normatively attractive alternative to the politics of hierarchy. And that in turn suggests that democracy's distinctive epistemic features are compatible with inherent human capacities and moral psychology.[12]

Democracies, ancient and modern, have the potential to do well because rational cooperation and social flourishing emerge when each of us enjoys an enhanced opportunity to fulfill our human potential. That potential prominently includes an ability to innovate and to learn. In a truly democratic community, among the things we would learn is that when each shares knowledge with others, our individual prospects expand as our society changes for the better.

---

[12] Aristotle on "natural democracy": Ober 2005a. Democracy and natural capacities: Ober 2007.

APPENDIXES

Appendix A. Aggregate Material Flourishing

THE SAMPLE is 164 poleis for which the Indices of *Inventory of Archaic and Classical Greek Poleis* (M. H. Hansen and Nielsen 2004) include indication of both constitutional form and territory size. Data were collected on the variables of fame, territory size, public buildings, and interstate activity, based on the relevant Index.

Fame is measured by a simple count of *Inventory* text columns. Bias is against the more famous states (as measured by, for example, number of mentions in classical authors), since even very obscure places receive a certain minimum text allocation. Since each entry was made by an individual scholar, there is some variation in what is included (and thus the length of entries), but overall editorial control was quite careful, and there is a good deal of consistency among entries. Correlation with column counts in two other standard and recent encyclopedic reference works (*Oxford Classical Dictionary* (3d ed.) and *Der neue Pauly: Enzyklopädie der Antike*) is high: see table A.4.

Territory size was based on Index 9, which ranks territories on a scale of 1–5; in order to gain more specificity in the upper end of the range, I have extended the scale to 9, on the basis of actual sizes noted in the *Inventory*. The 1–9 scale indicates the following size range of actual size, in square kilometers: 1 = < 25; 2 = 25–100; 3 = 100–200; 4 = 200–500; 5 = 500–1,000; 6 = 1,000–2,000; 7 = 2,000–4,000; 8 = 4,000–7,000; 9 = 7,000–12,000. See, further, M. H. Hansen 2006a, chapter 13.

International activity is based on scoring points for each of the following: 1 point for "proxeny given" and 1 point for "proxeny received" in Index 14; 1 point for each instance of establishing *theorodokoi* in Index 15; 1 point for each Panhellenic sanctuary at which of a victory by a citizen is recorded in Index 16. Bias is positive for well-documented poleis, whose activity is recorded in literary sources and inscriptions. Bias is against states with a good deal of international activity, that is, those that give and receive multiple proxenies, send out multiple *theorodokoi* to the same ritual centers, and states whose citizens have multiple victories at a given Panhellenic sanctuary. Some obscure poleis record no evidence of international activity.

Public buildings are based on 1 point for each building noted in Indexes 24 (political architecture) and 25 (temples, theaters, stoas, gymnasiums, stadiums, hippodromes); 2 points for building type indicated in plural (e.g., "temples"); 2 points for being noted as "town" or "fortified" in Index 23; 1 point if acropolis only is noted as fortified. Bias is positive for well-documented poleis whose buildings are mentioned in literary sources or inscriptions, and for poleis that have been carefully explored and/or excavated by archaeologists. Some obscure poleis record no public buildings. Bias is quite strongly against poleis with multiple buildings of the same type (e.g., more than two recorded temples).

The raw numerical score in each variable for each polis was then translated into a score on a standard 20-point scale. The highest raw score is the base for a score of 20; other raw scores are adjusted to the 20-point scale on a proportionate basis. The sum of a polis' four "20-point scale" scores is its overall "material flourishing" score. Each variable is thus weighted equally in computing the aggregate score.

Tables A.1–A.5 list correlations among the variables and break down international activity and public buildings for Athens, the top-20 group, and the "middling" (quartile 2 and 3) group of poleis.

Table A.1
Pearson correlations, 164 poleis

	Aggreg.	Territ.	Fame	Internat'l	Build
Aggreg.		0.77	0.83	0.83	0.80
Territ.	0.77		0.64	0.40	0.50
Fame	0.83	0.64		0.61	0.74
Internat'l	0.83	0.40	0.61		0.55
Build	0.80	0.50	0.74	0.55	
Constit.	0.31	0.12	0.31	0.30	0.31
Stasis	0.61	0.53	0.62	0.39	0.45

Notes: Aggregate: 80-point scale (Territory + Fame + International + Public buildings). Territory Size, Fame (*Inventory* columns), International Activity, Public Buildings: 20-point scale. Constitutional form: 5-point scale (democracy = 5 to tyranny = 1); stasis (recorded civil conflict) based on raw score. See appendix D.

Table A.2
International activity: Athens, top 20, quartiles 2 and 3

	Proxeny Give (cnt./tot.)	Proxeny Receive (cnt./tot.)	Theorodokoi (cnt./tot.)	Panhellenic Victories (cnt./tot.)	International (tot./med.)
Athens	yes	yes	2	4	8
Top 20	15/15	19/19	15/21	19/52	107/5
Q2&3 (n = 80)	23/23	46/46	28/31	24/40	140/2

Notes: (Q2&3 = poleis ranked 41–120 in aggregate score. Count, total, median.

Table A.3
Public buildings: Athens, top 20, quartiles 2 and 3

	Govt bldgs (cnt./tot.)	Temples (cnt./tot.)	Theaters (cnt./tot.)	Stoas (cnt./tot.)	Gymnasiums (cnt./tot.)	Stadiums (cnt./tot.)	Buildings (tot./med.)*
Athens	7	2	2	2	2	2	20
Top 20	13/31	19/34	11/13	13/22	8/9	6/7	156/7.5
Q2&3 (n = 80)	27/32	46/70	22/23	13/16	0	2/2	291/3

* Includes fortifications, miscellaneous other buildings.

TABLE A.4
Fame (text columns) for top 80 poleis

	H/N Aggreg.	Inventory	OCD³	Neue Pauly
H/N Aggreg.		0.83	0.77	0.76
Inventory	0.83		0.75	0.78
OCD³	0.77	0.75		0.87
Neue Pauly	0.76	0.78	0.87	

Sources: Hansen and Nielsen, *Inventory*; *Oxford Classical Dictionary*, 3rd edition; *Der Neue Pauly: Enzyklopädie der Antike*.
Note: Pearson correlations across standard reference works.

TABLE A.5
Comparisons of Athens, Syracuse, and Sparta, data for standard deviations

	H/N Aggreg.	Fame	Internat'l	Buildings	Hoards	Coins
St Dev	9.6	2.9	4.6	2.7	18.2	1098
Mean	27.8	5.3	8.5	5.2	17	506
Athens	75	20	20	20	107	8477
Syracuse	50.5	11.5	10	9	81	1756
Sparta	54.1	14.1	15	5		

APPENDIX B. DISTRIBUTION OF COINS IN HOARDS

THE EVIDENCE comes from the *Inventory of Greek Coin Hoards* (Thompson et al. 1973 = *IGCH*). The sample is all 852 hoards listed in the *IGCH* dated from 550 to 300 B.C. and eighty poleis (the top two quartiles, measured by aggregate material flourishing, from the sample described in Appendix A). Each hoard was coded according to the following variables: region within the Greek world (1 Greece, 2 Macedonia and North, 3 Thrace and Euxine, 4 South Russia, 5 Asia Minor, 6 Levant and the East, 7 Egypt and North Africa, 8 Italy, 9 Sicily), date of hoard burial (to either quarter century: n = 755 or century: n = 97), total number of coins (no distinction being made between coins of different metals), and for number of coins in the hoard issued by each of the eighty poleis in the sample.

Each polis in the sample received raw scores, as follows.

Hoard count: Number of hoards (from the 852-hoard sample) in which one or more coins issued by the polis appear. There is no strong bias associated with this indicator.

Number of coins: Total number of coins issued by the polis in all hoards. Many hoards were poorly recorded; the (often amateur) investigators who recorded the hoard tended to make note of rarities and to skip by common issues. Thus, notations in the *IGCH* are often vague: for example, "Athens, tetradrachms: many." Because there is no way to determine the actual number in such cases, indeterminate plurals were coded as "2." Bias is therefore strongly against those poleis with very large numbers of coins in hoards and very common coin types (like Athenian tetradrachms).

Region count: One point is scored for each region (maximum of 9, per above) in which a polis' coins appear in hoards. Bias is against poleis with high hoard-count or many coins in multiple regions, since a minimum of one coin in one hoard gains a polis a "region point."

Date count: One point is scored for each quarter-century in which a polis' coins appear in one or more hoards. Hoards datable only by century are ignored. Bias is against poleis with high hoard count or many coins in multiple date-periods.

Extraregional percentage: The percent of hoards in which a polis' coins are found that are located outside the polis' home region. While this variable is not taken as a positive or negative indicator of "monetary success," there is a good deal of variability in extraregional distribution. Some states (like Athens) are well represented in multiple regions (a fact partially caught by "region count"), whereas others, like Corcyra, are heavily represented in only one "external" region.

The extent of a polis' visibility in the coin hoards of the Greek world has some obvious correlation with its success as a minter and distributor of its money. The individuals (or groups) responsible for assembling the 852 archaic and classical hoards chose certain coins for retention (and thus for "hoarding"), presumably primarily on the basis of the assumed value of the coin as a financial instrument; see further, chapter 6. It is not easy to come up with an aggregate score for "monetary success" that would parallel "material flourishing." Hoard count seems overall by far the best single indicator, followed by coin numbers and then by date count and region count. Extraregional percentage should not be considered as having much, if any, weight in monetary success. Regional or global distribution may be strategic, but there is no reason to prefer either strategy in seeking to assess overall success. Tables B.1 and B.2 indicate correlations among the coinage variables, and among coinage variables and variables discussed in appendix A + D.

TABLE B.1
Pearson correlations, 80 poleis: Coin hoards

	Hoard Count	Coins Total	Region Count	Date Range Count	Hoards x-territ. %
Hoard count		0.76	0.64	0.75	0.16
Coins total	0.76		0.55	0.46	0.22
Region count	0.64	0.55		0.70	0.69
Date range	0.75	0.46	0.70		0.28
Hoards x-territ. %	0.16	0.22	0.69	0.28	

TABLE B.2
Pearson correlations, 80 poleis: Coin hoards and *Inventory* scores

	Hoard Count	Coins Total	Region Count	Date Range Count	Hoards x-territ. %
H/N Aggregate	0.57	0.53	0.43	0.34	0.18
Territory size 20 scale	0.34	0.22	0.32	0.26	0.19
Fame 20 scale	0.54	0.56	0.40	0.33	0.11
International 20 scale	0.29	0.27	0.23	0.17	0.12
Public buildings 20 scale	0.53	0.63	0.31	0.26	0.12
Civic insts. actual	0.20	0.30	0.36	0.15	0.29
Constitution 1–5 scale	−0.16	0.15	−0.07	−0.22	0.10

Appendix C: Prominence in Classical Greek Literature

THE FREQUENCY with which a polis' name appears in Greek literature in a given period serves as a proxy for its general prominence in the Greek world. The following measurements are drawn from the standard digitized corpus of Greek literature (*Thesaurus Linguae Graecae*), searching for all of the most common terms by which a polis was called (e.g., Athens, the Athenians, Attica; Sparta, the Spartans, Laconia, the Laconians, Lacedaemon, the Lacedaemonians—but not "the polis of Athena," "the polis by the Eurotas," etc.). Even with the sophisticated search mechanisms now available, this is a time-consuming and inevitably somewhat inexact process. Counts were therefore done only for the most prominent of the classical Greek poleis. Bias is strongly positive for poleis with a vibrant literary culture, and whose literary products were valued and therefore selected for transmission, by post-classical cultures.

It is immediately obvious that Athens is one of a group of literarily prominent poleis in the archaic period of the eighth through the sixth centuries B.C.; but in the fifth century, as the total volume of Greek literature expands immensely and literary production is increasingly centered in Athens, Athens begins to dominate all rivals. This trend intensifies in the post-imperial fourth century.

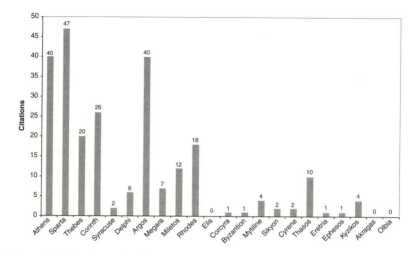

Figure C.1 Citations of polis name in literature, 8th–6th centuries B.C.

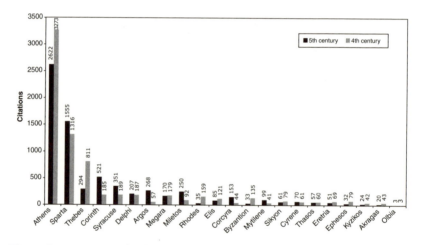

Figure C.2 Citations of polis name in literature, 5th and 4th centuries B.C.

Appendix D: Impact of Constitution and Historical Experience

SAMPLE AND source of evidence are the same as appendix A. Each polis in the sample was coded as follows.

Constitution type: Based on listing in M. H. Hansen and Nielsen (2004), *Inventory*, Index 11. The index lists, in abbreviated form, the known constitutional history of the polis. In some cases this is quite elaborate; in other cases we have evidence of only one "constitutional moment" in the polis' archaic and classical history. Each polis was given a single constitution score, on the basis of that information, on the following scale: 1 = tyranny; 2 = *basileia* (monarchy of some sort); 3 = oligarchy; 4 = moderate oligarchy/mixed regime of some sort; 5 = democracy. The scoring is inevitably subjective and results in some anomalies: Syracuse averages "3 = oligarchy" on the basis of its history of switching between tyranny and democracy. While this is a rough-and-ready approach, there seems no reason to suppose that systematic bias is being introduced that would favor either end of the scale.

Experience of democracy, oligarchy, tyranny: The polis is noted as having experienced the given form of government if Index 11 lists that form during the sixth, fifth, or fourth century. Very early constitutional forms are excluded as being historically unreliable. Bias is positive for well-documented poleis.

Decision-making institutions: On the basis of *Inventory* Index 12, each polis is listed as having or not having the following institutions: *boulē*, government council, often with probouleutic function; *dēmos*, assembly of citizens; *dikastēria*, courts of law; *thesmothetai*, lawmaking body distinct in composition from the citizen assembly. Bias is positive for well-documented poleis.

Stasis/Civil conflict: The number of known conflicts recorded in Index 11. Bias is so strongly positive for well-documented poleis that the actual number of conflicts is relatively meaningless; a somewhat better indicator is simply the indication that conflict is or is not recorded.

Destruction: A polis is recorded as having experienced destruction if it is listed as such in Index 20. Destruction ranges from physical ruin of infrastructure (sacking of a city, e.g., of Athens by Persians in 480 B.C.), to the total elimination of the population via killing and transportation (e.g., the destruction of Melos by Athens in 415). Bias is positive for well-documented poleis.

Tables D.1–D.4 document various correlations among variables, break out "material flourishing" by regime type, and look at the difference of historical experience across quartiles (ranked by aggregate material flourishing score).

TABLE D.1
Pearson correlations, 164 poleis:
Degree of democratization (5-point
scale) and *Inventory* scores

Aggregate score	0.31
Territory size	0.12
Fame (columns)	0.31
International activity	0.30
Public buildings	0.31
Civil conflict (*stasis*)	−0.02

TABLE D.2
Mean scores by regime type,* 164 poleis, 20 point-scale

Regime Type	Aggregated Score/4**	Territory Size	Fame (columns)	International Activity	Public Buildings
Tyranny n = 21	2.5	4.0	1.7	2.0	2.2
Monarchy n = 33	3.9	6.9	2.7	3.0	3.0
Oligarchy n = 56	4.8	6.2	3.6	5.6	3.8
Moderate oligarchy					
n = 33	6.5	8.0	4.9	7.8	5.1
Democracy n = 21	4.9	5.6	4.0	5.6	4.4
Democracy w/o					
Athens n = 20	4.2	5.1	3.2	4.9	3.7

* Regime type according to Constitution 1–5 scale as follows: Tyranny, 1–1.5; Monarchy, 1.7–2.5; Oligarchy, 3–3.4; Moderate Oligarcy, 3.5–4; Democracy, 4.3–5.

** Aggregated 80-point scale reduced to 20 points.

TABLE D.3

Aggregate score, constitution, history (experience of constitutional forms),
164 poleis, by quartile

	Aggregate Score (av./med.)	Regime Type* (av./med.)	Exper. Tyranny (tot./%)	Exper. Oligarchy (tot./%)	Exper. Democracy (tot./%)
Q1 (n = 40)	34.2/31.2	3.3/3.5	23/58	33/83	31/78
Q2 (n = 40)	21.3/20.6	3.3/3.0	18/45	22/55	26/65
Q3 (n = 40)	14.0/14.0	2.9/3.0	14/35	18/45	18/45
Q4 (n = 40)	7.0/7.0	2.4/2.0	16/40	13/33	10/25
All 164	18.7/17.1	3.0/3.0	72/44	88/53	88/53

* 1 = tyranny, 3= narrow oligarchy, 5 = democracy.

TABLE D.4

Aggregate score and risk factors, 164 poleis, by quartile

	Aggregate Score (av./med.)	Civil Conflict (count/tot.)	Destroyed (tot./%)
Q1 (n = 40)	34.2/31.2	34/145	13/33
Q2 (n = 40)	21.3/20.6	24/45	12/30
Q3 (n = 40)	14.0/14.0	17/30	12/30
Q4 (n = 40)	7.0/7.0	6/7	6/15
All 164	18.7/17.1	81/227	43/26

Appendix E. Athenian State Capacity and Democracy, 600–250 b.c.

On the basis of available evidence (presented in summary form in chapter 2), the history of Athenian activity in three spheres (military, public building, and domestic programs) was plotted over time, in two-year intervals. For each two-year period from 600 to 250 b.c., each of the three factors was rated on a 5-point scale, with zero being the least possible activity and 5 being the maximum level achieved by the Athenian state at any point in the 350-year period. The three scales were aggregated into an arbitrary 15-point scale; figure E.1 shows the results. The same approach was taken for democracy (fig. E.2). In this case the three components of the aggregate are the proportion of the adult male native population that is able to exercise full citizen-participation rights, the power of the demos to determine policy using procedures of majority rule (and thus the lack of "elite capture" of the system), and the authority and reliability of established processes of law.

The measurement process is inevitably subjective. We do not always have detailed historical evidence for a given two-year period. But overall, the results are based on a mass of historical and archaeological data, and so are not merely fanciful.

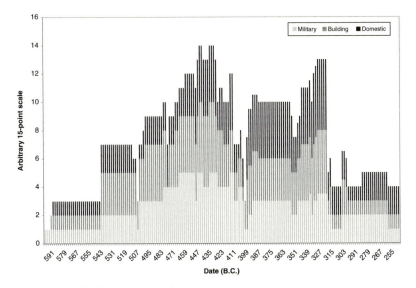

Figure E.1 Athenian state capacity over time.

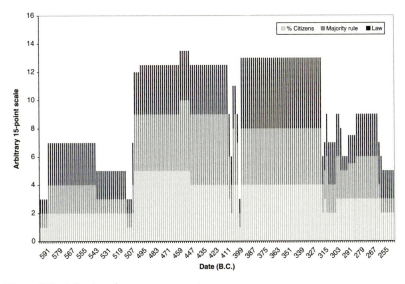

Figure E.2 Athenian democracy over time.

BIBLIOGRAPHY

Acemoglu, Daron, and James A. Robinson. 2006. *Economic Origins of Dictatorship and Democracy.* Cambridge and New York: Cambridge University Press.

Ackerman, Bruce A., and James S. Fishkin. 2004. *Deliberation Day.* New Haven: Yale University Press.

Adams, John. 2000. *The Revolutionary Writings of John Adams.* Indianapolis: Liberty Fund.

Aitken, Hugh G. J. 1985. *Scientific Management in Action: Taylorism at Watertown Arsenal, 1908–1915.* Princeton, N.J.: Princeton University Press.

Alcock, Susan E. 1993. *Graecia Capta: The landscapes of Roman Greece.* Cambridge and New York: Cambridge University Press.

Alcock, Susan E., and Robin Osborne (Eds.). 1994. *Placing the Gods: Sanctuaries and sacred space in ancient Greece.* Oxford and New York: Clarendon Press of Oxford University Press.

Alesina, Alberto, and Enrico Spolaore. 2003. *The Size of Nations.* Cambridge, Mass.: MIT Press.

Allen, Danielle S. 1996. "A Schedule of Boundaries: An exploration of time in Athens." *Greece and Rome* 43:157–68.

———. 2000a. "Changing the Authoritative Voice: Lycurgus' *Against Leocrates.*" *Classical Antiquity* 19:5–33.

———. 2000b. *The World of Prometheus: Politics of punishing in democratic Athens.* Princeton, N.J.: Princeton University Press.

———. 2004. *Talking to Strangers: Anxieties of citizenship since Brown v. Board of Education.* Chicago: University of Chicago Press.

Allen, Katarzyna Hagemajer. 2003. "Intercultural Exchanges in Fourth-Century Attic Decrees." *Classical Antiquity* 22:199–246.

Althusser, Louis. 1990 [1966]. *For Marx.* London: Verso.

Amemiya, Takeshi. 2007. *Economy and Economics of Ancient Greece.* London and New York: Routledge.

Anderson, Elizabeth. 2003. "Sen, Ethics, and Democracy." *Feminist Economics* 9:239–61.

———. 2006. "The Epistemology of Democracy." *Episteme: Journal of Social Epistemology* 3:8–22.

Anderson, Greg. 2003. *The Athenian Experiment: Building an imagined political community in ancient Attica, 508–490 B.C.* Ann Arbor: University of Michigan Press.

Andreades, Andreas M. 1933. *A History of Greek Public Finance.* Cambridge, Mass.: Harvard University Press.

Andreau, Jean. 2002. "Twenty Years after Moses I. Finley's The Ancient Economy." Pp. 33–49 in *The Ancient Economy,* edited by Walter Scheidel and Sita von Reden. Edinburgh: Edinburgh University Press.

Anton, John P. 1998. "Plato as a Critic of Democracy." *Philosophical Inquiry* 20:1–17.

Arendt, Hannah. 1958. *The Human Condition*. Chicago: University of Chicago Press.

Arrow, Kenneth Joseph. 1963 [1951]. *Social Choice and Individual Values*. New Haven: Yale University Press.

Austen-Smith, David. 1990. "Information Transmission in Debate." *American Journal of Political Science* 34:124–52.

Austin, J. L. 1975 [1962]. *How to Do Things with Words*. Cambridge, Mass.: Harvard University Press.

Austin, Michel, and Pierre Vidal-Naquet. 1977. *Economic and Social History of Ancient Greece: An introduction*. Berkeley: University of California Press.

Badian, E. 1995. "The Ghost of Empire: Reflections on Athenian foreign policy in the fourth century B.C." Pp. 79–106 in *Die athenische Demokratie im 4. Jahrhundert v. Chr.: Vollendung oder Verfall einer Verfassungsform?*, edited by Walter Eder. Stuttgart: F. Steiner.

Badian, E. 2000. "Back to Kleisthenic Chronology." Pp. 447–464 in *Polis and Politics [Festschrift Hansen]*, edited by P. Flensted-Jensen, T. H. Neilsen, and L. Rubinstein. Copenhagen: Museum Tusculanum Press.

Baiocchi, Gianpaolo. 2005. *Militants and Citizens: The politics of participatory democracy in Porto Alegre*. Stanford, Calif.: Stanford University Press.

Balot, Ryan K. 2004. "Courage in the Democratic *Polis*." *Classical Quarterly* 54:406–23.

———. 2006. *Greek Political Thought*. Maldon, Mass., and Oxford: Blackwell.

Bannerjee, Abhijit Vinayak, and others. 2006. "Making Aid Work." *Boston Review* 31:7–22.

Barber, Benjamin R. 1984. *Strong Democracy: Participatory politics for a new age*. Berkeley: University of California Press.

Barnard, Chester Irving. 1938. *The Functions of the Executive*. Cambridge, Mass.: Harvard University Press.

———. 1948. *Organization and Management: Selected papers*. Cambridge, Mass.: Harvard University Press.

Barnett, William P. 2008. *Red Queen among Organizations: How Competitiveness Evolves*. Princeton, N.J.: Princeton University Press.

Barnett, William P., and Elizabeth G. Pontikes. 2006. "The Red Queen, Success Bias, and Organizational Inertia." Stanford GSB Research Paper 1936.

Barro, Robert J. 1996. "Democracy and Growth." *Journal of Economic Growth* 1:1–27.

Bates, Robert H., Avner Greif, Margaret Levi, Jean-Laurent Rosenthal, and Barry R. Weingast. 1998. *Analytic Narratives*. Princeton, N.J.: Princeton University Press.

Baumol, William J. 1990. "St. John versus the Hicksians, or a Theorist malgré lui?" *Journal of Economic Literature* 28:1708–15.

———. 1993. *Entrepreneurship, Management, and the Structure of Payoffs*. Cambridge, Mass.: MIT Press.

———. 2004. "On Entrepreneurship, Growth and Rent-Seeking: Henry George updated." *American Economist* 48:9–16.

Benkler, Yochai. 2006. *The Wealth of Networks: How social production transforms markets and freedom*. New Haven: Yale University Press.

Berent, Moshe. 1996. "Hobbes and the 'Greek Tongues'." *History of Political Thought* 17:36–59.

———. 2000. "Anthropology and the Classics: War, violence and the stateless polis." *Classical Quarterly* 50:257–89.

Bers, Victor. 1985. "Dikastic Thorubos." Pp. 1–15 in *Crux: Essays Presented to G.E.M. de Ste. Croix*, edited by Paul Cartledge and F. D. Harvey. Exeter, U.K.: Imprint Academic.

———. 2000. "Just Rituals: Why the Rigmarole of the Fourth-Century Athenian Lawcourts?" Pp. 553–59 in *Polis and Politics [Festschrift Hansen]*, edited by Pernille Flensted-Jensen, Thomas Heine Nielsen, and Lene Rubinstein. Copenhagen: Museum Tusculanum Press.

Bertrand, Jean-Marie. 1999. *De l'écriture à l'oralité: Lectures des Lois de Platon*. Paris: Publications de la Sorbonne.

Bikhchandani, Sushil, David Hirshleifer, and Ivo Welch. 1992. "A Theory of Fads, Fashion, Custom, and Cultural Change as Informational Cascades." *Journal of Political Economy* 100:992–1026.

Binmore, K. G. 1994. *Game Theory and the Social Contract I: Playing fair*. Cambridge, Mass.: MIT Press.

———. 1998. *Game Theory and the Social Contract II: Just playing*. Cambridge, Mass.: MIT Press.

Blanshard, A.J.L. "Depicting Democracy." *Journal of Hellenic Studies* 124: 1–15.

Bleicken, Jochen. 1985. *Die athenische Demokratie*. Paderborn, Germany: Schöningh.

Blok, Josine, and André Lardinois (Eds.). 2006. *Solon: New historical and philological perspectives*. Leiden: E. J. Brill.

Bobonich, Christopher. 2002. *Plato's Utopia Recast: His later ethics and politics*. Oxford: Oxford University Press.

Boedeker, Deborah Dickmann, and Kurt A. Raaflaub (Eds.). 1998. *Democracy, Empire, and the Arts in Fifth-Century Athens*. Cambridge, Mass.: Harvard University Press.

Boegehold, Alan L. 1972. "The Establishment of a Central Archive at Athens." *American Journal of Archaeology* 76:23–30.

———. 1995. *The Lawcourts at Athens: Sites, buildings, equipment, procedure, and testimonia*. Princeton, N.J.: American School of Classical Studies at Athens.

———. 1996. "Resistance to Change in the Law at Athens." Pp. 203–14 in *Dēmokratia*, edited by J. Ober and C. W. Hedrick. Princeton, N.J.: Princeton University Press.

Boegehold, Alan L., and Adele C. Scafuro (Eds.). 1994. *Athenian Identity and Civic Ideology*. Baltimore, Md. and London: Johns Hopkins University Press.

Boehm, Christopher. 1993. "Egalitarian Behavior and Reverse Dominance Hierarchy." *Current Anthropology* 34:227–54.

———. 1999. *Hierarchy in the Forest: The evolution of egalitarian behavior*. Cambridge, Mass.: Harvard University Press.

———. 2000a. "Conflict and the Evolution of Social Control." *Journal of Consciousness Studies* 7:79–101.

Boehm, Christopher. 2000b. "The Origin of Morality as Social Control: Response to commentary discussion." *Journal of Consciousness Studies* 7:149–83.

Boersma, Johannes Sipko. 1970. *Athenian Building Policy from 561/0 to 405/4 B.C.* Groningen: Wolters-Noordhoff Publishing.

Bogaert, R. 1976. "L'essai des monnaies dans l'antiquité." *Revue Belge de Numismatique* 122:5–34.

Bowden, Hugh. 2005. *Classical Athens and the Delphic Oracle: Divination and democracy.* Cambridge: Cambridge University Press.

Bratman, Michael. 1999. *Faces of Intention: Selected essays on intention and agency.* Cambridge and New York: Cambridge University Press.

———. 2004. "Shared Valuing and Frameworks for Practical Reasoning." Pp. 1–27 in *Reason and Value: Themes from the moral philosophy of Joseph Raz,* edited by R. Jay Wallace, Philip Pettit, Samuel Scheffler, and Michael Smith. Oxford: Clarendon.

Brennan, Geoffrey, and Philip Pettit. 2004. *The Economy of Esteem: An essay on civil and political society.* Oxford and New York: Oxford University Press.

Bresson, Alain. 2000. *La cité marchande.* Paris: Diffusion de Boccard.

Brickhouse, Thomas C., and Nicholas D. Smith. 1989. *Socrates on Trial.* Princeton, N.J.: Princeton University Press.

Brock, Roger, and Stephen Hodkinson (Eds.). 2000. *Alternatives to Athens: Varieties of political organization and community in ancient Greece.* Oxford: Oxford University Press.

Brown, John Seely, and Paul Duguid. 1991. "Organizational Learning and Communities-of-Practice: Toward a unified view of working, learning, and innovation." *Organization Science* 2:40–57.

———. 2000. *The Social Life of Information.* Boston: Harvard Business School Press.

Bryan, Frank M. 2004. *Real Democracy: The New England town meeting and how it works.* Chicago and London: University of Chicago Press.

Buckler, John. 1980. *The Theban Hegemony, 371–362 B.C.* Cambridge, Mass.: Harvard University Press.

———. 1989. *Philip II and the Sacred War.* Leiden and New York: E. J. Brill.

———. 2003. *Aegean Greece in the Fourth Century B.C.* Leiden and Boston: Brill.

Budge, Ian. 1996. *The New Challenge of Direct Democracy.* Cambridge, U.K., and Cambridge, Mass.: Polity Press, in association with Blackwell Publishers.

Burke, Edmund M. 1985. "Lycurgan Finances." *Greek, Roman, and Byzantine Studies* 26:251–64.

———. 1992. "The Economy of Athens in the Classical Era: Some adjustments to the primitivist model." *Transactions of the American Philological Association* 122:199–226.

———. 2005. "The Habit of Subsidization in Classical Athens: Toward a thetic ideology." *Classica et Mediaevalia* 56:5–47.

Burt, Ronald S. 1992. *Structural Holes: The social structure of competition.* Cambridge, Mass.: Harvard University Press.

———. 1997. "The Contingent Value of Social Capital." *Administrative Science Quarterly* 42:339–65.

———. 2004. "Structural Holes and Good Ideas." *American Journal of Sociology* 110:349–99.

Butler, Judith. 1997. *Excitable Speech: A politics of the performative.* New York: Routledge.

Buttrey, T. V. 1981. "The Athenian Currency Law of 375/4 B.C." Pp. 33–45 in *Greek Numismatics and Archaeology: Essays in honor of Margaret Thompson,* edited by Otto Mørkholm and Nancy Waggoner. Wetteren, Belgium: Cultura.

———. 1982. "More on the Athenian Coinage Law of 375/4 B.C." *Numismatica e Antichità Classiche* 10:71–94.

———. 1993. "Calculating Ancient Coin Production: Facts and fantasies." *Numismatic Chronicle* 153:335–51.

———. 1999. "The Content and Meaning of Coin Hoards." *Journal of Roman Archaeology* 12:526–32.

Callataÿ, François de. 1997. "Quelques estimations relatives au nombre de monnaies grecques: Les collections publiques et privés, le commerce et les trésors." *Revue Belge de Numismatique* 143:21–94.

———. 2006. "Greek Coins from Archaeological Excavations: A *conspectus* of *conspecti* and a call for chronological charts." Pp. 177–200 in *Agoranomia: Studies in money and exchange presented to John Kroll.* New York: American Numismatic Society.

Camassa, Giorgio. 2007. *Atene: La costruzione della democrazia.* Rome: "L'Erma" di Bretschneider.

Camerer, Colin F, and Eric J. Johnson. 1991. "The Process-performance Paradox in Expert Judgment: How can experts know so much and predict so badly?" Pp. 195–217 in *Toward a General Theory of Expertise: Prospects and limits,* edited by K. Anders Ericsson and Jacqui Smith. Cambridge and New York: Cambridge University Press.

Camp, John McK. II. 1992. *The Athenian Agora: Excavations in the heart of classical Athens.* New York: Thames and Hudson.

———. 2001. *The Archaeology of Athens.* New Haven: Yale University Press.

Caplan, Bryan. 2007. *The Myth of the Rational Voter.* Princeton, N.J.: Princeton University Press.

Carey, Christopher. 1988. "A Note on Torture in Athenian Homicide Cases." *Historia* 37:241–45.

———. 1994. "Legal Space in Classical Athens." *Greece and Rome* 41:172–86.

———. 1998. "The Shape of Athenian laws." *Classical Quarterly* 48:93–109.

Cargill, Jack. 1981. *The Second Athenian League: Empire or free alliance?* Berkeley: University of California Press.

———. 1995. *Athenian Settlements of the Fourth Century B.C.* Leiden: E. J. Brill.

Cartledge, Paul. 2001. *Spartan Reflections.* London and Berkeley: Duckworth and University of California Press.

———. 2002. "The Economy (Economies) of Ancient Greece." Pp. 11–32 in *The Ancient Economy,* edited by Walter Scheidel and Sita von Reden. Edinburgh: Edinburgh University Press.

Cartledge, Paul, Edward E. Cohen, and Lin Foxhall (Eds.). 2002. *Money, Labour and Land: Approaches to the economies of ancient Greece.* London and New York: Routledge.

Cary, M. 1927/28. "Athenian Democracy." *History* 12:206–14.

Cavanaugh, Maureen B. 2001. "Order in Multiplicity: Aristotle on text, context, and the rule of law." *North Carolina Law Review* 79:577–662.

Cawkwell, George L. 1963. "Eubulus." *Journal of Hellenic Studies* 83:47–67.

Chandler, Alfred Dupont. 1962. *Strategy and Structure: Chapters in the history of the industrial enterprise.* Cambridge, Mass.: MIT Press.

Chang, Myong-Hun, and Joseph E. Harrington. 2005. "Discovery and Diffusion of Knowledge in an Endogenous Social Network." *American Journal of Sociology* 110:937–76.

Christ, Matthew R. 1990. "Liturgy Avoidance and Antidosis in Classical Athens." *Transactions of the American Philological Association* 120:147–69.

———. 1998. "Legal Self-Help on Private Property in Classical Athens." *American Journal of Philology* 119:521–45.

———. 2001. "Conscription of Hoplites in Classical Athens." *Classical Quarterly* 51:398–422.

———. 2006. *The Bad Citizen in Classical Athens.* Cambridge: Cambridge University Press.

Christensen, Kerry A. 1984. "The Theseion: A slave refuge at Athens." *American Journal of Ancient History* 9:23–32.

Christesen, Paul. 2003. "Economic Rationalism in Fourth-Century Athens." *Greece and Rome* 50:1–26.

Chwe, Michael Suk-Young. 2001. *Rational Ritual: Culture, coordination, and common knowledge.* Princeton, N.J.: Princeton University Press.

Coase, R. H. 1988. *The Firm, the Market, and the Law.* Chicago: University of Chicago Press.

Cohen, David. 1995. *Law, Violence, and Community in Classical Athens.* Cambridge and New York: Cambridge University Press.

———. 1997. "Democracy and Individual Rights in Athens." *Zeitschrift der Savigny-Stiftung für Rechtsgeschichte* 114:27–44.

Cohen, Edward E. 1973. *Ancient Athenian Maritime Courts.* Princeton, N.J.: Princeton University Press.

———. 1992. *Athenian Economy and Society: A banking perspective.* Princeton, N.J.: Princeton University Press.

———. 2000. *The Athenian Nation.* Princeton, N.J.: Princeton University Press.

———. 2005. "Commercial Law." Pp. 290–302 in *The Cambridge Companion to Ancient Greek Law,* edited by Michael Gagarin and David Cohen. Cambridge and New York: Cambridge University Press.

Cohen, Joshua. 1986. "An Epistemic Conception of Democracy." *Ethics* 97: 26–38.

———. 1996. "Procedure and Substance in Deliberative Democracy." Pp. 94–119 in *Democracy and Difference: Contesting the boundaries of the political,* edited by Seyla Benhabib. Princeton, N.J.: Princeton University Press.

———. 1997. "The Arc of the Moral Universe." *Philosophy and Public Affairs* 26: 91–134.

Cohen, M. D., and P. Bacdayan. 1994. "Organizational Routines as Stored Procedural Memory: Evidence from a laboratory study." *Organization Science* 5:554–68.

Cole, Susan G. 1996. "Oath Ritual and Male Community at Athens." Pp. 227–48 in *Dēmokratia: A conversation on democracies, ancient and modern*, edited by Josiah Ober and Charles W. Hedrick. Princeton, N.J.: Princeton University Press.

Cole, Susan Guettel. 2004. *Landscapes, Gender, and Ritual Space: The ancient Greek experience*. Berkeley: University of California Press.

Collins, James C. 2001. *Good to Great: Why some companies make the leap . . . and others don't*. New York: HarperBusiness.

Connor, W. Robert. 1987. "Tribes, Festivals, and Processions: Civic ceremonial and political manipulation in archaic Greece." *Journal of Hellenic Studies* 107:40–50.

———. 1988. "Early Greek Land Warfare as Symbolic Expression." *Past and Present* 119:3–27.

Conophagos, C. E. 1980. *Le Laurium antique, et la technique grecque de la production de l'argent*. Athens: Ekdotike Hellados.

Couzin, Iain D., Jens Krause, Nigel R. Franks, and Simon A. Levin. 2005. "Effective Leadership and Decision-Making in Animal Groups on the Move." *Nature* 433: 513–16.

Cox, Cheryl Anne. 1998. *Household Interests: Property, marriage strategies, and family dynamics in ancient Athens*. Princeton, N.J.: Princeton University Press.

Cronin, Thomas E. 1989. *Direct Democracy: The politics of initiative, referendum, and recall*. Cambridge, Mass.: Harvard University Press.

Csapo, Eric. 2007. "The Men Who Built the Theatres: *Theatropolai, Theatronai*, and *Arkhitektones*." Pp. 87–115 in *Epigraphy of the Greek Theatre*, edited by Peter Wilson. Oxford: Oxford University Press.

Csapo, Eric, and William J. Slater. 1994. *The Context of Ancient Drama*. Ann Arbor: University of Michigan Press.

Cyert, Richard Michael, and James G. March. 1963. *A Behavioral Theory of the Firm*. Englewood Cliffs, N.J.: Prentice Hall.

Dahl, Robert Alan. 1970. *After the Revolution? Authority in a good society*. New Haven: Yale University Press.

———. 1989. *Democracy and Its Critics*. New Haven: Yale University Press.

———. 1998. *On Democracy*. New Haven: Yale University Press.

Dahl, Robert Alan, and Edward R. Tufte. 1973. *Size and Democracy*. Stanford, Calif.: Stanford University Press.

Darley, John M., David M. Messick, and Tom R. Tyler. 2001. *Social Influences on Ethical Behavior in Organizations*. Mahwah, N.J.: Lawrence Erlbaum Associates.

Davenport, Thomas H., and Laurence Prusak. 1998. *Working Knowledge: How organizations manage what they know*. Boston, Mass: Harvard Business School Press.

Davies, John Kenyon. 1981. *Wealth and the Power of Wealth in Classical Athens*. New York: Arno Press.

———. 2003. "Greek Archives: From record to monument." Pp. 323–43 in *Ancient Archives and Archival Traditions: Concepts of record-keeping in the ancient world*, edited by Maria Brosius. Oxford: Oxford University Press.

Davies, John Kenyon. 2004. "Democracy without Theory." Pp. 319–36 in *Herodotus and His World*, edited by Peter Derrow and Robert Parker. Oxford: Oxford University Press.

De Laix, Roger Alain. 1973. *Probouleusis at Athens: A study of political decision-making*. Berkeley: University of California Press.

De Souza, Philip. 1999. *Piracy in the Graeco-Roman World*. Cambridge and New York: Cambridge University Press.

De Ste. Croix, G.E.M. 1972. *The Origins of the Peloponnesian War*. London: Duckworth.

———. 1983. *The Class Struggle in the Ancient Greek World: From the archaic age to the Arab conquests*. London: Duckworth.

Delli Carpini, Michael X., Cook F. Lomax, and L. R. Jacobs. 2004. "Public Deliberation, Discursive Participation, and Citizen Engagement: A review of the empirical literature." *Annual Review of Political Science* 7:315–34.

Dewey, John. 1954. *The Public and Its Problems*. Denver: A. Swallow.

Diani, Mario, and Doug McAdam (Eds.). 2003. *Social Movements and Networks: Relational approaches to collective action*. Oxford and New York: Oxford University Press.

Dietz, Thomas, Nives Dolsak, Elinor Ostrom, and Paul C. Stern. 2002. "The Drama of the Commons." Pp. 3–35 in *The Drama of the Commons*, edited by Elinor Ostrom and others. Washington, D.C.: National Academy Press.

Dixon, Nancy M. 2000. *Common Knowledge: How companies thrive by sharing what they know*. Boston: Harvard Business School Press.

Domingo Gygax, Marc. 2006a. "Les origines de l'évergétisme. Échanges et identités sociales dans la cité grecque." *Mètis: Anthropologie des mondes grecs anciens* 4:269–95.

———. 2006b. "Contradictions et asymétrie dans l'évergétisme grec: Bienfaiteurs étrangers et citoyens entre image et réalité." *Dialogues d'histoire ancienne* 32:9–23.

Doty, Ralph (Ed.). 2003. *Xenophon: Poroi: A new translation*. Lewiston, N.Y., and Lampeter, Wales: Edwin Mellen Press.

Dougherty, Carol, and Leslie Kurke (Eds.). 1993. *Cultural Poetics in Archaic Greece: Cult, performance, politics*. Cambridge and New York: Cambridge University Press.

Downs, Anthony. 1957. *An Economic Theory of Democracy*. New York: Harper and Row.

Drucker, Peter Ferdinand. 2003. *The Essential Drucker: The best of sixty years of Peter Drucker's essential writings on management*. New York: HarperBusiness.

Dubois, Laurent. 1996. *Inscriptions grecques dialectales d'Olbia du Pont*. Geneva: Librairie Droz.

DuBois, Page. 1991. *Torture and Truth*. New York: Routledge.

Ducat, Jean. 1990. *Les hilotes*. Athens and Paris: École française d'Athènes. Diffusion de Boccard.

———. 2006. *Spartan education: Youth and society in the classical period*. Swansea: Classical Press of Wales.

Dunbar, R.I.M. 1993. "Coevolution of Neocortex Size, Group Size and Language in Humans." *Behavioral Brain Science* 16:681–735.

Eadie, John William, and Josiah Ober (Eds.). 1985. *The Craft of the Ancient Historian: Essays in honor of Chester G. Starr*. Lanham, Md.: University Press of America.

Ehrenberg, Victor. 1973. *From Solon to Socrates: Greek history and civilization during the sixth and fifth centuries B.C.* London: Methuen [distributed by Barnes & Noble, New York].

Eich, Armin. 2006. *Die politische Ökonomie des antiken Griechenland.* Cologne: Böhlau.

Eich, Armin, and Peter Eich. 2005. "War and State-Bulding in Roman Republican Times." *Scripta Classica Israelica* 24:1–33.

Elster, Jon. 1985. *Ulysses and the Sirens: Studies in rationality and irrationality.* Cambridge: Cambridge University Press.

———. 1989. *Solomonic Judgements: Studies in the limitations of rationality.* Cambridge and New York: Cambridge University Press.

———. 1999. *Alchemies of the Mind: Rationality and the emotions.* Cambridge and New York: Cambridge University Press.

———. 2000. *Ulysses Unbound: Studies in rationality, precommitment, and constraints.* Cambridge and New York: Cambridge University Press.

Emmons, B. 1954. "The Overstruck Coinage of Ptolemy I." *American Numismatic Society Museum Notes* 6:69–84.

Engen, Darel Tai. 2004. "Seeing the Forest for the Trees of the Ancient Economy: Review article." *Ancient History Bulletin* 18:150–65.

———. 2005. "'Ancient Greenbacks': Athenian owls, the law of Nikophon, and the Greek economy." *Historia* 54:359–81.

Ericsson, Anders. 1999. "Expertise." Pp. 298–300 in *The MIT Encyclopedia of the Cognitive Sciences.* Cambridge, Mass.: MIT Press.

Ericsson, K. Anders, and Jacqui Smith (Eds.). 1991. *Toward a General Theory of Expertise: Prospects and limits.* Cambridge and New York: Cambridge University Press.

Estlund, David M. 2007. *Democratic Authority: A philosophical framework.* Princeton, N.J.: Princeton University Press.

Euben, J. Peter (Ed.). 1986. *Greek Tragedy and Political Theory.* Berkeley: University of California Press.

———. 2000. "Arendt's Hellenism." Pp. 151–64 In *Cambridge Companion to Hannah Arendt*, edited by Dana Richard Villa. Cambridge and New York: Cambridge University Press.

———. 2003. *Platonic Noise.* Princeton, N.J.: Princeton University Press.

Farenga, Vincent. 2006. *Citizen and Self in Ancient Greece: Individuals performing justice and the law.* Cambridge and New York: Cambridge University Press.

Fazal, Tanisha M. 2007. *State Death: The politics and geography of conquest, occupation, and annexation.* Princeton, N.J.: Princeton University Press.

Ferejohn, John. 1991. "Rationality and Interpretation: Parliamentary elections in early Stuart England." Pp. 279–305 in *The Economic Approach to Politics: A critical reassessment of the theory of rational action*, edited by Kristen R. Monroe. New York: HarperCollins.

Ferejohn, John, and Frances Rosenbluth. 2005. "Republicanisms." Working Paper.

Figueira, Thomas J. 1998. *The Power of Money: Coinage and politics in the Athenian empire.* Philadelphia: University of Pennsylvania Press.

Finley, M. I. 1953. "Land, Debt, and the Man of Property in Classical Athens." *Political Science Quarterly* 68:249–68.

———. 1978. "The Fifth-Century Athenian Empire: A balance sheet." Pp. 103–26, 306–10 in *Imperialism in the Ancient World*, edited by P.D.A. Garnsey and C. R. Whittaker. Cambridge: Cambridge University Press.

———. 1980. *Ancient Slavery and Modern Ideology.* New York: Viking Press.

———. 1985. *Democracy Ancient and Modern.* London: Hogarth.

———. 1999. *The Ancient Economy.* Berkeley: University of California Press.

Fishkin, James S. 1991. *Democracy and Deliberation: New directions for democratic reform.* New Haven: Yale University Press.

Fishkin, James S., and Peter Laslett (Eds.). 2003. *Debating Deliberative Democracy.* Malden, Mass.: Blackwell.

Fitzgerald, Thomas H. 1971. "Why Motivation Theory Doesn't Work." *Harvard Business Review* 49:37–44.

Flament, Christophe. 2007. *Le monnayage en argent d'Athènes. De l'époque archaïque à l'époque hellénistique (c. 550–c. 40 av. J.-C.).* Louvain-la-Neuve: Broché.

Fleck, Robert K., and F. Andrew Hanssen. 2006. "The Origins of Democracy: A model with application to ancient Greece." *Journal of Law and Economics* 49:115–46.

Fornara, Charles W., and Loren J. Samons. 1991. *Athens from Cleisthenes to Pericles.* Berkeley: University of California Press.

Forsdyke, Sara. 2000. "Exile, Ostracism and the Athenian Democracy." *Classical Antiquity* 19:232–63.

———. 2005. *Exile, Ostracism, and Democracy: The politics of expulsion in ancient Greece.* Princeton, N.J.: Princeton University Press.

Forsén, Björn, and G. R. Stanton (Eds.). 1996. *The Pnyx in the History of Athens: Proceedings of an international colloquium organized by the Finnish Institute at Athens, 7–9 October 1994.* Helsinki: Foundation of the Finnish Institute at Athens.

Forster, E. M. 1951. *Two Cheers for Democracy.* New York: Harcourt, Brace and Co.

Frank, Robert H. 1988. *Passions within Reason: The strategic role of the emotions.* New York: Norton.

Freitag, Markus. 2006. "Bowling the State Back In: Political institutions and the creation of social capital." *European Journal of Political Research* 45:123–52.

Friedman, Benjamin M. 2005. *The Moral Consequences of Economic Growth.* New York: Knopf.

Frost, Frank J. 1984. "The Athenian Military before Cleisthenes." *Historia* 33:283–94.

Fung, Archon. 2004. *Empowered Participation: Reinventing urban democracy.* Princeton, N.J.: Princeton University Press.

Fung, Archon, and Erik Olin Wright (Eds.). 2003. *Deepening Democracy: Institutional innovations in empowered participatory governance.* London and New York: Verso.

Funke, Peter. 1980. *Homónoia und Arche: Athen und die griechische Staatenwelt vom Ende des Peloponnesischen Krieges bis zum Königsfrieden (404/3–387/6 v. Chr.)*. Wiesbaden, Germany: F. Steiner.

Furley, William D. 1996. *Andokides and the Herms: A study of crisis in fifth-century Athenian religion*. London: Institute of Classical Studies.

Gabrielsen, Vincent. 1986. "*Phanera* and *Aphanes Ousia* in Classical Athens." *Classica et Mediaevalia* 37:99–114.

Gabrielsen, Vincent. 1994. *Financing the Athenian Fleet: Public taxation and social relations*. Baltimore: Johns Hopkins University Press.

———. 1997. *The Naval Aristocracy of Hellenistic Rhodes*. Aarhus, Denmark: Aarhus University Press.

———. 1999. *Hellenistic Rhodes: Politics, culture, and society*. Aarhus, Denmark and Oakville, Conn.: Aarhus University Press.

Gaddis, John Lewis. 2002. *The Landscape of History: How historians map the past*. Oxford and New York: Oxford University Press.

Gagarin, Michael. 1996. "The Torture of Slaves in Athenian Law." *Classical Philology* 91:1–18.

Gargiulo, Martin, and Mario Benassi. 2000. "Trapped in Your Own Net? Network cohesion, structural holes, and the adaptation of social capital." *Organization Science* 11:183–96.

Garlan, Yvon. 1995. *Les esclaves en Grèce ancienne*. Paris: La Découverte.

Garland, Robert. 1992. *Introducing New Gods: The politics of Athenian religion*. London: Duckworth.

Garnsey, Peter. 1988. *Famine and Food Supply in the Graeco-Roman World: Responses to risk and crisis*. Cambridge and New York: Cambridge University Press.

———. 1996. *Ideas of Slavery from Aristotle to Augustine*. Cambridge and New York: Cambridge University Press.

Garvin, David A. 2000. *Learning in Action: A guide to putting the learning organization to work*. Boston, Mass.: Harvard Business School Press.

Gauthier, Philippe. 1976. *Un commentaire historique des Poroi de Xénophon*. Geneva and Paris: Droz and Minard.

Gebhard, Elizabeth. 1974. "The Form of the Orchestra in the Early Greek Theater." *Hesperia* 43:428–40.

Geertz, Clifford. 1973. *The Interpretation of Cultures: Selected essays*. New York: Basic Books.

———. 1983. *Local Knowledge: Further essays in interpretive anthropology*. New York: Basic Books.

Gehrke, Hans-Joachim. 1985. *Stasis: Untersuchungen zu den inneren Kriegen in den griechischen Staaten des 5. und 4. Jahrhunderts v. Chr*. Munich: Beck.

Gerstner, Louis V. 2003. *Who Says Elephants Can't Dance? Leading a great enterprise through dramatic change*. New York: HarperBusiness.

Giddens, Anthony. 1979. *Central Problems in Social Theory: Action, structure, and contradiction in social analysis*. Berkeley: University of California Press.

———. 1990. *The Consequences of Modernity*. Stanford, Calif.: Stanford University Press.

Giddens, Anthony. 1992. *The Transformation of Intimacy: Sexuality, love, and eroticism in modern societies*. Stanford, Calif.: Stanford University Press.

Gigone, D., and R. Hastie. 1993. "The Common Knowledge Effect: Information sharing and group judgment." *Journal of Personality and Social Psychology* 65:956–74.

Gintis, Herbert. 2000. *Game Theory Evolving: A problem-centered introduction to modeling strategic behavior*. Princeton, N.J.: Princeton University Press.

Gintis, Herbert, Samuel Bowles, Robert Boyd, and Ernst Fehr (Eds.). 2004. *Moral Sentiments and Material Interests: The foundations of cooperation in economic life*. Cambridge, Mass.: MIT Press.

Gladwell, Malcolm. 2000. *The Tipping Point: How little things can make a big difference*. Boston and London: Little, Brown.

Glover, Jonathan. 2000. *Humanity: A moral history of the twentieth century*. New Haven: Yale University Press.

Goff, Barbara E. 2004. *Citizen Bacchae: Women's ritual practice in ancient Greece*. Berkeley and London: University of California Press.

Goldhill, Simon, and Robin Osborne (Eds.). 1999. *Performance Culture and Athenian Democracy*. Cambridge and New York: Cambridge University Press.

Goldman, Alvin I. 1999. *Knowledge in a Social World*. Oxford and New York: Clarendon Press.

Goldstone, Jack. 2002. "Efflorescences and Economic Growth in World History." *Journal of World History* 13:323–89.

Goleman, Daniel. 1995. *Emotional Intelligence*. New York: Bantam Books.

Gomes-Casseres, Benjamin. 1996. *The Alliance Revolution: The new shape of business rivalry*. Cambridge, Mass.: Harvard University Press.

Gomme, A. W. 1951. "The Working of the Athenian Democracy." *History* 36: 12–28.

Goodsell, Charles T. 1988. *The Social Meaning of Civic Space: Studying political authority through architecture*. Lawrence: University of Kansas Press.

Gordon, Stacy B., and Gary M. Segura. 1997. "Cross-National Variation in the Political Sophistication of Individuals: Capability or choice?" *Journal of Politics* 59:126–47.

Gould, Roger V. 1995. *Insurgent Identities: Class, community, and protest in Paris from 1848 to the Commune*. Chicago: University of Chicago Press.

Graham, Oliver J. 2007. *War, Food, and Politics of Early Hellenistic Athens*. Oxford: Oxford University Press.

Gramsci, Antonio. 1971. *Selections from the Prison Notebooks*. New York: International Publishers.

Grandjean, Catherine. 2006. "Athens and Bronze Coinage." Pp. 99–108 in *Agoranomia: Studies in money and exchange presented to John H. Kroll*, edited by Peter G. van Alfen. New York: American Numismatic Society.

Grandori, Anna, and Bruce Kogut. 2002. "Dialogue on Organization and Knowledge." *Organization Science* 13:224–32.

Granovetter, Mark S. 1973. "The Strength of Weak Ties." *American Journal of Sociology* 78:1360–80.

———. 1983. "The Strength of Weak Ties: A network theory revisited." *American Journal of Sociology* 78:1360–80.

———. 1985. "Economic Action and Social Structure: The problem of embeddedness." *American Journal of Sociology* 91:481–510.

Green, Donald P., and Ian Shapiro. 1994. *Pathologies of Rational Choice Theory: A critique of applications in political science*. New Haven: Yale University Press.

Green, Peter. 1996. *The Greco-Persian Wars*. Berkeley: University of California Press.

Greif, Avner. 2006. *Institutions and the Path to the Modern Economy: Lessons from medieval trade*. New York: Cambridge University Press.

Griffith, G. T. 1978. "Athens in the Fourth Century." Pp. 127–44 in *Imperialism in the Ancient World*, edited by Peter Garnsey and C. R. Whittaker. Cambridge and New York: Cambridge University Press.

Grofman, Bernard (Ed.). 1993. *Information, Participation, and Choice: An economic theory of democracy in perspective*. Ann Arbor: University of Michigan Press.

Gürerk, Özgür, Bernd Irlenbusch, and Bettina Rockenbach. 2006. "The Competitive Advantage of Sanctioning Institutions." *Science* 312:108–11.

Gutmann, Amy, and Dennis Thompson. 2004. *Why Deliberative Democracy?* Princeton, N.J.: Princeton University Press.

Haber, Stephen H. 1989. *Industry and Underdevelopment: The industrialization of Mexico, 1890–1940*. Stanford, Calif.: Stanford University Press.

Haber, Stephen H., Noel Maurer, and Armando Razo. 2003. *The Politics of Property Rights: Political instability, credible commitments, and economic growth in Mexico, 1876–1929*. Cambridge: Cambridge University Press.

Habicht, Christian. 1997. *Athens from Alexander to Antony*. Cambridge, Mass.: Harvard University Press.

Haidt, Jonathan. 2006. *The Happiness Hypothesis: Finding modern truth in ancient wisdom*. New York: Basic Books.

Hall, Edith. 1995. "Lawcourt Dramas: The power of performance in Greek forensic oratory." *Bulletin of the Institute of Classical Studies* 40:39–58.

Hallof, Klaus, and Christian Habicht. 1995. "Buleuten und Beamte der athenische Kleruchie aus Samos." *Athenische Mitteilungen* 110:273–304.

Handy, Charles B. 1998. *The Hungry Spirit: Beyond capitalism: A quest for purpose in the modern world*. New York: Broadway Books.

Hansen, Mogens Herman. 1975. *Eisangelia: The sovereignty of the people's court in Athens in the fourth century B.C. and the impeachment of generals and politicians*. Odense, Denmark: Odense University Press.

———. 1976a. *Apagoge, endeixis and ephegesis against kakourgoi, atimoi and pheugontes: A study in the Athenian administration of justice in the fourth century B.C.* Odense, Denmark: Odense University Press.

———. 1976b. "The Theoric Fund and the *graphē paranomon* against Apollodorus." *Greek, Roman, and Byzantine Studies* 17.

———. 1983. "*Rhetores* and *Strategoi* in Fourth-Century Athens." *Greek, Roman, and Byzantine Studies* 24:151–80.

———. 1984. "The Number of *rhetores* in the Athenian *ecclesia*, 355–322 B.C." *Greek, Roman, and Byzantine Studies* 24:227–38.

———. 1986. *Demography and Democracy: The number of Athenian citizens in the fourth century B.C.* Herning, Denmark: Systime.

Hansen, Mogens Herman. 1987. *The Athenian Assembly in the Age of Demosthenes*. Oxford: Blackwell.

———. 1999. *The Athenian Democracy in the Age of Demosthenes: Structure, principles, and ideology*. Norman: University of Oklahoma Press.

——— (Ed.). 2000. *A Comparative Study of Thirty City-State Cultures: An investigation*. Copenhagen: Kongelige Danske Videnskabernes Selskab.

———. 2002a. "Was the *Polis* a State or a Stateles Society?" Pp. 17–47 in *Even More Studies in the Ancient Greek Polis: Papers from the Copenhagen Polis Centre 6*, edited by Thomas Heine Nielsen. Stuttgart: F. Steiner.

——— (Ed.). 2002b. *A Comparative Study of Six City-State Cultures*. Copenhagen: Kongelige Danske Videnskabernes Selskab.

———. 2006a. *Polis: An introduction to the ancient Greek city-state*. Oxford: Oxford University Press.

———. 2006b. *The Shotgun Method: The demography of the ancient Greek city-state culture*. Columbia: University of Missouri Press.

———.2006c. *Studies in the Population of Aigina, Athens and Eretria*. Copenhagen: Royal Danish Academy.

———. 2006d. "Review of Samons 2004." *Bryn Mawr Classical Review*. 2006.01.32.

Hansen, Mogens Herman, H. L. Bjertrup, T. H. Nielsen, L. Rubinstein, and T. Vestergaard. 1990. "The Demography of the Attic Demes: The evidence of the Sepulchral Inscriptions." *Analecta Romana* 19:24–44.

Hansen, Mogens Herman, and Thomas Heine Nielsen. 2004. *An Inventory of Archaic and Classical Poleis*. Oxford: Oxford University Press.

Hansen, Morten T. 2002. "Knowledge Networks: Explaining effective knowledge sharing in multiunit companies." *Organization Science* 13:232–49.

Hanson, Victor Davis. 1995. *The Other Greeks: The family farm and the agrarian roots of western civilization*. New York: Free Press.

Hardin, G. 1968. "The Tragedy of the Commons." *Science* 162:1243–48.

Hardin, Russell. 1982. *Collective Action*. Baltimore: Johns Hopkins University Press.

———. 2002. "Street-Level Epistemology and Democratic Participation." *Journal of Political Philosophy* 10:212–29.

———. 2002. *Trust and Trustworthiness*. New York: Russell Sage Foundation.

Hargadon, Andrew, and Angelo Fanelli. 2002. "Action and Possibility: Reconciling dual perspectives of knowledge in organizations." *Organization Science* 13:290–303.

Harris, Diane. 1994. "Freedom of Information and Accountability: The inventory lists of the Parthenon." Pp. 213–26 in *Ritual, Finance, Politics: Athenian democratic accounts presented to David Lewis*, edited by Robin Osborne and Simon Hornblower. Oxford: Clarendon Press.

———. 1995. *The Treasures of the Parthenon and Erechtheion*. Oxford: Clarendon Press.

Harris, Edward M. 1999. "Notes on the New Grain-Tax Law." *Zeitschrift für Papyrologie und Epigraphik* 128:269–72.

———. 2002. "Workshop, Marketplace and Household: The nature of technical specialization in classical Athens and its influence on economy and society." Pp. 67–99 in *Money, Labour and Land: Approaches to the economies of*

Ancient Greece, edited by Paul Cartledge, Edward E. Cohen, and Lin Foxhall. London: Routledge.

Harris, William V. 1989. *Ancient Literacy*. Cambridge, Mass.: Harvard University Press.

Harrison, A.R.W. 1955. "Law-making at Athens at the End of the Fifth Century B.C." *Journal of Hellenic Studies* 75:26–35.

Harvey, F. D. 1966. "Literacy in the Athenian Democracy." *Revue des Études Grècques* 79:585–635.

Hayek, F. A. 1937. "Economics and Knowledge." *Economica* 4:33–54.

———. 1945. "The Use of Knowledge in Society." *American Economic Review* 35:519–30.

Head, Barclay Vincent. 1911. *Historia Numorum: A manual of Greek numismatics*. Oxford: Clarendon Press.

Hedrick, Charles W., Jr. 1994. "Writing, Reading, and Democracy." Pp. 157–74 in *Ritual, Finance, Politics: Athenian democratic accounts presented to David Lewis*, edited by Robin Osborne and Simon Hornblower. Oxford: Clarendon Press.

———. 1999. "Democracy and the Athenian Epigraphic Habit." *Hesperia* 68:387–439.

———. 2000. *History and Silence: Purge and rehabilitation of memory in late antiquity*. Austin: University of Texas Press.

———. 2004. "The American Ephebe: The Ephebic oath, U.S. education and nationalism." *Classical World* 97:384–407.

———. 2006. *Ancient History: Monuments and documents*. Oxford: Blackwell.

Henry, Alan S. 1983. *Honours and Privileges in Athenian Decrees: The principal formulae of Athenian honorary decrees*. Hildesheim and New York: G. Olms.

———. 2002. "The Athenian State Secretariat and Provisions for Publishing and Erecting Decrees." *Hesperia* 71:91–118.

Herman, Gabriel. 1994. "How Violent Was Athenian Society?" Pp. 99–117 in *Ritual, Finance, Politics: Athenian democratic accounts presented to David Lewis*, edited by Robin Osborne and Simon Hornblower. Oxford and New York: Clarendon Press.

———. 2006. *Morality and Behaviour in Democratic Athens: A social history (508–322 B.C.)*. Cambridge: Cambridge University Press.

Hesk, Jonathan. 2000. *Deception and Democracy in Classical Athens*. Cambridge: Cambridge University Press.

Hignett, Charles. 1952. *A history of the Athenian Constitution to the End of the Fifth Century B.C.* Oxford: Clarendon Press.

Hintzen-Bohlen, Brigitte. 1997. *Die Kulturpolitik des Euboulos und des Lykurg: Die Denkmäler- und Bauprojekte in Athen zwischen 355 und 322 v. Chr.* Berlin: Akademie.

Hitchner, R. Bruce. 2005. " 'The Advantages of Wealth and Luxury': The Case for Economic Growth in the Roman Empire." Pp. 207–22 in *The Ancient Economy: Evidence and models*, edited by Joseph Gilbert Manning and Ian Morris. Stanford, Calif.: Stanford University Press.

Hitz, Zena. 2004. "Plato and Aristotle on the Failings of Democracy." PhD dissertation in Philosophy, Princeton University, Princeton, N.J.

Hoepfner, Wolfram, and Ernst-Ludwig Schwandner (Eds.). 1994. *Haus und Stadt im klassischen Griechenland*. Munich: Deutscher Kunstverlag.

Hölkeskamp, Karl-Joachim. 1992. "Arbitrators, Lawgivers and the 'Codification of Law' in Archaic Greece." *Metis* 7:49–81.

———. 1999. *Schiedsrichter, Gesetzgeber und Gesetzgebung im archaischen Griechenland*. Stuttgart: F. Steiner Verlag.

Hopper, R. J. 1953. "The Attic Silver Mines in the Fourth Century B.C." *Annual of the British School at Athens* 48:200–54.

———. 1957. *The Basis of the Athenian Democracy*. Sheffield, U.K.: The University.

Horden, Peregrine, and Nicholas Purcell. 2000. *The Corrupting Sea: A study of Mediterranean history*. Oxford and Malden, Mass.: Blackwell.

Hornblower, Simon. 2002. *The Greek World, 479–323 B.C.* 3rd ed. London and New York: Routledge.

Hornblower, Simon, and Antony Spawforth (Eds.). 1999. *The Oxford Classical Dictionary*. 3rd ed. Oxford and New York: Oxford University Press.

Howgego, C. J. 1990. "Why Did Ancient States Strike Coins?" *Numismatic Chronicle* 150:1–25.

———. 1995. *Ancient History from Coins*. London and New York: Routledge.

Huber, John D., and Charles R. Shipan. 2002. *Deliberate Discretion: The institutional foundations of bureaucratic autonomy*. Cambridge: Cambridge University Press.

Humphreys, S. C. 1985. "Lycurgus of Butadae: An Athenian aristocrat." Pp. 199–252 in *The Craft of the Ancient Historian: Essays in honor of Chester G. Starr*, edited by John W. Eadie and Josiah Ober. Lanham, Md.: University Press of America.

———. 1993. *The Family, Women and Death: Comparative studies*. Ann Arbor: University of Michigan Press.

Hunter, Virginia J. 1994. *Policing Athens: Social control in the Attic lawsuits, 420–320 B.C.* Princeton, N.J.: Princeton University Press.

Hurwit, Jeffrey M. 1999. *The Athenian Acropolis: History, mythology, and archaeology from the Neolithic era to the present*. Cambridge and New York: Cambridge University Press.

Inglis, Fred. 2000. *Clifford Geertz: Culture, custom, and ethics*. Cambridge, U.K., and Malden, Mass.: Polity Press.

Jackson, Peter. 1999. *Introduction to Expert Systems*. Harlow, U.K., and Reading, Mass.: Addison-Wesley.

Jameson, Michael H. 1978. "Agriculture and Slavery in Classical Athens." *Classical Journal* 73:22–45.

———. 1997. "Women and Democracy in Fourth Century Athens." Pp. 95–117 in *Esclavage, guerre économie en Grèce ancienne. Homages à Yvon Aàrlan*, edited by Pierre Brulé. Rennes: University Press of Rennes.

Johnstone, Steven. 1998. "Cracking the Code of Silence: Athenian legal oratory and the history of women and slaves." Pp. 221–35 in *Women and Slaves in Greco-Roman Culture: Differential equations*, edited by Sandra R. Joshel and Sheila Murnaghan. London: Routledge.

———. 1999. *Disputes and Democracy: The consequences of litigation in ancient Athens*. Austin: University of Texas Press.

Jones, Nicholas F. 1999. *The Associations of Classical Athens: The response to democracy*. New York: Oxford University Press.

———. 2004. *Rural Athens under the Democracy*. Philadelphia: University of Pennsylvania Press.

Jongman, Willem M. 2006. "Roman Prosperity." Paper given at American Philological Association, Annual Meeting, San Diego.

Kagan, Donald. 1974. *The Archidamian War*. Ithaca, N.Y.: Cornell University Press.

———. 1981. *The Peace of Nicias and the Sicilian Expedition*. Ithaca, N.Y.: Cornell University Press.

———. 1987. *The Fall of the Athenian Empire*. Ithaca, N.Y.: Cornell University Press.

———. 1991. *Pericles of Athens and the Birth of Democracy*. New York: Free Press.

Kaiser, Brooks A. 2007. "The Athenian Trierarchy: Mechanism design for the private provision of public goods." *Journal of Economic History* 67:445–80.

Kallet-Marx, Lisa. 1994. "Money Talks: Rhetor, demos, and resources of the Athenian empire." Pp. 227–52 in *Ritual, Finance, Politics: Athenian democratic accounts presented to David Lewis*, edited by Robin Osborne and Simon Hornblower. Oxford: Clarendon Press.

Karayiannis, Anastassios D, and Aristides N. Hatzis. 2007. "Morality, Social Norms and Rule of Law as Transaction Cost-Saving Devices: The case of ancient Athens." Working Paper http://ssrn.com/abstract=1000749.

Kateb, George. 1992. *The Inner Ocean: Individualism and democratic culture*. Ithaca, N.Y.: Cornell University Press.

———. 2000. "Political action: Its nature and advantages." Pp. 130–48 in *Cambridge Companion to Hannah Arendt*, edited by Dana Richard Villa. Cambridge and New York: Cambridge University Press.

Katz, Marilyn. 1999. "Women and Democracy in Ancient Greece." Pp. 41–68 in *Contextualizing Classics [Festschrift for John Peradotto]*, edited by M. Falkner, Nancy Felson, and David Konstan. Lanham, Md.: Rowman and Littlefield.

Katzenbach, Jon R., and Douglas K. Smith. 2003 [1993]. *The Wisdom of Teams: Creating the high-performance organization*. Revised edition. Boston: Harvard Business School Press.

Keohane, Robert O. 1984. *After Hegemony: Cooperation and discord in the world political economy*. Princeton, N.J.: Princeton University Press.

———. 2002. *Power and Governance in a Partially Globalized World*. London and New York: Routledge.

Keyt, David. 1991. "Aristotle's Theory of Distributive Justice." Pp. 238–78 in *A Companion to Aristotle's Politics*, edited by David Keyt and Fred Dycus Miller. Oxford: Blackwell.

King, Barbara J. 1994. *The Information Continuum: Evolution of social information transfer in monkeys, apes, and hominids*. Santa Fe and Seattle: SAR Press. Distributed by the University of Washington Press.

King, Gary, Robert O. Keohane, and Sidney Verba. 1994. *Designing Social Inquiry: Scientific inference in qualitative research*. Princeton, N.J.: Princeton University Press.

Kinzl, Konrad H., and Kurt A. Raaflaub (Eds.). 1995. *Demokratia: Der Weg zur Demokratie bei den Griechen*. Darmstadt: Wissenschaftliche Buchgesellschaft.

Klarreich, Erica. 2006. "The Mind of the Swarm." *Science News* 170:307–49.

Kogut, Bruce, and U. Zander. 1992. "Knowledge of the Firm, Combinative Capabilities, and the Replication of Technology." *Organization Science* 3:383–97.

———. 1996. "What Firms Do: Coordination, identity, and learning." *Organization Science* 7:202–518.

Kopelman, Shirli, J. Mark Weber, and David M. Messick. 2002. "Factors Influencing Cooperation in Commons Dilemmas: A review of experimental psychological research." Pp. 113–56 in *The Drama of the Commons*, edited by Elinor Ostrom and others. Washington, D.C.: National Academy Press.

Kounas, Dionysios A. (Ed.). 1972. *Studies on the Ancient Silver Mines at Laurion*. Lawrence, Kan.: Coronado Press.

Krackhardt, David. 1992. "The Strength of Strong Ties: The importance of Philos in organizations." Pp. 216–39 in *Networks and Organizations: Structure, form, and action*, edited by Nitin Nohria and Robert G. Eccles. Boston: Harvard Business School Press.

Krehbiel, Keith. 1991. *Information and Legislative Organization*. Ann Arbor: University of Michigan Press.

Krentz, Peter. 2002. "Fighting by the Rules: The invention of the hoplite Agon." *Hesperia* 71:23–39.

Kroll, John H. 1972. *Athenian Bronze Allotment Plates*. Cambridge, Mass.: Harvard University Press.

———. 1993. *The Greek Coins*. Princeton, N.J.: American School of Classical Studies in Athens.

———. 2006. "Athenian Tetradrachms Recently Recovered in the Athenian Agora." *Revue Numismatique* 162: 157–63.

Kron, Geoffrey. 2005. "Anthropometry, Physical Anthropology, and the Reconstruction of Ancient Health, Nutrition, and Living Standards." *Historia* 54:68–83.

Krueger, Anne O. 1973. "The Political Economy of the Rent-seeking Society." *American Economic Review* 64:291–303.

Kuran, Timur. 1991. "Now Out of Never: The element of surprise in the East European revolution of 1989." *World Politics* 44:7–48.

———. 1995. *Private Truths, Public Lies: The social consequences of preference falsification*. Cambridge, Mass.: Harvard University Press.

Kurke, Leslie. 1999. *Coins, Bodies, Games, and Gold: The politics of meaning in archaic Greece*. Princeton, N.J.: Princeton University Press.

Labarbe, Jules. 1957. *La loi navale de Thémistocle*. Paris: Société d'Édition "Les Belles Lettres."

Lang, Mabel L., and Margaret Crosby. 1964. *Weights, Measures, and Tokens*. Princeton, N.J.: American School of Classical Studies at Athens.

Langdon, Merle K. 1994. "Public Auctions at Athens." Pp. 253–68 in *Ritual, Finance, Politics: Athenian democratic accounts presented to David Lewis*, edited by Robin Osborne and Simon Hornblower. Oxford: Clarendon Press.

Lanni, Adriaan M. 1997. "Spectator Sport or Serious Politics: *Hoi periestekotes* and the Athenian lawcourts." *Journal of Hellenic Studies* 117:183–89.

———. 2004. "Arguing from 'Precedent': Modern perspectives on Athenian practice." Pp. 159–72 in *The Law and the Courts in Ancient Greece*, edited by Edward M. Harris and L. Rubinstein. London: Duckworth.

———. 2006. *Law and Justice in the Courts of Classical Athens*. Cambridge: Cambridge University Press.

Lape, Susan. 2002/3. "Solon and the Institution of the Democratic Family Form." *Classical Journal* 98:117–39.

———. 2003. "Racializing Democracy: The politics of sexual reproduction in classical Athens." *Parallax* 9:52–63.

———. 2004. *Reproducing Athens: Menander's comedy, democratic culture, and the Hellenistic city*. Princeton, N.J.: Princeton University Press.

Laslett, Peter. 1973. *The World We Have Lost*. New York: Charles Scribner.

Lauffer, Siegfried. 1979. *Die Bergwerkssklaven von Laureion*. Wiesbaden, Germany: F. Steiner.

Lauter, Hans. 1985. *Lathuresa: Beiträge zur Architektur und Siedlungsgeschichte in spätgeometrischer Zeit*. Mainz, Germany: Verlag Philipp von Zabern.

Lavelle, Brian M. 2005. *Fame, Money, and Power: The rise of Peisistratos and "democratic" tyranny at Athens*. Ann Arbor: University of Michigan Press.

Lebow, Richard Ned, and Barry S. Strauss (Eds.). 1991. *Hegemonic Rivalry: From Thucydides to the nuclear age*. Boulder, Col.: Westview Press.

Leifer, Eric. 1988. "Interactional Preludes to Role Setting: Exploratory local action." *American Sociological Review* 53:865–78.

Leiwo, Martii, and Paulina Remes. 1999. "Partnership of Citizens and Metics: The will of Epicurus." *Classical Quarterly* 49:161–66.

Le Rider, G., and François de Callataÿ. 2006. *Les Séleucides et les Ptolémées: L'héritage monétaire et financier d'Alexandre le Grand*. Paris: Éditions du Roche.

Levi, Margaret. 1981. "The Predatory Theory of Rule." *Politics and Society* 10:431–65.

Levitt, Barbara, and James March. 1988. "Organizational Learning." *Annual Review of Sociology* 14:319–40.

Levitt, Steven D., and Stephen J. Dubner. 2005. *Freakonomics: A rogue economist explores the hidden side of everything*. New York: William Morrow.

Lévy, Edmond (Ed.). 2000. *La codification des lois dans l'antiquité: Actes du Colloque de Strasbourg 27–29 novembre 1997*. Paris: De Boccard.

Lewis, David M. 1963. "Cleisthenes and Attica." *Historia* 12:22–40.

Lewis, Sian. 1996. *News and Society in the Greek Polis*. London: Duckworth.

Lind, E. Allan, and Tom R. Tyler. 1988. *The Social Psychology of Procedural Justice*. New York: Plenum Press.

Lintott, A. W. 1982. *Violence, Civil Strife, and Revolution in the Classical City, 750–330 B.C.* London: Croom Helm.

Lippmann, Walter. 1956. *Essays in the Public Philosophy*. New York: New American Library.

Lipset, Seymour Martin. 1981 [1960]. *Political Man: The social bases of politics*. Baltimore: Johns Hopkins University Press.

List, Christian. 2005. "Group Knowledge and Group Rationality: A judgment aggregation perspective." *Episteme: Journal of Social Epistemology* 2:25–38.

List, Christian, and Robert E. Goodin. 2001. "Epistemic Democracy: Generalizing the Condorcet jury theorem." *Journal of Political Philosophy* 9:277–306.

List, Christian, and Philip Pettit. 2004. "An Epistemic Free-Riding Problem?" Pp. 128–58 in *Karl Popper: Critical Appraisals*, edited by Philip Catton and Graham Macdonald. London: Routledge.

Locke, Richard, and Monica Romis. 2006. "Beyond Corporate Codes of Conduct: Work organization and labor standards in two Mexican garment factories." Working Paper: MIT Sloan School of Management.

Loening, Thomas Clark. 1987. *The Reconciliation Agreement of 403/402 B.C. in Athens: Its content and application*. Stuttgart: F. Steiner Verlag.

Lohmann, Susanne. 1994. "Information Aggregation through Costly Political Action." *American Economic Review* 84:518–30.

———. 2000. "I Know You Know He or She Knows We Know You Know They Know: Common knowledge and the unpredictability of informational cascades." Pp. 137–73 in *Political Complexity: Nonlinear models of politics*, edited by Diana Richards. Ann Arbor: University of Michigan Press.

Loraux, Nicole. 1986. *The Invention of Athens: The funeral oration in the classical city*. Cambridge, Mass.: Harvard University Press.

———. 1993. *The Children of Athena: Athenian ideas about citizenship and the division between the sexes*. Princeton, N.J.: Princeton University Press.

Low, Polly. 2002. "Cavalry Identity and Democratic Ideology in Early Fourth-Century Athens." *Proceedings of the Cambridge Philological Society* 48: 102–22.

———. 2007. *Interstate Relations in Classical Greece*. Cambridge: Cambridge University Press.

Luraghi, Nino, and Susan E. Alcock (Eds.). 2003. *Helots and Their Masters in Laconia and Messenia: Histories, ideologies, structures*. Washington, D.C.: Center for Hellenic Studies.

Lyttkens, Carl Hampus. 1992. "Effects of the Taxation of Wealth in Athens in the Fourth Century B.C." *Scandinavian Economic History Review* 40:3–20.

———. 1994. "A Predatory Democracy? An essay on taxation in classical Athens." *Explorations in Economic History* 31:62–90.

———. 1997. "A Rational-Actor Perspective on the Origin of Liturgies in Ancient Greece." *Journal of Institutional and Theoretical Economics* 153:462–84.

———. 2006. "Reflections on the Origins of the Polis: An economic perspective on institutional change in ancient Greece." *Constitutional Political Economy* 17:31–48.

Ma, John. 2000. "Seleukids and Speech-Act Theory: Performative utterances, legitimacy and negotiations in the world of the Maccabees." *Scripta Classica Israelica* 19:71–112.

MacDowell, Douglas M. 1978. *The Law in Classical Athens*. Ithaca, N.Y.: Cornell University Press.

————. 2006. "Mining Cases in Athenian Law." Pp. 212–32 in *Symposion 2003: Vorträge zur griechischen und hellenistischen Rechtsgeschichte*, edited by Hans-Albert Ruprecht. Cologne: Böhlau.

Mackie, Gerry. 2003. *Democracy Defended*. Cambridge and New York: Cambridge University Press.

Mackil, Emily. 2003. "*Koinon* and *Koinonia*: Mechanisms and structures of political collectivity in classical and Hellenistic Greece." PhD dissertation in Classics, Princeton University, Princeton, N.J.

————. 2004. "Wandering Cities: Alternatives to catastrophe in the Greek polis." *American Journal of Archaeology* 108:493–516.

————. 2008. "The Greek *Koinon*." In *The Oxford Handbook of the Ancient State: Near East and Mediterranean*, edited by P. Bang and Walter Scheidel. Oxford: Oxford University Press.

Mackil, Emily, and Peter G. van Alfen. 2006. "Cooperative Coinages." Pp. 201–46 in *Agoranomia: Studies in money and exchange presented to John Kroll*, edited by Peter G. van Alfen. New York: American Numismatic Society.

Mactoux, Marie Madeleine. 1980. *Douleia: Esclavage et pratiques discursives dans l'Athènes classique*. Paris: Belles lettres.

Mader, Gotfried. 2006. "Fighting Philip with Decrees: Demosthenes and the syndrome of symbolic action." *American Journal of Philology* 127:376–86.

Mandel, Ernest. 1968. *Marxist Economic Theory*. New York: Monthly Review Press.

Manin, Bernard. 1997. *The Principles of Representative Government*. Cambridge and New York: Cambridge University Press.

Manning, Joseph Gilbert, and Ian Morris (Eds.). 2005. *The Ancient Economy: Evidence and models*. Stanford, Calif.: Stanford University Press.

Mannix, Elizabeth, and Margaret A. Neale. 2005. "What Differences Make a Difference? The promise and reality of diversity teams in organizations." *Psychological Science in the Public Interest* 6:31–55.

Mansbridge, Jane J. 1983. *Beyond Adversary Democracy*. Chicago: University of Chicago Press.

————. 1990. *Beyond Self-Interest*. Chicago: University of Chicago Press.

Manville, Brook, and Josiah Ober. 2003. *A Company of Citizens: What the world's first democracy teaches leaders about creating great organizations*. Boston: Harvard Business School Press.

Manville, Philip Brook. 1990. *The Origins of Citizenship in Ancient Athens*. Princeton, N.J.: Princeton University Press.

————. 1996. "Ancient Greek Democracy and the Modern Knowledge-Based Organization: Reflections on the ideology of two revolutions." Pp. 377–99 in *Dēmokratia: A conversation on democracies, ancient and modern*, edited by Josiah Ober and Charles W. Hedrick. Princeton, N.J.: Princeton University Press.

Manz, Charles C., and Henry P. Sims. 1995. *Businesses without Bosses: How self-managing teams are building high-performing companies*. New York: John Wiley and Sons.

March, James. 1991. "Exploration and Exploitation in Organizational Learning." *Organization Science* 2:71–87.

Marshall, C. W., and Stephanie van Willigenburg. 2005. "Judging Athenian Dramatic Competitions." *Journal of Hellenic Studies* 124:90–107.

Mattingly, Harold B. 1996. *The Athenian Empire Restored: Epigraphic and historical studies*. Ann Arbor: University of Michigan Press.

Mattusch, Carol C. 1982. *Bronzeworkers in the Athenian Agora*. Princeton, N.J.: American School of Classical Studies at Athens.

———. 1988. *Greek Bronze Statuary: From the beginnings through the fifth century B.C.* Ithaca, N.Y.: Cornell University Press.

Maurizio, Lisa. 1998. "The Panathenaic Procession: Athens' participatory democracy on display?" Pp. 297–317 in *Democracy, Empire, and the Arts in Fifth-Century Athens*, edited by Deborah Dickmann Boedeker and Kurt A. Raaflaub. Cambridge, Mass.: Harvard University Press.

McDonald, William A. 1943. *The Political Meeting Places of the Greeks*. Baltimore: Johns Hopkins University Press.

McLean, Iain, and Fiona Hewitt (Eds.). 1994. *Condorcet: Foundations of social choice and political theory*. Aldershot, Hants, U.K., and Brookfield, Vt.: Elgar.

McLennan, Andrew. 1998. "Consequences of the Condorcet Jury Theorem for Beneficial Information Aggregation by Rational Agents." *American Political Science Review* 92:413–18.

Meier, Christian. 1998. *Athens: A portrait of the city in its Golden Age*. New York: Metropolitan Books/H. Holt and Co.

Meiggs, Russell. 1973. *The Athenian Empire*. Oxford: Clarendon Press.

Meiggs, Russell, and David M. Lewis (Eds.). 1988. *A Selection of Greek Historical Inscriptions to the End of the Fifth Century B.C.* Oxford: Clarendon Press.

Mendelberg, Tali. 2002. "The Deliberative Citizen: Theory and evidence." *Political Decision Making, Deliberation and Participation* 6:151–93.

Michels, Robert. 1962 [1911]. *Political Parties: A sociological study of the oligarchical tendencies of modern democracy*. New York: Collier Books.

Mikalson, Jon D. 1975. *The Sacred and Civil Calendar of the Athenian Year*. Princeton, N.J.: Princeton University Press.

———. 1983. *Athenian Popular Religion*. Chapel Hill: University of North Carolina Press.

Miller, David. 2000. *Citizenship and National Identity*. Cambridge, U.K., and Malden, Mass.: Polity Press and Blackwell.

Miller, Margaret Christina. 1997. *Athens and Persia in the Fifth Century B.C.: A study in cultural receptivity*. Cambridge and New York: Cambridge University Press.

Millett, Paul C. 1989. "Patronage and Its Avoidance in Classical Athens." Pp. 15–48 in *Patronage in Ancient Society*, edited by A. Wallace-Hadrill. London: Routledge.

———. 1991. *Lending and Borrowing in Ancient Athens*. Cambridge and New York: Cambridge University Press.

Mirhady, David C. 1991. "Oath-Challenge in Athens." *Classical Quarterly* 41:78–83.

———. 1996. "Torture and Rhetoric in Athens." *Journal of Hellenic Studies* 116:119–31.

———. 2000. "The Athenian Rationale for Torture." Pp. 53–74 in *Law and Social Status in Classical Athens*, edited by Virginia J. Hunter and J. C. Edmondson. Oxford and New York: Oxford University Press.

———. 2007. "The Dikast's Oath and the Question of Fact." Pp. 48–59 in *Horkos: The oath in Greek society*, edited by Alan H. Sommerstein and Judith Fletcher. Bristol, U.K.: Bristol Phoenix Press.

Moe, Terry. 2005. "Power and Political Insitutions." *Perspectives on Politics* 3:215–33.

Mokyr, Joel. 2002. *The Gifts of Athena: Historical origins of the knowledge economy*. Princeton, N.J.: Princeton University Press.

Molho, Anthony, and Kurt A. Raaflaub (Eds.). 1991. *City States in Classical Antiquity and Medieval Italy*. Ann Arbor: University of Michigan Press.

Monoson, Susan Sara. 1994. "Citizen as *Erastes*: Erotic imagery and the idea of reciprocity in the Periclean funeral oration." *Political Theory* 22:253–76.

———. 2000. *Plato's Democratic Entanglements: Athenian politics and the practice of philosophy*. Princeton, N.J.: Princeton University Press.

Montgomery, Hugo. 1983. *The Way to Chaeronea: Foreign policy, decision-making, and political influence in Demosthenes' speeches*. Bergen, Norway: Universitetsforlaget.

Moreno, Alfonso. 2003. "Athenian Bread-Baskets: The grain-tax law of 374/3 B.C. reinterpreted." *Zeitschrift für Papyrologie und Epigraphik* 145:97–106.

———. 2008. *Feeding the Democracy: The Athenian grain supply in the fifth and fourth centuries B.C.* Oxford: Oxford University Preses.

Morris, Ian. 1987. *Burial and Ancient Society: The rise of the Greek city-state*. Cambridge: Cambridge University Press.

———. 1994. "The Athenian Economy Twenty Years after *The Ancient Economy*." *Classical Philology* 89:351–66.

———. 1998a. "Archaeology as a Kind of Anthropology (A Response to David Small)." Pp. 229–39 in *Democracy 2500? Questions and challenges*, edited by Ian Morris and Kurt A. Raaflaub. Dubuque, Iowa: Kendall/Hunt Pub. Co.

———. 1998b. "Remaining Invisible: The archaeology of the excluded in classical Athens." Pp. 193–220 in *Women and Slaves in Greco-Roman Culture*, edited by Sandra R. Joshel and Sheila Murnaghan. New York: Routledge.

———. 2003. "Mediterraneanization." *Mediterranean Historical Review* 18: 30–55.

———. 2004. "Economic Growth in Ancient Greece." *Journal of Institutional and Theoretical Economics* 160:709–42.

———. 2005a. "Archaeology, Standards of Living and Greek Economic History." Pp. 91–126 in *The Ancient Economy: Evidence and models*, edited by Joseph Gilbert Manning and Ian Morris. Stanford, Calif.: Stanford University Press.

———. 2005b. "The Athenian Empire (478–404 B.C.)." Princeton/Stanford Working Papers in Classics. 120508.

———. 2005c. "Military and Political Participation in Archaic-Classical Greece." Princeton/Stanford Working Papers in Classics. 120511.

———. In progress. *Why the West Rules (For Now)*.

Morris, Ian, and Joseph Gilbert Manning. 2005. "Introduction." Pp. 1–44 in *The Ancient Economy: Evidence and models*, edited by Joseph Gilbert Manning and Ian Morris. Stanford, Calif.: Stanford University Press.

Morris, Ian, and Barry B. Powell. 2005. *The Greeks: History, culture, and society.* New York: Prentice Hall.

Morris, Sarah, and John K. Papadopoulos. 2005. "Greek Towers and Slaves: An archaeology of exploitation." *American Journal of Archaeology* 109:155–225.

Morrison, James. 1999. "Preface to Thucydides: Rereading the Corcyraean conflict." *Classical Antiquity* 18:94–131.

Mossé, Claude. 1962. *La fin de la démocratie athénienne, aspects sociaux et politiques du déclin de la cité grecque au IVe siècle avant J.-C.* Paris: Presses Universitaires de France.

———. 1979. "Comment s'élabore un mythe politique: Solon, 'Père fondateur' de la démocratie athénienne." *Annales (ESC)* 34:425–37.

———. 1986. *La démocratie grecque.* Paris: MA Editions.

———. 1995. *Politique et société en Grèce ancienne: Le "modèle" athénien.* Paris: Aubier.

———. 2007. *D'Homère à Plutarque: Itinéraires historiques.* Paris and Bordeaux: Boccard.

Mueller, Dennis C. 2003. *Public Choice III.* Cambridge and New York: Cambridge University Press.

Munn, Mark Henderson. 2000. *The School of History: Athens in the age of Socrates.* Berkeley: University of California Press.

———. 2006. *The Mother of the Gods, Athens, and the Tyranny of Asia: A study of sovereignty in ancient religion.* Berkeley: University of California Press.

Mussche, H. F., Paule Spitaels, and F. Goemaere-De Poerck (Eds.). 1975. *Thorikos and the Laurion in Archaic and Classical Times: Papers and contributions of the colloquium held in March, 1973, at the State University of Ghent.* Ghent: Belgian Archaeological Mission in Greece.

Mutz, D., and P. Martin. 2001. "Facilitating Communication across Lines of Political Difference." *American Political Science Review* 95:97–114.

Namier, Lewis Bernstein. 1957. *The Structure of Politics at the Accession of George III.* London: Macmillan.

Neer, Richard T. 2002. *Style and Politics in Athenian Vase-Painting: The craft of democracy, ca. 530–460 B.C.E.* Cambridge and New York: Cambridge University Press.

Netz, Reviel. 2002. "Counter Culture: Towards a history of Greek numeracy." *History of Science* 40:321–52.

Nevett, Lisa C. 2000. "A Real Estate 'Market' in Classical Greece? The example of town housing." *Annual of the British School at Athens* 95:329–47.

———. 2005. "Between Urban and Rural: House form and social relations in Attic villages and *deme* centers." Pp. 83–98 in *Ancient Greek Houses and Households: Chronological, regional, and social diversity*, edited by Bradley A. Ault and Lisa C. Nevett. Philadelphia: University of Pennsylvania Press.

Nixon, Lucia, and Simon Prince. 1990. "The Size and Resources of Greek Cities." Pp. 137–70 in *The Greek City: From Homer to Alexander*, edited by Oswyn Murray and S.R.F. Price. Oxford and New York: Clarendon Press.

North, Douglass Cecil. 1981. *Structure and Change in Economic History.* New York: Norton.

———. 1990. *Institutions, Institutional Change, and Economic Performance.* Cambridge and New York: Cambridge University Press.

———. 2005. *Understanding the Process of Economic Change.* Princeton, N.J.: Princeton University Press.

North, Douglass Cecil, John Joseph Wallis, and Barry R. Weingast. In progress. *A Conceptual Framework for Interpreting Recorded Human History.*

North, Douglass Cecil, and Barry R. Weingast. 1989. "Constitutions and Commitment: The Evolution of Institutions Governing Public Choice in Seventeenth Century England." *Journal of Economic History* 49:803–32.

Nouhaud, Michel. 1982. *L'utilisation de l'histoire par les orateurs attiques.* Paris: Société d'Édition "Les Belles Lettres."

Novick, Peter. 1988. *That Noble Dream: The "objectivity question" and the American historical profession.* Cambridge: Cambridge University Press.

Nussbaum, Martha Craven. 2001. *Upheavals of Thought: The intelligence of emotions.* Cambridge and New York: Cambridge University Press.

———. 2006. *Frontiers of Justice: Disability, nationality, species membership.* Cambridge, Mass.: Harvard University Press.

Ober, Josiah. 1985. *Fortress Attica: Defense of the Athenian land frontier, 404–322 B.C.* Leiden: E. J. Brill.

———. 1989. *Mass and Elite in Democratic Athens: Rhetoric, ideology, and the power of the people.* Princeton, N.J.: Princeton University Press.

———. 1996. *The Athenian Revolution: Essays on ancient Greek democracy and political theory.* Princeton, N.J.: Princeton University Press.

———. 1998. *Political Dissent in Democratic Athens: Intellectual critics of popular rule.* Princeton, N.J.: Princeton University Press.

———. 2000a. "Political Conflicts, Political Debates, and Political Thought." Pp. 111–38 in *The Shorter Oxford History of Europe I: Classical Greece*, edited by Robin Osborne. Oxford: Oxford University Press.

———. 2000b. "Quasi-Rights: Participatory citizenship and negative liberties in democratic Athens." *Social Philosophy and Policy* 17:27–61.

———. 2001. "The Debate over Civic Education in Classical Athens." Pp. 273–305 in *Education in Greek and Roman Antiquity*, edited by Yun Lee Too. Leiden: E. J. Brill.

———. 2004. "I, Socrates . . . The Performative Audacity of Isocrates' *Antidosis*." Pp. 21–43 in *Isocrates and Civic Education*, edited by Takis Poulakos and David Depew. Austin: University of Texas Press.

———. 2005a. "Aristotle's Natural Democracy." Pp. 223–43 in *Aristotle's Politics: Critical essays*, edited by Richard Kraut and S. Skultety. Lanham, Md.: Rowman and Littlefield.

———. 2005b. *Athenian Legacies: Essays in the politics of going on together.* Princeton, N.J.: Princeton University Press.

———. 2005c. "Law and Political Theory." Pp. 394–411 in *Cambridge Companion to Ancient Greek Law*, edited by Michael Gagarin and David Cohen. Cambridge: Cambridge University Press.

Ober, Josiah. 2006a. "The Original Meaning of Democracy: Capacity to do things, not majority rule." APSA Paper (annual meeting). Princeton/Stanford Working Papers in Classics 090704 (= *Constellations* 15 [2008]:3–9).

———. 2006b. "Thucydides and the Invention of Political Science." Pp. 131–59 in *Brill's Companion to Thucydides*, edited by Antonios Rengakos and Antonis Tsamakis. Leiden: E. J. Brill.

———. 2007a. "Athenian Military Performance in the Archidamian War: Thucydides on democracy and knowledge." Princeton/Stanford Working Papers in Classics. 090702.

———. 2007b. Natural Capacities and Democracy as a Good-in-Itself." *Philosophical Studies* 132:59–73.

———. In progress. *Information, Choice, and Action in Greek Political Thought.*

Ober, Josiah, and Charles W. Hedrick, (Eds.). 1996. *Dēmokratia: A conversation on democracies, ancient and modern.* Princeton, N.J.: Princeton University Press.

Oliver, Graham J. 2006. "*Polis* Economies and the Cost of the Cavalry in Early Hellenistic Athens." Pp. 109–24 in *Agoranomia: Studies in money and exchange presented to John H. Kroll*, edited by Peter G. van Alfen. New York: American Numismatic Society.

———. 2007. *War, Food, and Politics in Early Hellenistic Athens.* Oxford: Oxford University Press.

Olson, Mancur. 1965. *The Logic of Collective Action: Public goods and the theory of groups.* Cambridge, Mass.: Harvard University Press.

Orlikowski, Wanda J. 2002. "Knowing in Practice: Enacting a collective capability in distributed organizing." *Organization Science* 13: 249–73.

Ortner, Sherry B. 1999. *The Fate of "Culture": Geertz and beyond.* Berkeley: University of California Press.

Osborne, Michael J., and Sean G. Byrne. 1996. *The Foreign Residents of Athens: An annex to the Lexicon of Greek personal names: Attica.* Leuven, Belgium: Peeters.

Osborne, Robin. 1985a. *Demos, the Discovery of Classical Attika.* Cambridge and New York: Cambridge University Press.

———. 1985b. "Law in Action in Classical Athens." *Journal of Hellenic Studies* 105:40–58.

———. 1987. *Classical Landscape with Figures: The ancient Greek city and its countryside.* London: G. Philip.

———. 1990. "The Demos and Its Divisions in Classical Athens." Pp. 265–93 in *The Greek City: From Homer to Alexander*, edited by Oswyn Murray and S.R.F. Price. Oxford and New York: Clarendon Press.

———. 1994. "Ritual, Finance, Politics: An account of Athenian democracy." Pp. 1–24, in *Ritual, Finance, Politics*, edited by Robin Osborne and Simon Hornblower. Oxford: Clarendon Press.

———. 1995. "The Economics and Politics of Slavery at Athens." Pp. 27–43 in *The Greek World*, edited by Anton Powell. London and New York: Routledge.

———. 1996. *Greece in the Making, 1200–479 B.C.* New York: Routledge.

———. 1998. *Archaic and Classical Greek Art.* Oxford and New York: Oxford University Press.

Osborne, Robin, and Simon Hornblower (Eds.). 1994. *Ritual, Finance, Politics: Athenian democratic accounts presented to David Lewis*. Oxford: Clarendon Press.

Osterloh, Margit, and Bruno S. Frey. 2000. "Motivation, Knowledge Transfer, and Organizational Form." *Organization Science* 11:538–50.

Ostrom, Elinor. 1990. *Governing the Commons: The evolution of institutions for collective action*. Cambridge and New York: Cambridge University Press.

———. 2003. "Toward a Behavioral Theory Linking Trust, Reciprocity, and Reputation." Pp. 19–79 in *Trust and Reciprocity: Interdisciplinary lessons from experimental research*, edited by Elinor Ostrom and James Walker. New York: Russell Sage Foundation.

Ostrom, Elinor, and others (Eds.). 2002. *The Drama of the Commons*. Washington, D.C.: National Academy Press.

Ostwald, Martin. 1986. *From Popular Sovereignty to the Sovereignty of Law: Law, society, and politics in fifth-century Athens*. Berkeley: University of California Press.

Padgett, John F., and Christopher K. Ansell. 1993. "Robust Action and the Rise of the Medici, 1400–1434." *American Journal of Sociology* 98:1259–1319.

Page, Benjamin I., and Robert Y. Shapiro. 1992. *The Rational Public: Fifty years of trends in Americans' policy preferences*. Chicago: University of Chicago Press.

Page, Scott E. 2007. *The Difference: How the power of diversity creates better groups, firms, schools, and societies*. Princeton, N.J.: Princeton University Press.

Papadopoulos, John K. 2003. *Ceramicus Redivivus: The early Iron Age potters' field in the area of the classical Athenian Agora*. Princeton, N.J.: American School of Classical Studies at Athens.

Parker, Robert. 1996. *Athenian Religion: A history*. Oxford: Clarendon Press.

———. 2006. *Polytheism and Society at Athens*. Oxford and New York: Oxford University Press.

Pateman, Carole. 1970. *Participation and Democratic Theory*. London: Cambridge University Press.

Patterson, Cynthia. 1981. *Pericles' Citizenship Law of 451–50 B.C.* New York: Arno Press.

———. 1998. *The Family in Greek History*. Cambridge, Mass.: Harvard University Press.

———. 2005. "Athenian Citizenship Law." Pp. 267–89 in *The Cambridge Companion to Ancient Greek Law*, edited by Michael Gagarin and David Cohen. Cambridge and New York: Cambridge University Press.

Pauly, August Friedrich von, Hubert Cancik, and Helmuth Schneider (Eds.). 1996. *Der neue Pauly: Enzyklopädie der Antike*. Stuttgart: J. B. Metzler.

Pearson, Lionel. 1941. "Historical Allusions in the Attic Orators." *Classical Philology* 36:209–29.

Pecírka, Jan. 1966. *The Formula for the Grant of Enktesis in Attic Inscriptions*. Prague: Universita Karlova.

Petrey, Sandy. 1988. *Realism and Revolution: Balzac, Stendhal, Zola, and the performances of history*. Ithaca, N.Y.: Cornell University Press.

———. 1990. *Speech Acts and Literary Theory*. New York: Routledge.

Pettit, Philip. 1997. *Republicanism: A theory of freedom and government.* Oxford and New York: Clarendon Press.

———. 2002. *Rules, Reasons, and Norms: Selected essays.* Oxford and New York: Oxford University Press.

Pettit, Philip, and Christian List. In progress. *Agency incorporated.*

Pettit, Philip, and David Schweikard. 2006. "Joint Action and Group Agency." *Philosophy of the Social Sciences* 36:18–39.

Phillips, Derek L. 1993. *Looking Backward: A critical appraisal of communitarian thought.* Princeton, N.J.: Princeton University Press.

Picard, O. 1997. "Monnaies de fouilles et histoire grecque: L'exemple de Thasos." Pp. 29–39 in *Numismatic Archaeology, Archaeological Numismatics: Proceedings of an international conference held to honour Dr. Mando Oeconomides in Athens 1995,* edited by Kenneth A. Sheedy and Ch. Papageorgiadou-Banis. Oxford: Oxbow.

Piérart, Marcel. 1974. *Platon et la cité grecque: Théorie et réalité dans la constitution des Lois.* Brussels: Académie royale de Belgique.

———. 2000. "Argos: Un autre démocratie." Pp. 297–314 in *Polis and Politics: [Festschrift Hansen],* edited by P. Flensted-Jensen, T. H. Nielsen, and L. Rubinstein. Copenhagen: Museum Tusculanum Press.

Pitkin, Hanna F. 1967. *The Concept of Representation.* Berkeley: University of California Press.

Polanyi, Michael. 1964. *Personal Knowledge: Towards a post-critical philosophy.* New York: Harper and Row.

———. 1966. *The Tacit Dimension.* Garden City, N.Y.: Doubleday.

Popkin, Samuel L. 1991. *The Reasoning Voter: Communication and persuasion in presidential campaigns.* Chicago: University of Chicago Press.

Powell, Anton. 2001. *Athens and Sparta: Constructing Greek political and social history from 478 B.C.* 2nd ed. London: Routledge.

Premack, David, and Ann James Premack. 1995. "Origins of Human Social Competence." Pp. 205–18 in *The Cognitive Neurosciences,* edited by Michael S. Gazzaniga and Emilio Bizzi. Cambridge, Mass.: MIT Press.

Pritchard, David. 2004. "Kleisthenes, Participation, and the Dithyrambic Contests of Late Archaic and Classical Athens." *Phoenix* 58:208–28.

———. 2005. "Kleisthenes and Athenian Democracy: Vision from above or below?" *Polis* 22:136–57.

Pritchett, W. Kendrick. 1953. "The Attic Stelai, Part I." *Hesperia* 22:225–99.

———. 1956. "The Attic Stelai, Part II." *Hesperia* 25:210–317.

Przeworski, Adam. 2000. *Democracy and Development: Political institutions and material well-being in the world, 1950–1990.* Cambridge: Cambridge University Press.

Przeworski, Adam, Susan Carol Stokes, and Bernard Manin (Eds.). 1999. *Democracy, Accountability, and Representation.* Cambridge and New York: Cambridge University Press.

Purcell, Nicholas. 1990. "Mobility and the Polis." Pp. 29–58 in *The Greek City: From Homer to Alexander,* edited by Oswyn Murray and S. R. F. Price. Oxford and New York: Clarendon Press.

Purser, Ronald E., and Steven Cabana. 1998. *The Self Managing Organization: How leading companies are transforming the work of teams for real impact.* New York: Free Press.

Putnam, Robert D. 1993. *Making Democracy Work: Civic traditions in modern Italy.* Princeton, N.J.: Princeton University Press.

———. 2000. *Bowling Alone: The collapse and revival of American community.* New York: Simon and Schuster.

———. 2007. "*E Pluribus Unum*: Diversity and Community in the Twenty-first Century. The 2006 Johan Skytte Prize Lecture." *Scandinavian Political Studies* 30:137–74.

Putterman, Louis. 1982. "Some Behavioral Perspectives on the Dominance of Hierarchical over Democratic Forms of Enterprise." *Journal of Economic Behavior and Organization* 3:139–60.

Quillin, James. 2002. "Achieving Amnesty: The Role of Events, Institutions, and Ideas." *Transactions of the American Philological Association* 132:71–107.

Raaflaub, Kurt. 1998. "The Thetes and Democracy (A Response to Josiah Ober)." Pp. 87–103 in *Democracy 2500? Questions and challenges*, edited by Ian Morris and Kurt A. Raaflaub. Dubuque, Iowa: Kendall/Hunt Pub. Co.

Raaflaub, Kurt, Josiah Ober, and Robert W. Wallace. 2007. *The Origins of Democracy in Ancient Greece.* Berkeley and Los Angeles: University of California Press.

Rawls, John. 1971. *A Theory of Justice.* Cambridge, Mass.: Belknap Press of Harvard University Press.

———. 1996. *Political Liberalism.* New York: Columbia University Press.

Rebenich, S. 1998. "Fremdenfeindlichkeit in Sparta? Überlungen zur Tradition der spartanischen Xenelasie." *Klio* 80:336–59.

Reden, Sitta von. 2002a. "Money in the Ancient Economy: A Survey of Recent Research." *Klio* 84:141–74.

———. 2002b. "Demos' *phialê* and the rhetoric of money in fourth-century Athens." Pp. 52–66 in *Money, Labour and Land: Approaches to the economies of ancient Greece*, edited by Paul Cartledge, Edward E. Cohen, and Lin Foxhall. London and New York: Routledge.

———. 2007a. "Consumption." In *The Cambridge Economic History of the Greco-Roman World*, edited by Walter Scheidel, Ian Morris, and Richard P. Saller. Cambridge: Cambridge University Press.

———. 2007b. *Money in Ptolemaic Egypt: From the Macedonian conquest to the end of the third century B.C.* Cambridge: Cambridge University Press.

Reed, C. M. 2003. *Maritime Traders in the Ancient Greek World.* Cambridge and New York: Cambridge University Press.

Reger, Gary. 1994. *Regionalism and Change in the Economy of Independent Delos, 314–167 B.C.* Berkeley: University of California Press.

Reiter, Dan, and Allan C. Stam. 2002. *Democracies at War.* Princeton, N.J.: Princeton University Press.

Rhodes, P. J. 1981. *A Commentary on the Aristotelian Athenaion Politeia.* Oxford and New York: Clarendon Press of Oxford University Press.

———. 1985. *The Athenian Boule.* Revised ed. Oxford: Clarendon Press.

Rhodes, P. J. 1994. "The Ostracism of Hyperbolus." Pp. 85–98 in *Ritual, Finance, Politics*, edited by Robin Osborne and Simon Hornblower. Oxford: Clarendon Press.

———. 2000. "Who Ran Democratic Athens?" Pp. 465–477 in *Polis and Politics [Festschrift Hansen]*, edited by P. Flensted-Jensen, T. H. Nielsen and L. Rubinstein. Copenhagen: Museum Tusculanum Press.

——— (Ed.). 2004. *Athenian Democracy*. Edinburgh: University of Edinburgh Press.

———. Forthcoming. "Demagogues and *demos* in Athens." In *Festschrift for John K. Davies*.

Rhodes, P. J., and David M. Lewis. 1997. *The Decrees of the Greek States*. Oxford: Clarendon Press.

Rhodes, P. J., and Robin Osborne. 2003. *Greek Historical Inscriptions: 404–323 B.C.* Oxford: Oxford University Press.

Richardson, M. B. 2000. "The Location of Inscribed Laws in Fourth-Century Athens: *IG* II² 244, on rebuilding the walls of Piraeus (337/6 BC)." Pp. 601–15 in *Polis and Politics [Festschrift Hansen]*, edited by P. Flensted-Jensen, T. H. Nielsen, L. Rubinstein. Copenhagen: Museum Tusculanum Press.

Riess, Werner. 2006. "How Tyrants and Dynasts Die: The semantics of political assassination in fourth-century Greece." Pp. 65–88 in *Terror et Pavor. Violenza intimidazione, cladestinà nel mondo antico*. Pisa: Edizioni ETS.

Roberts, Jennifer Tolbert. 1982. *Accountability in Athenian Government*. Madison: University of Wisconsin Press.

———. 1994. *Athens on Trial: The antidemocratic tradition in Western thought*. Princeton, N.J.: Princeton University Press.

Roberts, John. 2004. *The Modern Firm: Organizational design for performance and growth*. Oxford: Oxford University Press.

Robinson, Eric W. 1997. *The First Democracies: Early popular government outside Athens*. Stuttgart: F. Steiner.

———. 2000. "Democracy in Syracuse, 466–412 B.C." *Harvard Studies in Classical Philology* 100:189–205.

———. 2007. "The Sophists and Democracy beyond Athens." *Rhetorica* 25: 109–22.

———. forthcoming. *Democracy beyond Athens: Popular government in the Greek classical age*. Cambridge: Cambridge University Press.

Rodrik, Dani. 1999. "Democracies Pay Higher Wages." *Quarterly Journal of Economics* 114:707–38.

———. 2000a. "Participatory Politics, Social Cooperation, and Economic Stability." *American Economic Review* 90:140–44.

———. 2000b. "Institutions for High-Quality Growth: What they are and how to acquire them." *Studies in Comparative International Development* 35:3–31.

———. 2003. *In Search of Prosperity: Analytic narratives on economic growth*. Princeton, N.J.: Princeton University Press.

Rodrik, Dani, and Romain Wacziarg. 2005. "Do Democratic Transitions Produce Bad Economic Outcomes?" *American Economic Review Papers and Proceedings*. 95:50–56.

Roisman, Joseph. 2005. *The Rhetoric of Manhood: Masculinity in the Attic orators.* Berkeley and Los Angeles: University of California Press.

Rorty, Richard. 1979. *Philosophy and the Mirror of Nature.* Princeton, N.J.: Princeton University Press.

Rosen, Ralph Mark, and I. Sluiter (Eds.). 2003. *Andreia: Studies in manliness and courage in classical antiquity.* Leiden: E.J. Brill.

Rosivach, Vincent. 1999. "Enslaving *barbaroi* and the Athenian Ideology of Slavery." *Historia* 48:129–57.

Rothschild, Emma. 1973. *Paradise Lost: The decline of the auto-industrial age.* New York: Random House.

Rousseau, Jean-Jacques. 2002 [1762]. *The Social Contract and The First and Second Discourses,* edited by Susan Dunn and Gita May. New Haven: Yale University Press.

Rubinstein, Lene. 2000. *Litigation and Cooperation: Supporting speakers in the courts of classical Athens.* Stuttgart: F. Steiner Verlag.

———. 2007. "Arguments from Precedent in Attic Oratory." Pp. 359–71 in *Oxford Readings in the Attic Orators,* edited by Edwin Carawan. Oxford and New York: Oxford University Press.

Runciman, David. 2007. "The Paradox of Political Representation." *Journal of Political Philosophy* 15:93–114.

Runciman, W. G. 1990. "Doomed to Extinction: The polis as an evolutionary dead-end." Pp. 348–67 in *The Greek City: From Homer to Alexander,* edited by Oswyn Murray and Simon Price. Oxford: Oxford University Press.

Ruschenbusch, E. 1985. "Die Zahl der griechischen Staaten und Arealgrösse und Bürgerzahl der Normalpolis." *Zeitschrift für Papyrologie und Epigraphik* 59:253–63.

Ruzé, Françoise. 1997. *Délibération et pouvoir dans la cité grecque: De Nestor à Socrate.* Paris: Publications de la Sorbonne.

Ryan, Alan. 1995. *John Dewey and the High Tide of American Liberalism.* New York: W. W. Norton.

Ryfe, D. M. 2005. "Does Deliberative Democracy Work?" *Annual Review of Political Science* 8.

Saller, Richard P. 1982. *Personal Patronage under the Early Empire.* Cambridge and New York: Cambridge University Press.

———. 2005. "Framing the Debate over Growth in the Ancient Economy." Pp. 223–38 in *The Ancient Economy: Evidence and models,* edited by Joseph Gilbert Manning and Ian Morris. Stanford, Calif.: Stanford University Press.

Salmon, John. 2001. "Temples the Measures of Men: Public building in the Greek economy." Pp. 95–108 in *Economies beyond Agriculture in the Classical World,* edited by D. J. Mattingly and John Salmon. London and New York: Routledge.

Salomon, Nicoletta. 1997. *Le cleruchie di Atene: Caratteri e funzione.* Pisa: ETS.

Salthouse, Timothy A. 1991. "Expertise as the Circumvention of Human Processing Limitations." Pp. 286–300 in *Toward a General Theory of Expertise: Prospects and limits,* edited by K. Anders Ericsson and Jacqui Smith. Cambridge: Cambridge University Press.

Samons, Loren J. 2004. *What's Wrong with Democracy? From Athenian practice to American worship*. Berkeley: University of California Press.

Samons, Loren J. (Ed.). 2007. *The Cambridge Companion to the Age of Pericles*. Cambridge and New York: Cambridge University Press.

Saxonhouse, Arlene. 2006. *Free Speech and Democracy in Ancient Athens*. Cambridge: Cambridge University Press.

Scaff, Lawrence. 1981. "Max Weber and Robert Michels." *American Journal of Sociology* 86:1269–86.

Scheidel, Walter. 2004. "Demographic and Economic Development in the Ancient Mediterranean World." *Journal of Institutional and Theoretical Economics* 160:743–57.

———. 2005a. "Military Commitments and Political Bargaining in Ancient Greece." Princeton/Stanford Working Papers in Classics 110501

———. 2005b. "Real Slave Prices and the Relative Costs of Slave Labor in the Greco-Roman World." *Ancient Society* 35:1–17.

———. 2006. "Population and Demography." Princeton/Stanford Working Papers in Classics 040604.

Schelling, Thomas C. 1980. *The Strategy of Conflict*. Cambridge, Mass.: Harvard University Press.

Schmitt, Carl. 1985 [1926]. *The Crisis of Parliamentary Democracy*. Cambridge, Mass.: MIT Press.

———. 2004 [1932]. *Legality and Legitimacy*. Durham, N.C.: Duke University Press.

Schmitt-Pantel, Pauline. 1992. *La cité au banquet: Histoire des repas publics dans les cités grecques*. Rome: École française de Rome.

Schofield, Malcolm. 2006. *Plato: Political Philosophy*. London and New York: Oxford University Press.

Schultz, Kenneth A., and Barry R. Weingast. 2003. "The Democratic Advantage: The institutional foundations of financial power in international competition." *International Organization* 57:3–42.

Schumpeter, Joseph Alois. 1947. *Capitalism, Socialism, and Democracy*. New York: Harper.

Schwartzberg, Melissa. 2004. "Athenian Democracy and Legal Change." *American Political Science Review* 98:311–25.

———. 2007. *Democracy and Legal Change*. Cambridge and New York: Cambridge University Press.

Scott, James C. 1998. *Seeing Like a State: How certain schemes to improve the human condition have failed*. New Haven: Yale University Press.

Seaford, Richard. 2004. *Money and the Early Greek Mind: Homer, philosophy, tragedy*. Cambridge and New York: Cambridge University Press.

Searle, John R. 1995. *The Construction of Social Reality*. New York: Free Press.

Sen, Amartya Kumar. 1993. "Capability and Well-Being." Pp. 30–53 in *The Quality of Life: Studies in development economics*, edited by Martha Craven Nussbaum and Amartya Kumar Sen. Oxford and New York: Oxford University Press.

———. 1999. "Democracy as a Universal Value." *Journal of Democracy* 10:3–17.

Sewell, William. 1996. "Historical Events as Transformations of Structures: Inventing revolution at the Bastille." *Theory and Society* 25:841–81.

———. 1999. "The Concept(s) of Culture." Pp. 35–61 in *Beyond the Cultural Turn: New directions in the study of society and culture*, edited by Victoria E. Bonnell and Lynn Avery Hunt. Berkeley and Los Angeles: University of California Press.

Sharples, R. W. 1994. "Plato on Democracy and Expertise." *Greece and Rome* 41:49–56.

Shaw, Brent D. 1991. "The Paradoxes of People Power." *Helios* 18:194–214.

Shaw, Tamsin. 2006. "Max Weber on Democracy: Can the people have political power in modern states?" APSA Paper (annual meeting).

Shear, Julia L. 2003. "Prizes from Athens: The list of Panathenaic prizes and the sacred oil." *Zeitschrift für Papyrologie und Epigraphik* 142:87–105.

Shear, T. Leslie, Jr. 1970. "The Monument of the Eponymous Heroes in the Athenian Agora." *Hesperia* 39:145–220.

———. 1995. "Bouleuterion, Metroon, and the Archives at Athens." Pp. 157–89 in *Studies in the Ancient Greek Polis*, edited by Mogens Herman Hansen and Kurt A. Raaflaub. Stuttgart: F. Steiner Verlag.

Sickinger, James P. 1999. *Public Records and Archives in Classical Athens*. Chapel Hill: University of North Carolina Press.

Shipley, D. Graham J., and Mogens H. Hansen. 2006. "The *Polis* and Federalism." Pp. 52–72 in *The Cambridge Companion to the Hellenistic world*, edited by Glenn Richard Bugh. Cambridge: Cambridge University Press.

Shipton, Kirsty. 2001. "Money and the Élite in Classical Athens." Pp. 129–144 in *Money and its uses in the ancient Greek world*, edited by Andrew Meadows and Kirsty Shipton. Oxford and New York: Oxford University Press.

Sieloff, C. G. 1999. "'If only HP Knew What HP Knows': The roots of knowledge management at Hewlett-Packard." *Journal of Knowledge Management* 3:47–53.

Siewert, Peter. 1977. "The Ephebic Oath in Fifth-Century Athens." *Journal of Hellenic Studies* 97:102–11.

———. 1982. *Die Trittyen Attikas und die Heeresform des Kleisthenes*. Munich: C. H. Beck.

Simms, Ronda R. 1989. "Isis in Athens." *Classical Journal* 84:216–221.

Simon, Erika. 1983. *Festivals of Attica: An archaeological commentary*. Madison: University of Wisconsin Press.

Simon, Herbert Alexander. 1955. "A Behavioral Model of Rational Choice." *Quarterly Journal of Economics* 65:99–118.

———. 1976 [1947]. *Administrative Behavior: A study of decision-making processes in administrative organization*. New York: Free Press.

Sinclair, R. K. 1988. *Democracy and Participation in Athens*. Cambridge and New York: Cambridge University Press.

Smith, Douglas K. 2004. *On Value and Values: Thinking differently about we in an age of me*. Upper Saddle River, N.J.: Financial Times, Prentice Hall.

Smith, Douglas K., and Robert C. Alexander. 1988. *Fumbling the Future: How Xerox invented, then ignored, the first personal computer*. New York: W. Morrow.

Smith, Tara. 2006. *Ayn Rand's Normative Ethics: The virtuous egoist.* Cambridge and New York: Cambridge University Press.

Snodgrass, Anthony. 1980. *Archaic Greece: The age of experiment.* London and Toronto: J. M. Dent.

Sommerstein, Alan H. (Ed.). 2007. *Horkos: The oath in Greek society.* Bristol, U.K.: Bristol Phoenix Press.

Sowell, Thomas. 1980. *Knowledge and Decisions.* New York: Basic Books.

Stanton, G. R. 1984. "The Tribal Reform of Kleisthenes the Alkmeonid." *Chiron* 14:1–41.

Starr, Chester G. 1970. *Athenian Coinage, 480–449 B.C.* Oxford: Clarendon Press.

Stasavage, David. 2003. *Public Debt and the Birth of the Democratic State: France and Great Britain, 1688–1789.* Cambridge and New York: Cambridge University Press.

———. 2007. "Polarization and Publicity: Rethinking the benefits of deliberative democracy." *Journal of Politics* 69:59–72.

Steinbeck, John, and Edward Flanders Ricketts. 1976 [1941]. *The Log from the Sea of Cortez.* New York: Penguin Books.

Stewart, Andrew, and Rebecca S. Martin. 2005. "Attic Imported Pottery at Tel Dor Israel: An overview." *Bulletin of the American Institutes of Oriental Research* 337:79–94.

Stinchcombe, Arthur L. 2001. *When Formality Works: Authority and abstraction in law and organizations.* Chicago: University of Chicago Press.

Strauss, Barry S. 1985. "Ritual, Social Drama and Politics in Classical Athens." *American Journal of Ancient History* 10:67–83.

———. 1986. *Athens after the Peloponnesian War: Class, faction and policy 403–386 B.C.* London: Croom Helm.

———. 2004. *The Battle of Salamis: The naval encounter that saved Greece—and western civilization.* New York: Simon and Schuster.

Stroud, Ronald S. 1974. "An Athenian Law on Silver Coinage." *Hesperia* 43: 157–88.

———. 1998. *The Athenian Grain-Tax Law of 374/3 B.C.* Princeton, N.J.: American School of Classical Studies at Athens.

Sunstein, Cass R. 2000. "Deliberative Trouble? Why groups go to extremes." *Yale Law Journal* 110:71–119.

———. 2002. "The Law of Group Polarization." *Journal of Political Philosophy* 10:175–95.

———. 2006. *Infotopia: How many minds produce knowledge.* New York: Oxford University Press.

———. 2007. "Deliberating Groups versus Prediction Markets (or Hayek's Challenge to Habermas)." *Episteme: Journal of Social Epistemology* 3:192–213.

Surowiecki, James. 2004. *The Wisdom of Crowds: Why the many are smarter than the few and how collective wisdom shapes business, economies, societies and nations.* New York: Doubleday.

Syme, Ronald. 1939. *The Roman Revolution.* Oxford: Clarendon.

Tacon, J. 2001. "Ecclesiastic Thorubos: Interventions, interruptions and popular involvement in the Athenian assembly." *Greece and Rome* 48:173–92.

Tavares, José, and Romain Wacziarg. 2001. "How Democracy Affects Growth." *European Economic Review* 45:1341–79.

Taylor, Claire. 2001a. "Bribery in Athenian politics. Part I: Accusations, allegations, and slander." *Greece and Rome* 48:53–66.

———. 2001b. "Bribery in Athenian politics. Part II: Ancient reactions and perceptions." *Greece and Rome* 48:154–72.

———. 2007. "An Oligarchy of the City? The sociological impact of election and lot in Athenian democracy" *Hesperia* 76:323–46.

———. 2008. "A New Political World." Pp. 72–90 in *Debating the Athenian Cultural Revolution: Art, literature, philosophy, and politics 430–380 B.C.*, edited by Robin Osborne. Cambridge: Cambridge University Press.

Teegarden, David. 2007. "Defending Democracy: A Study of ancient Greek antityranny Legislation." PhD dissertation in Classics, Princeton University, Princeton, N.J.

Tetlock, Philip. 2005. *Expert Political Judgment: How good is it? How can we know?* Princeton, N.J.: Princeton University Press.

Thomas, Rosalind. 1989. *Oral Tradition and Written Record in Classical Athens.* Cambridge and New York: Cambridge University Press.

———. 1992. *Literacy and Orality in Ancient Greece.* Cambridge and New York: Cambridge University Press.

———. 2005. "Writing, Law, and Written Law." Pp. 41–60 in *The Cambridge Companion to Ancient Greek Law*, edited by Michael Gagarin and David Cohen. Cambridge and New York: Cambridge University Press.

Thompson, F. H. 2003. *The Archaeology of Greek and Roman Slavery.* London: Duckworth.

Thompson, Homer A., and R. E. Wycherley. 1972. *The Agora of Athens: The history, shape, and uses of an ancient city center.* Princeton, N.J.: American School of Classical Studies at Athens.

Thompson, Margaret, Otto Mørkholm, and Colin M. Kraay (Eds.). 1973. *An Inventory of Greek Coin Hoards.* New York: Published for the International Numismatic Commission by the American Numismatic Society.

Thompson, W. E. 1978. "The Athenian Investor." *Rivista di Studi Classici* 26:403–23.

Thür, Gerhard. 1977. *Beweisführung vor den Schwurgerichtshöfen Athens: Die Proklesis zur Basanos.* Vienna: Kerlag der Österreichen Akademie der Wissenschaften.

Tigerstedt, Eugene Napoleon. 1965. *The Legend of Sparta in Classical Antiquity*, vol. 1. Stockholm: Almqvist and Wiksell.

Tilly, Charles. 1990. *Coercion, Capital, and European States, A.D. 990–1990.* Boston, Mass.: Blackwell.

Tocqueville, Alexis de. 2000 [1835]. *Democracy in America.* New York: Harper and Row.

Todd, S. C. 1993. *The Shape of Athenian Law.* Oxford: Clarendon.

———. 1994. "Status and Contract in Fourth-Century Athens." Pp. 125–40 in *Symposion 1993: Vorträge zur griechische und hellenistische Rechtsgeschichte*, edited by G. Thür. Cologne and Vienna: Böhlau.

Too, Yun Lee. 2001. "Legal Instructions in Classical Athens." Pp. 111–32 in *Education in Greek and Roman Antiquity*, edited by Yun Lee Too. Leiden: E. J. Brill.

Traill, John S. 1975. *The Political Organization of Attica: A study of the demes, trittyes, and phylai, and their representation in the Athenian Council.* Princeton, N.J.: American School of Classical Studies at Athens.

———. 1986. *Demos and Trittys: Epigraphical and topographical studies in the organization of Attica.* Toronto, Canada: Athenians Victoria College.

Tully, James (Ed.). 1988. *Meaning and Context: Quentin Skinner and his critics.* Princeton, N.J.: Princeton University Press.

Tyler, Tom R., Roderick Moreland Kramer, and Oliver P. John. 1998. *The Psychology of the Social Self.* Mahwah, N.J.: Lawrence Erlbaum Associates.

Urbinati, Nadia. 2002. *Mill on Democracy: From the Athenian polis to representative government.* Chicago: University of Chicago Press.

———. 2006. *Representative Democracy: Principles and genealogy.* Chicago: University of Chicago Press.

van Alfen, Peter G. 2000. "The 'Owls' from the 1973 Iraq Hoard." *American Journal of Numismatics* 12:9–58.

———. 2002. "The 'Owls' from the 1989 Syria Hoard, with a Review of Pre-Macedonian Coinage in Egypt." *American Journal of Numismatics* 14:1–57.

———. 2004/5. "Herodotos' 'Aryandic' Silver and Bullion Use in Persian-Period Egypt." *American Journal of Numismatics* 16–17:7–46.

———. 2005. "Problems in Ancient Imitative and Counterfeit Coinage." Pp. 322–54 in *Making, Moving, and Managing: The new world of ancient economics, 323–31 B.C.*, edited by Zofia Archibald, John Davies, and Vincent Gabrielsen. Oxford: Oxbow.

Vanderpool, Eugene, James McCredie, and A. Steinberg. 1962. "Koroni: A Ptolemaic Camp on the East Coast of Attica." *Hesperia* 31:26–61.

Vernant, Jean-Pierre. 1982. *The Origins of Greek Thought.* Ithaca, N.Y.: Cornell University Press.

Veyne, Paul. 1992 [1976]. *Bread and Circuses: Historical sociology and political pluralism.* London: Penguin.

Waldron, Jeremy. 1992. "Minority Cultures and the Cosmopolitan Alternative." *University of Michigan Journal of Law Reform* 25:751–93.

———. 1995. "The Wisdom of the Multitude: Some reflections on Book III Chapter 11 of the Politics." *Political Theory* 23:563–84.

Walker, Rob. 2004. "The Hidden (in Plain Sight) Persuaders." *New York Times Magazine*, December 5:69–76ff.

Wallace, Robert W. 1997. "Poet, Public, and 'Theatrocracy': Audience performance in classical Athens." Pp. 97–111 in *Poet, Public, and Performance in Ancient Greece*, edited by Lowell Edmunds and Robert W. Wallace. Baltimore, Md.: Johns Hopkins University Press.

———. 2005. "'Listening' to the *archai* in Democratic Athens." Pp. 147–58 in *Symposion 2001: Vorträge zur griechischen und hellenistischen Rechtsgeschichte*, edited by Michael Gagarin and Robert W. Wallace. Cologne: Böhlau.

Wallace-Hadrill, A. (Ed.). 1989. *Patronage in Ancient Society.* London and New York: Routledge.

Wallach, John R. 2001. *The Platonic Political Art: A study of critical reason and democracy.* University Park: Pennsylvania State University Press.

Waltz, Kenneth Neal. 1979. *Theory of International Politics.* New York: Random House.

Weingast, Barry R. 1997. "The Political Foundations of Democracy and the Rule of Law." *American Political Science Review* 91:245–63.

Welwei, Karl-Wilhelm. 1999. *Das klassische Athen: Demokratie und Machtpolitik im 5. und 4. Jahrhundert.* Darmstadt: Primus Verlag.

Wenger, Etienne. 1998. *Communities of Practice: Learning, meaning, and identity.* Cambridge and New York: Cambridge University Press.

Westbrook, Robert B. 1991. *John Dewey and American Democracy.* Ithaca, N.Y.: Cornell University Press.

Whitby, Michael. 1998. "The Grain Trade of Athens in the Fourth Century." Pp. 102–28 in *Trade, Traders, and the Ancient City*, edited by Helen Parkins and Christopher John Smith. London and New York: Routledge.

White, Lawrence H. 2006. "Can Economics Rank Slavery against Free Labor in Terms of Efficiency?" Paper prepared for San Jose State University seminar, February 13, 2006.

Whitehead, David. 1977. *The Ideology of the Athenian Metic.* Cambridge, U.K.: Cambridge Philological Society.

———. 1983. "Competitive Outlay and Community Profit: *Philotimia* in democratic Athens." *Classica et Mediaevalia* 34:55–74.

———. 1986. *The Demes of Attica, 508/7–ca. 250 B.C.: A political and social study.* Princeton, N.J.: Princeton University Press.

———. 1993. "Cardinal Virtues: The language of public approbation in democratic Athens." *Classica et Mediaevalia* 44:37–75.

Williamson, Oliver E. 1975. *Markets and Hierarchies, Analysis and Antitrust Implications: A study in the economics of internal organization.* New York: Free Press.

———. 1981. "The Economics of Organization: The transaction cost approach." *American Journal of Sociology* 87:548–577.

———. 1985. *The Economic Institutions of Capitalism: Firms, markets, relational contracting.* New York and London: Free Press.

Wilson, Peter. 2000. *The Athenian Institution of the Khoregia: The chorus, the city, and the stage.* Cambridge: Cambridge University Press.

Winkler, John J., and Froma I. Zeitlin (Eds.). 1990. *Nothing to Do with Dionysos? Athenian drama in its social context.* Princeton, N.J.: Princeton University Press.

Wohl, Victoria. 1996. "*Eusebeias eneka kai philotimias*: Hegemony and democracy at the Panathenaia." *Classica et Mediaevalia* 47:25–88.

———. 1998. *Intimate Commerce: Exchange, gender, and subjectivity in Greek tragedy.* Austin: University of Texas Press.

———. 2002. *Love among the Ruins: The erotics of democracy in classical Athens.* Princeton, N.J.: Princeton University Press.

Wolin, Sheldon S. 1994. "Norm and Form: The constitutionalizing of democracy." Pp. 29–58 in *Athenian Political Thought and the Reconstruction of*

American Democracy, edited by J. Peter Euben, John Wallach, and Josiah Ober. Ithaca, N.Y.: Cornell University Press.

Wolin, Sheldon S. 1996. "Transgression, Equality, and Voice." Pp. 63–90 in *Dēmokratia: A conversation on democracies ancient and modern*, edited by Josiah Ober and Charles Hedrick. Princeton, N.J.: Princeton University Press.

Wolpert, Andrew. 2002. *Remembering Defeat: Civil war and civic memory in ancient Athens*. Baltimore: Johns Hopkins University Press.

Wood, Ellen Meiksins. 1988. *Peasant-Citizen and Slave: The foundations of Athenian democracy*. London and New York: Verso.

Worthington, Ian. 1994. *Persuasion: Greek rhetoric in action*. London and New York: Routledge.

———. 1996. *Voice into Text: Orality and literacy in ancient Greece*. Leiden and New York: E. J. Brill.

Worthington, Ian, Craig R. Cooper, and Edward Monroe Harris (Eds.). 2001. *Dinarchus, Hyperides, and Lycurgus*. Austin: University of Texas Press.

Wright, Gavin, and Jesse Czelusta. 2002. "Exorcizing the Resource Curse: Minerals as a knowledge industry, past and present." Working Paper, Department of Economics, Stanford University 02–008.

Wycherley, R. E. 1962. *How the Greeks Built Cities*. London: Macmillan.

Young, H. P. 1988. "Condorcet's Theory of Voting." *American Political Science Review* 82:1231–44.

Yunis, Harvey. 1996. *Taming Democracy: Models of political rhetoric in classical Athens*. Ithaca, N.Y.: Cornell University Press.

———. 2005. "The Rhetoric of Law in Fourth-Century Athens." Pp. 191–208 in *The Cambridge Companion to Ancient Greek Law*, edited by Michael Gagarin and David Cohen. Cambridge and New York: Cambridge University Press.

Zelnick-Abramowitz, Rachel. 2000. "Did Patronage Exist in Classical Athens?" *Antiquité Classique* 69:65–80.

INDEX

Note: Page numbers in bold type indicate explanations of terms. Page numbers in italic type indicate figures or tables.